ARMIES SOUTH, ARMIES NORTH

THE MILITARY FORCES OF THE CIVIL WAR COMPARED AND CONTRASTED

ALAN AXELROD, PhD

Guilford, Connecticut

For Anita and Ian

An imprint of Globe Pequot

Distributed by NATIONAL BOOK NETWORK

British Library Cataloguing in Publication Information Available
Library of Congress Cataloging-in-Publication Data is available on file.

ISBN 978-1-4930-1862-8 (hardcover)
ISBN 978-1-4930-2407-0 (e-book)

∞™ The paper used in this publication meets the minimum requirements of American National Standard for Information Sciences—
Permanence of Paper for Printed Library Materials, ANSI/NISO Z39.48-1992.

Printed in the United States of America

CONTENTS

INTRODUCTION

The American Civil War never ceases to start arguments. They typically focus on three areas: morality, the generals, and the armies.

Morality is a fertile subject for thought, discussion, and debate. Put the moral aspects of the Civil War in a book, however, and the result tends to reveal more about the author than about the historical realities of the decisions and events under discussion. In this book, considerations of morality, justice, humanity, and society do figure in chapters 4, 5, and 6 as well as in chapters 9 and 10, but the morality of the Civil War and the relative merits of the case for war made in the South and in the North are not the focus of what you are about to read.

As for the generals, the comparative merits of the principal commanders, the generals South and North, is the subject of my *Generals South, Generals North: The Commanders of the Civil War Reconsidered* (Lyons Press, 2011 and 2016). The present book, *Armies South, Armies North*, enters the third area of Civil War argument. It is an exploration of the armies with which America went to war for and against itself in 1861–65, and it is an attempt to assess their comparative merits.

In the interest of truth in labeling, I make no claim that this book will settle the argument over whether the South or the North had the better army, armies, or fighting men. Nor did I claim that my earlier book settled the argument over which side had the better generals. On the contrary, I suspect—really, I hope—this book will start some fresh arguments. Most of all, as with *Generals South, Generals North*, my main purpose in *Armies South, Armies North* is to make arguments about the Civil War less arbitrarily subjective by providing a framework for fact-based evaluation in a historical context. In this same spirit, as in the earlier book, I attempt to quantify the evaluation of the armies using a simple scale:

✶	wholly inadequate
✶ ✶	marginal
✶ ✶ ✶	mission-capable
✶ ✶ ✶ ✶	war-winning

I hope awarding stars will sharpen, not settle, the ongoing dialog among those of us who remain fascinated by the Civil War.

In creating my scale, I have chosen what I believe to be sentiment-free evaluative labels—"wholly adequate," "marginal," "mission-capable," and "war-winning"—that focus on performance and outcomes rather than on intention and opinion. I have also chosen evaluative labels that can be applied to all aspects of the armies, not just to the armies themselves. For the nature, performance, and fate of the Civil War's principal military formations cannot be evaluated in a historical, technological, economic, social, and cultural vacuum. Thus, part one, Brothers in Arms, focuses on the single military institution that gave birth to both the Confederate and Union armies: the United States military as it existed before the Civil War.

Part two, Brother against Brother, evaluates the American military as it divided itself into a Confederate army and a Union army. Dimensions considered here are the social, cultural, and economic conditions under which the two forces went to war; the manner in which the South and the North actually mobilized for war; the overall organization, size, demographic makeup, and command structure of the Confederate and Union armies; the demographic, cultural, and economic profile of the soldiers and officers in each; and the uniforms, equipment, and arms with which each army fought. In addition, part two includes chapters devoted to the African-American Civil War, military medicine in the two armies, and the fate of POWs on both sides.

Before the Civil War, the United States fielded no land forces that required organizational formations larger than the regiment. Practically overnight—and a very dark night it was—the Civil War demanded militaries of a size unprecedented in the Americas. This, in turn, required organizational formations much larger than the regiment. The largest of these was the "army." The final part of this book, part three, The Principal Armies, evaluates the most important armies on each side.

I have included a very brief afterword, The Calculus of Victory and Defeat, which offers the equivalent of a "bottom-line" evaluation of the military institutions with which the South and the North fought the Civil War. In business, barring error or nefarious intent, the bottom line is a *final* result: profit, loss, or break-even. In business, the bottom line is the finish line. I suspect (indeed, I hope) that the bottom line in this book will be the *starting* line, marking the beginning of fresh discussion and debate on the single most formative event—not excepting the War of Independence—in the history we Americans share.

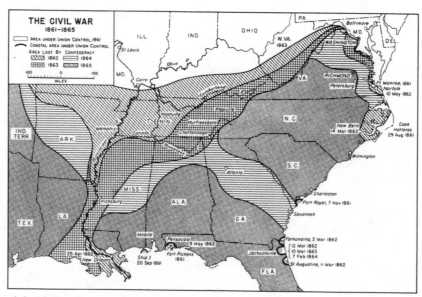

A divided nation at war, 1861–65.

Office of the Chief of Military History, United States Army

Part One

Brothers in Arms

Chapter 1
REVOLUTION, 1812, AND MEXICO

Before there was a "Union army" and a "Confederate army," there was a United States Army. On the eve of the nation's dissolution, at the very end of 1860, that army consisted of 16,000 officers and men. The product of a country whose people never liked the idea of maintaining a standing army in their midst—the obnoxious presence of redcoats among them was instrumental in driving the American colonists to war against their king in 1775—it was a military formation intended, really, to be little more than a police

B-4/58

Lieutenant General Winfield Scott, general-in-chief of the US Army at the start of the Civil War, had fought in every American conflict since the War of 1812.

force to manage, if not to curb, the depredations of "hostile" Indians on the frontier. This was the case even as late as 1860.

The core of the officer corps commanding the opposing troops of the North and the South had fought as comrades in arms during the US-Mexican War of 1846–48. Robert E. Lee and Ulysses S. Grant, Thomas "Stonewall" Jackson and William Tecumseh Sherman, James Longstreet and George B. McClellan, P. G. T. Beauregard and Ambrose Burnside, Braxton Bragg and George Meade were all among the Civil War general officers who got their start fighting Mexico together. Jefferson Davis, the president of the Confederacy, was a hero of the Battle of Buena Vista in the US-Mexican War, but perhaps even more remarkable was the Union army's first general-in-chief, Winfield Scott, "Old Fuss and Feathers," whose fifty-three-year military career began in 1808 and whose first war was the War of 1812 (1812–15). They were a band of brothers about to embark on a war tagged famously as the struggle of "brother against brother." Many of them never lost that fraternal feeling, even in the thick of bitterest battle.

In his 1885 *Personal Memoirs*, Grant recalled April 9, 1865, when Robert E. Lee came to him at the house of Wilmer McLean in Appomattox Courthouse, Virginia, to surrender his defeated Army of Northern Virginia. "What General Lee's feelings were I do not know. As he was a man of much dignity, with an impassable face, it was impossible to say whether he felt inwardly glad that the end had finally come, or felt sad over the result, and was too manly to show it. . . . my own feelings . . . were sad and depressed. I felt like anything rather than rejoicing at the downfall of a foe who had fought so long and valiantly, and had suffered so much for a cause, though that cause was, I believe, one of the worst for which a people ever fought." Grant found himself painfully self-conscious in Lee's presence, dressed, as the Confederate commander was, "in a full uniform which was entirely new, and . . . wearing a sword of considerable value, very likely the sword which had been presented by the State of Virginia. . . . In my rough traveling suit, the uniform of a private with the straps of a lieutenant-general, I must have contrasted very strangely with a man so handsomely dressed, six feet high and of faultless form." But soon the embarrassment melted as the two "fell into a conversation about old army times." The "conversation grew so pleasant that I almost forgot the object of our meeting." It was Lee who "called my attention to the object of our meeting, and said that he had asked for this interview for the purpose of getting from me the terms I proposed to give his army."[1]

THE UNITED STATES ARMY IS BORN

ARMY AT THE START OF THE AMERICAN REVOLUTION, 1775: ★

ARMY AT THE BATTLE OF YORKTOWN, 1781: ★ ★ ⸙

In the beginning was the militia. Following the Boston Tea Party of December 16, 1773, in which a band of political demonstrators destroyed a shipment of East India Company tea to protest British "taxation without representation," Parliament passed a series of Coercive Acts against Britain's American colonies, including the much-hated Quartering Act, authorizing the involuntary permanent quartering of British troops in Boston. British general Thomas Gage was named both commander in chief of British forces in America and royal governor of Massachusetts in April 1774. In response to the Boston crisis, fifty-six delegates from twelve

colonies (Georgia abstained) heeded the call of the Massachusetts Assembly (banned by Gage) for a Continental Congress, which convened at Carpenters' Hall, Philadelphia, on September 5, 1774. The congress condemned the Coercive Acts, urged Massachusetts to form an independent government, and advised colonists to arm themselves for protection while withholding taxes from the Crown until the acts were repealed.

On September 1, 1774, General Gage seized cannon and powder from arsenals in Cambridge and Charles Town, just outside of Boston. The Continental Congress responded by appropriating funds to buy new military supplies and authorizing John Hancock to head a Committee of Safety and to call out the militia. The militia members were dubbed "minutemen" because these citizen-soldiers pledged themselves to be armed, assembled, and prepared for battle on a minute's notice. A guerrilla war commenced against the British troops, and on April 18 Gage quietly assembled 600 to 800 troops on Boston Common under the command of Lieutenant Colonel Francis Smith and Major John Pitcairn. They set out for Lexington, where they were met by seventy or so minutemen on April 19. Fire was exchanged, and the outnumbered militiamen scattered. From Lexington, the British marched to Concord, where they met much more effective resistance and were forced to retreat to Boston, harried, all the way, by militia snipers.

The next month, the Second Continental Congress convened in Philadelphia and on June 14, 1775, created the Continental army, the direct precursor of the US Army. The congress authorized companies of riflemen and named George Washington their commander in chief. In addition, the Continental Congress took over the so-called Boston Army, a quasi-militia force at the time engaged against British forces in Boston. The Continental Congress quickly commissioned generals to serve under Washington. At this point the colonies had yet to declare their independence from Britain, so the origin of the US Army predates the birth of the United States itself, on July 4, 1776.

The Continental army constituted the "regular army," first of the United Colonies and then, after July 4, 1776, of the United States. It never supplanted the many state and local militias that also fought in the revolution—nor was it intended to. Over the course of the entire American Revolution, the Continental army consisted of (by modern estimate) 231,771 soldiers and officers—although a far lower number served at any one time. (Total militia forces numbered an estimated 145,000.) Appointed as Washington's top lieutenants were Artemas Ward (already commanding the Boston militia), Israel Putnam of Connecticut, Philip Schuyler of New York, and two recently retired officers of the British army, Charles Lee and Horatio Gates. By the end of 1775, Congress had 27,500 Continental army troops actively on its payroll, from all the colonies.

During the spring of 1775, New Englanders poured into Cambridge and adjacent towns to lay siege to Boston. By the end of May, some 10,000 colonial troops surrounded the city, and by June the number had swollen to between 14,000 and 16,000, all now become soldiers of the Continental army, and quartered chiefly at Cambridge. It was not this force, but some 2,400 militiamen serving in regiments from Connecticut, Massachusetts, New Hampshire, and Rhode Island, who fought the celebrated Battle of Bunker Hill on June 17, 1775, holding the British regulars to bloody Pyrrhic victory. The British took Bunker Hill and Breed's Hill in Charles Town, but at the heavy cost of 1,054 casualties out of some 3,000 deployed. Of 2,400 colonial defenders, 450 were killed, wounded, or captured.

Even as the Battle of Bunker Hill was being fought, the troops of the Continental army laid siege to Gage and his forces of about 11,000. On January 24, 1776, Henry Knox returned from Fort Ticonderoga and Crown Point, in New York, with the artillery that had been captured there, and the Continental army, now under Washington's command, used the weapons to fortify Dorchester Heights, overlooking Boston. Seeing himself surrounded and outnumbered, General Howe abandoned Boston, evacuating by ship from March 7 to March 17. The siege of Boston had consumed nearly eleven months.

In a contest with the army of the most powerful nation in the world, the Patriots had prevailed. But Washington and the Continental army would not enjoy another such triumph anytime soon. The Battles of Quebec (December 31, 1775), Long Island/Brooklyn Heights (August 27, 1776), White Plains (October 28, 1776), and Fort Washington (November 16, 1776) were all Continental army defeats. Through them all, however, General George Washington, a mediocre tactician, nevertheless emerged as a courageous commander who kept his army together, inspired, and viable.

He was also a realist. Washington accepted that he could not defeat the overwhelming military might of the British Empire, but he believed that if he could keep his army intact and fighting long enough, the liberal wing of the British government might well prevail and America would win its independence. In this task he struggled not only against the British, but against a Continental Congress that ran the Continental army as if it were a mere militia. Enlistment periods were brief, unrelated to the "duration" of the war, and expired both frequently and inopportunely. Congressional appropriations were parsimonious and inadequate, and their disbursement was routinely delayed.

British forces pursued Washington and his army across the Hudson River and into New Jersey. Here, in the late winter of 1776, Washington consolidated his forces, only to retreat farther, across the Delaware River and into Pennsylvania. Fortunately, Lord Charles Cornwallis, commanding the British forces in pursuit of the Continental army, decided to halt at the Delaware to await spring before finishing off Washington and the revolution.

By Christmastime, General Washington had no more than 6,000 troops fit for duty. Fearing that he would soon lose most of these when current enlistments expired, he boldly decided on a counteroffensive. On Christmas night he loaded 2,400 veteran troops and eighteen cannon into flat-bottomed Durham boats and crossed the Delaware back to New Jersey in the teeth of a vicious winter storm. He stealthily marched his men to Trenton, where Hessians, the Crown's much-feared German mercenaries, were camped, and there, at about eight o'clock on the morning of December 26, Washington surprised them and won a splendid victory. This was followed on January 3 by the Battle of Princeton, another American victory. From here Washington rode west to Morristown to make winter camp. For the present, the Revolution had been saved.

Early spring 1777 brought the Americans fresh troops and, thankfully, a willingness among many veterans to extend their enlistments in the Continental army. In Paris, congressional emissaries Benjamin Franklin and Silas Deane were gradually persuading the French government to conclude a formal alliance with the United States. Before this became a reality, Marie Joseph Paul Yves Roch Gilbert du Motier, Marquis de Lafayette, arrived in June with a party of other idealistic European adventurers. Foremost among these was Johann de Kalb (Johann von Robais, Baron de Kalb), from Bavaria. In December, Friedrich Wilhelm von Steuben, from the Prussian fortress city of Magdeburg, also arrived. The two Germans would impart their European military expertise to the officers and men of the Continental army. In particular,

Steuben, whom Washington appointed inspector general, advised on shelter, encampments, and equipment and then introduced a training program, which, during the bitter Valley Forge (Pennsylvania) winter of 1778–79, he distilled into *Regulations for the Order and Discipline of the Troops of the United States*. Familiarly dubbed the "Blue Book," this was the first manual of the United States Army. Second only to the actual creation of the army by the Continental Congress, the Blue Book was responsible for the emergence of an effective national military force.

Throughout 1777–80 the Continental army, in loose and imperfect coordination with the various state militias, continued to battle British and "Tory" forces (Americans who remained loyal to the king) in the northern and southern colonies. As was the case earlier in the war, the Patriot forces lost more battles than they won—except for, most notably, the two Battles of Saratoga (Freeman's Farm and Bemis Heights, September 19 and October 7, 1777, respectively) in New York, which resulted in the surrender of General John Burgoyne's army to Patriot generals Horatio Gates and Benedict Arnold. This had the effect of validating the military dimension of the American Revolution not only in the United States, but throughout much of the international community. The next great Patriot triumphs came in the south, at the Battle of King's Mountain (on the border of North and South Carolina, October 7, 1780) and the Battle of Cowpens (South Carolina, January 17, 1781). The first was a militia victory, but the second victory was a unique collaboration between "conventional" Continental army forces under General Nathanael Greene and the skilled guerrilla leader Daniel Morgan.

The Battle of Cowpens set British southern forces on their heels, ultimately moving General Charles Cornwallis to lead his army to make a stand at Yorktown, Virginia. Cornwallis chose the Yorktown peninsula because it gave him access to the Atlantic, where he and his men might be rescued by the Royal Navy, if need be. But, in the end, thanks to Washington's skilled coordination of Continental army operations with French land forces under Jean-Baptiste Donatien de Vimeur, comte de Rochambeau, and French naval forces under Admiral François Paul de Grasse, Cornwallis was trapped and formally surrendered on October 19, 1781. Yorktown did not end the war, but it broke Britain's national resolve to continue resisting the revolution. On September 3, 1783, the Treaty of Paris ended the American Revolution with Britain's recognition of United States independence.

WAR OF 1812

ARMY AT THE START OF THE WAR, JUNE 1812: ★

ARMY AT THE BATTLE OF NEW ORLEANS, JANUARY 1815: ★ ★ ⸝

After the victory at Yorktown, the Continental army was allowed to dwindle with the expiration of enlistments, except for small forces that garrisoned the Hudson River fortress at West Point, New York, and a handful of frontier outposts. The latter garrisons foreshadowed the principal role of the US Army throughout the rest of the eighteenth century and most of the nineteenth—a frontier force serving mainly to police the Indians.

On June 3, 1784, Congress transformed the Continental army into a diminutive peacetime force. This action followed a series of proposals from General Washington and others for a modest peacetime standing army, all of which Congress rejected. On June 2, 1784, having rejected one proposal for a 900-man army and then another, for a 350-man army with a mandate to raise an additional 700 recruits, Congress ordered all remaining members of the Continental army to be discharged, save for 25 caretakers

at Fort Pitt and 55 at West Point. The next day, however, Congress created a United States Army based on a modified militia plan. The legislation required four states to raise annually a total of 700 men for a year's service. The concept of a national army made up of regiments with distinctly state origins would remain operative up to and during the Civil War. The fact that most soldiers and their officers identified their greatest loyalty with their home state rather than with the federal government facilitated, in 1861, the breakup of the US Army into a Confederate army and a Union army.

On November 4, 1791, a force led by General Arthur St. Clair was all but wiped out at the Battle of the Wabash by Indians of the so-called Western Confederacy—933 killed or wounded out of 1,000 troops. This disaster prompted the disbandment of the Continental army and its replacement by the Legion of the United States, assembled from elements of the 1st and 2nd Regiments of the Continental army who were given training according to the military writings of Henry Bouquet, a Swiss-born British general during the French and Indian War. The legion was led by General Anthony ("Mad Anthony") Wayne, a standout officer of the American Revolution. Bouquet's work was supplemented by Steuben's Blue Book, which would continue to serve as the official manual not only for the legion but also most state militias of most states until 1840.

The US Army officially came into being in 1796, when the Legion of the United States was disbanded. Six years later, in 1802, the United States Military Academy was established at West Point, New York. The son of a Virginia plantation owner, Winfield Scott (1786–1866) studied briefly at the College of William and Mary and then apprenticed to a local lawyer, but soon discovered he had a taste for the military life. He did not attend the academy, but instead enlisted directly in the Virginia militia in 1807 before obtaining a commission as captain in the Light Artillery of the US Army in 1808. Four years later, the War Hawk faction of Congress passed a declaration of war against Britain on June 18, 1812. Officially, the chief cause was British failure to respect American neutrality rights at sea and, on land, to honor the frontier boundaries between Canada and the United States. The more compelling American motive, however, was territorial acquisition. In 1812 the region known as Spanish Florida extended as far west as the Mississippi River. Because Spain was an ally of Great Britain against Napoleon, the War Hawks believed that victory in a war against Britain would result in the acquisition of its ally's territory, which would be joined to the vast western territories already acquired by the United States with the Louisiana Purchase (1803). The War Hawks gave little thought to the fact that the strength of the US Army was only 7,000 regular troops, who were broadcast across a vast territory and were led by generals of very uneven ability, most having attained their rank through political connections rather than demonstrated military ability.

Among the US Army regulars was Scott, who was promoted to lieutenant colonel of the 2nd Artillery Regiment in July 1812. Congress, however, relied on militia companies and on short-term volunteers, not the recruitment of regulars like Scott, to swell the ranks of the land army. A grandiose and entirely unrealistic plan was implemented to take the war to British America with a three-pronged invasion of Canada: an incursion from Lake Champlain to Montreal, another penetration across the Niagara frontier, and a third into Upper Canada from Detroit. Undermanned, poorly led, and thoroughly uncoordinated, all three prongs failed.

Scott served primarily in the Niagara Campaign, commanding a landing party during the Battle of Queenston Heights (Ontario, Canada) on October 13, 1812. He quickly learned a bitter lesson about depending on militia units. No sooner did US forces reach the Canadian border than the militia troops refused to cross the international boundary. Left with an inadequate number of regulars, Scott, together with the New York militia commander, was forced to surrender. Taken as a prisoner of war, Scott was subsequently released in a prisoner exchange. The army recognized that the defeat and surrender had been no fault of Scott's, and he was promoted to colonel in March 1813. He performed brilliantly, planning and leading the capture of British-held Fort George, Ontario. The operation, in which Scott was wounded, was one of a handful of US Army success in the war.

On March 19, 1814, the twenty-seven-year-old Scott was promoted to brigadier general and commanded the 1st Brigade at the Battle of Chippawa (July 5, 1814), a US victory, and then at Lundy's Lane (July 25). Fought at Niagara Falls, Ontario, Lundy's Lane was a bloody tactical draw and a narrow British strategic victory. Seriously wounded, Scott was brevetted to major general.

Although his wounds prevented his return to combat for the duration of the conflict—ended on December 24, 1814, by the Treaty of Ghent, which restored Anglo-American relations to their *status quo ante bellum*—Scott emerged from the War of 1812 with a well-deserved reputation for competence and valor. In 1815 he was appointed to oversee the compilation of the first standard drill regulations for the US Army, and he was made chairman of an officer selection board and a Board of Tactics. Late in 1815, Scott was sent to Europe to study the methods of the French army, at the time the most admired military force in Europe. While abroad he acquired the practical military writings of Napoleon I, which he translated into English for use in training the army. In 1821, 1824, and 1826, Scott presided over the Board of Tactics.

All told, more than anyone else, Winfield Scott was responsible for creating the doctrine that guided the nineteenth-century American army. Nevertheless, he was passed over for promotion to top army command and, in 1828, tendered his resignation, which was refused. Two years later, he published *Abstract of Infantry Tactics, Including Exercises and Manueuvres of Light-Infantry and Riflemen, for the Use of the Militia of the United States*, an attempt to extend the professionalism of the regular US Army to the state militias.

INDIAN WARS

US ARMY, 1815–46: ✯ ✯

Winfield Scott was not a glamorous figure, and to the extent that most Americans are familiar with him today, it is as he was in his old age, arthritic, rotund, far too heavy to ride horseback, and with an affection for ornate dress uniforms that earned him the nickname of "Old Fuss and Feathers." In fact, no other single officer had a greater positive and formative impact on the United States Army, the army that would bring victory in the US-Mexican War and that would fight *both* sides of the Civil War.

Between the War of 1812 and the war with Mexico, the army carried out the principal mission for which it had been created: "policing" the "hostile" Indian tribes, an assignment more accurately described as suppressing Native Americans who resisted the expansion of the white American frontier. The army and a variety of militias fought the Black Hawk War in 1832 (Scott had planned to assume field command, but was prevented from doing so due to a cholera outbreak among his troops). He did lead the army in the Second Seminole War and the Creek War, both in 1836, and, two years later, led troops in the US Army's grimmest and perhaps most reprehensible mission, the forcible "removal" of the Cherokee Indians from their traditional lands in Georgia, Tennessee, and Alabama to "Indian Territory" in what is now Oklahoma. Later called the Trail of Tears, the removal (not all of it under Scott's command) cost perhaps 6,000 Cherokee lives en route to Indian Territory.

US-MEXICAN WAR

US ARMY, 1846–48: ✯ ✯ ✯

In 1840 Scott wrote the three-volume *Infantry-Tactics; or, Rules for the Exercise and Maneuvre of the United States Infantry*, which served as the new standard US Army manual. It was this work that would guide the army in fighting the US-Mexican War, and it remained the army's official manual until William J. Hardee published his *Rifle and Light Infantry Tactics for the Exercise and Manoeuvres of Troops When Acting as Light Infantry or Riflemen* in 1855. Popularly called *Hardee's Tactics*, this volume would be a principal guide for the armies of both the Union and the Confederacy during the Civil War. Like Scott, Hardee was a Southerner, and, also like Scott, he served in the US-Mexican War. In contrast to Scott, who remained loyal both to the Union and to the US Army at the outbreak of the Civil War, Hardee would resign his commission on January 31, 1861, to join the Confederate army. Thus the two officers instrumental in shaping US Army doctrine became enemies. Their writings, however, would continue to influence the commanders of both sides equally.

On June 25, 1841, following the death Major General Alexander Macomb, Scott, now the senior ranking officer in the army, succeeded him as commanding general. Promoted to major general, at the time the army's highest rank, Scott formally assumed office on July 5, 1841. His top priority was to ensure that the army would have a continuous supply of highly qualified officers and, accordingly, he turned his attention to strengthening and professionalizing the United States Military Academy at West Point.

On March 1, 1845, after Congress voted to admit the Republic of Texas as a state of the Union, Mexico repudiated the 1836 treaty by which it had granted Texas independence following defeat in the Texas War of Independence. Mexico also severed diplomatic relations with the United States. President James K. Polk continued efforts to peacefully negotiate US claims to Texas as well as to Upper California (in 1845 a Mexican province) even as he ordered a military force to be positioned along the Rio Grande to resist an anticipated invasion. Polk viewed Scott as a potential political rival, and, during the planning of the positioning operation—the first large-scale strategic movement of the United States Army—the two men fell into dispute. Polk denounced Scott publicly and relieved him of command of forces in the field. Zachary Taylor believed the relief was politically motivated and unjustified, but nevertheless obeyed the president and took command of the deployment. By the fall of 1845, he had deployed some 4,000 men, and when US-Mexican negotiations collapsed in February 1846, Polk ordered Taylor to advance. He led his men 100 miles down the coast to the Rio Grande, positioning most of his forces along the river, eighteen miles southwest of Point Isabel, opposite the Mexican town of Matamoros. On April 25 the Mexicans responded to the provocation by attacking a small advance party of 60 US Army dragoons. This prompted Taylor to appeal directly to Texas and Louisiana for 5,000 militia volunteers to augment his regular army forces. Nevertheless, he had only about 2,300 troops available on May 8 at Palo Alto when a Mexican force of some 4,000 engaged him.

Taylor was a courageous but cautious and conservative commander. Fortunately for him, he had a body of well-trained officers in the field (among them Ulysses S. Grant, a West Point graduate) and a substantial complement of artillery. Outnumbered though he was, Taylor repulsed the Mexican forces—but then failed to pursue his defeated opponent. He showed a similar absence of aggressiveness at Resaca de Palma on May 9, when he again declined to follow up with pursuit a victory against Mexican forces. Had he done so, Taylor might have finished off the very force that had begun the war. With war already under way, Congress voted a declaration of war and President Polk signed it on May 12, 1846. The prewar regular army consisted of between 6,562 and 7,224 troops (of whom more than 600 were officers). The authorized strength was increased at the time of the declaration to 15,540, a number that was augmented by the call-up of 50,000 one-year volunteers. This would be the largest regular federal force *actually fielded* to that time. Its objective was to obtain all Mexican territory north of the Rio Grande and Gila River, west to the Pacific Ocean. In the course of the war, 35,009 additional enlisted troops and 1,016 additional officers were recruited into the regular army. Of the twenty-eight states of the Union at the time, only Vermont, Maine, Connecticut, and Rhode Island did not provide any volunteer units for incorporation into the United States Volunteers. California, which did not join the Union until 1850, provided soldiers, as did Iowa, which didn't become a state until December 1846. The states recruited a total of 73,260 volunteers, including 3,131 officers.

Although he was officially denied field command, Scott was still commanding general of the US Army, and it was he who created the overall plan of war. Taylor was to march west from Matamoros to Monterrey, Mexico; once Monterrey was taken, all of northern Mexico would be vulnerable. Simultaneously, Brigadier General John E. Wool would march from San Antonio, Texas, to Chihuahua, Mexico; from here he could advance farther south, to Saltillo, near Taylor's force at Monterrey. Finally, Colonel Stephen Watts Kearny would advance out of Fort Leavenworth, Kansas, to take Santa Fe and, from there, continue all the way to San Diego, California. This third prong would later be modified after part of Kearny's force, under Colonel Alexander W. Doniphan, succeeded in making a remarkable advance deep into Mexico, via Chihuahua to Parras. As Scott had originally planned the war, capturing the Mexican capital, Mexico City, was not contemplated. Both President Polk and General Scott hoped that achieving all the objectives of the initial plan would force Mexico to capitulate quickly without the necessity for a deeper invasion.

Despite sweltering temperatures and the illness of many of his troops, which cut his available forces in half, Taylor took Monterrey on September 23. Unwisely, however, he granted the Mexican commander's request for an eight-week armistice. This gave the Mexicans time to rebuild their forces, and President Polk harshly criticized Taylor for having permitted the Mexican army to escape intact. Although Taylor and Wool were subsequently able to join forces at Monterrey, Polk, scorning Taylor's lack of aggression, now called on General Scott to personally lead an amphibious assault on Veracruz. Polk directed Taylor to detach 8,000 of his troops to join Scott's force. Scott would march inland for an attack on Mexico City while Taylor, who was left with 7,000 men, mostly US Volunteers rather than regular army troops, would go on the defensive at Monterrey. (In fact, Taylor chose to interpret President Polk's directions as advice rather than orders and decided to leave small garrisons at Monterrey and Saltillo while marching off with 4,650 men to Agua Nueva. This movement led to the Battle of Buena Vista (February 22–23, 1847) against the soldiers of the man now in command of all Mexican forces, General Antonio López de Santa Anna. Santa Anna's troops outnumbered Taylor's command three to one, but Taylor refused Santa Anna's demand for his surrender and, again thanks to superior American artillery and the bold

leadership of Taylor's well-trained field commanders, the larger Mexican force was defeated.

While Taylor was occupied fighting Santa Anna, Colonel Kearny led a spectacular march from Fort Leavenworth, Kansas, to Santa Fe, New Mexico, which fell to him without a shot. From Santa Fe, Kearny marched on to California, reaching San Diego in December 1846, only to find that a US naval squadron had already secured the California ports.

By March 2, 1847, when Scott commenced operations leading to the landing at Vera Cruz—the very first amphibious landing in US Army history—the Americans were already in control of northern Mexico. In a masterpiece of logistics and command, Scott landed 10,000 men at Vera Cruz during the night of March 9. He took Vera Cruz, then advanced on Jalapa (Xalapa), closing in on Mexico City. On April 17 Scott defeated a superior force at Cerro Gordo and took Jalapa and then Puebla. The citizens of Puebla, the second-largest city in Mexico, hated Santa Anna and therefore surrendered to Scott without resistance on May 15, 1847.

While Scott prepared to march out of Puebla and on to Mexico City, State Department official Nicholas P. Trist opened treaty negotiations with Santa Anna. In contrast to Taylor, Scott believed in seizing the moment to apply maximum pressure to Santa Anna, who was now the overall commander of Mexican forces. He therefore committed all of his troops to the advance against Mexico City, even though this meant leaving his line of communication, from Vera Cruz to Puebla, entirely undefended. He moved out on August 7 and won the Battle of Contreras on August 19–20 and the Battle of Churubusco later on the 20th. On September 8 Scott stormed and seized El Molino del Rey, a cannon foundry just west of Chapultepec Castle outside of Mexico City. On September 12–13 he began an assault on Chapultepec with an artillery barrage, then sent three columns over the approaches to the hilltop fortress, which was soon taken. Mexico City itself fell on September 14, 1847. As Scott had hoped, this hastened the peace negotiations and, on February 2, 1848, the Treaty of Guadalupe Hidalgo was concluded. Mexico ceded to the United States what was called "New Mexico," the territory that encompassed the present state of New Mexico and portions of the present states of Utah, Nevada, Arizona, and Colorado as well as all of Upper California (the present state of California). Mexico also formally renounced claims to Texas above the Rio Grande. In return, the United States paid Mexico $15 million and agreed to assume all claims of US citizens against Mexico.

More than any prior conflict, the US-Mexican War forged the armies that would fight the Civil War. Taylor, Jefferson Davis (colonel of the 155th Infantry Regiment, the "Mississippi Rifles"), and Scott emerged as heroes. Taylor would go on to be elected president of the United States shortly after the war, succumbing, however, to an unknown illness just seventeen months into his single term. Davis served in the House of Representatives, then as secretary of war under President Franklin Pierce, and in the US Senate from 1857 to 1861. He became

the first and only president of the Confederate States on February 22, 1862. As for Winfield Scott, he continued to command the US Army through the outbreak of the Civil War and through the war's first major battle, Bull Run, on July 21, 1861. Accepting responsibility for that defeat, the seventy-four-year-old, 300-plus-pound Scott, mocked now as "Old Fat and Feeble," voluntarily yielded operational command to George B. McClellan.

Yet it was undeniably Scott who had, more than any other officer, created the foundation of the armies that fought the Civil War, and it was the war with Mexico that had given twenty of the most prominent Civil War generals—in addition to the president of the Confederate States of America—their defining experience of command in war: Robert E. Lee, Stonewall Jackson, P. G. T. Beauregard, Fitz-John Porter, Albert Sydney Johnston, Braxton Bragg, Joseph Johnston, James Longstreet, William J. Hardee, and President Jefferson Davis on the Confederate side; Ulysses S. Grant, Ambrose Burnside, George Meade, George McClellan, William T. Sherman, Joseph K. Mansfield, Edwin Vose Sumner Sr., John F. Reynolds, Robert Anderson, John C. Frémont, and John Pope on the side of the Union.

Chapter 2

OFFICER CORPS

US ARMY OFFICER CORPS ON THE EVE OF CIVIL WAR: ★ ★ ⚔

On December 20, 1860, South Carolina became the first state to secede from the Union. Now it was clear. There would be no turning back from a bloody crisis rooted in the single greatest issue that the American Revolution (1775–83), Declaration of Independence (1775), Articles of Confederation (1777), and Constitution (1787) had not merely failed to resolve but had largely ignored: slavery.

In that December, the United States Army had an authorized strength of approximately 18,000 officers and men, but, at the time, only 16,367 were actually on the rolls. Of this number, 1,109 were commissioned officers.[1] Just five of these were general officers, with the highest rank actually serving being a solitary major general, who was the US Army's commanding general; the other four were brigadiers:

- Maj. Gen. Winfield Scott, commanding general, appointed 1841

- Brig. Gen. William S. Harney, appointed 1858

- Brig. Gen. Joseph E. Johnston, quartermaster general, appointed June 28, 1860*

- Brig. Gen. David E. Twiggs, appointed 1846**

- Brig. Gen. John E. Wool, appointed 1841

The remaining 1,104 members of the officer corps were either staff officers or line officers. In December 1860, 361 staff officers were distributed over the bureaus and departments of the War Department. Except for the Quartermaster Department, commanded by a brigadier general, each department or bureau was commanded by a colonel. Some of these colonels held "staff brevets" of brigadier general. A brevet is often described as a temporary promotion, but, more accurately, it is a warrant that gives an officer rank title higher than his actual rank—without, however, a commensurate advance in pay. Typically, a brevet is awarded for gallantry in the field; a *staff* brevet however, is a distinction for meritorious service of any kind. The brevetted generals (there were seven on the eve of the war) are not included in the count of five general officers just mentioned.

The other 743 officers were line officers—combat officers—who served in regiments. Of these, 351 were assigned to infantry regiments, 210 to artillery regiments, and 182 to mounted regiments, which included cavalry (soldiers who fought on horseback) and dragoons (soldiers who rode into position, but who dismounted to fight), as well as "mounted riflemen" (similar to dragoons). All regiments were commanded by colonels. Promotion in the antebellum US Army came at a notoriously glacial pace, so top-ranking staff officers were old men, averaging age 64, with six of them over 70. But even regimental commanders, colonels in the field, were on average only a year younger than their desk-bound counterparts. The actual age range for *combat* colonels was 42 to 80. The United States Army on the eve of the Civil War was commanded by

---

*Johnston resigned in May 1861 and was appointed general in the CSA on August 31, 1861.
**After surrendering men, equipment, and property to Confederates in Texas on February 18, 1861, Twiggs was dismissed from the USA on March 1, 1861; he was appointed CSA major general on May 22, 1861, retired on October 18, 1861, and died in July 1862.

old men—all older than the average white life expectancy in the United States, 40.8 years.[2] And at least some were twice that age!

A regimental headquarters in the US Army on the brink of Civil War consisted of a colonel, a lieutenant colonel, two majors, and an adjutant and quartermaster, both of whom were lieutenants. In infantry and artillery regiments, the adjutant and quartermaster were detailed from line companies. Mounted regiments, however, were allocated additional lieutenants expressly for headquarters staff service. The regimental officers presided over an enlisted staff that included a sergeant major, a quartermaster sergeant, and a chief musician. (Music was important in the nineteenth-century American military, with each infantry and artillery regiment authorized to enlist twenty musicians while mounted regiments had just two chief buglers.)

In theory, regiments in the West, which an 1850 law had made larger than those in the East, numbered as many as 900 men, but, in practice, no regiment before the Civil War ever reached that size. The typical US Army regiment before the Civil War consisted of 300 to 400 enlisted soldiers organized into either ten companies (in infantry and mounted regiments) or twelve batteries (in artillery regiments). Each company consisted of 30 to 40 soldiers commanded by one or two officers. On the eve of the war, there were ten infantry regiments, five mounted regiments, and four artillery regiments, fielding in total 197 "line" (that is, combat) companies. Because the principal mission of the United States Army at this time was to police the Indians west of the Mississippi River, only eighteen companies—all artillery units totaling about 720 soldiers—were stationed east of the Mississippi.

Officer Training

As will be discussed further in chapter 3, the United States Army was diminutive by design.

Among the compelling reasons for declaring independence in 1776 was King George III's quartering among the American people, "in times of peace, Standing Armies without the Consent of our legislatures." Moreover, the king "affected to render the Military independent of and superior to the Civil power."[3] The government of the independent United States had no desire to repeat this situation. The small federal army it maintained was intended mainly to function as a frontier police force to suppress Indian "depredations." The belief was that, in time of some greater emergency, the federal army could be quickly supplemented by existing state militias, and the states would be additionally responsible for recruiting volunteers into the federal service as needed to meet the demands of war or other contingency.

Although the states were capable of delivering raw manpower to the military when required to do so, there was no substitute for well-trained officers. In addition to policing Indians, the peacetime army also served as a vehicle for creating a cadre of professional military leaders capable of fighting wars. The US Military Academy at West Point, New York, was established in 1802. Although the academy has had its detractors, including none other than frontiersman and Tennessee congressman Davy Crockett (who unsuccessfully introduced a "Resolution to Abolish the Military Academy at West Point" on February 25, 1830[4]) and more recent luminaries,[5] 523 USMA graduates served in the US-Mexican War, of whom 452 were promoted or decorated for gallantry.[6] The majority of notable Civil War officers, Union and Confederate, were West Point graduates, with 294 serving as Union generals and 151 as Confederate generals.[7]

The curriculum to which these officers were exposed had been formulated by Brevet Brigadier General Sylvanus Thayer (1785–1872), the "Father of West Point," who served as superintendent of the academy from 1817 to 1833. He modelled the academy curriculum on France's

École Polytechnique (where he himself had studied from 1815 to 1817) and emphasized practical mathematics, engineering, and the study of historical battles, especially the then-recent campaigns of Napoleon (especially as filtered through the writings of Antoine-Henri Jomini). In addition, the French language and drawing were required—the former to aid in military studies (the most important scholarly writing on military subjects came from France at the time) and the latter to aid in mapmaking in the field. Most important of all, however, Thayer introduced some of the bedrock traditions of West Point, including the emphasis on honor, discipline, and

Lieutenant General Ulysses S. Grant would rise to top command of the Union armies. He is seen here at Cold Harbor, Virginia, during his Overland Campaign of 1864. NATIONAL ARCHIVES AND RECORDS ADMINISTRATION

personal responsibility. He also inaugurated the cumulative demerit system, by which strict standards of military deportment were to be individually inculcated through negative reinforcement. For some of the older Union and Confederate officers who served in the Civil War, Thayer was a profound influence, and the tactical thought of Napoleon as distilled by Jomini formed the basis of their conduct of the war.

Most of the Civil War–era officers who came through West Point were, however, influenced more by Denis Hart Mahan (1802–71) than by Thayer. Mahan never became superintendent of West Point, but he was the institution's towering professor of engineering as well as military science from 1832 to 1871. Almost everything senior US Army officers, including those who fought in the Civil War, knew about fortifications and entrenchment came from Mahan, as did his emphasis on the tactical importance of maneuver and the taking and holding of key strategic points. These latter two lessons may have done more harm than good during the Civil War, especially in their influence on inherently conservative officers such as George Brinton McClellan, who substituted maneuver for the kind of raw aggression Ulysses S. Grant so productively practiced, and who devoted more energy to seizing and holding ground than he did to doing what Grant usually tried to do, namely destroy the enemy army.

Among the most notable early graduates of West Point who served in the Civil War are (in order of their class):

- Maj. Gen. Joseph Gilbert Totten, 1805 (Union): A military engineer who served in the War of 1812 (1812–15) and the US-Mexican War (1846–48) as well as the Union army. He was chief of engineers of the US Army from 1832 to 1864.

- Brig. Gen. Gustavus Loomis, 1811 (Union): Superintendent of recruiting for the Union army, Loomis served in the field during the Black Hawk War (1832) and the Third Seminole War (1855–1858).

- Col. Lewis Gustavus DeRussy, 1814 (Confederate): Oldest West Point graduate in the Confederate States Army (CSA). Fought in the War of 1812 (1812–15) and the US-Mexican War (1846–48).

- Gen. Samuel Cooper, 1815 (Confederate): Adjutant general and inspector general of the CSA. Fought in the Second Seminole War (1835–42) and the US-Mexican War (1846–48).

- Maj. Gen. Richard Delafield, 1818 (Union): Was in charge of New York Harbor defenses (1861–64) and served as chief of engineers (1864–66) during the Civil War; was superintendent of USMA 1838–45, 1856–61, and (after a brief break) again in 1861.

- Brig. Gen. John H. Winder, 1820 (Confederate): Commander, Confederate Bureau of Prison Camps. Fought in the US-Mexican War (1846–48).

- Capt. Charles Dimmock, 1821 (Confederate): Engineer who designed the remarkable defenses of Petersburg, Virginia, site of the nine-month Petersburg Siege (June 9, 1864–March 25, 1865).

- Brig. Gen. John J. Abercrombie, 1822 (Union): Was a field commander at the Battle of Falling Waters, Peninsula Campaign, Battle of Seven Pines (where he was wounded), and Battle of Malvern Hill; late in the war, he commanded the Washington, DC, defenses and, during Grant's Overland Campaign, was in charge of various supply depots. He served in the Black Hawk War (1832), the Seminole Wars (variously, 1816–58), and the US-Mexican War (1846–48).

- Maj. Gen. David Hunter, 1822 (Union): Fought at the First Battle of Bull Run and commanded the Army of the Shenandoah. On his own authority, he emancipated slaves in three Confederate states *before* the Emancipation Proclamation (his "illegal" actions were rescinded by Abraham Lincoln). Before the Civil War, he fought in the Second Seminole War (1835–42) and the US-Mexican War (1846–48).

- Brig. Gen. George Wright, 1822 (Union): Served as commander of the Department of the Pacific during the Civil War, having fought in the Second Seminole War (1835–42), the US-Mexican War (1846–48), and the Yakima War (1855–58).

- Maj. Gen. Lorenzo Thomas, 1823 (Union): Adjutant general of the US Army during the Civil War and appointed interim US secretary of war by President Andrew Johnson. Fought in the Seminole Wars (variously, 1816–58) and the US-Mexican War (1846–48).

- Maj. Gen. Robert Anderson, 1825 (Union): Commandant of Fort Sumter at the outbreak of the Civil War. Served in the Black Hawk War (1832), the Second Seminole War (1835–42), and the US-Mexican War (1846–48).

- Maj. Gen. Benjamin Huger, 1825 (Confederate): General officer in the CSA relieved of field duty for poor performance at Norfolk and reassigned as a staff officer. Fought in the US-Mexican War (1846–48).

- Maj. Gen. Samuel P. Heintzelman, 1826 (Union): Fought at the First Battle of Bull Run, Peninsula Campaign, and Second Battle of Bull Run. He served in the Second Seminole War (1835–42) and the US-Mexican War (1846–48).

- Maj. Gen. Philip St. George Cooke, 1827 (Union): Fought in the Battles of Yorktown, Williamsburg, Gaines's Mill, and White Oak Swamp. He was the father of Confederate brigadier general John Rogers Cooke and the father-in-law of Confederate major general J. E. B. Stuart. Cooke fought in the Black Hawk War (1832) and the US-Mexican War (1846–48).

- Lt. Gen. Leonidas Polk, 1827 (Confederate): Called the "Fighting Bishop" because he was the Episcopal bishop of the Louisiana Diocese. He fought at the Battles of Perryville and Stones River, the Tullahoma Campaign, the Battle of Chickamauga, and the Chattanooga and Atlanta Campaigns. During the latter campaign, he was killed at the Battle of Marietta on June 14, 1864.

- Pres. Jefferson Davis, 1828 (Confederate): Although he held no rank in the Confederate military, he served as the president of the Confederacy and took a strong (if often misguided) hand in the conduct of strategy. He served in the Black Hawk War (1832) and the US-Mexican War (1846–48).

- Brig. Gen. Thomas F. Drayton, 1828 (Confederate): Military railroad engineer; he fought against his brother, US Navy captain Percival Drayton, at the Battle of Port Royal.

- Brig. Gen. Hugh W. Mercer, 1828 (Confederate): Commander of the District of Georgia who drafted free blacks into the Confederate service.

- Lt. Gen. Theophilus H. Holmes, 1829 (Confederate): A favorite of President Jefferson Davis, Holmes commanded the Trans-Mississippi Department, a post in which he enjoyed little success.

- Gen. Joseph E. Johnston, 1829 (Confederate): A brigadier general in the US Army, he was the highest-ranking US officer to resign his commission and join the Confederate forces. Johnston held several army commands and fought at the First Battle of Bull Run, the Peninsula Campaign, the Vicksburg Campaign, the Atlanta Campaign, and the Battle of Bentonville. He was a veteran of the Seminole Wars (variously, 1816–58) and the US-Mexican War (1846–48).

- Gen. Robert E. Lee, 1829 (Confederate): Commander of the Army of Northern Virginia and (in 1865) general-in-chief of the Confederate States Army; one of the greatest commanders of the Civil War. Fought in the US-Mexican War (1846–48).

Considered by some the greatest general America ever produced, Robert E. Lee is best remembered as commander of the Army of Northern Virginia, flagship force of the Confederacy. He was photographed in April 1865 by Mathew B. Brady, the iconic photographer of the Civil War. NATIONAL ARCHIVES AND RECORDS ADMINISTRATION

- Brig. Gen. Robert C. Buchanan, 1830 (Union): Fought at the Battles of Yorktown, Gaines's Mill, Glendale, and Malvern Hill, as well the Second Battle of Bull Run and the Battle of Fredericksburg. Buchanan fought in the Black Hawk War (1832), the Second Seminole War (1835–42), and the US-Mexican War (1846–48).

- Maj. Gen. John B. Magruder, 1830 (Confederate): Celebrated for action in the Peninsula Campaign. Magruder served in the Second Seminole War (1835–42) and the US-Mexican War (1846–48), as well as in the Imperial Mexican Army.

- Brig. Gen. William N. Pendleton, 1830 (Confederate): An Episcopal priest in civilian life, he was chief of artillery in the Army of Northern Virginia.

- Maj. Gen. Samuel Ryan Curtis, 1831 (Union): Fought in the Battles of Pea Ridge and Westport. Curtis commanded the Army of the Southwest and the Army of the Border. An Iowa congressman, he resigned his seat on August 4, 1861, to accept a commission in the Union army. Curtis fought in the US-Mexican War (1846–48).

- Col. Benjamin S. Ewell, 1832 (Confederate): Brother of Lt. Gen. Richard S. Ewell, he commanded the 32nd Virginia Infantry Regiment.

Younger Civil War officer graduates of West Point, who were influenced more by Mahan than by Thayer, include:

- Col. Abraham C. Myers, 1833 (Confederate): Was quartermaster general for the Confederate army. He served in the Second Seminole War (1835–42) and the US-Mexican War (1846–48).

- Brig. Gen. Goode Bryan, 1834 (Confederate): His regiment was a standout in the Battle of the Wilderness; it fought until it had completely exhausted its ammunition. Bryan served in the US-Mexican War (1846–48).

- Maj. Gen. George Meade, 1835 (Union): In command of the Army of the Potomac, defeated Lee at Gettysburg; also fought at Antietam, Fredericksburg, Chancellorsville, Overland Campaign, and Appomattox Campaign. Served in the Second Seminole War (1832–45) and the US-Mexican War (1846–48).

- Maj. Gen. Jones M. Withers, 1835 (Confederate): Served with distinction at the Battles of Shiloh and Stones River. Fought in the US-Mexican War (1846–48).

- Brig. Gen. Joseph R. Anderson, 1836 (Confederate): Superintendent of the Tredegar Iron Works, the primary iron-production facility of the Confederacy and crucial to its war effort.

- Brig. Gen. Danville Leadbetter, 1836 (Confederate): An important military engineer in the Western Theater of the Civil War.

- Gen. Braxton Bragg, 1837 (Confederate): One of the Confederacy's principal commanders in the war's Western Theater, commanded the Army of Mississippi and the Army of Tennessee. He fought at Shiloh, Perryville, Stones River, the Tullahoma Campaign, Chickamauga, Chattanooga, Second Battle of Fort Fisher, and Battle of Bentonville. Served in the Second Seminole War (1835–42) and the US-Mexican War (1846–48).

- Gen. Jubal A. Early, 1837 (Confederate): Served under Thomas A. "Stonewall" Jackson and Richard S. Ewell, fought in the Valley Campaigns (1864) and staged a daring assault on Washington, DC.

Throughout the war Early never surrendered, and after the war he led the "Lost Cause" movement of Confederate diehards. He served in the Seminole Wars (variously, 1816–58) and the US-Mexican War (1846–48).

- Maj. Gen. Arnold Elzey, 1837 (Confederate): Gallant officer to whom President Jefferson Davis awarded a battlefield promotion to brigadier general at the First Battle of Bull Run. Served in the Indian Wars and the US-Mexican War (1846–48).

- Maj. Gen. Joseph "Fighting Joe" Hooker, 1837 (Union): Fought at Williamsburg, Seven Days Battles, South Mountain, Antietam, and Fredericksburg before assuming command of the Army of the Potomac for the Battle of Chancellorsville, in which Lee defeated him. Subsequently fought at Gettysburg, Lookout Mountain, Chattanooga Campaign, and the Atlanta Campaign. Served in the Seminole Wars (variously, 1816–58) and the US-Mexican War (1846–48).

- Lt. Gen. John C. Pemberton, 1837 (Confederate): Commanded the defense of Vicksburg, which he ultimately surrendered to US Grant. Fought in the Seminole Wars (variously, 1816–58) and the US-Mexican War (1846–48).

- Maj. Gen. John Sedgwick, 1837 (Union): Fought at Yorktown, Seven Pines, Glendale, and Antietam (he was wounded in the latter two). Also fought at Fredericksburg, Chancellorsville, Salem Church, Gettysburg, the Wilderness, and Spotsylvania Court House, where he was killed. Served in the Seminole Wars (variously, 1816–58), the US-Mexican War (1846–48), the Utah (or Mormon) War (1857–58), and the Indian Wars.

- Maj. Gen. William H. T. Walker, 1837 (Confederate): Killed at the Battle of Atlanta. He fought in the Second Seminole War (1835–42) and the US-Mexican War (1846–48) and served as commandant of West Point.

- Gen. Pierre Gustave Toutant Beauregard, 1838 (Confederate): Commanded the assault on Fort Sumter that opened the Civil War; commanded the Confederate Army of the Potomac and the Army of Mississippi and fought at Fort Sumter, First Battle of Bull Run, Shiloh, Corinth, First and Second Battles of Charleston Harbor, First and Second Battles of Fort Wagner, Second Battle of Fort Sumter, Bermuda Hundred Campaign, Second Battle of Petersburg, and Battle of Bentonville. He served in the US-Mexican War (1846–48).

- Lt. Gen. William J. Hardee, 1838 (Confederate): Noted as a masterful tactician, he fought at Shiloh, Perryville, Stones River, Third Battle of Chattanooga, Peachtree Creek, Atlanta, Averasborough, and Bentonville. Served in the Second Seminole War (1835–42) and the US-Mexican War (1846–48).

- Maj. Gen. Irvin McDowell, 1838 (Union): Defeated at the First Battle of Bull Run. Fought in the US-Mexican War (1846–48).

- Maj. Gen. Henry Hopkins Sibley, 1838 (Confederate): Led the failed New Mexico Campaign and fought at the Battles of Valverde and Glorieta Pass; accused of drunkenness in fighting battles in Louisiana, he was court-martialed and relieved of command in 1863. Served in the US-Mexican War (1846–48) and invented the distinctive Sibley tent, which was widely adopted throughout the US Army. After the Civil

War he served as artillery adviser in the Egyptian Army (1869–73).

- Brig. Gen. Lewis Armistead, 1839 (expelled) (Confederate): Expelled from West Point in 1839 for breaking a plate over the head of fellow cadet Jubal Early, he was killed while leading his brigade at the Battle of Gettysburg. Served in the US-Mexican War (1846–48) and the Indian Wars.

- Maj. Gen. Edwin Canby, 1839 (Union): Fought largely in the Far Western Theater, including the Battle of Glorieta Pass. Served in the Second Seminole War (1835–42), the US-Mexican War (1846–48), the Utah (or Mormon) War (1857–58), the Navajo War of 1860, and, after the Civil War, the Modoc War (1873), in which he became the only US general killed in the Indian Wars.

- Maj. Gen. Henry Wager Halleck, 1839 (Union): General-in-chief of the US Army and, later, Army chief of staff. Fought at Shiloh and Corinth, and served in the US-Mexican War (1846–48).

- Brig. Gen. Alexander Lawton, 1839 (Confederate): After being severely wounded at Antietam, he served as the second quartermaster general of the CSA. From 1887 to 1889 he was US minister to Austria-Hungary.

- Lt. Gen. Richard S. Ewell, 1840 (Confederate): Brother of Col. Benjamin S. Ewell (1832), he commanded II Corps in the Army of Northern Virginia and fought at the First and Second Battles of Bull Run, Valley Campaign, Seven Days Battles, Cedar Mountain, Second Battle of Winchester, Gettysburg, the Wilderness, Spotsylvania Court House, and Sayler's Creek. Lost his left leg at Groveton. Ewell served

in the US-Mexican War (1846–48) and the Apache Wars (chiefly 1849).

- Col. William H. Gilham, 1840 (Confederate): Briefly commanded a brigade in the field, but is mainly noted as a trainer of Confederate troops; he taught at the Virginia Military Institute (VMI) and wrote the durable and influential *Manual of Instruction for the Volunteers and Militia of the United States* (1860). In 1864, while he was again teaching at VMI, his cadets fought at the Battle of New Market.

- Brig. Gen. Paul Octave Hébert, 1840 (Confederate): Graduated first in the Class of 1840 and fought at the Siege of Vicksburg and in Texas. After serving in the US-Mexican War (1846–48), he was governor of Louisiana from 1853 to 1856.

- Maj. Gen. Bushrod Johnson, 1840 (Confederate): Fought at Chickamauga and Petersburg, among other battles. He fought in the Second Seminole War (1835–42) and the US-Mexican War (1846–48).

- Maj. Gen. William Tecumseh Sherman, 1840 (Union): U. S. Grant's top lieutenant. He fought at Shiloh and in the Vicksburg, Chattanooga, Atlanta, and Carolina campaigns. His Savannah Campaign—the "March to the Sea"—brought total war to the people of the South. He served as commanding general of the US Army from 1869 to 1883.

- Maj. Gen. George Henry Thomas, 1840 (Union): Fought at Mill Springs, Perryville, and Stones River. His steadfast performance at Chickamauga earned him the sobriquet of the "Rock of Chickamauga." Thomas also fought at Missionary Ridge and Nashville. He commanded the Army of the Cumberland. He served in the US-Mexican War (1846–48).

- Maj. Gen. Don Carlos Buell, 1841 (Union): Fought at Shiloh, Corinth, and Perryville, and held command of the Army of the Ohio. Fought in the Seminole Wars (variously, 1816–58) and the US-Mexican War (1846–48).

- Brig. Gen. Nathaniel Lyon, 1841 (Union): First Union general killed in the war, at the Battle of Wilson's Creek. Lyon served in the Seminole Wars (variously, 1816–58) and the US-Mexican War (1846–48).

- Maj. Gen. John F. Reynolds, 1841 (Union): Fought at Seven Days, Second Battle of Bull Run, Fredericksburg, and Chancellorsville. One of the most highly respected senior Union generals, he was in command of the left wing of the Army of the Potomac at Gettysburg when he was killed early on day one of the battle. Reynolds served in the US-Mexican War (1846–48).

- Lt. Gen. Daniel Harvey Hill, 1842 (Confederate): Fought at Big Bethel, Seven Pines, Seven Days, South Mountain, Antietam, Fredericksburg, Gettysburg, Chickamauga, and Bentonville, but had a reputation for being difficult and generally cantankerous. Served in the US-Mexican War (1846–48).

- Lt. Gen. James Longstreet, 1842 (Confederate): Best known as Lee's top lieutenant, Longstreet led Longstreet's Brigade, Longstreet's Division, I Corps of the Army of Northern Virginia, and the Department of East Tennessee. He served in the US-Mexican War (1846–48).

- Maj. Gen. John Pope, 1842 (Union): Commanding officer of the Army of the Mississippi and the Army of Virginia, Pope was disastrously defeated at the Second Battle of Bull Run. "Exiled" to the West, he fought in the Dakota War of 1862 and the Apache Wars (variously, 1849–1924).

- Maj. Gen. William Rosecrans, 1842 (Union): Commanding officer of the Army of the Cumberland; Rosecrans fought at Stones River, Tullahoma Campaign, and Chickamauga—from which he made a premature retreat.

- Maj. Gen. Gustavus Woodson Smith, 1842 (Confederate): Military engineer who had the distinction of being the first (temporary) commander of the Army of Northern Virginia, before Lee assumed command. Fought in the US-Mexican War (1846–48).

- Lt. Gen. Alexander P. Stewart, 1842 (Confederate): Fought at the Battles of Perryville, Chickamauga and Ezra Church, Battle of Franklin, and Battle of Nashville. Considered one of the ablest Confederate commanders in the Western Theater, he was the last commander of the Army of Tennessee. Served only briefly in the US Army after graduating from West Point; was a college professor before the Civil War.

- Maj. Gen. Earl Van Dorn, 1842 (Confederate): Defeated at Pea Ridge and the Second Battle of Corinth. Fought in the US-Mexican War (1846–48) and the Indian Wars. Was murdered in May 1863 by a man he had cuckolded.

- General of the Army of the United States Ulysses S. Grant, 1843 (Union): Before achieving top command, Grant fought at Belmont, Forts Henry and Donelson, Shiloh, Vicksburg, and Chattanooga. As top commander he led the Overland Campaign, which led to the Union's final victory. He served in the US-Mexican War (1846–48) and was elected to two terms as the eighteenth president of the United States, in 1868 and 1872.

- Maj. Gen. Frederick Steele, 1843 (Union): Fought at Wilson's Creek, Chickasaw Bayou, Arkansas Post, Vicksburg Campaign, Camden Expedition, and Fort Blakely. He is credited with wresting a large portion of Arkansas from Confederate control.

- Lt. Gen. Simon Bolivar Buckner, 1844 (Confederate): Fought at Battles of Fort Donelson, Perryville, and Chickamauga. Served in the US-Mexican War (1846–48).

- Maj. Gen. Winfield Scott Hancock, 1844 (Union): Fought at Gettysburg, Wilderness, and Spotsylvania Court House. Served in the US-Mexican War (1846–48) and ran unsuccessfully for US president in 1880.

- Maj. Gen. Alfred Pleasonton, 1844 (Union): Cavalry commander who fought in the Peninsula Campaign and at Antietam (in which he was wounded), Chancellorsville, Brandy Station, Byram's Ford, and Marais des Cygnes. Served in the US-Mexican War (1846–48).

- Brig. Gen. Barnard Bee, 1845 (Confederate): During the First Battle of Bull Run, conferred on Thomas Jackson his famous nickname, *"Stonewall"*—and was killed in that very battle. Bee served in the US-Mexican War (1846–48) and the Utah (or Mormon) War (1857–58).

- Maj. Gen. Fitz John Porter, 1845 (Union): Fought at Yorktown, Gaines's Mill, Malvern Hill, Second Battle of Bull Run, and Antietam. Served in the US-Mexican War (1846–48).

- Gen. Edmund Kirby Smith, 1845 (Confederate): Commanded the Trans-Mississippi Department. Served in the US-Mexican War (1846–48) and the Indian Wars.

- Maj. Gen. William Farrar "Baldy" Smith, 1845 (Union): Fought at First Battle of

Bull Run, White Oak Swamp, Antietam, Fredericksburg, Gettysburg, Wauhatchie, Cold Harbor, and Petersburg. His complacent leadership at Petersburg lost an opportunity for an early breakthrough in what became a prolonged siege.

- Maj. Gen. John G. Foster, 1846 (Union): Fought extensively in the Carolinas and participated in Sherman's March to the Sea. He saw distinguished service during the US-Mexican War (1846–1848).

- Lt. Gen. Thomas J. "Stonewall" Jackson, 1846 (Confederate): The most innovative and daring tactician of the Civil War, Jackson fought in many battles, including First Bull Run, Valley Campaign, Seven Days, Northern Virginia Campaign, Maryland Campaign, Fredericksburg, and Chancellorsville, where he was fatally wounded by friendly fire. He served in the US-Mexican War (1846–48) and was a professor at the Virginia Military Institute from 1851 to 1861.

- Maj. Gen. George B. McClellan, 1846 (Union): Dubbed the "Young Napoleon," McClellan organized and trained the Army of the Potomac, but handled it overcautiously. Fought at Rich Mountain, the Peninsula Campaign (including the Seven Days Battles), and Antietam. Served in the US-Mexican War (1846–48). Democratic candidate for the presidency in 1864.

- Gen. George Pickett, 1846 (Confederate): Most famous for his role in "Pickett's Charge" at the Battle of Gettysburg. Pickett first earned national fame during the US-Mexican War (1846–48) for his gallantry at Chapultepec; also fought in the brief Pig War (1859).

- Maj. Gen. George Stoneman, 1846 (Union): Fought in Seven Days Battles and at Fredericksburg, Chancellorsville, and Atlanta Campaign.

- Maj. Gen. Ambrose Burnside, 1847 (Union): After fighting at First Bull Run, Roanoke Island, New Bern, South Mountain, and Antietam, Burnside reluctantly accepted Abraham Lincoln's insistent offer of command of the Army of the Potomac, which Burnside led to disastrous defeat at the Battle of Fredericksburg. He then accepted lesser commands and fought at Campbell's Station, Fort Sanders, the Wilderness, Spotsylvania Court House, Cold Harbor, and the Siege of Petersburg—during which he was largely blamed for the failure of the Battle of the Crater. He served in the US-Mexican War (1846–48) and, after the Civil War, was a US senator from Rhode Island and then governor of that state.

- Maj. Gen. John Gibbon, 1847 (Union): Probably best known as a commander during the Plains Indian Wars after the Civil War, Gibbon fought in many of the major Civil War battles and was commander of the famed Iron Brigade. Before the war he served in the US-Mexican War (1846–48) and the Seminole Wars (variously, 1816–58).

- Maj. Gen. Henry Heth, 1847 (Confederate): First Confederate commander to make contact with Union forces at Gettysburg. Fought in the US-Mexican War (1846–48) and the Indian Wars.

- Lt. Gen. Ambrose P. Hill, 1847 (Confederate): Corps commander in the Army of Northern Virginia, Hill was killed at Petersburg just seven days before Lee's surrender of the Army of Northern Virginia at Appomattox Court House. Served in the US-Mexican War (1846–48) and the Seminole Wars (variously, 1816–58).

- Maj. Gen. John Buford, 1848 (Union): A tough and skilled cavalry commander, Buford's stand at the beginning of the Battle of Gettysburg prevented a total Union rout. He also fought at Second Bull Run, South Mountain, Antietam, Brandy Station, Upperville, and the Bristoe Campaign. He saw service during the Bleeding Kansas crisis in the 1850s and the Utah (or Mormon) War (1857–58).

- Brevet Maj. Gen. Eugene A. Carr, 1850 (Union): Carr fought at Wilson's Creek, Pea Ridge, Port Gibson, Champion's Hill, Siege of Vicksburg, Camden Expedition, Spanish Fort, and Fort Blakeley. For action in the Battle of Pea Ridge, he received the Medal of Honor. Both before and after the Civil War, he fought in the Indian Wars.

- Maj. General George Crook, 1852 (Union): A general well known for his service during the Plains Indian Wars after the Civil War, Crook fought at South Mountain, Antietam, Chickamauga, Cloyd's Mountain, Opequon, Fisher's Hill, Cedar Creek, and the Appomattox Campaign.

- Gen. John Bell Hood, 1853 (Confederate): Bold but rash commander in the Atlanta Campaign and the Franklin-Nashville Campaign. Was the youngest army commander on either side—thirty-three years old when he assumed leadership of the Army of Tennessee. Fought in the Indian Wars before the Civil War.

- Maj. Gen. James B. McPherson, 1853 (Union): Fought at Forts Henry and Donelson, Shiloh, Vicksburg, and the Battle of Marietta. He was killed during the Battle of Atlanta.

- Lt. Gen. John Schofield, 1853 (Union): Decorated with the Medal of Honor for his actions at Wilson's Creek, Schofield also fought in the Atlanta Campaign and the Battles of Franklin, Nashville, and Wyse Fork. During Reconstruction Schofield served briefly as military governor of Virginia. He subsequently served as US secretary of war (1868–69), superintendent of West Point (1876–81), and commanding general of the US Army (1888–95).

- Gen. Philip Sheridan, 1853 (Union): Principal Union cavalry commander during the Civil War, Sheridan fought in the Chattanooga, Overland, and 1864 Valley campaigns. His operations in the Shenandoah Valley were relentless, as was his pursuit of Lee in the Appomattox Campaign. After the Civil War he was equally relentless in prosecuting the Plains Indian Wars.

- Maj. Gen. Oliver O. Howard, 1854 (Union): Fought in the First Battle of Bull Run and received the Medal of Honor for his actions in the Battle of Seven Pines (which cost him his right arm). He fought at Antietam, Chancellorsville, Gettysburg, and the Chattanooga and Atlanta Campaigns, followed by the March to Sea. After the war he founded Howard University and fought in the Indian Wars against Chief Joseph and the Nez Perce.

- Maj. Gen. George Washington Custis Lee, 1854 (Confederate): Son of Robert E. Lee, graduated first in his West Point class; was captured at the Battle of Sayler's Creek.

- Maj. Gen. William Dorsey Pender, 1854 (Confederate): Mortally wounded at Gettysburg. Served in the Indian Wars.

- Maj. Gen. J. E. B. Stuart, 1854 (Confederate): Dashing cavalry commander; fought in First Battle of Bull Run, the Peninsula Campaign, Northern Virginia Campaign, Maryland Campaign, Fredericksburg, Chancellorsville, Gettysburg, and in the Overland Campaign. His reconnaissance failures at Gettysburg contributed to Lee's defeat there. Fought in the Bleeding Kansas conflict (1850s).

- Brevet Maj. Gen. Alfred Thomas Torbert, 1855 (Union). Torbert's most important service was as a division commander in the Overland Campaign. He briefly held command of the Army of the Shenandoah at the end of the war.

- Maj. Gen. Fitzhugh Lee, 1856 (Confederate): Nephew of Robert E. Lee; fought at First Battle of Bull Run, Antietam, Gettysburg, and Opequon and led the final charge of the Army of Northern Virginia at Farmville (April 9, 1865). He fought in the Indian Wars before the Civil War, and in the Spanish-American War (1898) after it. He was Virginia's governor from 1886 to 1890.

- Brig. Gen. Edward Porter Alexander, 1857 (Confederate): Fought at Fredericksburg, Chancellorsville, Gettysburg, and the Siege of Petersburg.

- Maj. Gen. George Armstrong Custer, 1861 (Union): Became the Civil War's "Boy General" and fought at Antietam and Chancellorsville; at Gettysburg he led the decisive charge that broke the final resistance of Lee's forces there. Custer also fought at the Wilderness, Petersburg, and the Appomattox Campaign. He was even more famous for his actions during the Indian Wars of 1870s and his fatal defeat at the Little Bighorn in 1876.

Non-Academy Generals

The US Military Academy was the major source of the officers of the United States Army on the eve of the Civil War and was therefore a major source of high-ranking officers in both the Union and Confederate armies. At the outbreak of the war, 296 serving US Army officers resigned. Of these, 239 joined the Confederate army in 1861 and 31 joined after 1861. Of this total, 184 were West Point graduates. Of the 809 active officers who remained in the US Army, 640 were West Point graduates. At the outbreak of the war, some 900 West Point graduates were civilians. Of these, 114 returned to active service in the Union army and 99 joined the Confederate army.[8]

As the Union army mobilized and the Confederate army was created from scratch and state militias, both forces had to look beyond West Point for experienced leaders. Some of the lowest-ranking officers from the US Army were jumped in rank. Retired veterans of the US-Mexican War were called upon to serve as were the civilian graduates of the nation's few military schools. These schools included:

- Virginia Military Institute (VMI): Established in 1839 in Lexington, Virginia, VMI had 1,902 alumni by the outbreak of the Civil War. Of this number, 1,781 would fight for the Confederacy. One-third of the field officers commanding Virginia's Civil War regiments were graduates.[9]

- The Citadel, the Military College of South Carolina: Founded in 1842 in Charleston, the Citadel graduated 6 Confederate general officers, 49 field-grade officers (colonels and majors), and 120 company-grade officers (captains and lieutenants).[10]

- Norwich University, Northfield, Vermont: In the North, other than West Point, the only notable military institution of higher learning was Norwich University, which was established as a private military college in 1819. Among its graduates, 523 became officers in the Union army and 34 in the Confederate army.[11]

As in the American Revolution, military leaders on both sides found some officer material among immigrants with European military experience. Twenty of the Union army's officers were European émigrés.[12]

Finally, there was also a category of so-called political generals in both the Union and the Confederate armies. These men were commissioned for political reasons rather than for their military experience or demonstrated martial merit. The best-known Confederate political generals include:

- William Barksdale, Mississippi congressman

- John C. Breckinridge, former vice president under James Buchanan

- Thomas Reade Rootes Cobb, Confederate congressman from Georgia

- Gideon Pillow, general in the US-Mexican War

- Sterling Price, former US congressman and Missouri governor

On the Union side the most prominent names include:

- Nathaniel Prentice Banks, former governor of Massachusetts

- Benjamin Franklin Butler, state senator from Massachusetts and brigadier general in the Massachusetts militia

- James A. Garfield, Ohio state senator who became the twentieth president of the United States—and the second president to suffer assassination

- John A. Logan, Illinois congressman

- Daniel Sickles, New York congressman who had been tried (and acquitted) for the murder of Philip Barton Key II (son of Francis Scott Key, author of "The Star-Spangled

Banner"), who was having an affair with his wife

- Franz Sigel, a German émigré who led units largely composed of German immigrants

- Lew Wallace, an Indiana legislator whose performance at the Battle of Monocacy (Maryland) helped to save Washington, DC, from Jubal Early's raid. After the Civil War, Wallace wrote the sensationally popular novel *Ben-Hur*.

Although much derided, most political generals and political colonels did their best to be or to become competent and courageous leaders. That more than a few failed is hardly surprising. That so many—on both sides—succeeded is, however, one of the more remarkable facts of the Civil War.

Chapter 3

On the Eve of Secession

CONFEDERATE READINESS FOR WAR: ⋆

UNION READINESS FOR WAR: ⋆ ⸎

In 1860, but before December 20, when South Carolina became the first of eleven states to secede from the Union, the United States was still a whole nation and had but one regular army, the United States Army, consisting of 16,367 soldiers, of whom 1,108 were commissioned officers.[1]

OPERATIONAL ORGANIZATION

The army at that moment in time was broadly divided between staff (administrative) and line (combat) functions. Staff functions were led by a cadre of colonels (and one brigadier general) who supervised a total of 353 staff officers and some civilian employees of the War Department:

- Col. Samuel Cooper, adjutant general: chief administrative officer of the USA

- Brig. Gen. Joseph E. Johnston, quartermaster general: responsible for non-food stores, equipment, uniforms, and supplies as well as the transport of same

- Col. [Brevet Maj. Gen] George Gibson, commissary general: responsible for procurement, storage, and distribution of food for troops

- Col. Benjamin Franklin Larned, paymaster general: responsible for payroll accounting and distribution of pay

- Col. Henry Knox Craig, chief of Ordnance Department: duties included "to enlist artisans and laborers; to direct the inspection and proof of all cannon and small arms; to direct the construction of gun carriages, equipments, implements, and ammunition; to make estimates and contracts for, and purchases of ordnance supplies and stores, and to issue them to the army; to exact from armories and arsenals quarterly returns of property and to receive from all responsible officers reports of damages to ordnance material; to establish ordnance depots"[2]

- Col. [Brevet Brig. Gen.] Joseph G. Totten, chief engineer: commanded the Corps of Engineers and was responsible for a wide array of construction and logistical functions

- Col. [Brevet Brig. Gen.] Sylvester Churchill, inspector general: commanded the Inspector General's Department, which was responsible for ensuring the combat readiness of the army and for investigating noncriminal and some criminal matters

- Col. [Brevet Brig. Gen] Thomas Lawson, surgeon general: commanded the Medical Department

The army's line (combat) functions were carried out by regiments. In the diminutive pre–Civil War army, the regiment was the largest permanent operational unit. Only after the armies of the Civil War were fully mobilized into forces of Napoleonic dimension did brigades, divisions, corps, and armies come into use. On the eve of the Civil War, there were ten infantry regiments, five mounted regiments, and four artillery regiments. The infantry and mounted regiments consisted of ten companies each. Artillery regiments had twelve companies—called, in artillery parlance, "batteries."

The paper strength of each army regiment was 1,000 men, 100 per company. Universally, however, as actually deployed, the regiments and their constituent companies were very substantially understrength, with each regiment consisting of 300–400 men in ten companies of 30 to 40 men each.[3] In part, the understrength status was intentional, as a parsimonious approach to its budget induced the army to maintain its force below the 18,000 men Congress had authorized. In part, however, regiments and companies were understrength because soldiers tended to drift in and out—mostly out, due to a high rate of desertion. Once the Civil War began in earnest, regiments unable to muster ten companies with at least 30 men each were designated as battalions.

Mounted regiments might be cavalry (troops who fought from horseback), dragoons (troops who rode to battle mounted, but dismounted to fight as infantry), or "mounted riflemen" (similar to dragoons). In the course of the Civil War, the use of dragoons and mounted riflemen diminished, and all mounted regiments were simply designated as cavalry regiments. All regiments were commanded by colonels, who presided over a headquarters staffed by a lieutenant colonel, two majors, an adjutant (lieutenant), and a quartermaster (lieutenant). The line companies were commanded by captains.

GEOGRAPHICAL ORGANIZATION

The US Army of 1860 was apportioned into seven geographical departments. Roughly from east to west, these were:

- The Department of the East, which by and large covered all territory east of the Mississippi River. Department headquarters was at Troy, New York.

- The Department of the West, which extended westward from the Mississippi River and encompassed the states of Minnesota, Iowa, Missouri, Arkansas, and Louisiana in addition to the Kansas and Nebraska Territories as well as the "Unorganized Territory" between Minnesota and the Nebraska Territory. Department headquarters was in St. Louis, Missouri.

- The Department of Texas, which encompassed the state of Texas and "Indian Territory" (roughly corresponding at this time to the present state of Oklahoma). Department headquarters was at San Antonio.

- The Department of New Mexico, which corresponded roughly to the present state of New Mexico. Department headquarters was at Santa Fe.

- The Department of Utah, which covered most of Utah Territory. Department headquarters was at Camp Floyd.

- The Department of Oregon, which covered the state of Oregon and all of Washington Territory. Department headquarters was at Fort Vancouver.

- The Department of California, which covered the western portions of New Mexico Territory and Utah Territory as well as the state of California. Department headquarters was at the Presidio in San Francisco.

In 1860 the population of the United States was, of course, overwhelmingly concentrated east of the Mississippi River, and all of the major battles of the Civil War would be fought in this section of the country, with most of the biggest battles close to the Eastern Seaboard. Prior to the Civil War, however, the principal mission of the US Army was as a constabulary or police force charged with protecting white western settlers as well as transportation and mail routes from Indian hostilities. Moreover, three treaties in the 1840s–1850s added hundreds of thousands of square miles to the western territories of the United States, bringing more settlers to the region: the Oregon Treaty (June 15, 1846), which settled the long-standing dispute between the US and UK over the Oregon boundary with Canada; the Treaty of Guadalupe Hidalgo (February 2, 1848), which ended the US-Mexican War (1846–48); and the Gadsden Purchase of 1854. Before the US-Mexican War, the US Army maintained fifty-six military posts throughout the United States, of which just twelve were west of the Mississippi River. After the treaties mentioned above and the acquisition of so much new territory, many new western posts and forts were established. By 1860 there were seventy-six west of the Mississippi, about 13,000 troops. With virtually all of the military action west of the Mississippi River, all but eighteen of the 197 line companies of the US Army were stationed in that vast part of the country. Thus, on the verge of civil war, fewer than 1,000 regular, combat-ready US Army soldiers were permanently stationed east of the Mississippi. As for the militia from which a war-fighting force was to be built, it existed, but was poorly organized and mustered lower numbers than it had during the War of 1812—when it proved ineffective in combat.[4]

FACILITIES

The majority of the seventy-six forts established west of the Mississippi by 1860 offered no more than basic shelter to house officers and men, who spent most of their time on patrol over wide areas. In some cases the primitive forts offered accommodations for military families as well as civilian camp followers. There was little or no standardization in the design and building of the forts, and the builders were typically the soldiers themselves. Construction materials depended on location. Where trees were available, timber

was the material of choice. Elsewhere, sod, brick, adobe, and even brush were used. Contrary to the image portrayed in popular fiction and film, most frontier forts were not fortified and there was no gated stockade. Western army forts were not defensive refuges so much as they were refuges from the elements.

There were exceptions, however. At more established trading centers, for example, more substantial facilities were constructed. In 1849 the army purchased a trading post along the Laramie River in what is now the state of Wyoming. The post had already been fortified with high walls, which, according to Western showman William "Buffalo Bill" Cody—who, in his early career was a civilian scout for the US Army—were "twenty feet high and four feet thick, encompassing an area two hundred and fifty feet long by two hundred wide." Cody called the fort "an oasis in the desert."[5] In the Pacific coast city of San Francisco, the Presidio, headquarters for the Department of California, became an army showplace and was, in fact, a highly civilized example of the coastal fortifications that the army garrisoned on both the West and East Coasts.

Indeed, the most highly developed US Army facilities up to the era of the Civil War were of two kinds: coastal defenses and armories and arsenals (which included foundry facilities, some quite large). By the start of the Civil War, there were more than eighty coastal forts and fortifications, including Fort Sumter, the anchor of a suite of fortifications defending Charleston Harbor. The Confederate assault on Fort Sumter on April 12–14, 1861, aimed at ejecting the federal garrison there, was the start of the Civil War. The relatively elaborate development of coastal artillery in the era leading up to the Civil War was the product of an assumption among US political and military leaders that the greatest existential threat to the United States would surely come from some foreign enemy and would be delivered by sea. The possibility of massive *internal* rebellion seems never to have been contemplated, despite the nation's history of bitter, divisive, and apparently insoluble disputation between North and South over the issue of slavery.

Up to the Civil War, the number one mission of the regular army continued to be that of a frontier constabulary. Missions two and three were the garrisoning of coastal fortifications and the maintenance, operation, and security of a system of armories (for the purpose of repairing and even manufacturing small arms and ammunition) and arsenals and foundries (for the manufacture, testing, and maintenance of cannon and the projectiles used in them). The armories functioned not only to supply the regular army, but, in time of need, to arm state militia companies. Some arsenals included laboratories in which existing weapons were tested and evaluated and new weapons were developed.

In 1859 the US military maintained the Allegheny Arsenal, Pittsburgh, Pennsylvania; Augusta Arsenal, Georgia; Baton Rouge Arsenal, Louisiana; Benicia Arsenal, California; Charleston Arsenal, South Carolina; Detroit Arsenal, Dearbornville, Michigan; Fayetteville Arsenal, North Carolina; Fort Monroe Arsenal, Old Point Comfort, Virginia; Frankford Arsenal, Philadelphia; Harpers Ferry Armory, Virginia; Kennebec Arsenal, Augusta, Maine; Little Rock Arsenal, Arkansas; Mount Vernon Arsenal, Alabama; New York Arsenal, Governors Island, New York; Pikesville Arsenal, Maryland; Saint Louis Arsenal, Missouri; San Antonio Arsenal, Texas; Springfield Armory, Massachusetts; Vancouver Arsenal, Washington Territory; Washington Arsenal, Washington, DC; Watertown Arsenal, Massachusetts; and Watervliet Arsenal, New York. Collectively, the arsenals held 561,400 muskets and 48,862 rifles.[6] Those facilities located in the South were confiscated by the Confederacy at the outbreak of the war.

Pierre Gustave Toutant Beauregard commanded the ad hoc Confederate army that fired upon Fort Sumter, in Charleston Harbor, during April 12–14, 1861, thus beginning the Civil War. NATIONAL ARCHIVES AND RECORDS ADMINISTRATION

All of the arsenals included foundries capable of repairing cannon or casting new barrels; however, during the war both the United States and the Confederate States governments let contracts to many private foundry firms as well. With its far superior industrial base, the North had a huge advantage; yet the famed Tredegar Iron Works in Richmond, Virginia, achieved remarkable levels of output and served as the Confederacy's principal military foundry.

WEAPONS DEVELOPMENT

Modern military historians often criticize the pre–Civil War US Army for its resistance to innovation. This is unfair on three counts. First, armies must be prudent before putting troops into life-or-death situations with relatively untested technology. Second, even proven new technologies may present operational or other complexities that counterbalance the value of innovation. Third, by the 1850s army leadership was probably more receptive to new weapons technology than was the leadership of European armies. In the decade before the Civil War, the army began gradually upgrading its standard infantry shoulder weapon by replacing smoothbore muskets with rifled ones. Rifled bores—bores with spiral grooves that imparted a spin to projectiles, thereby stabilizing them in flight, making the weapons more accurate and increasing their effective range—had been around for years before the army began to adopt the technology. Nevertheless, rifled weapons presented a serious problem. Because a bullet fired from a barrel had to be of slightly larger diameter than the bore in order to engage the rifled grooves, the shooter had to manhandle each round down the barrel, pounding the bullet home with his ramrod. This significantly slowed the rate of fire, was not always an easy task to perform under combat conditions, and could lead to misfires.

Soldiers with smoothbores could achieve a rate of fire three or four times that of soldiers equipped with the early-generation rifles or rifle-muskets. By the 1850s improvements in rifling and, even more, the development of minié ball ammunition largely overcame the slow loading problem. (Named after one of its inventors, Claude-Étienne Minié, the minié "ball" was actually a bullet-shaped round with a hollow iron cup at its base. The round was the same size as the rifled bore and therefore fit easily into the barrel when loaded. When fired, the hollow iron cup expanded, so that the base engaged the rifling grooves, and the projectile therefore spun as it exited the muzzle.) In 1854, after extensive tests, the army began converting many of

its existing smoothbores into rifled weapons at the federal armories in Springfield, Massachusetts, and Harpers Ferry, Virginia (today West Virginia). In 1855 the Springfield facility also began production of the purpose-built Springfield Model 1855 rifle-musket, of which 4,000 were available by the end of 1858.

Another advance in rate of fire and simplification of loading was the development of breech-loading versus muzzle-loading weapons. Prototype breechloaders underwent tests at the federal arsenals in 1854, but the boards of experts who reviewed the results could not agree on a model to replace the muzzleloaders for the infantry. Breech-loading carbines for mounted troops gained more traction, however. The carbine barrels were shorter and therefore easier to handle from horseback, and breech loading in the saddle was far more feasible than muzzle loading.

In 1855 the army began issuing a repeating rifle on a limited trial basis. Repeating rifles were fed by magazines instead of rounds individually loaded by hand. They were therefore capable of repeated firing without reloading, and this achieved a very rapid rate of fire. Nevertheless, early repeaters were plagued by reliability problems: The repeating mechanism jammed easily, and the paper cartridges then in use tended to burn the shooter's hands or, even worse, ignite while still in the cylinder—with catastrophic results. When metallic cartridges were developed in 1858, the army began seriously considering both repeaters and muzzleloaders. In 1860, George W. Morse, inventor of a metallic cartridge, was awarded a contract to convert quantities of US Army muzzleloaders to breechloaders at the Harpers Ferry Armory. A year later, however, Morse joined the Confederacy, and, that same year, Harpers Ferry fell to Confederate troops. Nevertheless, shortly before the war, in 1860, two dependable magazine-fed repeaters, the Spencer and the Henry rifles, became widely available. The US Army did not rush to acquire them, however. Concerned over complications in manufacture and misguided by fears that a rapid rate of fire would lead troops to waste ammunition, the army restricted both breechloaders and repeating rifles to cavalry units and a few other specialized units.

The technology of artillery progressed significantly between the US-Mexican War (1846-48)—in which US cannon and ammunition proved significantly superior to Mexican artillery—and 1860. The US Army acquired in 1857 the "Napoleon" gun-howitzer as its standard field artillery weapon. Named after Emperor Napoleon III (1808–73), the most respected military figure of the 1850s and 1860s, the American Napoleon was fashioned after French examples used in the Crimean War (1853–56). A very versatile weapon, the Napoleon could be fired at low trajectory (for use against personnel, for instance), like a conventional cannon, or at high trajectory (for siege work and use against fortifications), like a howitzer or a mortar. The army's Napoleons were cast of bronze, were not rifled, and could fire a solid twelve-pound projectile, an explosive shell, or case shot and canister antipersonnel rounds (which dispersed grapeshot or shrapnel when fired).

The army did not merely imitate the French prototypes, it worked to improve on them, developing casting methods that extended the life of the weapons and enabled the use of larger charges for greater range and destructive velocity. Moreover, by the mid-1850s the army began testing *rifled* cannon. A board of ordnance officers recommended in 1860 that half of the US Army artillery in forts (not field artillery) be converted from smoothbores to rifled bores. Foundry experts countered that such conversion would weaken the barrels, so, instead of conversion, work was done to phase out bronze cannon and develop cast-iron barrels instead. Army facilities began turning out iron-barreled rifled

guns during the winter of 1860–61. A captain of the US 3rd Artillery Regiment, Robert P. Parrott, developed a manufacturing method to add a wrought-iron reinforcing hoop on the breech of cast-iron barrels. Wrought iron was stronger than cast iron, and the hoop thus increased the durability of the barrel, enabling the use of the largest possible powder charges. Parrott guns would be widely used to fire from forts during the Civil War.

DOCTRINE

"God fights on the side with the best artillery," Napoleon Bonaparte famously declared, and it was artillery that dominated US Army strategic and tactical thinking during the decade preceding the Civil War. In 1849, Major Alfred Mordecai, an artillery specialist serving on the army's Ordnance Board, published his *Artillery for the United States Land Service,* which became the bible of the army's artillery arm. Two years later, in 1851, the War Department published new regulations for artillery drill, and in 1859 the army's artillery experts published a complete course in artillery instruction and training. A full official manual, *Instructions for Field Artillery,* appeared in 1861 and became *the* manual in both the Union and Confederate armies during the war.

Since the end of the era of Napoleon III's uncle, Napoleon I, strategic and tactical doctrine developed and taught at West Point was primarily based on the great campaigns of Bonaparte as these were presented in the works of Antoine-Henri Jomini (1779–1869), who served as an officer in both the French and the Russian armies. Napoleon himself frequently reiterated his principal objective in warfighting, which was to focus on "only one thing, namely the enemy's main body. I try to crush it, confident that secondary matters will then settle themselves."[7] In other words, Napoleon advocated an intensively

Major General Henry Wager "Old Brains" Halleck, who was slow to recognize the military genius of his subordinate, Ulysses S. Grant. NATIONAL ARCHIVES AND RECORDS ADMINISTRATION

aggressive strategy and tactics of assuming and maintaining the offensive—not with the objective of obtaining territory or territorial advantage, but of simply killing the enemy army. Through the intellectual filter of Jomini, however, the exclusive focus on the offensive was diffused and tempered by more cautious defensive considerations, and it was this version of the Napoleonic playbook that was taught at West Point, first by Sylvanus Thayer and then by Dennis Hart Mahan.

Indeed, throughout the combined tenure of Thayer and Mahan (1817–71), even as academy cadets were relentlessly exposed to Napoleon's campaigns and his ethos of attack, the classroom use of Jomini and the relative profusion of

coastal defenses (as discussed under "Facilities," above) revealed the overriding defensive orientation of the US Army at the mid-nineteenth century. Major General Henry Wager Halleck, who would rise to become general-in-chief of the US Army in July 1862, graduated with the West Point Class of 1839, emerging as a thoroughly indoctrinated protégé of Dennis Hart Mahan. Because Mahan was the academy's leading professor of engineering and of military tactics and strategy, it was clearly no accident that his strategic theories were intimately linked to his ideas on fortification. This linkage was carried into Halleck's own 1846 treatise, widely read and used by Civil War officers, *Elements of Military Art and Science*. Five of the fifteen chapters in *Elements* are devoted to fortifications, especially coastal fortifications. Halleck argues that a good system of coastal fortification can defeat any assaulting navy or amphibiously invading army.[8]

With its emphasis on coastal defense, Halleck's *Elements* exposes the bedrock of US Army doctrine on the eve of civil war. First, it was generally assumed that any major enemy would almost certainly attack and attempt to invade by sea. The possibility of massive internal insurrection or rebellion was not contemplated. Second, it was assumed that defensive weapons are inherently superior to offensive weapons—that massed firepower directed from cover would almost certainly defeat an offensive assault.

The first assumption, of course, was shattered by the outbreak of a civil war involving numbers far greater than anyone had imagined possible and employing industrial-age weapons more destructive and more numerous than ever contemplated before the conflict. These weapons included the mass-produced rifles and rifle-muskets, which enabled more soldiers to fire more accurately from greater range than in previous conflicts. Halleck and other theorists and commanders of his generation assumed that defense carried out from within strong fortifications would always have the edge over attackers. The technological advances in the decade leading up to the Civil War took much of the advantage from the defenders and gave it to the attackers, yet the US Army entered the Civil War as a force led by officers trained according to the assumptions of Jomini, Mahan, and Halleck, assumptions largely outmoded by technological progress.

LEADERSHIP

The doctrinal influence of Thayer, Mahan, Halleck, and William J. Hardee was extensive. (An 1838 West Point graduate, Hardee, whose 1855 *Rifle and Light Infantry Tactics for the Exercise and Manoeuvres of Troops When Acting as Light Infantry or Riflemen* was authoritative, resigned his US Army commission on January 31, 1861, and joined the Confederate army on March 7). Nevertheless, it was Major General Winfield Scott, since 1841 commanding general of the army, who did the most to create the US Army as it stood on the eve of the Civil War.

He had fought and led in every major American conflict after the Revolution: the War of 1812, the "Indian Removal" (during the Andrew Jackson administration), and the US-Mexican War. He would lead the Union army into the Civil War itself. As the army's commanding general, he did more than any other military or civilian official to transform an ill-equipped, ill-trained, dispirited federal police force into a small but credible United States Army. What is more, he did this both as an administrator and as a field officer. During the war with Mexico, he not only led that army to triumph, but also commanded more than 100 of the men, Northerners and Southerners, who would serve as generals during the Civil War, including Ulysses S. Grant, William T. Sherman, Robert E. Lee, and Thomas J. "Stonewall" Jackson—not to mention the president of the Confederacy, Jefferson Davis. He imparted to these men a sense of professionalism and boldness, tempered, however, by a decidedly non-Napoleonic moderation. His objective was certainly to defeat the enemy, but not necessarily to crush it. When Scott personally presided over the negotiations that brought the 1846–48 war with Mexico to an end, he opened the proceedings by declaring, "Too much blood has already been shed in the unnatural war between the two great republics of this continent."[9] It was in this spirit that Scott would bring what remained of the US Army to war against the forces of the breakaway South. His principal strategy was not to punish the "rebels" with aggressive attacks aimed at killing them, but to isolate the South with a naval blockade that, he hoped, would make it impossible for its army to fight. For this, Winfield Scott would be derided both by the North and the South. Yet, over time, the blockade was a highly effective instrument of war. It proved to be the only strategically viable alternative to total war and complete destruction that anyone offered in the course of the Civil War.

Part Two

Brother against Brother

Chapter 4

ESPRIT AND ECONOMICS

CONFEDERATE UNITY AND
ESPRIT: ✭ ✭ ✭

CONFEDERATE ECONOMY: ✭

UNION UNITY AND ESPRIT: ✭ ✭ ⅟

UNION ECONOMY: ✭ ✭ ✭

This chapter does not pretend to explain the causes of the Civil War. That is a subject for entire libraries. But to understand the two armies that went to war from 1861 to 1865, it is necessary to appreciate the ideological, industrial, economic, and cultural context in which they came into being, existed, and fought.

IDEOLOGY AND REGIONAL ALLEGIANCE

Of the two words *United* and *States*, the noun described the nation far more accurately than the adjective, not only on April 12, 1861, but ever since 1788, when the Constitution was ratified in a form that passively accepted the existence of slavery, that failed to recognize slavery as a fatally divisive issue, and that did nothing to decide upon the future of slavery. Thus the *United* States came into existence essentially divided. What is worse, the line surveyed by the English astronomers Charles Mason and Jeremiah Dixon in 1767 for the purpose of resolving a boundary dispute between the colonies of Maryland and Pennsylvania became a far more consequential demarcation associating a geographical division with a division between the embrace and the rejection of slavery.

For the most part, by 1861 slavery was universal south of the Mason–Dixon Line and nonexistent north of it. To this day, some historians and probably even more Southerners argue that

the Civil War was never "all about" slavery, but rather involved such issues as ethnic homogeneity (among whites the South was more homogenous than the ethnically diverse North), rural versus urban "values," plantation culture versus a culture born of industrialization, regional commercial competition, and states' rights versus the authority of the central government. To be sure, all of these issues played roles in dividing the two regions against one another. Yet all were ultimately related to slavery or its absence, and none of these issues except slavery itself would

Jefferson Davis of Mississippi, president of the Confederate States of America, as photographed by Mathew B. Brady before the war. NATIONAL ARCHIVES AND RECORDS ADMINISTRATION

have driven the two regions to war. Slavery was essential to the plantation system of the South, which, in turn, was the very heart of the social and economic order of the South, the Southern way of life.

By virtue of their having declared in common their independence from Great Britain, by virtue of having united against the forces of king and Parliament to win that common independence, and by virtue of having together drafted and ratified a constitution creating a single government for themselves, the South and the North were geographical regions of one nation. Moreover, they had a great deal in common: the same language, a heritage of revolution, and a predominantly Protestant population. Yet the range of Puritan belief is wide, and religious practice in the predominantly Anglican South differed markedly from the Puritan orientation of New England. Elsewhere in the North, religious attitudes varied yet more widely, even within the confines of Christianity. The white people of the South were also rooted to their place—geographically, historically, politically, ideologically, and spiritually—whereas those in the North tended to be more peripatetic within the region and less wedded to any particular tradition.

Above all, however, it was the issue of slavery that most profoundly divided the two regions morally, economically, and politically. On March 3, 1858, Senator William H. Seward of New York delivered to the Senate a speech entitled "Freedom in Kansas," in which he spoke of (among many other things) the inherent value of a workforce, educated, industrious, and, above all, democratic, the workforce that was the people of the North. To such a free people, the United States, he said, owed "the strength, wealth, greatness, intelligence, and freedom" it enjoyed. Seward pointedly contrasted this with the slave states, in which the "masters . . . secure all political power, and constitute a ruling aristocracy."[1] On the next day, March 4, Senator James Henry Hammond, a South Carolina planter, answered Seward by declaring that

in all social systems there must be a class to do the menial duties, to perform the drudgery of life. That is, a class requiring but a low order of intellect and but little skill. Its requisites are vigor, docility, fidelity. . . . It constitutes the very mud-sill of society and of political government; and you might as well attempt to build a house in the air, as to build either the one or the other, except on this mud-sill. Fortunately for the South, she found a race adapted to that purpose to her hand. A race inferior to her own, but eminently qualified in temper, in vigor, in docility, in capacity to stand the climate, to answer all her purposes. We use them for our purpose, and call them slaves. We found them slaves by the common "consent of mankind," which, according to Cicero, "lex naturae est." The highest proof of what is Nature's law. . . .

Senator [Seward] said yesterday that the whole world had abolished slavery. Aye, the name, but not the thing; all the powers of the earth cannot abolish that. . . . for the man who lives by daily labor, and scarcely lives at that, and who has to put out his labor in the market, and take the best he can get for it; in short, your whole hireling class of manual laborers and "operatives," as you call them, are essentially slaves. The difference between us is, that our slaves are hired for life and well compensated; there is no starvation, no begging, no want of employment among our people, and not too much employment either. Yours are hired by the day, not cared for, and scantily compensated, which may be proved in the most painful manner, at any hour in any street of your large towns. . . . We do not think that whites should be slaves either by law or necessity. Our slaves are black, of another and inferior race.[2]

At issue was not only—or even primarily—the morality or immorality, the rightness or wrongness, of slavery, but the question of which region of the country, South or North, was superior and should therefore prevail as *the* model for the future of the United States. The South was economically dependent on slave labor. The North, with its larger population and greater economic power, by opposing slavery threatened the South's very economic basis. But beyond this, it threatened to transform the pastoral plantation aristocracy into another New York City, a place, Hammond said, where "you meet more beggars in one day, in any single street . . . than you would meet in a lifetime in the whole South."[3] At the root of the dispute between the two regions was slavery—the foundation of a Southern civilization most Southerners, even those who did not own plantations and could not afford slaves, believed superior to that of the North, just as most Northerners believed their civilization of freedom and hard work was both morally and economically superior to what they saw as a slothful way of life cruelly built on the backs of slaves. As for religion, it was the God of Abraham that was worshipped on both sides of the Mason–Dixon Line, and people on both sides were convinced that this God was on their side. In the South the way of slavery was the way of the law of God and of nature. In the North slavery was seen as the very condition the first people of Abraham, the Jews of the Old Testament, had justly fought to escape. God, clearly, had been with the Jews and opposed to the wicked pharaoh who oppressed them. On these warring articles of national, moral, and ultimately religious faith there could be no compromise.

Two Populations

The 1860 census counted some thirty-two million Americans, two-thirds of whom lived in the North. Fourteen percent of the total population were slaves, 95 percent of whom lived in the South. (The remaining 5 percent lived in the so-called border states—Delaware, Maryland, Kentucky, and Missouri—states that would not secede from the Union but in which slavery was legal.) In two Southern states, the slave population exceeded the white population: South Carolina was 57 percent slave, and Mississippi was somewhat more than 50 percent.[4]

Although the United States was predominantly rural in 1860, 26 percent of Northerners lived in cities or towns, compared to only 10 percent in the South. New Orleans was the biggest Southern city, with 168,675 people in 1860, and no other urban center had more than 50,000 residents. Contrast the North, where nine cities had populations upward of 100,000, including the three largest: New York City at 813,669; Philadelphia, 565,529; and Brooklyn (separate from New York until 1898), 266,661.

As mentioned, the white Southern population was relatively homogeneous and nonimmigrant, whereas the northern population was far more diverse. From 1821 to 1860, 5,054,029 immigrants came to the United States, the great majority from western and central Europe. Of these, just one in eight settled in slave states—presumably because most were looking for work and could not hope to compete with slave labor. Although most immigrants settled in the large cities of the North, a significant number migrated to the western frontier, bringing with them "Northern" rather than "Southern" values. Overall, the great influx of immigrants into the United States added most to the diversity of the Northern population, especially in the cities.

It is also significant that the level of education was higher in the North than in the South. Both regions had surprisingly high literacy rates for the era: 80 percent of the Southern white population could read and write, compared with 95 percent in New England and a somewhat lower percentage in other sections of the North.

Yet only 39.7 percent of Southern white children were enrolled in school, whereas 75 percent of Northern children were. Moreover, Southern children who attended school did so only about 80 days out of the year, compared to 160 in the North. Public education financed and mandated by the states was in every Northern state, but virtually nonexistent throughout the South.

Two Recruitment Pools

The free Northern states had about 19 million people. The border states—slave states that did not secede from the Union—added another 3.2 million to the Union population count. The Southern population was about 9 million, of whom 3.2 million were slaves. In the North, potential military manpower in 1860—that is, the male population between ages eighteen and forty-five, the eligibility range initially set—consisted of some 3 million men. In the South, it was approximately 1 million.[5]

Two Economies

As two opposing cultures and two opposing populations were developing in America, so were two economies. The economy of the entire United States in the first sixty years of the nineteenth century enjoyed vigorous growth, principally in the industrial sector. The gross national product (GNP) doubled every fifteen years during that span, and per capita income grew during this period at an average rate of 1.7 percent annually. The growth in per capita income was largely in the nonagricultural sector, especially industry. In 1810 only 21 percent of the working population was employed outside of agriculture. By 1860 that number had grown to 45 percent.

Looked at on a per capita basis, the average net worth among white adult Southerners in 1860 was $3,978, versus a $2,040 average for adult Northerners. But the average fails to indicate the overall economic health of either region. Wealth was distributed more widely and equitably over the population in the North than it was in the South. The Southern economy was a slave economy. All of the South's slaves were owned by just one-third of Southern families. These families invested a portion of the wealth produced by their slaves in maintaining their slaves and adding to their number; the remainder was reallocated among themselves and only among themselves. This meant that the two-thirds of the white population who did not own slaves did not participate in the apparent prosperity of the region. Moreover, while wealthy Southerners invested in their own agricultural establishments (including the slaves who worked them), they invested very little in industry and transportation.

Cotton vs. Iron

It was South Carolina's Senator James Henry Hammond who famously crowned cotton king in the South. And so it was. The production of "King Cotton" claimed a relatively small portion of farmland in southern North Carolina; a broad swath in South Carolina; most of Georgia, Alabama, and Mississippi; perhaps 20 percent of arable land in Tennessee; about half of Arkansas farmland; much of upper Louisiana; and most of the eastern half of Texas. Even the Florida panhandle had cotton plantations.

Three other principal cash crops claimed significant labor but much less of the region's land and economy. Rice cultivation was confined to the low-country coastline extending from southeastern North Carolina through the entire coast of South Carolina and Georgia. Tobacco was cultivated at the northern edge of North Carolina and into a large band of Virginia (where it was the state's only considerable slave cash crop); tobacco was also very important in western Kentucky and northwestern Tennessee.

Sugar plantations thrived along the Gulf Coast of Louisiana and extended northward into the southwestern portion of Mississippi.

Cotton made Southern slave-owning planters very wealthy. Whereas Northern farmers (who were producing food commodities such as wheat, corn, and beef) invested in farm machinery to facilitate production, Southern planters doubled down on slave labor. By 1860 the average Northern farmer owned $0.89 worth of farm machinery per acre, whereas the average Southern plantation owner had just $0.42 worth. In the South the demand for slaves drove up their price dramatically, making slave labor increasingly inefficient in economic terms. In contrast, mechanization made Northern farming more efficient, which made Northern farmland more productive, thereby increasing its value. Moreover, while Northern farmers grew a variety of crops on their land, the Southern planters, by devoting massive acreage to one soil-intensive crop—cotton—quickly leached the nutrients from their land, exhausting it rapidly. On average, an acre of farmland was worth $25.67 in the North, but less than half that in the South, $10.40.

There were those in the South who saw that the prosperity created by King Cotton had a limited horizon and therefore counseled their wealthy planter brethren to diversify investment to include mining, manufacturing, and railroad building. This advice, however, was mostly ignored. The South was a net exporter of the major slave crops it produced, but was overwhelmingly a net importer of manufactured goods—bringing these in (before the war) from the North as well as from Europe (mostly Great Britain) and, during the war, relying almost exclusively on European imports.

In the North major investments were being made in industry, steamship transportation, and railroads, as well as in the financial infrastructure

The Union army included an organization called the United States Military Railroad (USMRR), which operated rail lines seized by the government during the war. This USMRR locomotive, the W. H. Whiton (built by the William Mason Works in 1862) was often detailed to pull President Lincoln's private rail car—which also served as the funeral car that carried him from Washington, DC, to Springfield, Illinois, for burial. LIBRARY OF CONGRESS

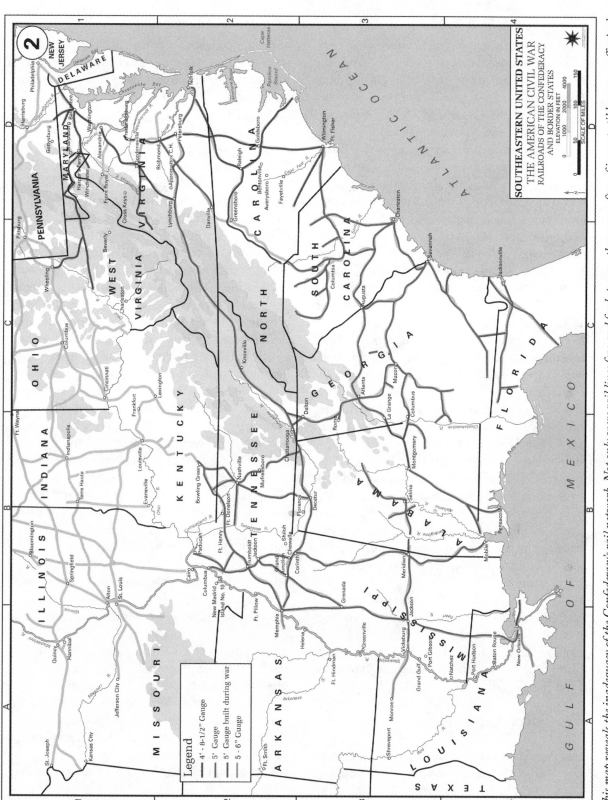

SOUTHEASTERN UNITED STATES
THE AMERICAN CIVIL WAR
RAILROADS OF THE CONFEDERACY
AND BORDER STATES

ELEVATION IN FEET

| 0 | 50 | 1000 | 2000 | 4000 |

SCALE OF MILES
0   50   100   150

Legend
4' - 8-1/2" Gauge
5' Gauge
5' Gauge built during war
5 - 6' Gtauge

This map reveals the inadequacy of the Confederacy's rail network. Not only were rail lines few and far between, they were often of incompatible gauges, effectively disconnecting one line from another. UNITED STATES MILITARY ACADEMY

that went with them: banks, insurance companies, and speculative investment firms. The South had relatively few such institutions. Indeed, of the 1,642 banks and bank branches in the United States in 1860, 1,421—86.6 percent—were in the Northern states.[6]

The existence of a large private-sector financial network would be of great importance to the North in fighting the war to come. The same was true of the North's investment in railroads, steamboats, and canals. Fought over a large area and with great numbers of men, supplies, and equipment, the Civil War drew on both industrial capacity and transportation to a degree unprecedented in modern warfare anywhere in the world, but especially in North America. In 1830 the entire United States had but 23 miles of railroad track. Just thirty years later, in 1860, it had 30,626 miles—about two-thirds of which was in the North, even though the geographical area south of the Mason–Dixon Line was about 300,000 square miles larger than the area north of it. Moreover, whereas Northern railroad tracks had been laid for the most part using a single standard gauge (the width between rails), the small Southern railway companies did little to standardize gauges among themselves. This necessitated changing trains at numerous points over any distance, laboriously unloading and reloading passengers and freight, something that greatly reduced the efficiency and speed of rail travel in the South.

By the numbers, the South in 1860 had 18,000 manufacturing establishments employing 111,000 workers; the North had 111,000, employing 1.3 million. In short, about 90 percent of the nation's manufacturing in 1860 came from the North.[7]

Two Social Contracts

Senator Hammond enthusiastically conceded that the South was "old-fashioned," but perhaps it was even older-fashioned than he thought it was. With an economy based on slaves laboring primarily on large plantations the owners governed as if they were princes or barons, and with the non-slave-owning two-thirds of the population sharing the racist views of the one-third who owned slaves, Southern culture both fed and fed upon a world view that had more in common with the feudalism of Europe's Middle Ages than with modern American democracy. White Southerners, rich and poor alike, spoke of sharing "traditions" or a "way of life." In fact, they shared a highly ritualized, rigidly hierarchical world view in which black slavery was ordained by both nature and God and in which people of every station in life had a similarly ordained place. It was, by definition, a socially immobile existence, a feudal hierarchy out of which both a mythology and an ethos of chivalry developed.

The North had no cultural institution remotely resembling Southern feudalism. To be sure, there was a wide gap between the richest and the poorest in the North, and the wealthy could buy not only material comforts, but political influence and even administrative and judicial preferences unavailable to most of the less well-off. Nevertheless, the region embraced a principle of equality. Some people, doubtless, did so hypocritically, yet the principle existed, and it was as real as the possibility that anyone, regardless of background and current station in life, could better themselves, and could even grow rich. In direct contrast with Southern society, Northern society was highly mobile. The dream among Northerners was that the mobility tended inexorably upward. The dream, however, was not always the reality. Whereas the Southern social compact kept people in their place, severely limiting both upward social expectation as well as aspiration, it was also structured to ensure that a person's place, whatever it was, would sustain him or her at a level suited to it.

There were few surprises in Southern society. Hammond was probably correct in his observation that one encountered far more beggars in the urban North than in the rural South. On the other hand, the possibilities for social change and individual betterment beyond one's class, one's place, were few in the South and far more numerous in the North.

In 1860 the South was focused on maintaining the status quo, whereas the North had its sights set on change. The South would break away from the Union not to change things, but to avoid the changes it feared—and probably rightly so—the North was determined to force upon it. At the war's start, the North fought the South as it would fight any rebellion against the national government. By the second year of the war, however, with the introduction of emancipation, President Abraham Lincoln nudged the war in a new direction. While the South continued to fight *against* change, the North began to fight *for* change—for the end of slavery, which meant (as some Northerners saw it) the belated perfection of American independence and the Constitution that grew from it.

At some level and in varying degrees, the soldiers, both gray and blue, who fought the Civil War fought for a cause, a way of life, a world order. In the South it was a cause, a life, an order long familiar and jealously guarded. In the North it was two causes—one to restore the nation, the other to redefine the nation at long last as the perfection of liberty and

President Abraham Lincoln is pictured with his 1865 cabinet, as photographed by Mathew B. Brady. Clockwise from under the eagle's right wing (upper left of the photograph): Secretary of State William H. Seward, Secretary of the Treasury Hugh McCulloch, Secretary of the Navy Gideon Welles, Postmaster General William Dennison, Attorney General James Speed, Secretary of the Interior John P. Usher, and Secretary of War Edwin M. Stanton. NATIONAL ARCHIVES AND RECORDS ADMINISTRATION

equality. It was to accomplish something the Founding Fathers had left undone. It was something new.

Chapter 5

THE SOUTH MOBILIZES

SPEED AND EFFICIENCY OF MOBILIZATION FOR WAR: ✷ ✷ ✷

South Carolina had been leading the South's secession conversation since the 1830s and had repeatedly tried to stir the other Southern states to take a stand against the Union. The election of Abraham Lincoln in November 1860 brought the secession issue to a crisis, but it did not instantly create unanimity in the South. On December 20, 1860, South Carolina passed an ordinance of secession, as did Mississippi, Florida, Alabama, Georgia, and Louisiana in January 1861 and Texas on February 1. Virginia, Arkansas, Tennessee, North Carolina, Missouri, and Kentucky held back, not fully persuaded that Abraham Lincoln would play the part of tyrant.

Four of the so-called border states—Delaware, Kentucky, Maryland, and Missouri, all slaveholding—never seceded. Four others—Arkansas, North Carolina, Tennessee, and Virginia—did not secede until after the April 14, 1861 fall of Fort Sumter. Their hesitancy did not discourage the so-called fire-eaters—the most passionate secessionists—who rationalized that a buffer between the Union and the Confederacy consisting of states that were militarily neutral but nevertheless friendly to slavery might prevent Northern forces from invading the secessionist South. At the very least, the existence of such a border might well buy time for the pro-secession forces to build a more complete consensus around the idea of a Confederacy, seize and occupy all former federal installations in the South—forts, ports, armories, and depots—recruit volunteers, and mobilize an army.

ABRAHAM LINCOLN: CONFEDERATE RECRUITER

As Lincoln's election provoked South Carolina's secession, his decision to defend Fort Sumter in Charleston and Fort Pickens in Pensacola against Confederate seizure and his subsequent call for 75,000 militia volunteers on April 15, 1861, moved Virginia to secede on April 17. The other three states that would make up the Confederacy—Arkansas, Tennessee, and North Carolina—would leave the Union in May.

With the series of secessions came thousands of volunteers, who organized or joined local militia companies, which presented themselves to anyone designated as an officer of the Confederate army. By this time a constitutional convention had already met at Montgomery, Alabama (February 9, 1861), and elected by acclamation Jefferson Davis as provisional Confederate president. Educated at West Point (Class of 1828), Davis served in the US Army until 1835. He became a Mississippi cotton planter and in 1845 was elected to the US House of Representatives. He resigned in 1846 to rejoin the army as a colonel, distinguishing himself in the US-Mexican War (1846–48). Davis served very ably as secretary of war (1853–57) in the administration of Franklin Pierce and was elected to the US Senate in 1857, serving there until Mississippi seceded from the Union in 1861.

Davis drew on this military education and experience to create the regular Army of the Confederate States of America (ACSA), which was modeled closely on the United States Army he knew so well from the war with Mexico. He planned ultimately to create the ACSA as a small

This chromolithograph published in 1896 shows four versions of the flag of the Confederate States of America. Also portrayed are the Confederacy's heroes: Standing at the center are (left to right) Stonewall Jackson, P. G. T. Beauregard, and Robert E. Lee, surrounded by bust portraits of the principal figures of the Confederacy (clockwise from upper-left corner): General Braxton Bragg, General P. G. T. Beauregard, President Jefferson Davis, Vice President Alexander H. Stephens, Lieutenant General Thomas J. "Stonewall" Jackson, General Sterling Price, Lieutenant General Leonidas Polk, Lieutenant General William J. Hardee, General J. E. B. Stuart, General Joseph E. Johnston, Lieutenant General Kirby Smith, Brigadier General John H. Morgan, General Albert Sidney Johnston, General Wade Hampton, General John B. Gordon, Lieutenant General James Longstreet, General A. P. Hill, and General John Bell Hood.

standing force, like the US Army; however, to meet the demands of the impending Civil War, he prevailed on the Confederate Congress to enact legislation (February 28, 1861) authorizing a Provisional Army of the Confederate States (PACS), which would serve the same purpose as the US Volunteer Army. The PACS would be a large force assembled solely to prosecute the current war, after which it would be dissolved. On March 6 the Confederate Congress also officially sanctioned the ASCA and, soon after, authorized Davis to call up 100,000 men for twelve months' service. In May the call-up of an additional 400,000 was authorized—these men to serve for three years or the duration of the war.

Most histories and discussions of the Civil War make no distinction between the ACSA and PACS, but refer to them collectively as the Confederate army or the Confederate States Army (CSA). From the soldiers' point of view, the main difference between the ASCA and the PACS was that service in the ASCA was for a minimum of three years, whereas service in the PACS had become three years or the duration. That most who volunteered for service volunteered to *fight Yankees*, not to *be soldiers*, is made dramatically apparent by the disparity in numbers between volunteers for the two organizations. Some 1,000 enlisted men and 750 officers joined the ASCA, whereas the rest of the half million authorized by May 1861 all volunteered for the PACS. Nobody expected the war to last anything like three years, let alone longer.

A MATTER OF HONOR

In the early days of the war, there was never any shortage of volunteers. This has often puzzled historians, who debate whether most Confederate volunteers were driven by political ideology, especially states' rights; economics, especially the economic incentive to preserve slavery; or something more personal, such as "the defense of

one's home and family, or the honor and brotherhood to be preserved when fighting alongside other men."[1]

The diary of one Confederate officer's wife suggests the magnitude of the persuasive potency of ideology: "Dear Old Virginia, long did she strive to keep her place in the Union, but trampled rights, a broken Constitution, and a dishonorable Government compelled her to join her sister states in a new Confederacy."[2]

"The unanimity of the people was simply marvelous," author George C. Eggleston wrote of the outbreak of war in the South. "So long as the question of secession was under discussion opinions were both various and violent. The moment secession was finally determined upon, a revolution was wrought. There was no longer anything to discuss, and so discussion ceased. Men got ready for war, and delicate women with equal spirit sent them off with smiling faces."[3]

A Confederate War Department clerk marveled at the enthusiasm and fire of the volunteers: "From the ardor of the [Southern] volunteers . . . they might sweep the whole Abolition concern beyond the Susquehanna, and afterwards keep them there," he wrote. "This [Lincoln's call-up of 75,000 volunteers] is the irrevocable blow! Every reflecting mind here should know that the only alternatives now are successful revolution or abject subjugation."[4]

"It is not far to demand a reason for actions above reason," Carlton McCarthy, a Confederate private, recalled in a postwar memoir. "No man can exactly define the cause for which the Confederate soldier fought." But McCarthy tried nevertheless and concluded that he, personally, fought against the "accumulated wrongs and indignities" that were prompting his "brethren and friends" to answer "the bugle-call and the roll of the drum. To stay [behind] was dishonor and shame." Indeed, for most volunteers, the leading motive came down to *honor*. The Confederate soldier "would not obey the dictates of tyranny. To disobey was death. He disobeyed and fought for his life." Rebellion against "tyranny" was honorable. To yield to Northern demands to end slavery was to bow to "the dogmas of fanatics, and so [the young Southern man] became a 'rebel.' Being a rebel, he must be punished. Being punished, he resisted. Resisting, he died."[5] If McCarthy's analysis and self-analysis of motivation are correct, the Southern perception of Northern tyranny was an offense against Southern honor that could be answered only with rebellion. Since this rebellion was considered treason, it was punishable by death. Since the object of the rebellion was large and powerful, death was almost certain. Yet the fatalism entailed in serving the demands of honor overcame all reluctance and fear.

For a time.

OVERWHELMED AND UNDERESTIMATED

Jefferson Davis's initial call for 100,000 volunteers was met by an overwhelming response. Volunteers swamped makeshift recruiting offices, and in the early weeks of the war, recruiters turned away some 200,000 hopefuls. In the first place, the infant Confederacy had no way of clothing, sheltering, or feeding, much less arming, so many men at one time. In the second place, nobody dreamed that the war would last very long. Based on the slow, even reluctant, and often inept response of Union forces to the rebellion, Confederate politicians and military commanders alike dared assume that the North would either soon back down or would, in fact, be defeated. For this reason, Confederate leaders grossly underestimated the need for troops.

Those who burned with a passion to fight the Yankees, but who could find no place in the ACSA or the PACS, might still join a private militia company raised by some locally prominent citizen who had a hankering to be addressed as captain. If the "captain" was wealthy enough,

he supplied the company's uniforms, equipment, and firearms; if not, the men themselves used or purchased their own weapons, made do with whatever civilian clothing could pass for uniforms, and chipped in for rations. In some places these private companies would attach themselves and subordinate themselves to the ACSA or PACS. In other places, however, especially in the backcountry, they would operate independently, sometimes counterproductively, and at times were even a drain on manpower that could be more productively used in the PACS.

WHAT DO WE DO NOW?

But, in the early weeks and months of the war, the PACS had more volunteers than it could handle. As with the Union army's sharp distinction between the diminutive regular US Army and the enormous US Volunteer Army (Chapter 6), the division between the ACSA and the PACS created a crisis in leadership. PACS officers were almost uniformly inexperienced. Regimental commanders, like company commanders, were elected by the men of the regiment. Their election was based not on their military credentials—many had few or none—but on their popularity with their troops. Indeed, "candidates" for the office of regimental colonel routinely campaigned as they might for civilian political office. To many who observed such military electioneering, the spectacle appeared unseemly.

Yet there was a peculiar resistance among many enlisted men to accept promotion based on demonstrated performance and prowess in battle—at least early in the war. "To offer a man promotion in the early part of the war was equivalent to an insult," Carlton McCarthy wrote. "The higher the social position, the greater the wealth, the more patriotic it would be to serve in the humble position of a private; and many men of education and ability in the various professions, refusing promotion, served under the command of men greatly their inferiors, mentally, morally, and as soldiers." At the same time, it "took years to teach the educated privates in the army that it was their duty to give unquestioning obedience to officers because they were such, who were awhile ago their playmates and associates in business. It frequently happened that the private, feeling hurt by the stern authority of the officer, would ask him to one side, challenge him to personal combat, and thrash him well. After awhile these privates learned about extra duty, half rations, and courts-martial."[6]

Inexperience at the top led to a resistance to discipline in the ranks of the PACS. The enlistees had enthusiastically volunteered to fight, not to perform laborious fatigue duties or to engage in even more tedious drills. The experience of combat would, in time, provide the experience both officers and enlisted men needed. But on-the-job training is worse than inefficient in life-or-death situations. It is costly in blood and treasure.

How to Supply?

Outfitting, supplying, provisioning, and arming its rapidly mobilizing armies was a daunting proposition for the Confederacy, given an industrial base and transportation infrastructure far inferior to that of the North. As a region, the antebellum South was a net exporter of agricultural commodities and a net importer of manufactured goods. Its main prewar supplier of industrial products, the northern United States, was now largely cut off.[7] The region's few indigenous manufacturers did their best to gear up for war, and the Tredegar Iron Works, in Richmond, Virginia, even reached remarkable levels of production.[8] But Southern leaders recognized as early as the run-up to the war that the Confederacy would have to rely on European suppliers, mainly British and French, for weapons, ammunition, and warships.

Obtaining war materiel from overseas presented two obstacles. The first, discussed in the next section, was how to pay for it all. The Confederacy's supply of gold and hard currency was limited, and the foreign credit of this breakaway region was practically nonexistent. The second obstacle was the Union's naval blockade of Southern ports. The idea for the blockade came not from a Union naval leader, but from the army's general-in-chief, Winfield Scott, and it came at the very outbreak of the war. Understanding that it would take time to mobilize a credible invasion force, Scott proposed delaying any major offensive against the Confederacy until sufficient forces could be built up. In the short term, he recommended a maritime blockade of the South to starve the region both literally and economically. If it were unable to export cotton and other trade goods or to import foodstuffs and European-manufactured arms and ammunition, the South would be reeling by the time the armies of the North were ready to invade.

The naval blockade was a brilliant plan on paper, but the reality was that the US Navy would need hundreds, perhaps thousands, of ships to adequately patrol the vast Southern coastline. In the spring of 1861, the Union's navy consisted of just forty-two seaworthy vessels of war, but, as the war went on, the navy grew, and the blockade became increasingly effective. As the months went by, the Confederacy had more and more trouble supplying its army—not to mention feeding its people.

Throughout the war intrepid Confederate and foreign sea captains would make daring runs against the Northern blockade. But first, the Confederate government had to launch a diplomatic offensive to round up European allies or, at the very least, obtain recognition as a sovereign nation by European trading partners and potential creditors. On March 16, 1861, the Confederate government sent three emissaries to Europe authorized to offer tariff-free trade with the breakaway nation. As attractive as the offer was, there were no takers, and so President Jefferson Davis appointed James M. Mason of Virginia minister to England and Louisiana's John Slidell minister to France and, in October, sent both to Europe to try again.

There was reason to hope for success this time. Both France and England relied heavily on the South as a trading partner. Indeed, British textile mills practically ran on Southern cotton. Moreover, both Britain and France were monarchies in a Europe that, as recently as 1848, had been convulsed by a wave of republican revolutions. Instead of prejudicing these governments against a rebellion in North America, the secession of the South, which portrayed itself as a conservative aristocracy of planters, seemed like a blow against the radicalizing forces of the North's industrial democracy. Both culturally and ideologically, therefore, the imperial governments of Britain and France were sympathetic to the Confederacy.

As it turned out, the Slidell-Mason mission was quickly intercepted by a US Navy warship, which arrested the British mail packet *Trent* just after it left Havana, Cuba, bound for England. Union sailors boarded the *Trent*, removed the two Confederate emissaries, and took them to Fort Warren in Boston Harbor, where they were held. Outraged by the forcible arrest of a British-flagged vessel, Parliament demanded an apology and the release of the prisoners. Against the advice of Secretary of State William Seward, President Lincoln ordered the release of Mason and Slidell—although he declined to apologize. Still, he wanted to avoid antagonizing Britain. "One war at a time," he counseled Seward.[9]

The Confederacy did buy weapons from both Britain and France, and it covertly purchased ships from British shipyards. Intrepid foreign as well as Confederate captains did their best to "run" the Union blockade, often succeeding at landing cargoes in Southern harbors. But

the process was slow, expensive, and risky—and, as the war continued, it was less and less effective as the blockading fleet grew larger. Supplying the Confederate armies would remain a crippling problem throughout the war.

HOW TO PAY?

With foreign trade strangled—although by no means strangled to death—the Confederacy resorted to printing paper currency, "treasury notes," to finance the war. This began as early as March 9, 1861. The currency was supplemented by the sale of bonds and the levying of taxes. When bond sales proved disappointing, the treasury resorted to printing more currency. The treasury notes had to compete with currency issued by some states and even by some counties within states—not to mention the efforts of numerous counterfeiters. Inflation rapidly set in. Against US currency, the Confederate dollar was worth just 80 cents by late 1861, 20 cents in 1863, and 1.5 cents in 1865.[10]

In August 1861 the Confederate government passed its first tax law, levying a 0.5 percent tax on real property, including slaves (who represented 35 percent of the property on which Confederate taxes were levied). Some state governments paid the required taxes on behalf of their citizens at a rate the Confederate government reduced by 10 percent; however, the states borrowed funds to do this, thereby adding their own debts to the Confederate government's debt. In April 1863 tax revenues were increased through taxes levied not only on property, but on occupations (in the form of licenses), income, and produce. Still, try as it might, the Confederate government never generated through taxation more than 7 percent of the revenue it needed.

In desperation the Confederacy resorted, beginning on March 26, 1863, to the compulsory "impressment" for military use of manufactured goods and agricultural produce in return for increasingly valueless Confederate currency or for government certificates redeemable at some later date. Goods impressed were routinely assessed at about 50 percent of their market rate, but since payment was in currency of rapidly diminishing value or virtually valueless promissory certificates, impressment amounted to confiscation, and it worked a great hardship on Southerners, their businesses, and the Confederate economy generally. Black markets emerged for everything, and inflation became hyperinflation, reaching catastrophic heights.

AN END TO ENTHUSIASM

Desertion was a problem in the Confederate forces from the beginning. In the early years men wandered away from their units out of boredom, pressing family need, or simple lack of discipline. By 1863, however, as soldiers went unpaid and often unfed, and amid growing hardship on the home front, they deserted in ever larger numbers. In July of that year, after the defeats at Vicksburg and Gettysburg, an estimated 50,000 to 100,000 men just walked away. On October 6, 1864, the Richmond *Enquirer* reported that President Davis had announced that "two-thirds of the Army are absent from the ranks." If this was true, Confederate deserters had come to outnumber Confederate soldiers.[11]

Anticipating critical shortages of manpower, the Confederacy enacted a conscription law on April 16, 1862, nearly a year before the Union did the same. The law obliged all white males ages eighteen to thirty-five to give three years of service. Before the end of the year, the upper age limit was advanced to forty-five, and in February 1864, to fifty, while the lower limit was rolled back to age seventeen. None of the Confederate draft laws made an attempt to be equitable. Like those later enacted in the North, they provided two alternatives to service—for anyone with the

means to pay for them. A draftee could stay out of the army by paying the government a commutation fee or by hiring an acceptable substitute to serve in his place. In the Confederacy, men who either owned or oversaw twenty slaves or more were also automatically exempt.[12]

Declining rates of enlistment, increasing rates of desertion, and a generally shrinking pool of men and boys (some were fourteen or even younger) suitable for military enrollment brought on one of the great ironies of the Confederate struggle. The Conscription Acts of 1862 and 1864 drafted (from their owners) slaves as well as free blacks to replace white soldiers in such noncombat support roles as laborers, cooks, teamsters, and even musicians. Slaves and conscripted free blacks were put to work building, repairing, and maintain fortifications, railroads, and river defenses, and they were also assigned to foundries and arsenals to assist in arms manufacture.[13]

In January 1864 Major General Patrick Cleburne, commanding a division of the Army of Tennessee, proposed "that we immediately commence training a large reserve of the most courageous of our slaves, and . . . guarantee freedom within a reasonable time to every slave in the South who shall remain true to the Confederacy in the war." He added that only by "making the negro [*sic*] share the danger and hardships of the war" could sufficient numbers of troops be raised. Cleburne's proposal was not accepted, but on March 13, 1865, a desperate Confederate Congress did authorize the recruitment—not the conscription—of "Negro Soldiers," whose "loyal service" was to be rewarded by some largely unspecified form of emancipation, provided that the Union was defeated. A few African-American soldiers were recruited, and a handful even fought on April 5, 1865, during the retreat from Richmond, but the war came to an end before any significant number of African Americans saw action as Confederate riflemen.[14]

Chapter 6

THE NORTH MOBILIZES

SPEED AND EFFICIENCY OF MOBILIZATION FOR WAR: ★ ★ ⸶

Reading chapters 4 and 5 would lead us to believe that the North was far more prepared to go to war than the South. Economically, industrially, and demographically, this was quite true. But in more strictly military terms, it was not true at all. The North did have a small army and navy on which to build a force for war, whereas the South had to start from nothing more than some state militias; nevertheless, at the outbreak of war, some of the best officers either came out of retirement or left the US Army to join the Confederacy as generals. These included the likes of Robert E. Lee, Thomas J. Jackson, and 149 others.[1] Moreover, the US-Mexican War (1846–48) had been fought largely at the instigation of Southerners, and it was the South that provided most of the volunteers for the conflict. This meant that many Southerners, still in the prime of life, had combat experience as company-level officers and noncommissioned officers.

Arguably even more important than experience, the Southerners tended to be more urgently motivated than the Northerners. Most Northerners entered the war with just one compelling goal, to restore the Union, and not everyone who served was convinced that this was worth the effort. Even the abolitionist editor of the *New York Tribune* counseled, "Let the erring sisters go in peace," meaning that the seceded states should be allowed to secede and shift for themselves.[2] What is more, it very soon became apparent that restoring the Union would mean crushing—not merely chastising—the Confederacy, and there was by no means unanimity of purpose among Northern troops or politicians on how to accomplish this. Only during the second year of the war did freeing the slaves and ending slavery also become a war aim—and not everyone of military age welcomed the prospect of risking life and limb to achieve this end. "Willing to Fight for Uncle Sam but Not for Uncle Sambo!" was a typical headline in a Pennsylvania newspaper.[3]

In any case, strategically, the North was obliged to assume the offensive, to take the fight south to the Confederacy. Mounting an invasion and an offensive required substantially more military resources than merely defending territory, which was the military role of the Confederacy. One modern scholar has estimated that invasion and offensive required about "three times as many men and resources" as merely defending one's home turf. This was "almost exactly equal to the [manpower] advantage enjoyed by the North."[4] Moreover, while the North had to achieve absolute, annihilating victory, the South had merely to endure, to survive, to outlast the North, to win by not losing. The South was, in fact, in the same situation as George Washington's armies in the American Revolution. They did not have to defeat a superior enemy. They only had to outlast its will to continue the fight.

In the South fighting the Civil War was seen as a matter of honor and survival—economic survival and the survival of a world view, a way of life. Most of the two-thirds of Southerners who did not own slaves were poor, and their poverty (they believed) was due mainly to the economic and trade policies forced upon them by the North. Northern politicians favored high import tariffs, which made it possible for Northerners to export their manufactured goods cheaply even as it forced down both the demand for and prices of the main Southern exports, cotton, tobacco, sugar, and rice. Thus the wealthy planters and the landless Southern poor were united in their feeling of being deliberately oppressed by the North. Nobody had to convince the Southern man of military age that his well-being and that of his family depended on prevailing in battle against the North. He was already living this truth.

In contrast, in the North men were motivated by more abstract imperatives: patriotism and the inherent value of preserving a democratic republic hard won by revolution. Some, it is true, were additionally motivated by an intense moral and even religious passion to free the oppressed slaves. For them fighting took on the dimension of a crusade. But these men were in the minority. Indeed, only among the African-American troops, who were largely barred from enlisting until 1863 and then only in segregated units under white officers, did an urgency of motivation equivalent to that of Southern whites exist. The "colored soldiers," 186,097 by the end of the war, were fighting for both freedom and survival—the very objectives the Confederate soldier saw himself fighting for. (The dramatic story of the United States Colored Troops is covered in chapter 13.)

RALLYING TO THE COLORS

"Where there is no vision, the people perish," King Solomon proclaimed in Proverbs 29:18. The people of the Confederacy went to war with a vision—of liberation from an oppressor who meant to take away their livelihood and their way of life, who meant to enslave them even as he forced them to free the black men, women, boys, and girls who were their slaves under the law of God and nature. The young men of the North were propelled less by a vision than they were compelled by a patriotic sense of duty. For many, this was sufficient. For others, early in the war, there was also the promise of adventure and even fun. "New recruits were caught up in a festive air created by rallies and speeches that were organized in their wards and townships."[5] Nobody

wanted to be left out of a once-in-a-lifetime event they all believed would be over very quickly.

In obedience to their Southern vision, South Carolina Confederates bombarded Fort Sumter into submission during April 12–14, 1861. In this they "struck a blow" against oppression. On April 15 President Abraham Lincoln responded to the fall of Fort Sumter not with a stirring call to war, but by invoking the Militia Act of 1795 and the Militia Act of 1803. Section 2 of the former law specified:

That, whenever the laws of the United States shall be opposed or the execution thereof obstructed, in any state, by combinations too powerful to be suppressed by the ordinary course of judicial proceedings, or by the powers vested in the marshals by this act, the same being notified to the President of the United States, by an associate justice or the district judge, it shall be lawful for the President of the United States to call forth the militia of such state to suppress such combinations, and to cause the laws to be duly executed. And if the militia of a state, where such combinations may happen, shall refuse, or be insufficient to suppress the same, it shall be lawful for the President, if the legislature of the United States be not in session, to call forth and employ such numbers of the militia of any other state or states most convenient thereto, as may be necessary, and the use of militia, so to be called forth, may be continued, if necessary, until the expiration of thirty days after the commencement of the ensuing session.[6]

Section 24 of the subsequent Militia Act of 1803, which was approved on March 3 of that year, empowered the president to call out the militia to defend law and order in the District of Columbia when necessary.[7]

Backed by these laws, Lincoln called for 75,000 volunteers. General-in-chief Winfield Scott had called for a military of 85,000

Newly minted soldiers march out from Fort Massachusetts on the periphery of Washington, DC, in the first year of the war, 1861. The fort was renamed Fort Stevens in 1863 and was the target of an unsuccessful raid led by Jubal Early on July 11–12, 1864. NATIONAL ARCHIVES AND RECORDS ADMINISTRATION

men—25,000 regulars and 60,000 volunteers. President Lincoln's initial call-up brought US Army strength to 91,816 men (75,000 plus the more than 16,000 already in the regular army). His belief was that Scott underestimated the numbers needed to fight the war. Soon, however, it would be apparent that the war required far more than either man had imagined. In any case, the militia responded to the call-up, but the response from non-militia members was even greater—this despite the fact that Lincoln resorted to the militia laws, which implied that he was not so much taking the nation to war, let alone leading it on a crusade, as he was merely acting to put down an insurrection that violated federal law. If this legalistic approach

was intended to avoid provoking the South, it failed, as Southerners took it instead as a declaration of war against the South and, accordingly, responded by rallying to their flag in large numbers.

On both sides, North and South, the initial call-up of militia volunteers was for ninety days. This was the specification of the United States militia law, and the Confederacy followed suit. It was also the result of assumptions on both sides that the war would be a very short one.

Lincoln privately confessed his relief that Fort Sumter had fallen during the congressional recess. He decided *not* to call the legislative body into special session and, for the next three months, ran the war from the White House.

A month after his initial call-up, he issued an executive order expanding the size of the regular army to 22,000 troops, and he showed more foresight than most by asking for an additional 42,000 volunteers to serve not for ninety days, but for three years. In the absence of Congress, Lincoln further directed the Treasury to advance $2 million for the immediate purchase of supplies for the troops.[8]

UNPREPARED AND OVERWHELMED

It is impossible to say whether the absence of Congress during the first three months of the war increased or decreased the efficiency of the Union's response to the crisis. It is a fact that throughout the spring of 1861, the response to Lincoln's call for volunteers was overwhelming. It is also a fact that the federal government was utterly unprepared to cope with the tremendous influx of troops. Would congressional oversight have made it more prepared? Who knows?

Mobilization consists of two broad components: troop mobilization and materiel mobilization. It is a truism of all military mobilizations that the recruitment and mustering of troops soon overtake the mobilization of materiel. In both the South and the North, this was the case, but in the Confederacy, the lack of preparation may be explained and excused by the fact that the South had to build a military nearly from scratch. In the case of the Union, the Northern government was simply, shamefully, and woefully unready. The volunteers, both in groups of organized militias and individually, mustered at designated gathering places in their states and localities. At these places they awaited transportation—typically by rail—to Washington, DC, which, at the outbreak of the war, was *the* designated point from which the army would march. In contrast to the local mustering, which was often quite well organized, the incoming recruits were greeted in Washington by sheer chaos. Because the United States had no large standing army in 1861, there were no permanent facilities—encampments, barracks, and supply depots—to accommodate substantial numbers of troops. Officials commandeered whatever buildings and spaces within buildings were available in and around the capital. Vacant land was acquired to establish training camps, but instead of hiring civilian contractors to build them, the army quartermasters brought in lumber and other materials, and the first recruits, who had come to learn to fight, were instead given hammers and nails and told to use the lumber to build their own barracks. The results were not beautiful, but they were nevertheless remarkable. Regimental "camps" sprang up all over the capital, each with an officers' barracks and ten or a dozen troop barracks, complete with cook shacks (adjacent but separate, to reduce the risk of fire) and stables (for cavalry regiments). The barracks were invariably arranged around a central parade ground.

THE SHOCK OF BATTLE

Congress became active in the Civil War only after it came into session some eighty days following the surrender of Fort Sumter. Even then, there was little enough sense of urgency. If this sounds like dereliction of duty, maybe it was. But it was up to the Union forces to bring the fighting to the Confederate forces, and, except for some relatively minor engagements, the Union army did no such thing. For this reason, it would be fair to apply to the first ninety days of the conflict the appellation that the British applied to the first few months of World War II in western Europe: *the phony war*. This changed abruptly on July 21, 1861, when Confederate forces handed the Union a humiliating defeat at the First Battle of Bull Run, a short carriage ride from the nation's capital. The Union army was led by a respected general, Irvin McDowell, and (at least initially) outnumbered the Confederate forces. Nevertheless, Union casualties tallied to more than 2,700 while Confederate losses were under 2,000. That was a shock. Even more shocking was the harsh realization that the "rebellion" would not be easily crushed or might not be crushed at all and that, whatever the outcome, the war would certainly not be brief.

In his message to Congress on July 4, weeks before Bull Run, President Lincoln had recommended that Congress "give the legal means for making this contest a short and a decisive one; that you place at the control of the Government for the work at least 400,000 men and $400,000,000." He also, for the first time, strove to elevate the aim of the war to a new, loftier, and more urgent level, calling it "a People's contest . . . a struggle for maintaining in the world, that form, and substance of government, whose leading object is, to elevate the condition of men."[9] The defeat at Bull Run spurred Congress to authorize an army of 500,000 and allowed for the extension of the term of enlistment to "the duration of the war."

THE ROLE OF THE STATES IN MOBILIZATION

But the problem was not numbers alone. Until the First Battle of Bull Run, the federal government did not take the "rebellion" seriously enough to create a sound administration for the War Department. Under Lincoln's predecessor, President James Buchanan, Secretary of War John B. Floyd's mismanagement of the department's resources created a scandal that resulted in his indictment for "malversation" (corruption). A Virginian who would become a brigadier general in the *Confederate* army, Floyd was suspected of essentially sabotaging the US military establishment to make it vulnerable in the event of the outbreak of civil war. In his memoirs Ulysses S. Grant wrote that Floyd had "scattered the army so that much of it could be captured when

hostilities should commence, and distributed cannon and small arms from Northern arsenals throughout the South so as to be on hand when treason wanted them."[10]

Floyd was replaced before the end of the Buchanan administration by Joseph Holt, who managed to bring no reform whatsoever. By the time the war began, about a third of the War Department's personnel had left government service or had joined the Confederacy. The administrative staff necessary to an efficient mobilization was simply missing, and President Lincoln's appointment of Simon Cameron as his secretary of war in March 1861 proved disastrous. For the ten months of Cameron's service—he was replaced on January 14, 1862, by the fiercely able Edwin McMasters Stanton—the beleaguered War Department was beset by corruption on a scale that dwarfed the "malversation" of Floyd. When Lincoln asked Pennsylvania congressman Thaddeus Stevens for his opinion on Cameron's honesty, the crusty abolitionist replied drily, "I don't think that he would steal a red-hot stove." Taking umbrage, Cameron demanded Stevens retract the remark, to which the Pennsylvanian responded to the president, "I believe I told you he would not steal a red-hot stove. I will now take that back."[11]

Although Stanton eventually achieved remarkable reforms, this would take time, and, during the first year and more of the war, the mobilization effort largely fell to the states by default. They not only rose to the occasion, they approached the task precisely as the federal government did *not*—that is, *proactively*. Wisconsin, for instance, passed legislation allocating $100,000 to aid in raising and supporting the troops it would send into federal service—and it passed this bill on April 13, 1861, the day *before* Fort Sumter surrendered.[12] Other states, including New York, Rhode Island, Massachusetts, Pennsylvania, and New Jersey, soon followed with militia call-ups as well as appropriations to aid in securing supplies and materiel. Once federal authorities set militia quotas, most states responded by volunteering to send even more men than requested. In addition, aid and offers of aid came from the private sector, as banks, businesses, civic organizations, and even individuals donated money to aid the war effort. The Cincinnati City Council donated $255,000 to the federal government to use as it saw fit in financing the war.[13]

Well into 1862, the states were far more effective at recruiting than the federal government. For one thing, both the states and some localities within them offered enlistees a bounty for joining, whereas the federal government, early in the war, did not. Beyond this, however, was the fact that the American people entered the Civil War identifying more closely with their home states than with the nation. The Illinois man joined the militia to defend Illinois, not the United States. It was the long, bloody process of the Civil War itself that changed this mindset. Soldiers who entered the war in defense of their home state emerged from the experience feeling that they had fought for and saved the nation.

There is no question that, throughout the first year of the war, the states bore the brunt of mobilization. They did so independently of one another and, to a large extent, in a spirit of competition. In mobilization the states leaned heavily on both the banks operating within their borders and their wealthiest citizens to aid in financing their recruitment efforts. They also turned to various charitable and civic organizations, including the United States Christian Commission and the United States Sanitary Commission for aid in helping to feed and clothe the troops and, most of all, to care for them when they were sick or wounded. The army's own medical department was unequal to what proved a monumental task. In addition, these organizations provided aid to the families of soldiers. It was the work of these private-sector organizations that made

it possible for many men to enlist by providing a measure of assurance that they and their dependents would be looked after in ways the government could not promise them.

BREAKDOWN OF VOLUNTEERISM

By September 1861 enlistments fell off sharply. There were at least four reasons for this. First, the war had quickly lost the appeal of adventure. Second, many young men were returning from battle maimed, and many others were not returning at all. Third, reports of acute ration shortages and other supply shortages were rife; in some places and at some times, entire units were turned away from designated rendezvous points—without receiving resupply. Finally, the Union army was doing remarkably little to carry the fighting to the South.

Secretary Stanton was the new broom who was supposed to sweep away all that was bad. Part of his strategy to straighten out the War Department and the army support apparatus was to suspend recruiting efforts for two months, so that the proper staffing and support infrastructure could be put in place. Unfortunately, only the portion of Order 33 directing a halt in recruitment and the shuttering of recruiting offices was ever transmitted. The portion of the order specifying the two-month timeframe was, for some reason, withheld. Commanders of undermanned forces in the field were stunned by the order, and by the time it was clarified, Union morale had taken a bad hit. Efforts to revive voluntary enlistment at anything like the rates that were needed fell flat. For the first time in the war, the federal government offered a bounty for enlistment, which proved a reasonably effective (if costly) method of mustering in warm bodies—but the quality of the recruits declined. No question that those who applied surely wanted the cash, but as for serving their country and becoming good soldiers—not so much.

Lincoln, Congress, and the military leadership hoped that the bounty offer would allow them to avoid doing what the Confederates had already done: introduce conscription. It did not, however, and Congress accordingly passed a conscription law on March 3, 1863. Like the Confederate conscription law, it gave the financially privileged a way of avoiding service, either by hiring a substitute or by paying the government a $300 commutation fee. The less well-off were obliged to serve, and conscription was therefore reviled as unjustly exploiting the ordinary working man. Riots, especially in poorer areas and poorer neighborhoods, erupted in New York, New Jersey, Pennsylvania, Iowa, Illinois, Indiana, and Ohio.

The worst and most notorious draft riot began in New York City on Monday, July 13, 1863. A newspaper reporter, Joel T. Headley, described how "a ragged, coatless, heterogeneously weaponed army" of rioters "heaved tumultuously along toward Third Avenue," tearing down telegraph poles as they crossed the Harlem & New Haven Railroad track, then surging "angrily up around the building where the drafting was going on." They broke into the draft office, seized the draft lottery wheel, and destroyed whatever books, papers, and lists they encountered. Finding a safe, some of the rioters attempted to break into it. When this failed they put the building to the torch and then stormed the Second Avenue armory, looted it, and proceeded to ransack a variety of Third Avenue stores, including jewelry and liquor establishments.[14]

This was all bad enough, but there was far worse to come. A large mob began randomly attacking any African Americans they encountered. Some were beaten, some beaten to death. Others were lynched—strung up from lampposts. Most of the rioters were recent immigrants, many of them refugees from the catastrophic poverty of Ireland. They not only believed the draft treated them unfairly, they also were convinced that they were being called to fight and die in a war aimed at taking the bread from the mouths of their families by giving their jobs to legions of freed black slaves, who were willing to work for wages even lower than theirs. On the afternoon of July 13, an immigrant mob set fire to Manhattan's Colored Orphan Asylum, cheering as the blaze destroyed the building. Fortunately, asylum personnel were able to evacuate hundreds of children through a rear exit and none were killed or injured.

Heavy rains curbed the rioting on Tuesday, but the mayhem revived with dry weather on Wednesday, as rioters ravaged the black neighborhoods, tearing down ramshackle clapboard houses with their bare hands. That evening, however, a large contingent of Union troops marched into New York City, having arrived directly from Gettysburg. They positioned artillery—the very cannon they had just used against the Confederates who charged Cemetery Ridge—and fired antipersonnel grapeshot into the mob. Bayonets fixed, they stormed houses. They positioned sharpshooters on rooftops. The violence subsided and then ceased after at least 2,000 had been wounded and about 120 killed.[15]

In the end, conscription accounted for only 52,068 of the 2,778,304 enlisted Union soldiers who served during the Civil War. An additional 86,724 conscripts paid the $300 commutation fee to receive exemption, and 42,581 hired substitutes. Overall, the Union army, like its Confederate counterpart, remained a majority volunteer force.[16]

SUPPLYING THE MOBILIZATION

Recruiting soldiers for the initial mobilization through the spring and summer of 1861 was far less problematic than furnishing the arms and other supplies for that mobilization. In the Confederacy the problem of supply was largely a problem of money—or the lack of it. In the

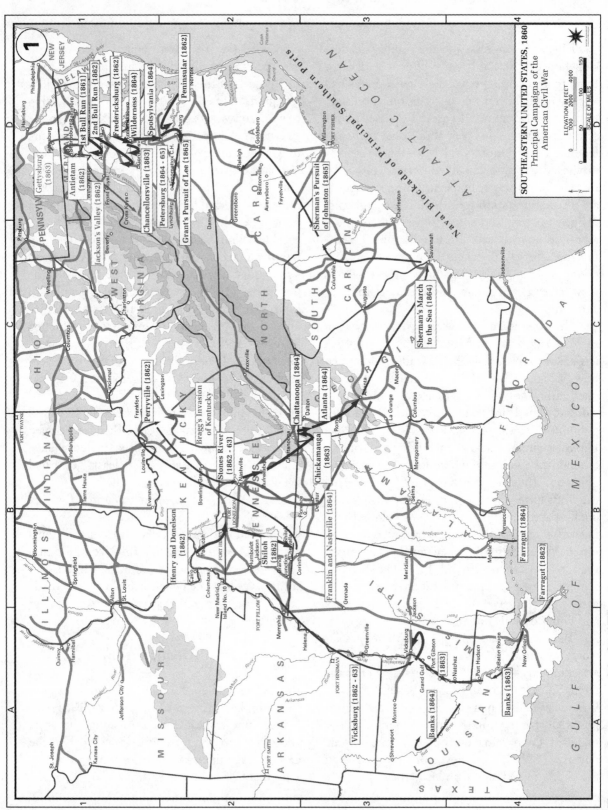

The principal campaigns of the Civil War. UNITED STATES MILITARY ACADEMY

North ample funds were available, but the logistics were daunting. The public and the politicians understood the need for soldiers. It was more difficult to persuade them of the equally pressing need for support personnel, both civilian and military, to solve the problems of supplying an army in the rapid process of growing from about 16,000 men to nearly 3 million.

At the beginning of the war, the federal government took the same approach to the logistical aspect of mobilization as it took to troop mobilization. It just stepped aside and left the problem to be solved by the states. As the states were called on to furnish militia units for the federal service, so they were made responsible for equipping them, transporting them, and even sheltering them. In many cases the states—or even localities within the states—were also charged with clothing them. For this reason, Union uniforms at the start of the war were anything but "uniform."

In June 1861 Brevet Major General Montgomery C. Meigs, a son of the South (born in Augusta, Georgia) who became a US Army engineer and remained loyal to the Union, was appointed quartermaster general of the US Army. His unenviable mission was to bring order to the chaotic system of individual states supplying the Union army. His first decision was to continue to rely on the states until a truly practical federal system could be created and put into operation. He worked closely with governors to coordinate their supply efforts and to assure them that they would be fully reimbursed for whatever they supplied. With this modicum of order instilled, Meigs turned to the task of prioritizing supply needs and then contracting with a legion of private manufacturers, merchants, and sutlers (provisioners) to satisfy them. Initially, the contracting system was plagued by outrageous fraud and scandal, but by mid-1862, order, efficiency, and accountability were largely in place. By the middle year of the war, what had been wildly inefficient chaos during the months of mobilization was thoroughly transformed—thanks to the indefatigable work of Meigs—into a model of efficiency. It would serve the US Army as a template for logistics well into the twentieth century.

Chapter 7

THE CONFEDERATE ARMY

AT ITS BEST: ★ ★ ★ ★

AT ITS WORST: ★ ⸙

No event and no span of history has been more intensively studied than the Civil War, and yet, because many Confederate records were destroyed in the fall of Richmond in 1865, there is no definitive tally of the strength of the Confederate States Army (CSA)—in either its regular component, the Army of the Confederate States of America (ACSA), or its volunteer component, the Provisional Army of the Confederate States (PACS). In any case, it is likely that few records were ever kept, since, throughout the war, the Confederate War Department and the CSA were notoriously lax in the matter of record keeping.

Historians have estimated total enlistments for the period of the war at between 1,227,890 and 1,406,180 men. And reports issued by the War Department at the end of each year from 1861 to 1864 survive. At the end of 1861, 362,768 troops were active on Confederate rolls. At the end of 1862, the number was 449,439; in 1863, 464,646; and at the end of 1864, 400,787. "Last reports," from around April 1865, tallied 358,692 men.[1] The number of individual soldiers who served at some time during the war has been estimated at between 500,000 and 2,000,000, but most historians believe the more accurate count is somewhere between 750,000 and 1,000,000.[2] This, however, is no indication of the size of the CSA on any given date.

A man might enlist or be inducted into the Confederate army at any time; however, there were major government calls for men at six points during the war:

1. March 6, 1861: 100,000 volunteers and militia

2. January 23, 1862: 400,000 volunteers and militia

3. April 16, 1862: With passage of the First Conscription Act, white men, aged eighteen to thirty-five, became subject to conscription for the duration of the war.

4. September 27, 1862: With passage of the Second Conscription Act, the upper age limit of those eligible for conscription was expanded to forty-five; implementation of the new law was delayed until July 15, 1863.

5. February 17, 1864: A Third Conscription Act further expanded eligibility for conscription, to encompass ages seventeen to fifty.

6. March 13, 1865: The Confederate Congress authorized the voluntary enlistment of up to 300,000 African-American troops. The authorization was never fully implemented.

Union sources document that a total of 174,223 Confederate soldiers surrendered to the Union army at war's end. With desertion, disease, and combat losses, this may well have been all that was left of the CSA by the spring and early summer of 1865.[3]

DOCTRINE AND COMMAND

Because the act of secession meant the separation of the South from the Union, the controlling military doctrine of the CSA at the start of the war was strictly defensive. The army's mission was not to bring the battle to the North, but to defend the Confederacy against invasion and to hold all Confederate territory against Northern attempts to seize it. Those who enthusiastically volunteered for service in the CSA and state militias did so in the spirit of defending their homeland. When Robert E. Lee shifted away from a defensive to an offensive strategy by invading Maryland in the campaign that culminated in the Battle of Antietam (September 17, 1862), many Confederate soldiers felt betrayed, as they had volunteered strictly to defend the South, not to invade the North.

As a defensive force, the CSA was not formally assigned a general-in-chief until nearly the end of the war. The fact was that President Jefferson Davis, a West Point graduate, a hero in the US-Mexican War (1846–48), and a man who considered himself thoroughly competent in military matters and highly sophisticated in the making of strategy, assumed de facto overall command of the CSA as well as the diminutive Confederate States Navy. Throughout the war, for better or worse (and most modern historians judge that it was far more often for worse), Davis was a hands-on armchair general who had the final word concerning overall Confederate military strategy.

Only two generals were ever designated as overall field commanders. History's most famous Confederate general, Robert E. Lee, did not debut in a leadership position until March 13, 1862, when Jefferson Davis named him his military adviser. Up to May 31, 1862, acting in this role, Lee did manage to exercise a high degree of direct control over Confederate military strategy. On June 1 he was given a field command, of the Army of Northern Virginia, the most important of the CSA's armies and the army destined to fight the central battles of the war's Eastern Theater. Arguably, this position made Lee the CSA's most senior commander, but he was by no means the general-in-chief of the CSA. That position would finally be

conferred on him by a January 23, 1865, act of the Confederate Congress, which took effect on January 31. Simultaneously, Lee continued to command the Army of Northern Virginia, and while his surrender of that army to the Union's General Ulysses S. Grant at Appomattox Court House on April 9, 1865, ended Lee's appointment as general-in-chief, his act of surrender extended only to the Army of Northern Virginia, not the entire CSA.

The only other Confederate general appointed to serve as anything approaching general-in-chief was Braxton Bragg. A commander universally unpopular with his fellow officers (both in the CSA, during the Civil War, and in the US Army before that), Bragg had a friend and champion in President Davis. After Bragg's miserable performance against Grant in the Chattanooga Campaign (September 21–November 25, 1863), however, Bragg asked President Davis to relieve him of command of the Army of Tennessee on November 28. The president obliged him on December 1, 1863. Three months later, Davis recalled Bragg to Richmond and handed him orders (February 24, 1864) charging him "with the conduct of military operations in the armies of the Confederacy." This made him something like a general-in-chief, but his nominal role was military adviser to President Davis. In effect, Bragg, having failed in the field, was kicked upstairs to a putatively higher command.[4] He was subsequently replaced as Davis's military advisor on January 31, 1865, when Lee was, finally and formally, appointed general-in-chief of the CSA.

Jefferson Davis's attempt through most of the war to function as the CSA's de facto central commander created a systemic strategic and doctrinal weakness in the Confederate war effort. The theater in which the Civil War was fought was vast, and the size of the armies involved was unprecedented in American military experience up to that time. Urgently needed

Fort Sumter, April 14, 1861—under the flag of the new Confederacy. NATIONAL ARCHIVES AND RECORDS ADMINISTRATION

was a central commander or a central command structure (similar to the modern US Joint Chiefs of Staff) to effectively coordinate operations of the different armies over the entire theater, with respect to both combat operations and logistics. This became increasingly imperative after Lee shifted doctrine and strategy from defense to a more aggressive posture. If the various Confederate armies could have been effectively coordinated toward common objectives, the South's war effort might well have been more successful.

While it is true that President Davis's ego and, in particular, his inflated confidence in himself as a military leader were in large part responsible for his failure to authorize a strong and unambiguous central command and put it in the hands of a capable general, he also had to contend with the very politics that had driven Confederate secession in the first place. Southern governors, representatives, and senators who passionately believed in states' rights resisted relinquishing control of the military forces their

states contributed to the cause. With the principal component of the CSA being the voluntary Provisional Army of the Confederate States, the CSA often functioned more like a collection of state militias than a national army.

ORGANIZATION

The organization of the CSA reflected that of the US Army, in which most of its senior officers had served. Field personnel were organized into three major combat arms: infantry, cavalry, and artillery. In addition, there were six administrative functions:

- Ordnance Bureau: Provided armies with weapons and the means of transporting, maintaining, and repairing them (as well as, in some cases, manufacturing them).

- Commissary Bureau (also called Subsistence Department): Supplied the army and navy with food.

- Quartermaster Bureau: Furnished all supplies not furnished by the Ordnance Bureau and Commissary Bureau.

- Engineer Bureau: Planned, built, and repaired all fortifications and defensive works; provided operational maps; cleared major obstacles in the path of CSA movement, and erected obstacles to block the movement of the enemy.

- Signal Service: Charged with establishing and maintaining communication among army units, including supervision of telegraphic communications.

- Provost Marshal: Performed military police functions, including securing prisoners charged with crimes (not POWs), preventing desertion and apprehending deserters, and (sometimes) creating and maintaining intelligence networks (spymaster function).

At the outbreak of the war, the largest organizational field unit was the regiment, but within a short time, the CSA was organized into armies (see next section and part III). Within each army the smallest organizational unit was the *company*. On paper a *company* consisted of 100 soldiers. Functionally, each company was typically divided into platoons and platoons into squads. In the artillery a company was usually called a battery. Each company was commanded by a captain and at least two lieutenants.

Ten companies were organized into a *regiment*, with a paper strength of 1,000 men. As actually deployed in the field, companies as well as the regiments they constituted were almost always understrength due to disease, desertion, combat casualties, and a shortage of replacements. It was not unusual for a CSA regiment to consist of only 300–400 men. Although not the smallest army unit, the CSA regiment was the basic army unit. In the CSA, regiments were raised by the states and so were usually designated by a number and a state ("12th Virginia," for instance). A regiment was commanded by a colonel, with a lieutenant colonel serving as his second in command, and at least one major in a subordinate command position.

In the CSA some units were designated as *battalions*. The term was used either as a synonym for *regiment* or to designate a regiment considered too small (often as a result of combat casualties) to be called a regiment.

The CSA prescribed the grouping of four regiments into a *brigade*. For practical reasons, however, when the manpower of the regiments became excessively depleted, more than four regiments often constituted a single brigade. A brigade was normally commanded by a brigadier general, although the exigencies of combat sometimes elevated a colonel to brigade command. In an emergency a lieutenant colonel or even a major might command a brigade.

A *division* consisted of two, three, or four brigades and was commanded by a major general.

A *corps*, which came into existence in the CSA late in 1862, consisted of two, three, or four divisions and was commanded by a lieutenant general (although some corps were commanded by major generals).

An *army* consisted of two, three, or four corps—although, in practice, a single corps might operate independently from any army and might even be called an army. A standard army (consisting of at least two corps) was commanded by a full general. The existence of full generals in the CSA was a departure from US Army practice as it existed at the outbreak of the Civil War, when the highest authorized USA rank was lieutenant general.

CSA Armies

The chapters in part III cover in detail the major armies of the CSA and the USA. The following list, however, presents *all* the CSA armies (and their commanders) that operated at various times during the war:

- Army of Arkansas: Sterling Price, Edmund Kirby Smith

- Army of Central Kentucky: Simon B. Buckner, Albert Sidney Johnston

- Army of East Tennessee (later redesignated Army of Kentucky): Edmund Kirby Smith

- Army of Eastern Kentucky: Humphrey Marshall

- Army of the Kanawha: Henry A. Wise, John B. Floyd, Robert E. Lee

- Army of Kentucky (originally Army of East Tennessee): Edmund Kirby Smith

- Army of Louisiana: Braxton Bragg, Paul O. Hébert

A Confederate soldier lies with his weapon at Petersburg, Virginia. The photograph, by Mathew B. Brady, was controversial because of its graphic representation of the war's horror. The dead were a popular subject for Civil War photographers—less for the sensational effect of such images than because the slow photographic emulsions of the era made it all but impossible to photograph the live action of combat. LIBRARY OF CONGRESS

- Army of Middle Tennessee: John C. Breckinridge

- Army of Mississippi (also known as the Army of the Mississippi, even though Confederate armies were generally named after states or regions, not rivers), March–November 1862:[5] P. G. T. Beauregard, Albert Sidney Johnston, Braxton Bragg, William J. Hardee, Leonidas Polk

- Army of Missouri: Sterling Price

- Army of Mobile: Jones M. Withers, Braxton Bragg, John B. Villepigue, Samuel Jones, William L. Powell, John H. Forney

- Army of New Mexico: Henry H. Sibley

- Army of Northern Virginia (originally, Army of the Potomac):[6] Joseph E. Johnston, Gustavus W. Smith, Robert E. Lee

- Army of the Northwest: Robert S. Garnett, Henry R. Jackson, William W. Loring, Edward Johnson

- Army of the Peninsula: John B. Magruder, Daniel H. Hill

- Army of Pensacola: Adley H. Gladden, Braxton Bragg, Samuel Jones

- Army of the Potomac[7] (later renamed Army of Northern Virginia): P. G. T. Beauregard, Joseph E. Johnston

- Army of Shenandoah: Joseph E. Johnston

- Army of Tennessee: Braxton Bragg, Samuel Gibbs French, William J. Hardee, Daniel H. Hill, John Bell Hood, Joseph E. Johnston, Richard Taylor

- Army of the Trans-Mississippi (also known as the Army of the Southwest): Thomas C. Hindman, Theophilus Holmes, Edmund Kirby Smith

- Army of the Valley (also known as II Corps, Army of Northern Virginia): Jubal Early

- Army of the West: Earl Van Dorn, John P. McCown, Dabney H. Maury, Sterling Price

- Army of West Tennessee: Earl Van Dorn

- Army of Western Louisiana: Richard Taylor, John G. Walker

DIVERSITY IN THE CSA

The CSA was remarkably homogeneous in terms of ethnicity, with 91% of Confederate soldiers native-born white men and just 9% foreign-born white men—mostly Irish, with a small admixture of men born in Germany, France, Mexico, and Great Britain.[8]

The Confederacy resisted using African Americans, slave or free, in the army but made extensive use of civilian slaves as logistical laborers and even as hospital and nursing aides. As mentioned earlier in the chapter, very late in the war, on March 13, 1865, the Confederate Congress authorized the voluntary enlistment of up to 300,000 African-American troops, but the war ended before this authorization could be significantly implemented. Chapter 13 is devoted to the role of African-American soldiers and military auxiliaries in both the Confederate and Union militaries.

Native Americans served in both the Union and Confederate armies. Estimates as to their number vary from 28,693[9] down to 18,000. In the latter estimate, perhaps 6,000 served with the Union and 12,000 with the Confederacy.[10] Other sources report that no more than 3,600 Native Americans served in the Union army.[11]

The Creeks and the Choctaws had a particular stake in a Confederate victory, since many of them were slaveholders. President Jefferson Davis reached out to Native Americans early in the war through Albert Pike, a Massachusetts-born military officer who had served with the US Army in the US-Mexican War (1846–48). Despite his New England birth, Pike was a pro-slavery states' rights advocate and therefore sided with the Confederacy at the outbreak of the Civil War. Because of his military background and his prewar experience negotiating agreements between various tribes and the US government, Pike received a brigadier general's commission in the CSA and was appointed to negotiate treaties between the Confederate government and Native American tribes. Pike concluded treaties with the Creek, Choctaw, Catawba, Seminole, and Cherokee tribes, among others. Some members of these tribes fought on the side of the Confederacy. Stand Watie, a Cherokee leader, was commissioned a colonel in the CSA and commanded a Cherokee battalion. Promoted to brigadier general, he rose to command the "Indian Division of Indian Territory" (mostly modern Oklahoma) and, on June 23, 1865—while commanding the 1st Brigade of the Army of the Trans-Mississippi—signed a ceasefire with Union forces. Watie has the historical distinction of being the very last Confederate general to lay down his arms.

Chapter 8

THE UNION ARMY

AT ITS BEST: ★ ★ ★ ★

AT ITS WORST: ★ ★

Despite the enormous upheaval of secession, a continuity prevailed between the prewar government of the United States and the Union government as it existed and functioned during the Civil War. In contrast with the government hurriedly cobbled together by the Confederacy, the Union had in place an extensive bureaucracy that was thoroughly accustomed to accounting for people and funds and for record keeping generally. For this reason, Union statistics concerning the army are far more plentiful and accurate than those pertaining to the CSA. Moreover, since the North was the victor in the Civil War, Washington escaped the devastation that Richmond suffered—a level of destruction that consumed many of the existing Confederate records, inadequate as they might have been. So we can determine with high accuracy that the enlistment strength of the USA during the Civil War was between 2,128,948 and 2,778,304,[1] almost certainly at least twice the estimated number of soldiers in the CSA.

As addressed in chapter 3, the US Army, on the eve of the Civil War, consisted of 16,367 soldiers, of whom 1,108 were commissioned officers,[2] and, at the outbreak of war, President Lincoln initially called for 75,000 volunteers. Chapter 6 details the call-ups, the vast majority of which were enlisted not into the regular US Army (sometimes referred to as the National Army), but into the United States Volunteers (USV), a more-or-less ad hoc force that debuted in 1794 and reappeared with each new war until 1903, when it was replaced by a combination of the US Army Reserve and the National Guard,

whose limited reserve role was formally defined in the Militia Act of 1903. Prior to 1903, the United States had no permanent, standing military reserve. The USV came into being only in time of war. When a war ended, the USV was dissolved—until such time as a new war created the need for the USV again.

In practice, during the Civil War no operational distinction was made between the regular US Army and the USV. Because the overwhelming majority of soldiers were members of the USV, they were commanded both by regular army officers and by USV officers. Indeed, the USV was sometimes a means of rapid, if ultimately temporary, promotion for regular army officers. George Armstrong Custer, a graduate of West Point (thirty-fourth out of thirty-four in the Class of 1861), served as second and then first lieutenant in cavalry regiments. After promotion to a staff captain, he served as a cavalry captain. He served through all of these ranks in the regular army, before vaulting to brigadier general in the US Volunteers on June 29, 1863. He would become a major general in the USV at the very end of the war, on April 15, 1865, but all the while he retained his "permanent" regular rank of captain, even as he was also awarded brevet promotions in the regular army during the Civil War, to brevet major (July 3, 1863), brevet lieutenant colonel (May 11, 1864), brevet colonel (September 19, 1864), and brevet brigadier general and brevet major general (March 13, 1865). On October 19, 1864, Custer was also brevetted to major general in the USV. Thus regular army and USV command often ran in parallel throughout the Civil War.

Shortly after the Civil War ended, the USV was dismantled, as it always was in peacetime, and Custer took a leave of absence from the army, returning to it as lieutenant colonel of the newly created 7th Cavalry on July 28, 1866. Far from being a demotion from his brevet and USV ranks as major general, his status as lieutenant colonel represented a considerable promotion from his last permanent US Army rank as a mere captain. Officers like Custer who were members of the regular army could hold different rank in the USV while still serving in the regular army. It was also possible for USV officers to transfer to the regular army, although quite probably at a reduction in rank. Operationally in the Civil War, the regular army and the USV functioned together as the United States Army, just as the Army of the Confederate States of America (ACSA, the regular Confederate army) and the Provisional Army of the Confederate States (PACS) functioned together, operationally, as the Confederate States Army (CSA).

DOCTRINE AND COMMAND

The pre–Civil War United States Army was primarily a frontier constabulary assigned to protect settlements, settlers, railroads, and commerce from Indian attacks. Although this would imply a defensive orientation, in practice frontier army patrols took an aggressive, proactive, *offensive* approach to dealing with "hostile" Indian groups that raided settlers and other white enterprises in or adjacent to "Indian country." This said, even though US Army doctrine tended to be offensive rather than defensive, it was geared to small-unit tactics. Relatively small cavalry patrols engaged relatively small Indian raiding parties or pursued relatively small groups of Indians who had strayed from the reservation. Even in the US-Mexican War, which featured a number of set battles between conventional military formations, there was nothing approaching the very large combat operations that would characterize the major battles of the Civil War.

Fighting army against army on a Napoleonic scale was entirely new to the USA. Nevertheless, because the mission was to suppress a Southern insurgency and to restore US government sovereignty and control in the rebellious region, the USA had an offensive mission. The Union army was, for all practical purposes, a force of invasion and conquest. Maintaining a defensive posture was out of the question.

At the outbreak of the war, volunteers eagerly answered the call for recruits. They wanted to play a part in what they believed would be a quick suppression of the "rebellion" followed by a righteous "chastisement" of the South. Most seasoned US Army officers felt much the same way. They believed that a significant show of force in a punitive expedition marching into Dixie would be sufficient to end the insurgency. Dissenting voices were few at the outbreak of the war, but among them was no less a figure than the superannuated general-in-chief of the army himself, Winfield Scott. Scott believed that the war would not be quickly won and that it would require very substantial forces to invade the South.

While these were being built up, Scott took a more mature view, balancing the economic, population, and industrial advantages of the North against the South's deficiencies in these areas. Critically, he understood that these advantages were not yet embodied in the military. Building up the Northern army would take time, and even though the same was true in the South, the Confederacy had the advantage of fighting a war in defense of its "homeland," and it would be doing so close to sources of supply. Although the population of the Southern states was much smaller than that of the Northern states, Dixie was a very large geographical area, which would likely yield to invasion only by a large, well-coordinated army. Scott wanted to enlist time as an ally because time was necessary to build an army. He therefore advocated delaying any major offensive against the Confederacy until sufficient forces had been developed. However, this did not mean idling during the interval. Scott proposed in the short term to mount a massive maritime blockade of the South. While the North built up its land forces, the blockade would slowly strangle the South, starving it both actually and economically. It would be able neither to export cotton and other trade goods nor to import foodstuffs and European-manufactured arms and ammunition. By the time the armies of the North were prepared to invade, the South would be staggered by hunger and want.

Scott called for cutting off the South's ports along the Atlantic and the Gulf of Mexico while, as soon as possible, sending 60,000 newly recruited troops along with a flotilla of naval gunboats down the Mississippi River to capture New Orleans, the single most strategic port in the Confederacy. These simultaneous operations would throttle the Confederacy economically while also cutting it in half geographically. Control the Mississippi, and the Confederate states of the east would be isolated from those of the west. As inevitable attrition set in and the Union army continued to build up, any number of offensive operations could be planned and executed upon an all-but-prostrate enemy.

It was, in fact, a brilliant plan—on paper. In execution, however, it stumbled over two imposing obstacles. First, the Southern coastline was rich in gulfs and inlets, making it some 3,500 miles long. Ten major ports lay below the Mason–Dixon Line. The US Navy would need hundreds, perhaps thousands, of ships to adequately blockade such a coast. As of spring 1861, the Union's navy consisted of forty-two seaworthy vessels of war. Blockade? The best the navy could come up with was a sieve.

Abraham Lincoln understood this, but he also recognized that Scott offered what no one else had, namely a plan. Lincoln therefore approved the plan, but, in so doing, laid bare the second problem. It seemed that, in all the North, only Scott and Lincoln actually had faith in the plan. The press, both in the Union and the Confederacy, mocked it as "Scott's Anaconda," and political cartoonists pictured the blockade as a great constrictor—its head comically portrayed as that of the president or the general—coiling around Dixie's coast. Editorials lambasted it as impractical, which, in fact, it was, in the short term, until the Union could build additional ships. But the more biting criticism was that the blockade was inglorious, craven, even cowardly. The newspapers wanted boldness and bloodshed.

What they got instead was humiliation. Union ground forces entered the fray on June 10, 1861, at Big Bethel, in Hampton and York Counties, Virginia, hoping to root out Confederates threatening Union-held Fort Monroe, in Hampton. The green Union troops performed miserably in an hour-long exchange in which 52 of them were wounded and 18 killed out of 2,500 engaged against just 1,200 Confederates. The Southerners lost only 1 man killed and 7 wounded.

The Union was off to a bad start. There would be more minor skirmishes, some of which ended more successfully, in the run-up to the first major battle, at Bull Run on July 21, which ended ignominiously in a Union comeuppance of shocking dimension.

The disaster prompted Lincoln to summon George B. McClellan, who had won two small skirmishes history calls battles, at Philippi and Rich Mountain, in western Virginia (today West Virginia). As the Union press saw it, these minor triumphs were steps in the right direction, and that made their author, McClellan, look like the Union's savior. Short, handsome, and pompous—the papers dubbed him the "Young Napoleon"—McClellan gleefully wrote to his wife, Ellen Marcy McClellan, "I find myself in a new and strange position here—Presdt,

George Brinton McClellan, whom the Northern press hailed as the "Young Napoleon." President Lincoln complained that he had "a bad case of the slows." NATIONAL ARCHIVES AND RECORDS ADMINISTRATION

Cabinet, Genl Scott & all deferring to me—by some strange operation of magic I seem to have become the power of the land. . . . I almost think that were I to win some small success now I could become Dictator or anything else that might please me—but nothing of that kind would please me—therefore I won't be Dictator. Admirable self-denial!"[3]

In the fullness of time, the "Young Napoleon" would prove a disappointment, but in the short term, he performed organizational wonders. First, he addressed the neglected defensive element of Union doctrine, creating a system of forty-eight forts and strong points to defend Washington, DC, which was, after all, vulnerable, wedged between Confederate Virginia across the Potomac to the southwest and Confederate-sympathizing Maryland to the northwest,

northeast, and southeast. Next, he built the Army of the Potomac from 50,000 men in July 1861 to 168,000 in November, by far the greatest military force the United States had raised up to that time.

And he wanted even more. Although McClellan prudently protected Washington, he decried Scott's Anaconda as timid and called instead for the expansion of the Army of the Potomac to 273,000 men, with whom he promised to wipe out the rebellion in a single campaign. Moreover, unlike Scott's blockade, which was directed against the civilian population of the South, McClellan's massive Napoleonic thrust would defeat the rebel army without adversely impacting the people of the South themselves.

ORGANIZATION

Under McClellan the Union created a magnificent force in the Army of the Potomac, which became the model for the USA's other armies. Tragically, the Army of the Potomac would be misused by McClellan and all of his successors prior to George Meade, but its mere creation nevertheless served to transform a small standing army into the largest national military force the United States would have until the world wars of the twentieth century.

McClellan did not alter the conventional structure of the US Army any more than the Confederates did. The smallest organizational unit was the *company*, on paper 100 men commanded by a captain and, typically, a pair of lieutenants. Typically, a company was divided into two or more *platoons*, each commanded by a lieutenant or sergeant. A platoon might be divided into two or more *squads*, each under a sergeant or a corporal. In an artillery unit, the company was called a *battery*, and in a cavalry unit, a platoon was referred to as a *troop*. Although, at the start of the war, many companies came close to meeting their paper strength of 100 men, by the second year of the war, many were at half strength or even lower.

As in the CSA, the *regiment* was the principal organizational unit of the Union army. On paper it consisted of ten companies—1,000 men, total—but as the companies became understrength in the course of the war, so the size of a regiment was reduced. If a regiment became so depleted that it could no longer muster ten companies, even understrength companies, it was redesignated as a *battalion*. Union (but not Confederate) cavalry regiments were composed of twelve companies. As in the CSA, regiments were raised by the states and named after them, as in, for example, the 54th Massachusetts. A regiment was commanded by a colonel, who was assisted by a lieutenant colonel and a major.

Two to six regiments were organized into a *brigade*, under the command of a brigadier general. In contrast to the Confederacy, in which a brigade was generally composed of regiments from the same state, a Union brigade might be composed of regiments from several states.

Two to six brigades made up a *division*, commanded by either a brigadier or major general in the Union army (but almost always a major general in the CSA). Union brigades were typically smaller than those in the CSA, which were sometimes the size of a corps.

Commanded by a brigadier general or major general in the Union army (but a lieutenant general in the CSA), a *corps* was the largest organizational unit in an army. It did not exist in the USA until McClellan, following French

General McClellan laid siege to Yorktown, Virginia, with these large siege mortars, intended to lob massive projectiles into fortified positions. By the time McClellan began his siege on April 5, 1862, the Confederates were stealthily withdrawing. The "Young Napoleon" wasted a month attacking a mostly deserted objective.

practice, persuaded President Lincoln to authorize the formation of corps in March 1862. Each corps consisted of two or more divisions and was officially identified by a roman numeral—although some were familiarly called by their commander's name.

An *army* was made up of multiple corps—usually at least two, occasionally just one, and sometimes many more, as in the case of the Army of the Potomac, which consisted of seven corps. Union armies were usually named after rivers (Army of the Potomac, Army of the James), whereas Confederate corps were often named after the geographical area in which they were based (Army of Northern Virginia, Army of Tennessee). In the CSA an army was commanded by a full general, but throughout the Civil War, the highest authorized rank in the USA was lieutenant general, and this was the rank of an army commander.

USA Armies

The principal Union armies and their commanders were as follows:

- Army of Northeastern Virginia (also called the Department and Army of Northeastern Virginia): Irvin McDowell

- Army of the Potomac (Department and Army of the Potomac): George B. McClellan, Ambrose E. Burnside, Joseph Hooker, George G. Meade

- Army of the Southwest (Army of Southwest Missouri): Samuel R. Curtis, Frederick Steele, Eugene A. Carr, Willis A. Gorman

- Army of the Mississippi (1862): John Pope, William S. Rosecrans

- Army of the Mississippi (1863): John A. McClernand

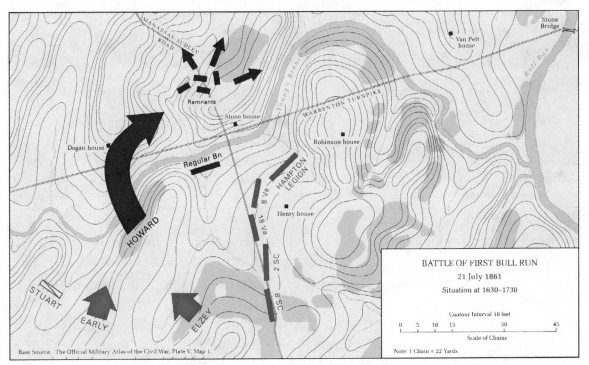

The First Battle of Bull Run—the Union retreats. UNITED STATES ARMY CENTER OF MILITARY HISTORY

Union private D. W. C. Arnold. Call him "Billy Yank," the G. I. Joe of the Civil War. He poses in front of a brass field-piece. NATIONAL ARCHIVES AND RECORDS ADMINISTRATION

- Army of Virginia: John Pope

- Army of the Frontier: John M. Scho-field, James G. Blunt, Schofield, Francis J. Herron

- Army of the Tennessee: Ulysses S. Grant, William T. Sherman, James B. McPherson, John A. Logan (July 22–27, 1864), Oliver O. Howard, Logan

- Army of the Cumberland: William S. Rosecrans, George H. Thomas

- (1st) Army of the Ohio (1861–62): Don Carlos Buell

- (2nd) Army of the Ohio (1863–65): Ambrose E. Burnside, John G. Foster, John M. Schofield

- Army of the James: Benjamin F. Butler, Edward Ord

- Army of the Shenandoah: Philip H. Sheridan, Alfred T. A. Torbert

- Army of Georgia: Henry W. Slocum

DIVERSITY IN THE UNION ARMY

As direct descendants of the pre–Civil War US Army, the CSA and USA had more similarities than differences; however, the most dramatic contrast between them was in the ethnic makeup of the forces. Whereas the CSA was remarkably homogeneous—overwhelmingly (91 percent) made up of white native-born Americans—the Union Army consisted less than half (45.4 percent) of native-born white Americans. Of the remaining whites, 9.7 percent were German, 9.1 percent Irish, 4.1 percent Dutch, 2.3 percent Canadian, 2.3 percent British, 1.8 percent French or French Canadian, 0.9 percent Nordic, 0.3 percent Italian, 0.3 percent classified as "Jewish," 0.2 percent Polish, and only 0.1 percent Native American. An additional 6.4 percent were members of other nationalities.

Congress passed two acts on July 17, 1862, authorizing the enlistment of "Colored" troops, but the first African-American soldiers were not actually enlisted until January 1863, immediately following the promulgation of the final Emancipation Proclamation. In all, some 186,097 African-American soldiers served in the Union army, making up about 9.5 percent of the force. The role of black soldiers is discussed fully in chapter 13.[4]

In the twentieth and twenty-first centuries, the army and other services were and remain true ethnic melting pots. To a remarkable degree, this was also the case in Union army during the Civil War; nevertheless, first- and second-generation immigrants sometimes formed their own units, occasionally on the brigade level but more usually on the level of the regiment. This gave special cohesion to these units and was considered beneficial to esprit de corps. Notable examples include:

- Irish Brigade (69th New York, 63rd New York, 88th New York, 28th Massachusetts, 116th Pennsylvania regiments)

- Swiss Rifles (15th Missouri)

- Gardes Lafayette (55th New York)

- Garibaldi Guard (39th New York)

- Martinez Militia (1st New Mexico)

- Polish Legion (58th New York)

- German Rangers (52nd New York)

- Cameron Highlanders (79th New York Volunteer Infantry)

- Scandinavian Regiment (15th Wisconsin)

In general, immigrants were among the most enthusiastic soldiers in the Union army, eager to show themselves as patriots and anxious to preserve the Union to which they or their parents had immigrated.

Chapter 9

Johnny Reb and His Commanders

AVERAGE QUALITY AND CAPABILITY OF OFFICERS AND MEN: ★ ★ ★ ⅞

A war of brother against brother. Such is the traditional characterization of the opposing armies that fought the Civil War. A cliché, yes, but like most clichés, it was born of some truth. First, there is the literal truth that, in not a few instances, the Civil War divided families, pitting actual brothers against one another. John J. Crittenden, US senator from Kentucky (1855–61) and subsequently representative from Kentucky's 8th Congressional District beginning in 1861 until his death on March 3, 1863, made heroic efforts to resolve the secession crisis of 1860–61 and thereby, he hoped, avert civil war. On December 18, 1860, he introduced in the House a package of six constitutional amendments and four congressional resolutions, the so-called Crittenden Compromise, intended to mollify the South by protecting slavery. Tabled on December 31 and ultimately rejected, the Crittenden Compromise never had a serious chance of passage, but remains valuable as a gauge of the desperation felt by many whose loyalties, interests, and allegiances were divided across the Mason–Dixon Line. With the outbreak of the war, one of Crittenden's sons, George, resigned his commission as lieutenant colonel in the USA to join the CSA, while his brother, Thomas Leonidas, joined the Union army in September 1861, as did another son, Eugene. A grandson, John Crittenden Coleman, enlisted as a Confederate, while another, John Crittenden Watson, graduated from the US Naval Academy and fought under Rear Admiral David Farragut in the capture of New Orleans.

But there is an even deeper and broader truth to the brother-against-brother formula. Probably no people in history who chose to war against one another had more in common with one another than the people of the North and the South. "We are not enemies, but friends," Lincoln closed his first inaugural address on March 4, 1861. "We must not be enemies. Though passion may have strained, it must not break our bonds of affection. The mystic chords of memory, stretching from every battle-field and patriot grave to every living heart and hearthstone all over this broad land, will yet swell the chorus of the Union when again touched, as surely they will be, by the better angels of our nature."[1] The ordinary soldiers on both sides came from similar socioeconomic backgrounds, they spoke the same language, and they shared a common revolutionary past. Both claimed to revere the Constitution. Both cherished popular democracy and were not, therefore, fighting to change the government. Yet they chose to minimize what they shared in common and instead magnify their differences.

WHY JOHNNY REB ENLISTED

Much as the "typical" American soldier in World War II was dubbed G. I. Joe, the nicknames "Johnny Reb" and "Billy Yank" were coined during the Civil War to symbolize the common soldiers who fought in the conflict. *Johnny Reb & Billy Yank*, a popular novel published in 1905 by Confederate veteran Alexander Hunter, did much to preserve these nicknames in American popular culture, as did *The Life of Johnny Reb: The Common Soldier of the Confederacy* (1943) and *The Life of Billy Yank: The Common Soldier of the Union* (1952) by historian Bell I. Wiley.[2]

Whereas Billy Yank enlisted mainly to preserve the Union and punish the rebellious South—and only secondarily, if at all, to free the slaves—Johnny Reb enlisted to defend his homeland against what his political leaders told him was, and what he himself generally believed to be, Northern tyranny and aggression. It would not be accurate to say that most Confederate soldiers enlisted expressly to preserve slavery; however, as historian Larry Logue notes, "beneath Confederate soldiers' political rhetoric lay a deeper, more personal concern for their society's racial equilibrium: the fear of life with the bottom rail on top echoes through southerners' explanations of why they were in the army." Will Crutcher, a Mississippi planter's son who joined the CSA (with one of his father's slaves in tow as servant), warned that "the time for action on the part of our entire race is *swiftly passing*, and unless they all awake and get up on their feet like men, they may be compelled to forever crawl upon the ground like worms."[3] There was, in fact, a fear that the "Union invaders meant to reverse the southern order." Slavery would not simply be abolished, but "former masters [would be] forced to exist somewhere beneath northerners and one-time slaves." Union troops were characterized as "fanatical mercenaries who are now attempting to subjugate us to a worse than Russian despotism," and "the Union's 'cry is still for blood-conquest: Subjugation' at any cost."[4]

Whatever drove Confederate enlistment hardest, it was a powerful force, especially at the beginning of the war. The Union population was about 18.5 million (excluding the 2.5 million free persons in the border states) versus 5.5 million free persons in the Confederate states, and yet it has been estimated that between 30 and 40 percent of all the soldiers who fought in the Civil War fought as Confederates. This means that a "majority of southern military-age males joined the army, a much larger proportion than served in the North."[5]

WHO JOHNNY REB WAS

A popular and enduring misconception about the composition of the CSA is that it was an army of boys and old men. In fact, the average age of men at enlistment in both the Union and Confederate armies was very nearly the same. The average Union enlistee was just under twenty-six; the average Confederate recruit was just over twenty-six. Records show that the average height and weight for a Union recruit was five feet, eight inches, 145 pounds. Because this was the average for a nineteenth-century American man in his mid-twenties, there is no reason to believe that Confederate recruits were any smaller or larger. But whereas 29 percent of Union recruits were married men, even more—36-plus percent—of their Confederate counterparts had wives and families. It may be that predominantly rural Southerners married younger than men in the more industrialized, more urban North. Or perhaps the higher percentage of married men enlisting may simply reflect the higher overall percentage of enlistment in the South compared with the North. Moreover, the demand for manpower was always greater in the South than in the North, and Northern married men were under less social pressure to enlist than married Southerners.[6]

Johnny Reb was, on average, less well educated than Billy Yank, largely because public education south of the Mason–Dixon Line was significantly less well developed than in the North and because Southerners during this period put less emphasis on education than Northerners did. The belief that illiteracy predominated in the Southern ranks, however, is mistaken. Most Confederate troops, like most Union troops, were literate.[7]

The majority of recruits in both the Union and Confederate armies were farmers or agricultural workers. In the CSA this majority was larger than in the USA, reflecting the

predominantly agricultural economy of the
South. In both armies as well, skilled laborers made up the second most numerous group.
These included carpenters, masons, machinists,
cartwrights, coopers, shoemakers, smiths, and
the like. Since the greatest need in both armies
was for infantry riflemen, little effort was made
to match a recruit's civilian vocation with his
military assignment—except in very specific
instances.[8] A butcher, for example, might be
assigned to food preparation duties or even provisioning. A blacksmith might be assigned to a
cavalry unit.

In contrast to members of the enlisted ranks,
officers generally came into both armies from the
professions. Lawyers, clergymen, engineers, and
even college professors were in demand. Physicians were always needed and were, of course,
assigned to medical duties.[9]

By 1863 Confederate soldiers were desert-
ing in ever larger numbers. In July of that year,
after Vicksburg and Gettysburg, an estimated
50,000 to 100,000 of them walked away, though
desertion rates had been quite high from the
beginning of the war and continued so through
to the end. On October 7, 1864, for instance,

*Contrary to persistent mythology, the majority of Civil War soldiers, Confederate and Union alike, were unaccustomed
to handling firearms, let alone skilled at doing so. A select few Civil War troops were assigned as sharpshooters—who
themselves became targets. This fallen sharpshooter at Gettysburg was a Confederate.*

the Richmond *Enquirer* reported that President Davis had announced that "two-thirds of the Army are absent from the ranks."[10] If this was true, Confederate deserters had come to outnumber Confederate soldiers.

As discussed in chapter 5, faced with a reduced rate of voluntary enlistment, the Confederacy enacted a conscription law on April 16, 1862, nearly a year before the Union did the same. As with the Union army, the majority of CSA soldiers enlisted voluntarily. It is likely, however, that many chose to enlist rather than await inevitable conscription.

How Johnny Reb Fought

Whether a soldier served in the USA or the CSA, he was required to be right-handed. First, in accordance with the universal prejudices of the era, the use of the right hand as the dominant hand was considered correct, while the use of the left was aberrant at worst and a bad habit at best. Second, the design of all available long arms was intended to accommodate right-handed shooters.[11]

Among the myth and lore that has accumulated about the Civil War is the contention that the Confederate common solider was a superior warrior to the Union enlisted man. That this belief forms part of the "rebel" legend and mystique does not mean it is untrue. Indeed, many contemporary observers noted a marked difference between the Confederate style of fighting and that of the Union soldier. "Three points I noted with regard to our opponents," USA captain John W. DeForest wrote. "They aimed better than our men; they covered themselves (in case of need) more carefully and effectively; they could move in a swarm, without much care for alignment and touching elbows. In short, they fought more like redskins [Native Americans], or like hunters, than we. The result was they lost fewer men, though they were far inferior in numbers."[12]

The statistics do not bear out DeForest's assertion that the Confederate fighting style resulted in fewer casualties than the Union suffered. As costly as the Civil War was in lives, just 5 percent of all Union soldiers were killed in action or died of their wounds, whereas nearly 12 percent of Confederate troops became fatal combat casualties.[13] Nevertheless, other observers do corroborate Captain DeForest's general observations, if not his conclusion concerning losses. Colonel Arthur J. L. Fremantle, a British observer embedded with the CSA, thought that the Confederate soldier looked like a "genuine rebel," with "a sort of devil-may-care, reckless, self-confident look."[14] The upside of this mindset or attitude was a certain dash, initiative, fighting spirit, and, above all, independence rather than blind obedience. "The best *mind* and the best *blood* in the country are in the army," a Confederate congressman wrote, "and much of both are found in the [enlisted] ranks. They have not lost the identity of the citizen in the soldier."[15] The downside, however, was a chronic "want of discipline among Confederate troops, a peculiar indifference to 'their obligations as soldiers.'" One soldier called the Confederate army "simply a vast mob of rather ill-armed young gentlemen from the country."[16]

If the Confederate soldier's resistance to conventional military discipline was as pronounced as more than a few observers suggest, it may have been the result of having come of age among the "independent small farmers who composed the vast majority of the antebellum Southern population. They came from a society that was not merely rural but, in many areas, still frontier, and isolation of settlements, absence of established traditions, and opportunities for rapid social mobility encouraged a distinctive Southern type of self-reliance."[17] Perhaps this analysis is accurate. Perhaps not. What is undeniable, however, is that the Confederate army consisted of men committed to rebellion against what they perceived to be an oppressive central government. By definition, "rebels" are not inclined toward discipline, and the mass of Confederate soldiers were not about to trade one set of tyrants for another.

Perhaps because of such officers as Robert E. Lee and Thomas J. "Stonewall" Jackson, commanders who inspired admiration, awe, and great devotion in the soldiers they led, there is a widespread and persistent belief that the South enjoyed an advantage in leadership. It is often casually remarked that many US Army officers resigned their commissions to join the CSA. *Many* is, however, a relative term. Of the roughly 824 West Point graduates on the USA active list at the outbreak of the Civil War, only 184 became Confederate officers, fewer than one in four. Of the approximately 900 West Point graduates who were civilians at the outbreak of the war, approximately 114 rejoined the USA and 99 accepted CSA commissions. The Union army thus started out with 754 West Point graduates, whereas the CSA had 283.[18]

This said, functioning successfully as a military officer was probably more difficult in the CSA than in the USA. USA soldiers were more likely than CSA soldiers to obey officers based merely on the authority conferred by their rank. In contrast, CSA officers had to earn the compliance of their men by earning their loyalty. The default position for a CSA enlisted man tended toward grudging compliance or even outright disobedience. "In fact, to an extent almost unparalleled in any other major war, the Confederate common soldier was the master of his officers," according to historian David Donald. This mindset was reinforced by the militia system context in which the CSA partially arose. "The peacetime militia, a quasi-social, quasi-political organization, has always elected officers, and the Confederate army was constituted on the same basis. . . . Only the high ranking field officers were appointed by [the central government in]

Richmond." This meant that enlisted men rarely hesitated to take "direct action against their superiors. Confederate court martial records are full of such cases as that of Private George Bedell of Georgia, who called his commanding officer a 'damned son of a bitch, a damned tyrant, a damned puppy, a damned rascal.'" Sometimes rebellion against an officer went beyond the verbal. A martinet could be painfully ridden "on a rail until he promised 'better behavior.'" Alternatively, the men in a unit might petition higher command for the officer's resignation.[19]

The loyalty and love Confederate soldiers of the Army of Northern Virginia showed their commanding officer, Robert E. Lee, is well known to history. Nevertheless, Lee complained as late as November 1864, "The great want in our army is firm discipline."[20]

Training was a challenge in both the USA and CSA, but was especially difficult among young Southerners who wanted to fight, not obey, drill, or march. Confederate general Richard Taylor fretted over the "collection of untrained men" that populated so much of the CSA. In their untrained state, he complained, they are "neither more nor less than a mob, in which individual courage goes for nothing. In movement each person finds his liberty of action merged in a crowd, ignorant and incapable of direction. Every obstacle creates confusion, speedily converted into panic by opposition."[21]

As it turned out, the first step toward adequate training was not to force discipline on the enlisted men, but to weed out poor officers whose only qualification was social position or political influence. "We are required to drill for hours a day," Rufus W. Carter, 19th Louisiana Volunteers, wrote to his "Cousin Fanny" on June 22, 1862, "and the strictest observance to duty is most rigidly exacted of both officers and men." Indeed, Carter pointed out that officers "had to undergo examination before a board of officers. Many were rejected on account of incompetency."[22]

A regimen of drill was established in soldier camps, not only among new recruits but on an ongoing basis. The leading training manual used in the CSA was *Rifle and Light Infantry Tactics* by William J. Hardee,[23] originally published in 1861 when Hardee was still credited on the title page as a brevet lieutenant colonel in the US Army, even though he resigned his commission on January 31, 1861, accepted a colonel's commission in the CSA, and was eventually promoted to lieutenant general. The training was basic and included how to salute, how to march in formation, and how to handle a musket. The wisest officers put the greatest emphasis on the latter, since the speed with which a soldier could fire, reload, and fire again was the common denominator in the success or failure of a battle. Drill began on the level of the company, but often included exercises in which entire regiments or even brigades participated—although such large-scale maneuvers and "sham battles" were more common in the Union army than in the CSA, which could ill afford to stage them.

How Johnny Reb Lived

Combat occupied relatively little of a soldier's time. Camp life predominated, and it was "one everlasting monotone, yesterday, today, and tomorrow." Time in camp was occupied with drill, "fatigue" (labor) details, and burials. Men rotated to the front for demanding yet tedious "picket" (sentry) duty, typically serving two days out of every six. Back in the encampment itself, whatever time was left before night fell was devoted to writing letters, keeping diaries, reading, whittling, sketching, and mending uniforms. Men also played checkers, dominoes, dice, and card games such as poker, cribbage, and euchre. If they were feeling more energetic, they might play football or baseball. Singing was another pastime—"Aura Lee," "The Yellow Rose of Texas," and "All Quiet along the Potomac" were rebel favorites.[24]

When not encamped, an army was usually on the move. Stonewall Jackson remarked that the "hardships of forced marches are often more painful than the dangers of battle." The speed of Jackson's prescribed pace for infantry was two miles per fifty minutes, followed by ten minutes of rest—flat on one's back, a position, Jackson held, that rests the man "all over."[25]

"Troops on the march were generally so cheerful and gay that an outsider, looking on them as they marched, would hardly imagine how they suffered," wrote Army of Northern Virginia soldier Carlton McCarthy.

In summer time, the dust, combined with the heat, caused great suffering. The nostrils of the men, filled with dust, became dry and feverish, and even the throat did not escape. The "grit" was felt between the teeth, and the eyes were rendered almost useless. There was dust in eyes, mouth, ears, and hair. The shoes were full of sand, and the dust, penetrating the clothes, and getting in at the neck, wrists, and ankles, mixed with perspiration, produced an irritant almost as active as cantharides. The heat was at times terrific, but the men became greatly accustomed to it, and endured it with wonderful ease. Their heavy woolen clothes were a great annoyance; tough linen or cotton clothes would have been a great relief; indeed, there are many objections to woolen clothing for soldiers, even in winter.[26]

And if "the dust and the heat were not on hand to annoy, their very able substitutes were: mud, cold, rain, snow, hail and wind took their places. Rain was the greatest discomfort a soldier could have; it was more uncomfortable than the severest cold with clear weather." As for night marches, these were "attended with additional discomforts and dangers, such as falling off bridges, stumbling into ditches, tearing the face and injuring the eyes against the bushes and projecting limbs of trees, and getting separated from your own company and hopelessly lost in the multitude."[27]

As miserable as woolen uniforms were in summertime, Confederate footwear was even worse in any season. The CSA supplied (when it could) crude brogans, with tops that reached just above the ankles. Unlike the more modern footwear supplied to Union forces, which Confederates called "crooked shoes" because they were specifically designed for right and left feet,[28] the brogans were meant to be worn on either the left or right foot. Only with repeated wear did the shoes conform—somewhat—to the shape of one foot or the other. "Very few men had comfortable or fitting shoes," McCarthy wrote, "and fewer had socks, and, as a consequence, the suffering from bruised and inflamed feet was terrible. It was a common practice, on long marches, for the men to take off their shoes and carry them in their hands or swung over the shoulder. Bloody footprints in the snow were not unknown to the soldiers of the Army of Northern Virginia!"[29]

"An army travels on its stomach," Napoleon famously declared, but McCarthy recalled that "Rations in the Army of Northern Virginia were alternately superabundant and altogether wanting." Clearly, the CSA's Commissary Bureau (also called the Subsistence Department) was never very reliable. "The quality, quantity, and frequency of [provisions] depended upon the amount of stores in the hands of the commissaries, the relative position of the troops and the wagon trains, and the many accidents and mishaps of the campaign." This was true from early in the war and worsened considerably as Robert E. Lee took the Army of Northern Virginia farther from home, including into Maryland and Pennsylvania. As the South's prospects became increasingly precarious during the last year and a half of the conflict, "so uncertain was the [ration and pay] issue as to time, quantity, and composition, that the men became in large measure

independent of this seeming absolute necessity, and by some mysterious means, known only to purely patriotic soldiers, learned to fight without pay and to find subsistence in the field, the stream, or the forest, and a shelter on the bleak mountain side."[30]

Foraging—living off the land—was commonplace, and when fish, fowl, or farm animals could not be caught, captured, or pilfered, soldiers improvised with nuts, berries, and leaves. Sassafras tea became a staple. Even so, to "be one day without anything to eat was common," per McCarthy. "Two days' fasting, marching and fighting was not uncommon, and there were times when no rations were issued for three or four days. On one march, from Petersburg to Appomattox, no rations were issued to Cutshaw's battalion of artillery for one entire week, and the men subsisted on the corn intended for the battery horses, raw bacon captured from the enemy, and the water of springs, creeks, and rivers."[31]

Poor nutrition, malnutrition, privation, and exposure threatened the health of soldiers in both armies, but none more than the Confederates. "Take special care of your health," a loving Southern father wrote to his son at the outbreak of the war:

More soldiers die of disease than in battle. A thin piece of damp sponge in the crown of your hat during exposure to the hot sun, the use of thick shoes and a water-proof coat in rainy weather, the practice of drinking cold water when you are very warm as slowly as you sip hot tea, the thorough mastication of your food, the avoiding of damp tents and damp grounds during sleep, and frequent ablutions of your person are all the hints I can give you on this point.[32]

An estimated 620,000 men died during the Civil War, twice as many succumbing to disease than suffering death in combat. Even more were periodically rendered unfit for duty due to illness.[33] (Medical care in the two armies is the subject of chapter 14.)

RESOLVE AND DESERTION

On October 9, 1864, Major General William Tecumseh Sherman sent Lieutenant General Ulysses S. Grant a telegram proposing to march clear across Georgia, from Atlanta to Savannah, for the purpose of bringing about the "utter destruction of its roads, houses, and people." His intention, in short, was to "make Georgia howl."[34] The underlying motive of this infamous March to the Sea (November 15–December 21, 1864) was to demonstrate to Georgia and to the entire South that its so-called Confederate government was now powerless to defend the people who had pledged to it their allegiance.

Long before the fall of Atlanta and the March to the Sea, the Confederate soldier had already experienced the impotence of the government he served. Clothed in rags, sometimes shoeless, often foodless, and rarely paid, what kept him going? "Leaving out of view every other consideration, he realized with exquisite delight, that he was resisting manfully the coercive force of other men, and was resolved to die rather than yield his liberty," Carlton McCarthy offered. "To strengthen his resolve he had ever present with him the unchanging love of the people for whom he fought; the respect and confidence of his officers; unshaken faith in the valor of his comrades and the justice of his cause."[35]

McCarthy had served in the Army of Northern Virginia. He was there. He suffered, and he endured. We therefore have good reason to assume that he spoke the truth of his own sentiments and those of the men he saw around him. But such men, the ones who remained to the bitter end, were a band that had long been dwindling. Part of the reality of the life

of Johnny Reb was desertion. It was a problem that plagued both the Union and Confederate armies. Estimates place Union desertion during 1861–65 at 200,000 men and Confederate desertion at 104,000.[36] If we assume that the enlistment strength of the USA was somewhat more than twice that of the CSA, the rate of desertion is about equal in both armies. As it is, the numbers may have been higher or lower, since it was often impossible to account for all the dead, captured, hospitalized, or missing and distinguish them from those who had simply walked away.

According to one modern essayist, "Poor food, boredom, unhealthy camp conditions, fear of death, and homesickness caused desertion on both sides," but in the CSA soldiers were closer to their homes and therefore uniquely and painfully aware of the misery in which their families and loved ones dwelled despite the soldiers' efforts to defeat the Yankees. Doubtless, this guilty awareness exacerbated the rate of desertion, especially late in the war. "When the promise of food, clothing, and shelter for the families of southern soldiers went unfulfilled, it weakened those soldiers' commitment to the army."[37]

The armies of the Civil War learned to exploit every weakness in their enemy. Both the CSA and the USA made strategic use of desertion. The Confederate government offered sanctuary to Northern deserters, the promise of jobs and (sometimes) even land. The Union government was even more aggressive in its inducements to Confederate desertion, offering amnesty in exchange for an oath of allegiance. Those who deserted were promised that they could return home after the war. During the conflict the army provided deserters with transportation to Union-occupied areas of the South, and even offered payment for any military equipment deserters brought with them. Those Confederate deserters who could not return home or did not want to do so were permitted to remain in the North as civilians or to join the US Army as so-called Galvanized Yankees, troops designated for service not in the war against the Confederacy but instead sent to the western frontier, to fight in the US government's ongoing conflict with the Plains Indians and other "hostile" tribes.

Some deserters, from both the Union and Confederate armies, holed up in the remote mountains and hills of Georgia, Alabama, Tennessee, and Kentucky. "Deserter country," it was called, and many of those who took refuge there lived by terrorizing and stealing from the civilian population in these areas. It was the ragged edge of the Civil War.

Chapter 10

BILLY YANK AND HIS COMMANDERS

AVERAGE QUALITY AND CAPABILITY OF OFFICERS AND MEN: ✭ ✭ ✭

The United States Army of 1861 was too small to be an instrument of war. This was by design. For one thing, American tradition shunned the idea of maintaining a large standing army in peacetime; for another, the geopolitical situation of the United States made a major war unlikely. The United States was economically and industrially superior to Mexico, its immediate neighbor to the south, and the same was true of its relationship to the chronically unstable states of Central and South America. Ever since the War of 1812 ended in 1815 with restoration of the *status quo ante bellum*, US relations with Canada, much smaller in population, had been cordial. As for the states of Europe and Asia, the existence of two vast oceans made acts of aggression highly unlikely—and the United States, for its part, with a vast trans-Mississippi frontier still open for settlement, had no imperialist designs on the rest of the world.

Indeed, the United States had not fought a major war for more than a decade, when it ensured the sovereignty and security of the state of Texas *and* wrested from Mexico the Southwest above the Rio Grande and Alta California through its victory in the war of 1846–48. The regular army entered the US-Mexican War with about half the strength, 8,613 soldiers, of the army of 1861. By 1848 federal forces grew to about 32,000 men (regular army, US Volunteers, and a small contingent of marines) supplemented by 59,000 state militia troops. While it is true that, without the aid of the militia, the regular army alone could not have prevailed against the Mexican forces—which at times numbered as many as 60,000 men, some equipped (though not trained) to high

European standards—the USA's officer corps and its enlisted veterans were justified in claiming the lion's share of credit for the ultimate victory. For the force of about 90,000 that won the US-Mexican War was formed around the core of the tiny regular army and its officers.

During long intervals of peace, the small USA carried and preserved the identity, tradition, and professionalism of a national military without presenting the burden of a large standing army. The war with Mexico proved that the army could fight and win a conflict between large forces—though nobody, at the outbreak of the Civil War, could imagine just how large those forces would be. It also demonstrated that the nation, upon need, could mobilize a large force around the tight professional kernel that was the USA.

The problem was that a portion of the USA, small as it was, suddenly broke away in 1860–61 to join a rebellion against the United States. Popular mythology holds that the secession of the Confederacy was followed by a mass exodus from the USA, especially among West Point–trained officers. The truth, however, is that of some 824 West Pointers on the army's active list, only 184 subsequently accepted commissions in the CSA. In addition, about 900 West Point graduates were civilians at the start of the war. Of these, 114 rallied to the USA, and just 99 accepted CSA commissions. The Union army began the Civil War with 754 West Point graduates to the Confederate army's 283.[1] As for enlisted soldiers, very few left the USA to join the Confederacy.

In sum, the Union entered the Civil War with a national army core, including its leadership, substantially intact—and still bigger than the miniscule force with which it had entered the

These Union soldiers were photographed on Mason's Island (today, Theodore Roosevelt Island) in 1861. Behind them is the Potomac Aqueduct Bridge and Georgetown University on top of the hill. During the war the island served as a storage and distribution site, and also as a training camp for Union troops. LIBRARY OF CONGRESS

war against Mexico. In contrast, the Confederacy had to start virtually from scratch, although, as in the North, it had a system of state militias on which to begin the necessarily rapid buildup.

WHY BILLY YANK ENLISTED

As was the case in the South, Northern men enthusiastically answered calls for volunteers. By existing law, militia volunteers for federal service obligated themselves to no more than a three-month enlistment. Yet when President Lincoln issued a call for US Volunteers to serve three years unless sooner discharged, "thousands of loyal men sprang to arms," observed John D. Billings, a veteran of an artillery unit in the

Army of the Potomac. It was "so large a number, in fact, that many regiments raised were refused until later."[2]

What drove the volunteers, according to many modern scholars, was a sense of duty "closely linked with concepts of masculinity, morality, conscience, and romance." Whereas Southerners tended to enlist from motives of honor and, according to some recent scholars, fear of a compelled reversal of the racial order in the South, such that "former masters [would be] forced to exist somewhere beneath northerners and one-time slaves," Northerners were driven by "a communal conscience analogous to a compact made with God, [a] consciousness of duty, which resonated . . . with the parallel development of social reform in the North. To shirk duty was to violate the collective conscience and to offend morality by omission." On the other hand, doing one's duty "served as part of the identity of manhood and established the place of the individual in society."[3]

Simple patriotism was also a motive. It was a sentiment whipped up in local war meetings featuring "Musicians and orators [who] blew themselves red in the face with their windy efforts. . . . The old veteran soldier of 1812 was trotted out and worked for all he was worth, and an occasional Mexican War veteran would air his nonchalance at grim-visaged war. At proper intervals the enlistment roll would be presented for signatures. . . . Sometimes the patriotism of such a gathering would be wrought up so intensely by waving banners, martial and vocal music, and burning eloquence, that a town's [recruitment] quota would be filled in less than an hour."[4] Yet in an era in which most Americans identified primarily with their state and only secondarily with their nation, Northern appeals to patriotism were also given a more local slant. "Citizens of Massachusetts should feel pride in attaching themselves to regiments from their own state," one recruiting poster explained, "in order to maintain the proud supremacy which the Old Bay State now enjoys in the contest for the Union and the Constitution."[5]

Ideology—especially abolitionism—and a thirst for adventure were less popular motives for enlistment, yet still significant. For some the experience of combat itself—"seeing the elephant"[6]—was a masculine rite of passage. For others the prospect of war was more of a lark, a thrill, an escape from the dull routines of home, farm, and factory.

Who Billy Yank Was

"We all declare for liberty," Abraham Lincoln said in an 1864 speech, "but in using the same word we do not all mean the same thing."[7] With this sentence Lincoln intended to express the central paradox of the Civil War: a nation in combat with itself over the same value interpreted differently. We can apply the sentence directly to the soldiers of the two armies that fought the war. For all their differences, the men of both armies declared for liberty.

In other ways, too, they were practically the same. At five feet, eight inches in height and 145 pounds in weight, the average Union recruit fit the physical norm for men of his age in 1860s America. The average recruit in the Confederate army was just over twenty-six, while the average recruit in the USA was just under that age. Both averages are considerably higher than the average age of the US Army recruit of 2013, which was 20.7 years old.[8] Fewer than a third of Union recruits in the first year of the war were married (29 percent).

Union soldiers were, by and large, better educated than Confederate soldiers. This is not surprising since the North had far more colleges, universities, and public libraries than the South and, even more important, had an extensively developed system of public education at the elementary and secondary levels. Whereas every Northern state had laws in place mandating schooling for varying minimum numbers of years, no Southern state had such laws in the 1860s, and public funding of education was practically nonexistent. In neither army, however, was outright illiteracy a serious problem, as most white Americans, Southerners and Northerners alike, could read and write. This did not necessarily make them particularly receptive to military training, however. "Raised in a country that proclaimed its independence, less than a century before, with a ringing declaration that all men are created equal and possess 'certain unalienable rights,' the citizen soldiers, on both sides, were characterized by a firm belief in their own worth and stubborn individualism that did not surrender easily to the strictures of military discipline," according to the *Civil War Desk Reference.*[9]

Ultimately, however, Union soldiers proved rather more tractable than Confederates, perhaps because more of them had more schooling, with its inherent discipline in a social setting; more of them were urban or at least residents of thickly settled areas (in contrast, many parts of the mid-nineteenth-century South still resembled the sparsely settled frontier); and more of them were at least acquainted with the discipline of employment in factories and other multi-employee enterprises. Still, it took the shock of large-scale combat to shake the Union army into demanding a level of rigorous training for its soldiers. At the First Battle of Bull Run (July 21, 1861), Union troops meandered rather than marched to the front, they were agonizingly slow to get into position, they bumbled, they were uncoordinated in attack and response to counterattack, they were unable to execute even fairly simple maneuvers, and, in defeat, they ran ("skedaddled," in parlance of the day) rather than retreated in anything approaching good order. The result was a lopsided Confederate victory and a complete Union humiliation: 2,708 Union troops killed, wounded, or missing versus 1,982 CSA casualties, with the Union forces ignominiously driven from the field. President Lincoln called on George B. McClellan to take the army in hand. The "Young Napoleon" built the Army of the Potomac and instituted within it a rigorous program of training and drill. The USA had entered First Bull Run as a rabble. In the aftermath it began to become an army.

Whereas the overwhelming majority of CSA enlisted recruits were farmers and agricultural laborers, many Union soldiers were tradesmen, factory workers, and clerks in civilian life—though most were, as in the South, small farmers. As in the CSA, those who became officers directly from civilian life were typically members of the professions—lawyers, engineers, college professors, bankers, and physicians. The latter served in the medical corps, but the others served wherever they were sent. In both the North and the South, influential men financed the raising of militia companies, which were incorporated into the CSA and USA. Typically, these men had no military experience, but because they had raised the unit, they were automatically appointed to command it as captain. In some cases they were accorded even higher rank. The CSA and, even more, the USA were also burdened by so-called political generals. These were men given commissions as general officers for the purpose of rewarding them politically or cajoling the support of certain communities or blocs of voters. Examples of political generals include John Adams Dix, Nathaniel Prentice Banks, and Benjamin F. Butler. All appointed generals of the US Volunteers, none possessed military experience, and all three were mediocre or worse as leaders. The one quality they shared was membership in the Democratic Party, and their appointment, Lincoln believed, was crucial to securing support for the war from reluctant moderate Democrats.

Some political generals were chosen in order to cement the loyalty and provoke the enthusiasm of major immigrant communities. Native-born white Americans made up 45.4 percent of the Union contingent that fought in the Civil War, 9.5 percent were African Americans, and just 0.1 percent were Native American. This left 45 percent who were either immigrants or who strongly identified with their maternal or paternal ethnic or national origins. German-born and Irish-born men constituted the two largest immigrant groups represented in the army, 9.7 percent and 9.1 percent, respectively. Franz Sigel and Carl Schurz were both commissioned generals, not because of their military experience (which in both cases included service in the abortive German revolts of 1848 in Europe)

In both armies, Civil War uniforms exhibited a tremendous range of styles, from the plaid "hickory shirt" worn by Private Emory Eugene Kingin, 4th Michigan Infantry, to the unidentified soldier in a Zouave uniform popular with several regiments, both in the USA and the CSA. BOTH NATIONAL ARCHIVES AND RECORDS ADMINISTRATION

but because of their political prominence in the German community. Sigel was a decidedly mediocre leader, but his popularity in the German immigrant community was a strong recruiting tool, and the men of XI Corps were almost all German immigrants who were fiercely loyal to Sigel, proudly proclaiming at every opportunity, "I fight mit Sigel!" Schurz, who served in the Lincoln administration as ambassador to Spain from July to December 1861, led a predominantly German division within XI Corps and proved to be both a competent and courageous leader.

Thomas F. Meagher and Michael Corcoran had both served as officers in the New York State Militia prior to the Civil War. They were commissioned as generals in the US Volunteers because of their great popularity among Irish immigrants. Both were able to rally large numbers of Irishmen to the Union cause.

Most of the 186,097 African Americans[10] who served in the Union army were admitted following the implementation of the final Emancipation Proclamation on January 1, 1863. This important group is discussed at length in chapter 13.

In response to flagging voluntary enlistments, the Union enacted a conscription law on March 3, 1863. Like the Confederate conscription law passed a year earlier, it gave the well-to-do a way of avoiding service, either by hiring a substitute or by paying a $300 commutation fee—this at a time when a common laborer earned approximately a dollar a day. It should be noted that the Union army, which enlisted a total of 2,778,304 men during the war, remained overwhelmingly a volunteer force. Just 52,068 conscripts were actually held to service during the entire war; an additional 86,724 conscripted men paid the $300 commutation fee to receive exemption, and 42,581 hired substitutes. Nevertheless, passage of the conscription laws, widely and accurately perceived as unjustly exploiting the ordinary working man, touched off demonstrations, even riots, in New York, Iowa, Illinois, Indiana, and Ohio.

HOW BILLY YANK FOUGHT

In the months and years following the First Battle of Bull Run, as the USA became more demanding in its training, Union troops arguably became increasingly effective at volley fire (simultaneous fire in line), but were probably never, on average, equal to the Confederate common soldier in individual marksmanship. For all their training, even as late as July 1863, many Union soldiers who fought in the Battle of Gettysburg failed ever to fire their weapons. After the battle, when the Union army and citizens of Gettysburg teamed up for the heartbreaking work of collecting bodies for burial and recovering their weapons from the field, they counted 27,574 rifles (some sources put the number at 37,574), of which 24,000 were fully loaded. Of the loaded weapons, 12,000 were loaded more than once (two or more minié balls) and half of these had been loaded between three and ten times. One weapon was found stuffed with twenty-three balls and cartridges! The mass of weapons recovered were Union issue. Did this suggest that a large number of *Union* soldiers were simply so ill-trained and so rattled by the chaos of combat that they forgot to fire? Or, in the depths of fear, did they deliberately go through the motions of loading and aiming without actually firing? Some have suggested that the loaded weapons are evidence of a psychological aversion to killing.[11] As one participant in the online forum *Civil War Talk* commented in 2012, "There seems to have been a sense that Union soldiers couldn't shoot straight. . . . The Wikipedia article asserts that Billy Yank fired 1,000 rounds for every Johnny Reb killed."[12]

At Shiloh, one Union soldier recalled, the peace of a Union encampment was shattered by "a dull, heavy 'Pum!' then another, and still another. Every man sprung to his feet as if struck by an electric shock, and we looked inquiringly into one another's faces." It was the second year of the war, April 6, 1862, and these Billy Yanks could not recognize when they were being fired upon.[13]

A "mounted staff officer came galloping wildly down the line from the right. He checked and whirled his horse sharply around right in our company street, the iron-bound hoofs of his steed crashing among the tin plates lying in a little pile where my mess had eaten its breakfast that morning. . . . The officer cast one hurried glance around him, and exclaimed, 'My God! This regiment not in line yet! They have been fighting on the right over an hour!'"

Well, the companies were formed, we marched out on the regimental parade ground, and the regiment was formed in line. The command was given: "Load at will; load!" We had anticipated this, however, as the most of us had instinctively loaded our guns before we had formed company. All this time the roar on the right was getting nearer and louder. Our old colonel rode up close to us, opposite the center of the regimental line,

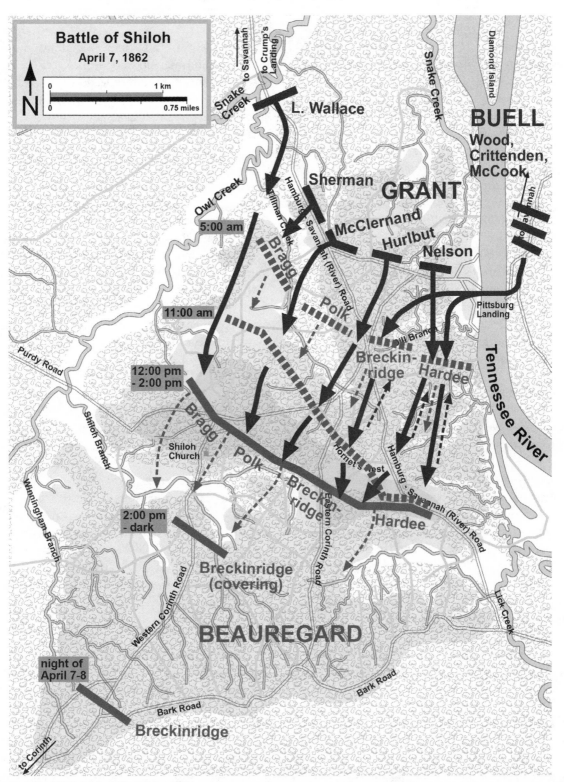

Battle of Shiloh, April 7, 1862. Map Hal Jespersen, www.cwmaps.com

and called out, "Attention, battalion!" We fixed our eyes on him to hear what was coming. It turned out to be the old man's battle harangue. "Gentlemen," said he, in a voice that every man in the regiment heard, "remember your State, and do your duty today like brave men." That was all. A year later in the war the old man doubtless would have addressed us as "soldiers," and not as "gentlemen," and he would have omitted his allusion to the "State," which smacked a little of Confederate notions.

Calm but forceful leadership could address some deficiencies of training and experience. Appearing in the right place and at the right time, a good officer could bring even bewildered Union soldiers to a recognition of their duty and transform at least some of them into effective fighting men.

HOW BILLY YANK LIVED

Certain universals mark the daily life of a soldier, no matter where he is. In both the CSA and the USA, soldiering was far less often a matter of fighting the enemy than it was fighting the exhaustion and other hardships attendant on frequent movement, physical labor, exposure to the elements, and, when encamped for any length of time, utter boredom. Drill and "fatigues"—manual labor that was sometimes necessary (such as building and maintaining camp buildings) and sometimes strictly make-work—were official methods of combatting idleness. For while boredom was unpleasant for the individual soldier, it was seen by those who commanded him as a dangerous threat to necessary and productive discipline.

RECREATION

In both the South and the North, commanders were not opposed to soldiers enjoying comradery-building recreation. They encouraged entertainment of all kinds, including music, dancing, and amateur theatricals. Occasionally, socially connected military leaders were able to persuade professional singers and actors to visit camps and put on high-quality shows. Since even among the enlisted men the rate of literacy was high, especially in the North, debating societies and literary societies—what today would be called book clubs—were formed. Reading, diary keeping, and letter writing were all popular pastimes when men needed solitude. Team sports, especially baseball, were popular, and, in winter, organized snowball fights were frequent occurrences. They were staged as full-on sham battles, with rival "armies" pitted against one another. In these contests officers participated with enlisted personnel—and they typically carried their command privileges into the game.

GAMBLING

Like their Confederate counterparts, Union commanders universally forbade gambling, and, like their Confederate counterparts, universally turned a blind eye to violations of the proscription. Soldiers would bet on anything—card games, of course, dice, the outcome of baseball games, and even the results of battle.

Also curtailed and regulated, if not strictly forbidden, on both sides was drinking alcohol in camp. Not only did the regulations fail to curb the consumption of alcohol, however, it is clear that camp life converted many a teetotaler into an imbiber.

SEX

Sex was another pastime, as evidenced in the high rate of venereal disease in some Union camps. Union army medical records reveal diagnosis and treatment of 73,382 syphilis cases and 109,397 gonorrhea cases during 1861–65, making for a VD rate of 82 cases per 1,000 men. This was actually slightly lower than the general civilian rate both before and after the war, which was 87 per 1,000.[14] Nevertheless, prostitution was a growth enterprise during the war years, partly because of demand and partly (some have assumed) because, with their breadwinning husbands away at war, women needed an income, often to support themselves *and* their children. At least one historian has suggested that "public women" (as prostitutes were sometimes euphemistically called) who sympathized with the Confederacy set about deliberately disseminating VD in the Union ranks.[15] In any event, there is no doubt that prostitution flourished near major Union camps, especially those in or adjacent to large cities. By 1864 Washington, DC, reportedly had 450 brothels, with another 75 in Union-held Alexandria across the Potomac. An estimated 5,000 prostitutes were active in Washington at this time and another 2,500 in Alexandria.[16]

Major General Joseph "Fighting Joe" Hooker, who commanded the Army of the Potomac during the disastrous Battle of Chancellorsville (April 30–May 6, 1863), came into the Civil War with a notorious reputation as a gambler, an imbiber, and a patron of bordellos. The latter, it was said, was the origin of the term *hooker* as a synonym for *prostitute*. Some "have suggested that the word arose from the disreputable atmosphere of Hooker's headquarters encampments during the Civil War, which were said to be so rife with prostitutes that people took to calling the women who were hanging about 'hookers.'" Other etymologists simply point to the profusion of Washington and Alexandria bordellos patronized by Army of the Potomac troops. Actually, however, *hooker* was a term "in widespread use in Britain and America long before the Civil War as a synonym for *streetwalker*, a woman who entices, snares, or *hooks* her clients."[17]

While not sanctioning prostitution, at least one Union officer, Lieutenant Colonel George Spalding, commanding the Union's 12th

Tennessee Cavalry in 1863, bowed to reality and had local Nashville prostitutes regularly examined and certified disease-free by an army physician.[18] It should be noted that while patronage of prostitutes was rife among Union soldiers, it was also very common among CSA soldiers, at least those stationed close to cities.

FOOD

As for sustenance, it cannot be said that Union soldiers ate well. *Rifle and Light Infantry Tactics* by William J. Hardee was the principal training manual used by the CSA; however, Hardee wrote it before the war, while he was serving in the USA, so we can safely assume that its specification for a USA soldier's daily rations applied to the Union army during the Civil War:[19]

- 20 ounces of pork (always salted) or beef (fresh or, more often, salted)

- 12 ounces of hard bread

- 1 ounce of "desiccated" (dehydrated) vegetables or 1.5 ounces of desiccated potatoes, both in a compressed cube

- These rations were supplemented by (per 100 rations): 8 quarts of beans or peas; 10 pounds of rice or hominy; 10 pounds of green coffee beans or 8 pounds of roasted coffee beans; 10 pounds of sugar; 2 quarts of salt; and 1 quart of vinegar

In the field individual soldiers were supplied with salt pork and hardtack—a simple, bland biscuit (more commonly called a "cracker") made of flour, water, and (usually) salt. It was virtually imperishable—and so hard that the crackers were referred to as "sheet iron" or "teeth dullers."

Understandably, soldiers supplemented their unpalatable rations with foraged (that is, pilfered) food from farms and other sources, as well as with delicacies from food packages sent from home or furnished by patriotic charitable organizations. New Yorker Gail Borden Jr., who had invented a process for condensing milk in 1853 and founded in 1857 a company for producing it, furnished condensed milk to the Union army. The military trade proved a boon to his business, which greatly expanded during the war and established condensed milk as a staple product in civilian life.

ENCAMPMENTS

Despite the efforts of the USA's Commissary Bureau, food-borne illness was a continual problem in military encampments, as were inadequate sanitary facilities. In planning camps, commanders sought high, dry ground—but often had to settle for wet, even swampy areas that did not lend themselves to adequate drainage and therefore created sanitation problems. Still, Union encampments tended to be at least orderly in appearance. They were planned to enhance operational cohesiveness and esprit de corps by keeping companies together, with each company assigned tents and other structures along a single lane called the "company street." The siting of latrines—which were usually nothing more elaborate than slit trenches—was always a compromise between convenience (not too far a walk from the shelters along the company street) and considerations of health (not too close as to create a nuisance or cause contamination). Care had to be taken that runoff from slit trenches did not pollute streams used for drinking water.

Union manuals dictated the disposition of shelters for officers, noncommissioned officers, and enlisted men along the company street. In permanent encampments, winter quarters were constructed of plank wood or logs. A single sixteen-by-twenty-foot room was intended to accommodate sixteen enlisted men. Each building had its own fireplace and chimney. Although tents were supplied to each company, the soldiers themselves they were expected to build the wooden winter quarters, using tools and plans furnished to them. They were also required to provide the labor

for the building of "officers' huts," which were constructed on the same sixteen-by-twenty-foot floor plan, but partitioned into two rooms, with a separate fireplace for each. Company captains rated their own room, whereas junior officers doubled up, two per room.

Throughout most of the year, especially during campaigns in the warm South, soldiers were sheltered in tents. These ranged from the humble dog tent, or shelter tent, which was used (almost exclusively by the Union army) to house enlisted troops. Of very basic construction, it was open at both ends and was composed of two shelter halves leaned against one another (it was said) like playing cards. The dog tent provided about six square feet of living space, was accessed by crawling on hands and knees, and offered no comfort whatsoever, but it could be erected in a matter of minutes and knocked down in even less time.

Far more elaborate was the Sibley tent, named after its inventor, Henry Hopkins Sibley, a USA officer who patented the design in 1856. (Henry Hopkins Sibley, who resigned his USA commission at the outbreak of the Civil War to command a Confederate cavalry brigade, is not to be confused with Henry Hastings Sibley—no relation—who remained loyal to the Union and served in the Indian Wars during the period of the Civil War.) The Sibley tent was conical, standing a lordly twelve feet high and offering an ample diameter of eighteen feet at its base. Supported by a single central telescoping pole, it could be erected and dismantled quickly and packed compactly. Moreover, it required no guy ropes for stability, but was instead held down by twenty-four pegs at its base. The most ingenious feature of the Sibley tent was a "cowl" set over its central pole, which vented smoke from the cooking and heating fire that could be built at the base of the pole. The Sibley tent was enormously popular with Union forces, which deployed some 44,000 of them during the war.

RESOLVE AND DESERTION

Although the USA delayed introducing conscription until early 1863, about a year after it was debuted by the Confederacy, the law was both unpopular (see the discussion of the draft riots in chapter 6) and, for anyone with sufficient money, easily circumvented. Its introduction reflected the sharp drop-off in voluntary enlistment by the beginning of the third year of the war. As already noted, however, conscription accounted for only 52,068 of the 2,778,304 enlisted Union soldiers who served during the Civil War, so that the Union army, like its Confederate counterpart, remained to the end primarily a force of volunteers. This notwithstanding, the USA suffered approximately the same rate of desertion (proportional to its far greater size) as the CSA—about 200,000 men, compared to 104,000 CSA deserters. That Southerners would begin to desert in large numbers is understandable, especially during the last year or year and a half of the war, when conditions throughout the South grew more desperate by the day. The similar desertion rate in the North, where civilians suffered few if any privations, may indicate that the slowly swelling tide of victory provided little encouragement to soldiers weary of killing and weary, too, of the many hardships of the soldier's life.

Chapter 11

Confederate Uniforms, Equipment, and Arms

QUALITY AND QUANTITY: ✶ ✶

Just as the Confederates and Union men who fought one another in the Civil War were more alike than they were different from one another, so their uniforms, equipment, and arms had more similarities than distinctions. The colors of the "official" uniforms—gray for the Confederacy, blue for the Union—soon became icons of the war itself, which was often characterized as a fight between "the blue and the gray." The enduring trope remains current to this day. It is, in fact, an example of what classical rhetoricians called a metonymy, the substitution of an attribute of something or someone for the thing or person itself. The government of a monarchy is called "the crown," the opposing armies of the Civil War were the blue and the gray. In the case of the Civil War, however, the effect of this figure of speech has not been to emphasize the differences between the two combatants but rather to draw attention to their sameness, as if to suggest that, in this war of "brother against brother," the only significant distinction was in the color of the uniforms.

In fact, the concept of the "blue and the gray" actually minimizes both the grave issues and the terrible cost of the war. The irony that underlies the concept is that the physical basis of the metonymy often did not exist. At the beginning of the war especially, the soldiers of both sides wore a variety of uniforms. Many Confederates wore blue uniforms, and many Union soldiers wore the uniforms of their particular state militia regiment, some of which were gray, some were various shades of blue, and some were other colors altogether. In the first major battle of the war, the First Battle of Bull Run (July

21, 1861), the *lack* of uniformity in the uniforms of the combatants on both sides created serious confusion on the battlefield. (Indeed, Confederate Thomas J. Jackson—who acquired his "Stonewall" sobriquet at Bull Run—rode into battle dressed, most probably, in the US Army blue uniform he wore as a professor at the Virginia Military Institute, and the blue uniforms of the Confederate 33rd Virginia Regiment allowed them to overrun a key Union position unopposed until it was too late.) Moreover, in the case of the Confederacy, soldiers early in the war often donned whatever clothing was available to them, mixing military-looking items of wear with their own civilian clothes. Late in the war, when the Confederate supply system had largely broken down, the uniformity of "uniforms" again diminished.

Uniforms and Insignia

One of the paradoxes of the Civil War is that the breakaway South emulated in most things the institutions and practices of the Union from which it had separated. The Confederate States Constitution, for example, was in large part a duplication of the United States Constitution. Likewise, the Confederate States Army (CSA) lived, fought, and looked much like the United States Army (USA). The first official uniforms essentially copied the USA uniforms, except for the use of gray rather than blue. The USA uniforms, in turn, were modeled closely on those of the military of the Second French Republic and the Second French Empire, both of which were presided over by the nephew of Napoleon I, Louis-Napoléon (president of the republic, 1848–52), who became Emperor Napoleon III

(1852–70). The cut of the wide-skirted, double-breasted greatcoat, the rakish kepi—with flat, sunken top and squared-off visor—and the full, loose trousers tapering at the bottom all closely copied the French style. The USA did turn from France to Prussia in using Prussian blue for the greatcoat, but it was distinctive in its use of sky blue for the trousers.[1]

On June 6, 1861, a Confederate general order was issued specifying, among other things, new requirements for uniforms. Nicola Marschall, a German-born artist living in Mobile, Alabama—and a man intensely sympathetic to the Confederate cause—designed the "Stars and Bars" Confederate national flag and was also commissioned to design a distinctive CSA uniform. In fact, what Marschall created drew on the very same European sources that had influenced the USA uniform, although he added to the overall French look certain Austrian details—especially the elaborate Austrian knots gracing the lower sleeves of officer uniforms. The USA-style kepi was retained.

Marschall's elegantly tailored design, which featured a choke-collared, double-breasted coat —longer than a jacket, but shorter than the Union greatcoat—may have been officially prescribed, but it was rarely executed in practice. For the first year of the war, Confederate enlisted men as well as officers were expected to hire tailors to make their uniforms following the specified design. The CSA reimbursed enlisted men twenty-one dollars per six months for the uniforms, but officers were expected to pay out of their own pockets. Some who purchased uniforms made more of an effort to follow the Marschall design than others. Early in 1862 the Confederate quartermaster instituted a program of mass production of uniforms, which were issued to enlisted soldiers. Officers continued to buy their uniforms individually until March 6, 1864, when a new regulation enabled them to acquire uniforms at a discounted price (at cost).

The mass-produced uniforms were manufactured as cheaply as possible. Indeed, the decision to continue using gray as the main color for the uniform was in part dictated by the cheapness of the required dyestuffs. As the war ground on and the increasingly strapped Confederacy looked for additional ways to save money, the quartermaster turned to sumac and logwood as homegrown sources of the cheapest possible gray dye. That this resulted in variable colors that were more brown-gray than neutral gray led to the uniforms being described as "butternut." This, in turn, became the source of a nickname for Confederate soldiers by the middle of the war—Butternuts.

One benefit of the gray used in the mass-produced uniform was that its dull shade—far more drab than the "cadet gray" Marschall specified—provided a degree of camouflage. Armies did not normally adopt camouflage during the Civil War, and this effect was serendipitous rather than intentional. Far less fortunate was the choice of wool for the uniform, which was hardly suited to the climate prevailing throughout most of the South most of the year. One argument the quartermaster made in favor of wool was that it kept soldiers warm during the night, so that they would not suffer unduly from the difference between daytime and nighttime temperatures. That rationale was, however, a stretch; the compelling reasons for the choice of wool were its durability and cheapness. Still, heatstroke was common among Civil War soldiers in the South, and by 1863 the uniform coat was abbreviated to a waist-length jacket. This was certainly more comfortable in the hot weather—and, because less material was used, it was also cheaper. Yet another concession to cost was the eventual abandonment of Marschall's double-breasted design for a simple single row of buttons, at least for enlisted men.

Officers, especially officers of field rank (major and above), often spent large sums to commission elegant bespoke uniforms from fine tailors. These mostly followed the high-collared, double-breasted Marschall design and incorporated embroidered gold "lace" or braid—called Austrian knots—on the sleeves in patterns prescribed for each grade of officer. Officers wore the insignia of their rank on the collars and sleeves of their dress uniforms only (omitted in the field):

- Second lieutenant: a single horizontal gold bar embroidered on each collar flap; a single gold Austrian knot design on each sleeve

- First lieutenant: a double horizontal gold bar embroidered on each collar flap; a single gold Austrian knot design on each sleeve

- Captain: a triple gold bar embroidered on each collar flap; a double Austrian gold knot design on each sleeve

- Major: a single gold star embroidered on each collar flap; a triple gold Austrian knot design on each sleeve

- Lieutenant colonel: two gold stars embroidered on each collar flap; a triple gold Austrian knot design on each sleeve

- Colonel: three gold stars embroidered on each collar flap; a triple gold Austrian knot design on each sleeve

- General: three gold stars surrounded by a gold wreath embroidered on each collar flap; a quadruple gold Austrian knot design on each sleeve. The insignia was the same for all grades of general, brigadier, major general, lieutenant general, and (full) general.

Confederate officers indicated their service branch or arm by the color of the facings (the portion of the lining visible to the observer) on their coats or jackets, including the collar and cuffs. Red indicated artillery; yellow, cavalry;

Major General John B. Gordon wears the dress uniform of a Confederate lieutenant general. Officers in both armies paid for their own uniforms, the high-ranking officers often spending a small fortune on custom tailoring.
NATIONAL ARCHIVES AND RECORDS ADMINISTRATION

light blue, infantry; and black, medical. Buff facings were used for staff officers and engineers, as well as for general officers, who were not associated with a specific service arm. The Confederate States Marines, a very small branch, had Prussian blue facings. Some officer uniforms featured piping to accent collars and the exposed edge of a buttoned jacket or coat. The piping also used the color associated with the service arm.

Early in the war, Confederate uniform trousers were sky blue, like those worn by Union officers and enlisted men. Later, they were dyed in a variety of brown, gray, or medium-blue shades. Officers through the grade of colonel had quarter-inch stripes running down the seams of their trousers. Like uniform facings, these were in the color of their service arm. Quartermaster, commissary, and engineer officers wore a single broad (one-and-a-quarter-inch) magenta stripe on the outer seam of the trousers. Generals were distinguished by a pair of five-eighths-inch stripes on each trouser leg.

Noncommissioned officers were identified by inverted chevrons worn on their sleeves. A sergeant major—the highest-ranking NCO—wore three chevrons topped by three inverted rockers (arcs). The next lower NCO, the quartermaster sergeant, wore three chevrons topped by three horizontal chevrons. An ordnance sergeant had three chevrons below a star; a first sergeant, three chevrons below a diamond device; a sergeant, three chevrons; a corporal, two chevrons. Musicians and privates wore no insignia of rank. The color of the chevrons was generally that of the service arm. Noncommissioned officers wore a single one-and-one-quarter-inch cotton stripe on the outer seam of each trouser leg in the color of their service arm.

Officers often had specially made swords worn with elaborate silk sashes. Cavalry officers wore gold, infantry wore burgundy, artillery officers wore red, and chaplains wore black sashes. General officers wore gray, cream, or buff sashes. Sergeants wore an issued NCO sword suspended from a leather belt. They were also permitted (but not required) to wear worsted wool waist sashes in either red (for both artillery and infantry) or yellow (cavalry). Medics sometimes wore green or blue sashes.

Leather waist belts were worn by enlisted ranks and were fastened by a variety of brass buckles bearing the initials CS (for Confederate States) or CSA (Confederate States Army). As brass buckles became scarce late in the war, many Confederate soldiers appropriated them from dead Union soldiers. Since these were stamped with "US," the Confederates wore them upside down.

There were distinguishing variations among infantry, cavalry, and artillery uniforms in addition to the color of facings, braid, piping, and trouser stripes. As originally specified, the infantry uniform was double-breasted (two rows of brass or gold buttons) in "cadet" gray with sky-blue facings; trousers were sky blue, as was the kepi. After the quartermaster took over mass production of uniforms, the specification was greatly simplified: a gray jacket, single-breasted; medium-blue, gray, or brown trousers; any available cap or slouch hat was acceptable. Originally, Jefferson brogans—ankle-top shoes—were specified as footwear; later, any available footwear was acceptable.

The earliest Confederate cavalry uniforms were designed and made or commissioned by the cavalrymen themselves, and it was not until 1862 that they became standardized in cadet gray for the frock coat, to be worn with light-blue pants. Although the kepi (in cavalry yellow) was prescribed, cavalrymen preferred a broad-brimmed slouch hat and were permitted to wear it. Boots, rather than brogans or other shoes, were worn.

As with the cavalry, the earliest artillery uniforms were custom made and personalized. By 1862 they were being mass produced and issued by the quartermaster. The coats were cadet gray lined with a layer of red around the sleeve. Trousers were light blue, and high boots were prescribed, though not always worn. Indeed, many artillerymen wore civilian clothing because of the labor involved in manhandling cannon, especially in the heat. Although kepis (in artillery red) were prescribed, artillerymen were permitted to wear straw hats in the summer.

Various state and local militia units adopted and retained very distinctive uniforms early in the war. As supplies and skilled craftsmen became scarce, such uniforms often had to be sacrificed. Most frequently seen was the Zouave uniform, a colorful ensemble copied from light infantry French and French colonial regiments serving in French North Africa. These featured short, open-front jackets and very baggy trousers

The "uniforms" of these enlisted soldiers of the 49th Virginia Infantry—a mixture of Confederate military dress and civilian clothing—were typical of the Army of Northern Virginia. LIBRARY OF CONGRESS

(called *serouel*). Some Zouave units wore kepis, while others adopted more eccentric "oriental" headgear. Flamboyant waist sashes were also common. Zouave units were even more plentiful in the Union army.

In the Western and Trans-Mississippi Theaters, Confederate uniforms were often highly irregular and, indeed, consisted of little more than civilian hunting or work clothes. The hickory shirt—a coarse, strong, loose shirt made of heavy twilled cotton typically woven in a broad checked pattern—became virtually the equivalent of a uniform in frontier areas away from the main theaters of the war.

EQUIPMENT

As essentially a frontier constabulary whose soldiers spent most of their time in the field, the USA fitted out the individual fighting man with equipment intended to promote self-reliance and independent sustainability. Both the CSA and the Union army continued this practice in equipping their men.[2]

Confederate infantrymen carried a sack of cotton duck, which was suspended from a shoulder strap over the right shoulder to the left hip. Called a haversack, it was intended mainly to hold field rations. The Union army's haversacks were made of linen painted and sealed with linseed oil to waterproof them.[3] Because the raw cotton duck haversacks issued by the CSA were porous—which often resulted in spoiled rations—the USA haversacks were coveted by CSA troops, who foraged them from fallen Union soldiers in the aftermath of combat.

Also slung from the right shoulder to the left hip by a strap of leather or cotton was a canteen, which rested on top of the haversack. The CSA canteens were crudely fashioned of tin and wood, so that they resembled miniature drums. In contrast, the USA canteens were swathed in wool cloth to insulate the contents. As with the haversacks, CSA soldiers eagerly sought to salvage Union canteens.

Another item of officially issued CSA equipment was a knapsack, also called a blanket roll. It was overstuffed with "a fatigue jacket, several pairs of white gloves, several pairs of drawers, several white shirts, undershirts, linen collars, neckties, white vests, socks, etc. . . . Strapped on the outside were one or two blankets, an oilcloth, and extra shoes. Most of the knapsacks weighed between thirty and forty pounds, but some were so full that they weighed fifty pounds!" attested Army of Northern Virginia veteran Carlton McCarthy. He also observed that the "knapsack vanished early in the struggle [jettisoned by marching troops]. It was inconvenient to 'change' the underwear too often, and the disposition not to change grew, as the [clothing-stuffed] knapsack was found to gall the back and shoulders, and weary the man before half the march was accomplished. The better way was to dress out and out, and wear that outfit until the enemy's knapsacks, or the folks at home supplied a change."[4] It was indeed possible for the CSA soldier to take whatever extra clothing he needed, roll up the articles into a blanket, and then wear the blanket as a kind of bandolier over the left shoulder, the ends tied together at the right hip. The CSA issued rough woolen blankets, which

most soldiers replaced with something more comfortable they purchased, something families sent them, or something stolen from a civilian home. The most fortunate CSA soldiers were issued very well-made knapsacks imported from the London firm of S. Isaac, Campbell & Co., suppliers to the British army. These were waterproof and designed so that they fit square to the soldier's back using leather straps that passed over and under the shoulders. Some even were equipped with wooden frames.

CSA infantry soldiers were supplied (by regulation, if not always in fact) with forty rounds of long-arm ammunition, which had to be carried in a cartridge box. Soldiers who were issued British-made Enfield rifle muskets were equipped with domestic copies of standard British army cartridge boxes. Those troops who were issued other long arms were furnished with crude copies of the standard USA "black box." It had straps on the back so that it could be carried on a strap that hung from the left shoulder to the right hip or on a waist belt, positioned at the center of the soldier's back. This type of box held forty paper-wrapped cartridges in two round tin containers, each holding twenty cartridges. Beneath the flap of the USA cartridge box was a pocket that held musket tools and cleaning equipment. Confederate copies were simpler. A single tin container held all forty cartridges, the fastener belts were more basic—intended to fasten either to the belt or to the shoulder strap, but not both—and the tool pocket was often omitted entirely. Whereas the USA flap was emblazoned with a brass USA badge, the CSA models typically had one of lead or wood. To save on the use of increasingly scarce leather, the outer flap of a CSA cartridge box often was made of painted cloth. If a soldier had the means and the inclination, he could purchase a specially made cartridge box from the Richmond, Virginia, firm of H. M. Richmond and Sons, which featured an oval brass emblem stamped "CS."

By regulation, a black leather waist belt was part of the CSA soldier's uniform. In practice, however, undyed leather was often substituted and, late in the war, plain cotton webbing. The official buckle was a simplified version of the USA buckle, with CS or a state seal, name, or initials substituted for the US that appeared on Union buckle shields. In many cases, a plain frame buckle, often fashioned of iron, was used without any shield. Strapped to the waist belt was a thin iron pick, used to clear a fouled musket nipple, and a cap box, a small leather pouch holding copper percussion caps for the rifle-musket. It was worn on the front right hip, next to the belt buckle. As usual, the CSA version of this piece of equipment was simpler and cheaper than the USA version. The CSA cap boxes lacked the sheepskin interior wrapper designed to prevent the caps from falling out when the flap was opened. In addition to Southern-made boxes, the CSA imported some from England, which were buff in color and designed to be secured on the cartridge-box sling instead of the waist belt.

Also affixed to the waist belt, on the left hip, beneath the haversack, was a leather scabbard to hold the bayonet when it was not affixed to the rifle-musket. Typically, in place of the brass fittings found on the more elaborate USA scabbards, the CSA versions used humble white metal.

INFANTRY WEAPONS

Many volumes have been devoted to the subject of Civil War weapons.[5] What we will note here is that despite the technological conservatism that prevailed in both the USA and CSA, the infantrymen of both armies benefitted from the widespread use of two innovations, the percussion rifled musket and the minié ball (or minié bullet). Up to—and even during—the Civil War, there was much debate concerning the comparative advantages of smoothbore versus rifled long arms. As explained in chapter 3, during the

1850s the USA had slowly begun transitioning from smoothbore muskets to rifle muskets, the bores of which had internal spiral grooves (rifling) to impart a spin to the projectile, which stabilized its flight, making it more accurate and increasing its effective range. The advantages over smoothbore fire are obvious, but because a bullet fired from a barrel had to be of slightly larger diameter than the bore in order to engage the rifled grooves, muzzle loading was more difficult and time-consuming than smoothbore loading because the shooter had to pound each loaded bullet home with his ramrod. This slowed the rate of fire and increased the chances of misfire. Indeed, a soldier with a smoothbore achieved a rate of fire three or four times that of soldiers using rifle muskets. The bullet-shaped minié ball changed this. Like the conventional smoothbore ball, the minié round was smaller than the rifled bore, but its base was designed to expand when fired, so that, as it exited the muzzle, the rim of the base engaged the rifling and thus spun the projectile.

Although Confederate soldiers continued to use smoothbore muskets, especially early in the war, they increasingly adopted rifle-muskets, some of which were appropriated from captured federal arsenals in Confederate territory, others of which were imported from the Enfield works in England and from the Lorenz firm in Austria. (Enfield sold firearms to both the North and South throughout the war.)

Much has been made of the South's limited industrial capacity, which surely did negatively impact the Confederate supply of weapons. Nevertheless, the South seized about 200,000 muskets (mostly smoothbores) from federal arsenals at the outbreak of the war and, despite the Union "Anaconda" naval blockade of Southern ports, managed to import sufficient quantities of long arms from abroad to ensure that the South never lost a Civil War battle because it lacked either ammunition or arms. Although most of the

Confederate records of arms purchases were lost during the war, the Confederacy's chief of ordnance, Josiah Gorgas, reconstructed statistics (at the request of USA officers preparing a war history) after hostilities had ended. Gorgas's figures showed that a total of 323,231 "infantry arms" had been purchased or captured—in addition to what the Confederacy seized at the outbreak of the war.[6]

In addition to the muskets, rifle-muskets, and rifles manufactured by US arsenals and contractors and seized or captured by the Confederates, the South imported .753-caliber Pattern 1839 and 1842 smoothbore muskets from British manufacturers and .577-caliber Pattern 1853 rifle muskets from Enfield in Great Britain as well as the .577 Enfield Volunteer Rifle. From Austrian makers the CSA imported .71-caliber smoothbores converted to percussion-fired weapons as well as the Austrian .54-caliber Lorenz Rifle-musket, Model 1854, and the .69-caliber Prussian Rifle-musket, Model 1839/55. Other European models were purchased in smaller quantities.

The Confederacy also manufactured limited quantities of rifles and muskets domestically. These included:

- The Fayetteville Rifle: A .58-caliber muzzle-loading percussion rifle manufactured in a quantity of about 20,000

- The Richmond Rifle-Musket: A .58-caliber muzzle-loading percussion rifle manufactured in a quantity of about 42,000

- The Tyler, Texas, Enfield Rifle and Austrian Rifle: Domestic copies of the .577-caliber Enfield and .54 Austrian rifles

- The Cook Infantry Rifle: A .577-caliber muzzle-loading percussion rifle, similar to the Enfield, turned out in a quantity of perhaps 20,000 by Cook & Brother, Athens, Georgia

The long arms of the CSA infantry were almost exclusively muzzleloaders (front-loading) rather than breechloaders (rear-loading). Although loading through the breech was faster and less cumbersome, the Confederacy, like the Union, generally shunned breechloaders for infantry use. Commanders feared that the ease of loading and firing would lead soldiers to waste ammunition. Acting on this questionable assumption, senior officers in both militaries effectively made a decision to trade lives for ammunition.

If both the North and South were reluctant to embrace breechloaders for the infantry, they were even more resistant to deploying large numbers of the recently invented Henry repeating rifle, which carried one round of .44-caliber ammunition in the chamber and fifteen more rounds in a tube magazine, which rapidly fed the ammunition into firing position with each shot. Thus a soldier could fire sixteen times before reloading. Again, the objection was that soldiers would squander ammunition. The more serious concern, however, was the complexity of the repeating mechanism, which was, in fact, prone to jamming, especially if soldiers failed to clean their weapons—as many did fail to do.

In addition to long arms, CSA soldiers used a wide variety of revolvers. Sidearms were not issued to enlisted soldiers—although some purchased their own or used weapons they happened to own—but revolvers were regularly carried by infantry officers. In addition to those seized or captured from the Union, .44- and .45-caliber revolvers were imported from European suppliers. In addition, three Southern firms manufactured .36-caliber weapons: Rigdon, Ansley & Co.; Griswold & Gunnison; and Spiller & Burr.

CAVALRY WEAPONS

Although swords (straight blade) and sabers (curved blade) were issued to noncommissioned officers as well as commissioned officers in the CSA infantry, they were rarely used in combat and were mainly ceremonial. They were wielded by cavalrymen. The Confederacy imported most of its cavalry sabers from England, France, Belgium, and Germany. Whatever their source, most emulated French patterns.[7]

The CSA made more extensive use of cavalry than the Union did. Cavalry units were used especially for reconnaissance and raiding. Revolvers were issued to all cavalrymen, including officers, but the main weapons for the CSA mounted service were the musketoon and carbine. Both of these weapons had short barrels: twenty-two to twenty-five inches, compared with thirty-nine inches for Enfield rifle-muskets. A length reduction of between fourteen and seventeen inches made the carbine

feasible for use by a mounted trooper, who had to be able to draw the weapon from a saddle holster, fire, and reload it speedily. The breech-loaders that were generally eschewed for infantry use were enthusiastically embraced by the cavalry. Loading and reloading a muzzleloader was difficult enough for an infantryman. It was nearly impossible for a cavalryman mounted on his horse. Repeating carbines—avoided by the infantry—became popular cavalry weapons with the Union, but were not widely available to the CSA. The principal carbine the CSA imported for cavalry use was the Enfield Cavalry Carbine, Pattern 1858, a .577-caliber muzzleloader. Two domestic manufacturers also supplied carbines to the CSA cavalry. The .577-caliber muzzle-loaded Richmond Carbine was manufactured in a quantity of more than

Confederate firepower. These columbiads (large-caliber smoothbore cannon) belonged to the battery at Warrenton, Florida, which defended the entrance to Pensacola Bay. NATIONAL ARCHIVES AND RECORDS ADMINISTRATION

2,500 by the Richmond Armory and Arsenal in 1863, and about 3,000 .52-caliber Confederate (Richmond) Sharps Carbines were turned out by the S. C. Robinson Arms Manufactory at Richmond. These were copies of the Sharps Carbine, Model 1859.

ARTILLERY

As explained in chapter 3, advances in industrial processes in the mid-nineteenth century allowed advances in cannon making, most of which bypassed the industrially disadvantaged Confederacy. According to Confederate chief of ordnance Josiah Gorgas, the CSA had 1,306 field artillery pieces and 341 large pieces (columbiads and siege guns) in 1863.[8]

The USA called the Twelve-Pounder Field Gun, Model 1857—the most widely used field artillery piece of the Civil War—a "Napoleon." Its namesake was not Napoleon I, but his nephew, Napoleon III, who commissioned the weapon's development for the French army. Most Union Napoleons had smoothbore brass barrels—and the Confederacy did manage to seize or capture some of them. For copies manufactured by the Tredegar Iron Works in Richmond, however, the material used was iron. This put the Confederacy at a disadvantage. Brass barrels were less prone to bursting than iron. This meant that Union artillerists could pack more powder into their brass cannon than their Confederate counterparts dared to load into their iron-barreled weapons. The resulting reduction in muzzle velocity sacrificed both range and destructiveness. Whereas a Union Napoleon had an effective range of at least 1,619 yards, Confederate gunners had to settle for less. Northern foundries turned out more than a thousand Napoleons. Confederate manufacturers, including Tredegar, produced about half this number.

Napoleons were all portable field artillery pieces. Both the Union and Confederate armies also used heavy artillery, which included weapons too big and heavy to be easily transportable—some were mounted on railroad flatcars—as well as fixed weapons used in fortifications for coastal defense. The South's 341 large pieces included so-called columbiads, which fired shells ranging from eight to eleven inches in diameter, and a variety of siege weapons. The Confederacy's heavy artillery had been seized from Union fortifications at the outbreak of the war, imported from Europe, or, in a few cases, manufactured in Southern foundries.

Examples included heavy naval guns adapted for use on land, transportable Coehorn mortars (for siege work), and several rifled cannon, such as the Brooke rifle, a muzzle-loading naval and coastal defense cannon designed and manufactured in the South and capable of firing ammunition ranging from 6.4 to 8 inches (a smoothbore version could fire 10-inch and 11-inch projectiles). These large guns, used on land as well as afloat, were cast at the Tredegar Foundry in Richmond and compared favorably to the North's state-of-the-art rifled cannon known as Parrott Rifles.

The Confederacy made use of seized USA smoothbore coastal guns—Model 1829 thirty-two pounders and Model 1831 forty-two pounders—to defend major cities. These weapons could be loaded with the whole range of artillery ammunition in addition to solid shot—conventional cannonballs—including:

- Shells: hollowed-out versions of solid shot, into which gunpowder was tightly packed. Solid shot did its damage by force of impact only; shells were packed with gunpowder, fused, and designed to explode in flight, sending jagged iron fragments—shrapnel—in all directions. They were antipersonnel weapons, intended to kill or injure as many men as possible within the blast radius of the ammunition.

- Case shot: another form of antipersonnel ammunition. This thin-walled projectile was filled with lead or iron balls packed tightly in a compound of sulfur or in asphalt. The case shot included a small fused "bursting charge" of gunpowder, which exploded in flight, scattering the balls. In effect, case shot transformed a cannon into a gargantuan shotgun.

- Canister shot: consisted of lead or iron balls packed in sawdust inside a tin or tinned iron cylinder. The cylinder was nailed to a wooden plug on one end and crimped over an iron plate on the other. When the cannon was fired, the thin canister disintegrated as it emerged from the muzzle, spraying the balls over a wide area.

Although the Confederacy was undeniably outgunned by Union artillery, the South, a region that had steadfastly resisted large-scale industrialization, nevertheless achieved a remarkable level of industrial weapons production and employed a combination of daring and skilled seamanship to evade the Union blockade and managed to import from European suppliers large quantities of arms and ammunition of all kinds.

Chapter 12

UNION UNIFORMS, EQUIPMENT, AND ARMS

QUALITY AND QUANTITY: ★ ★ ★

In his *Personal Memoirs* of 1885, Ulysses S. Grant paints a vivid picture of his meeting with Robert E. Lee in the home of Wilmer McLean at Appomattox Court House, Virginia, to agree on terms for the surrender of the Army of Northern Virginia. When he had left camp that morning, Grant wrote, he "had not expected so soon the result that was then taking place, and consequently was in rough garb. I was without a sword, as I usually was when on horseback on the field, and wore a soldier's blouse for a coat, with the shoulder straps of my rank to indicate to the army who I was. When I went into the house I found General Lee. We greeted each other, and after shaking hands took our seats. I had my staff with me, a good portion of whom were in the room during the whole of the interview." Grant was acutely self-conscious in Lee's presence, dressed, as the Confederate commander was, "in a full uniform which was entirely new, and . . . wearing a sword of considerable value, very likely the sword which had been presented by the State of Virginia. . . . In my rough traveling suit, the uniform of a private with the straps of a lieutenant-general, I must have contrasted very strangely with a man so handsomely dressed, six feet high and of faultless form."[1]

The irony was poignant. By this stage of the war, the Confederate States Army (CSA) was quite literally threadbare. Uniforms were typically in tatters. Many soldiers lacked shoes. The United States Army (USA), in contrast, had become a true national army, with uniforms that were at long last *uniform*. Yet, at this climactic summit, the Union general-in-chief wore the plain coat of a USA private, distinguished only by the shoulder straps of a lieutenant general.

Lee, at the head of a broken army, wore a magnificent new uniform. The defeated commander dressed like a conqueror while the victorious general appeared in the humblest of garb.

UNIFORMS AND INSIGNIA

The uniform in which the USA went to war in 1861 was the result of regulations promulgated in 1858 and revised in 1861.[2] Three uniforms were called for: campaign (battle dress), parade (dress uniform), and fatigue (work clothes).

The campaign uniform consisted of four main components: headgear, coat, greatcoat, and trousers. Although the most familiar and popular headgear was the flat kepi in the French pattern, the regulation specified a black felt Model 1858 Dress Hat, familiarly known as the "Hardee hat" and, during the Civil War, also called the "Jeff Davis hat" because the style was often seen on Confederate soldiers. Presumably, the hat was named after William J. Hardee, who was commandant of cadets at West Point from 1856 to 1860 but resigned his USA commission on January 31, 1861, to join the CSA. The hat had a high, stiff crown and broad brim, the right side of which was secured to the crown with an eagle pin. Other embellishments included the insignia of the wearer's service arm affixed to the front of the crown, a decorative hatband, and, sometimes, a feather. These hats were more popular in the Western Theater of the war than in the Eastern Theater, where the kepi was usually worn on campaign. The heavy felt hat was not very comfortable in the hot Southern climate.

The prescribed coat was dyed in Prussian blue. Tight fitting, its skirts extended nearly to the knee. The edges of the high, stand-up collar were piped with trim in the color of the service arm: light blue for infantry, yellow for cavalry, red (or scarlet) for artillery. Engineer collars were piped in yellow or gold, and ordnance personnel had crimson piping. For infantry company officers the coat was single-breasted, with shoulder straps signifying rank and service arm. Mounted officers—cavalry and mounted artillery—wore short jackets, which were better suited to riding. Field officers and generals wore double-breasted coats. Black velvet collar and cuffs were optional, not required.

A greatcoat was also authorized for enlisted personnel. It was sky blue, with a standing collar and a fixed short cape. Officers were authorized to wear a similarly cut garment, but in dark blue.

Trousers in sky blue were to be worn by all enlisted men and company-grade officers (lieutenants and captains). Noncommissioned officers wore trousers with a vertical stripe in the color of the service arm. Field-grade, senior staff, and general officers wore trousers in the same Prussian blue shade as the coat. The trousers of general officers had a gold double stripe along the outer seams. The trousers of all other officers were piped in colors representing their service arm.

The parade uniform featured the Hardee hat, trimmed in the arm of service colors. Some units (including mounted artillery) wore stiff shakos on parade. The coat was that used on campaign, except that, for enlisted ranks, it featured metallic epaulets resembling scales and, for officers, French-style epaulets as well as a sash in the color of the wearer's service arm. The greatcoat was the same one worn on campaign, as were the trousers.

The fatigue uniform consisted of a forage cap, which was a version of the kepi, dressed down by the removal of the stiffener, so that the crown was floppy. Officers typically found this look undignified and therefore purchased a fancier version of the forage cap called a chasseur cap. Enlisted caps featured an insignia pinned to the top of

the crown; the chasseur cap had the insignia on the front. Generals who wore the chasseur cap dressed it up with a black velvet band.

The fatigue coat was a sack coat in dark blue with a loose fit and a soft ("fall") collar rather than the standing choke collar. The sack coat had no pockets.

The fatigue greatcoat (when worn at all) was the same as that worn on campaign.

Fatigue trousers were sky blue for enlisted men and dark blue (matching the coat) for officers. Made of wool, they were baggier than the trousers worn on campaign or on parade, and they featured pockets.

As the war ground on and the government closely eyed expenditures, the campaign uniform yielded to the fatigue uniform, which, increasingly, became the combat uniform. Throughout the war various units wore distinctive uniforms, including green coats for sharpshooters (snipers). The color was a gesture toward camouflage, and the boldest innovation was the use of dull rubber ("Goodyear") buttons instead of brass; they were designed not to reflect the sun. Numerous Union regiments wore Zouave uniforms emulating those of North African French colonial units. These featured such elaborate accoutrements as a turban or a tasseled fez; a short, form-fitting jacket (in some versions without buttons); a flamboyant sash, whose ten-foot length required wrapping around the waist several times; leggings, typically in white; and *jambieres,* a short leather cuff for the calf, akin to spats. Trousers were very loose pantaloons. Depending on the degree of outlandish elaboration, the Zouave uniform could be unwieldy in combat—although the loose pantaloons and short jacket were better suited to Southern heat than the long woolen coat and high collar of the standard uniform.

Finally, a few units emulated Scottish Highlander dress. The 79th New York Regiment, for instance, wore a Scots doublet instead of the conventional shell jacket, and a Glengarry cap and kilts, complete with sporran for parade. On campaign, tartan trousers (called *trews*) were worn, with a kepi rather than the Glengarry cap.

In footwear Union soldiers fared more comfortably than their Confederate counterparts. The Union infantry was issued what Confederates referred to as "crooked shoes," shoes specifically manufactured in a right and left fit rather than intended to be broken in by repeated wear to fit on the left or the right foot. High-top "Jefferson Davis boots" were standard. In contrast to the Confederate "Jefferson shoes," which reached barely to the ankle, the uppers of Union footwear extended above the ankle. Most versions were "rough-out"—the rough side of the leather on the outside—but some were smooth leather. The uppers were reinforced with heel irons and the soles had hobnails to improve traction and durability. Cavalry and artillery units were issued calf-length riding boots, although some cavalry units adopted thigh-high cavalier or trooper boots as a nod to European cavalry regiments.

Infantry enlisted men wore a black leather waist belt with an oval buckle stamped with "US." Officers and NCOs in all branches, together with enlisted cavalry troopers, were issued sword belts featuring a rectangular brass eagle decoration.

The rank insignia for officers was displayed on epaulettes (parade uniforms) or shoulder straps (campaign and fatigue dress). Three ranks of general were authorized in the US Army. A lieutenant general wore three stars, a major general two, and a brigadier one. The insignia of a USA colonel was a spread eagle; a lieutenant colonel wore a silver oak leaf; a major, a gold oak leaf; a captain, two gold bars; and a first lieutenant, a single gold bar. The most junior officer, a second lieutenant, wore no insignia of rank. The shoulder straps themselves were trimmed in gold braid surrounding a field colored according to service arm:

- Dark blue: general officers and general staff
- Sky blue: infantry
- Yellow: cavalry
- Orange: dragoons (rarely used in the Civil War)
- Scarlet (red): artillery
- Dark green: sharpshooters
- White: judge advocates
- Emerald green: medical corps
- Crimson: ordnance
- Olive green: pay corps
- Buff: aides-de-camp
- Buff with white trim: adjutants
- Buff with black trim: engineers
- Buff with scarlet trim: inspectors
- Buff with sky blue trim: quartermasters

Officers were authorized to wear Austrian knots of gold braid on their sleeves, in the manner of Confederate officers; however, unlike their Confederate counterparts, they rarely adopted this practice since it made them conspicuous targets for snipers.

Noncommissioned officer ranks were indicated by chevrons worn on the upper sleeve (above the elbow). The highest NCO rank, sergeant major, had three inverted chevrons topped by three inverted (arced) rockers. The regimental or company quartermaster sergeant wore three inverted chevrons topped by three horizontal stripes; an ordnance sergeant had three inverted chevrons with a star centered between them; a first sergeant had three inverted chevrons into which a diamond device was inserted; and a sergeant had three inverted chevrons. Corporals had two chevrons, and musicians and privates wore no insignia. The chevrons were colored according to service arm:

- Sky blue: infantry

- Red: artillery

- Yellow: cavalry

- Yellow or gold: engineers

- Crimson: ordnance

In the course of the war, the USA began issuing corps badges, each of a distinctive shape to identify each corps. The object of the badges was to reduce battlefield confusion—and to create esprit de corps. As the badges quickly proved both popular and effective, Major General Daniel Butterfield designed distinctive badges for each division within a corps by varying the color of the badge:

- Red: 1st Division

- White: 2nd Division

- Blue: 3rd Division

- Green: 4th Division of VI, IX, and XX Corps

- Yellow: 4th Division of XV Corps

- Multicolor: Headquarters or Artillery elements within some corps

Corps badges were originally worn on the top of the kepi, the side of the Hardee hat, or over the left breast, but some soldiers wore them elsewhere. Enlisted men wore badges made of cloth, while officers often purchased badges made of other material, including fine metal fashioned by jewelers. Some of these were personalized in various ways.

EQUIPMENT

Union and Confederate soldiers went into the field similarly equipped, except that the USA equipment was almost always of higher quality.[3] Each Union soldier carried about fifty pounds of equipment into the field. This included the following items.

Knapsack: Essentially a backpack, the knapsack was carried on the back and was loaded with extra clothing, blankets, and whatever else a soldier decided to carry with him, including extra rations that did not fit into his haversack. Unlike the cheaply made Confederate knapsacks, USA Model 1855 knapsacks were well made of a double layer of cloth that was coated with thick black paint to render them water resistant. Like their Confederate counterparts, weary Union soldiers often abandoned their knapsacks and instead rolled up everything they needed in their blanket, which they wore over the shoulder, bandolier-fashion.

Blanket: The USA issued a rough woolen blanket to each soldier. Typically gray, it was embroidered with a "US" stitched in the center and somberly decorated with dark stripes on either end. The blanket could be carried in the knapsack or rolled up (often along with other odds and ends), the ends tied together, and then worn over the shoulder as a bandolier.

Rubber ground cloth: One item Confederate troops did not receive was a rubber ground cloth, which made sleeping on wet ground more tolerable. Union soldiers typically wrapped it around the blanket roll, both to make carrying easier and to protect the blanket from rain.

Haversack: This cloth bag was equipped with a strap so that it could be worn over the right shoulder, the bag resting on the left hip above the canteen. It held field rations and eating utensils. Whereas Confederate haversacks were cheaply fashioned of canvas duck, Union models were rendered water resistant with a coat of black paint. This helped to keep the rations dry.

Canteen: In contrast to Confederate canteens, crude drum-shaped vessels made of tin and wood, Union canteens were fashioned entirely of tin and covered with woolen cloth to improve the insulation of the contents. The cloth was typically dyed Prussian blue. The canteens were oblate in shape and easy to handle and carry.

Cartridge box: Union cartridge boxes were leather and held forty cartridges in two twenty-cartridge tin containers. A boxplate, stamped "US," on the front cover kept the flap closed. A pocket inside that flap held a small pick for cleaning the firing mechanism of the rifle-musket. The cartridge box was worn from a bandolier-style sling, with a decorative eagle breastplate attached. The box could be slung from the shoulder, with the box on the right hip, or it could be attached to the waist belt.

Waist belt: Nineteenth-century men generally wore suspenders to hold up their trousers. For the Civil War soldier, the waist belt was strictly a utility belt, used to hold cap box, bayonet, and sometimes the cartridge box. The belt might also be used to suspend a sword. Whereas Confederate belts were often made from painted cloth (as leather became increasingly scarce), USA belts were always of finished leather. A belt plate or shield covered the buckle. The shield was oval in shape and stamped with "US." Officers and noncommissioned officers had rectangular sword-belt plates featuring an American eagle inside a wreath, worn on the front.

Cap box: Worn on the waist belt, the cap box held the copper percussion caps needed to fire a musket or rifle-musket. Late in the war, Confederate cap boxes were often made of painted cloth. Union models were always leather.

Bayonet and scabbard: When not fixed in place at the end of a musket, the bayonet was stored in a leather scabbard decorated with a bright brass finial on the end.

INFANTRY WEAPONS

The industrial output of the North vastly outpaced that of the agricultural South, and much of the North's industry was dedicated during the war years to arms production. An 1866 War Department report to Congress summarized the material costs of the war, including for the production of arms and munitions. In addition to producing hundreds of millions of bullets and more than a billion percussion caps, Northern industry turned out more than 10,000 artillery pieces and millions of muskets, rifle-muskets, and rifles. In all, more than four million long arms were accounted for, about half of which were made by federal arsenals and half produced by domestic private manufacturers or imported from Europe. This second half—1,869,453 weapons in all—cost taxpayers $30,990,623.11.[4]

Springfield rifle-musket: This single-shot, muzzle-loading percussion cap weapon had a rifled bore and fired a .58-caliber minié ball. It was one of the standard long arms in the Union infantry arsenal and was the first weapon the Springfield Arsenal built from scratch as a rifle-musket. The earlier generation of rifle-muskets had been produced by rifling the barrel bores of existing .69-caliber Springfield smoothbore muskets. The first Model 1861 Springfields were delivered late in 1861 and by 1862 were on their way to becoming the weapon most commonly carried by Union infantry in the Eastern Theater.

With its thirty-eight-inch barrel, the Springfield was highly accurate, capable of hitting a target at a range of 500 yards. The later revision, Model 1863, was the last muzzle-loading weapon used by the US army. Approximately 1.5 million Springfields were produced during the war by the Springfield Armory and twenty private subcontractors. Even so, early in the war the Union did not have enough of the new weapons and so issued older versions, Model 1855 and Model 1842. Smoothbores were also dusted off and brought out of storage, including the obsolete but still serviceable Springfield Model 1812.

Enfield rifle-musket: Second only in quantity to the Springfield series of rifle-muskets used by the Union army was the British-made Enfield rifle-musket, which was imported by both sides. The standard long arm of the British Army from 1853 to 1867, its .577-caliber bore allowed the use of the .58-caliber ammunition common in both the North and the South. Combined, the USA and CSA imported more than 900,000 Enfields during 1861–65.

Lorenz rifle: This Austrian import was the third most widely used long arm in the Civil War. The Union imported 226,924 Lorenz rifles, and it is estimated that the Confederacy managed to smuggle through the blockade at least 100,000. Quite similar to the Enfield rifle-musket, the Lorenz had a .54-caliber bore, smaller than either the Enfield or the Springfield. Both sides often modified it by enlarging the bore to accommodate the same .58-caliber rounds used by the other two weapons. This process produced uneven results, however. While the Lorenz was often superbly made out of the factory, those that were bored "aftermarket" sometimes suffered problems of inconsistent caliber. Late in the war, a distressing number of Lorenz rifles were received directly from the factory in poor condition.

Revolvers: Union infantry officers used a variety of revolvers, most of them percussion arms loaded with paper- or linen-wrapped cartridges and separate percussion caps. The US armories did not produce revolvers; all of those used in the war were manufactured privately. The most popular revolvers were turned out by the Samuel Colt company, including the Colt Army Revolver, Model 1847; the Colt Model 1851 ("Navy"); the Colt Army Revolver, Model 1860 ("New Model Army"); and the Colt Navy Revolver, Model 1861 ("New Model Navy"). Some infantry officers preferred the navy models over the army models. Remington also produced a "New Model" Army Revolver, in 1863. All of the infantry revolvers were .44-caliber six-shot weapons.

CAVALRY WEAPONS

Although some Union cavalrymen carried standard infantry rifles, most were equipped with carbines. The shorter barrel of these weapons—twenty-two to twenty-five inches, compared with thirty-nine inches for the standard Enfield—made them less accurate, but far easier to manage on horseback. They were also, for the most part, single-shot breech-loading weapons rather than muzzleloaders. This made it much easier for a trooper to reload in the saddle. The carbines were produced by a few companies, but the most widely used in the Union cavalry were the Sharps (Models 1852, 1859, and 1863, all .52 caliber), the Burnside (five models produced from 1861 through 1864, all .54 caliber), and the Smith (weapons capable of using an innovative cartridge made of India rubber, .50 caliber).

Toward the end of 1863, Spencer introduced its seven-shot repeater, which met with much resistance from the leadership of the US cavalry. Objections included the temptation among troopers to waste ammunition and the potential unreliability of the relatively complex repeater mechanism. One forward-thinking Union cavalry colonel, John T. Wilder, personally purchased enough Spencer carbines at thirty-five dollars each to arm his entire mounted infantry brigade. When he then threatened to reimburse himself with deductions from his troopers' pay, the government, to avoid a scandal, ponied up for the weapons. His unit earned renown as the "Lightning Brigade" for the rapid rate of fire its troopers achieved.

As the Union cavalry took advantage of the latest innovations in long arms, it also continued to use the cavalry saber, the most archaic weapon in the army arsenal. The saber was regarded less as an offensive tactical weapon than as an instrument of terror and intimidation. Indeed, unlike sword-wielding Union troopers, Confederate cavalrymen rarely drew their sabers and used revolvers instead for close combat.

Union sabers included the Model 1840 Cavalry Saber, modeled (like many edged weapons of the period) on a French saber used by hussar (elite cavalry) regiments. A heavy saber designed for slashing rather than thrusting, its sturdy flat-backed blade made it highly fatiguing to use and earned it the sobriquet of "Old Wristbreaker." During the Civil War it was gradually replaced by the Model 1860 (also known as the Model 1862) Light Cavalry Saber. As its name suggests, the weapon was lighter, smaller, and easier to handle. By war's end 300,000 of the 1860 model had been manufactured, including some particularly elegant officer models by no less than Tiffany and Company.

Artillery

Civil War–era artillery was broadly divided into two categories, field (or "light") artillery and heavy artillery. The former were tactical weapons, highly transportable, and intended to move with a campaigning army. The latter were extremely heavy pieces that were not readily transportable. Cannon intended for coastal defense were essentially fixed in fortifications. Large siege cannon and mortars could be transported, but slowly and with great effort.

Within the category of field artillery were three subgroups:

1. *Mounted batteries* moved with advancing infantry. The artillery itself was pulled by horses while the artillerymen marched on foot—unless very quick movement was required, in which case they climbed aboard gun carriages and caissons.

2. *Horse batteries* were intended to accompany cavalry units. The artillery crews were all mounted, and the guns moved rapidly ahead.

3. *Batteries of position* consisted of the heaviest field guns—weapons that were transportable, but could not be repositioned or transported readily. They were used when an infantry unit was in position to invest the fortified positions of the enemy. The smaller mortars and howitzers, cannon capable of firing at high trajectories, were used in these batteries to attack the fortified positions of a well-entrenched enemy.

Of the combatant forces, only the Union had a full complement of all three categories of field artillery. Because of its deficiencies in manufacturing capacity, the Confederacy was perpetually at a serious disadvantage in the quantity and quality of this service arm.

As mentioned in chapter 11, the twelve-pounder Napoleon was the most extensively used field piece on both sides in the Civil War. The USA's Model 1857 was a smoothbore brass-barrel cannon that fired a twelve-pound, 4.2-inch projectile to an effective range of 1,619 yards. At the time, brass was the preferred metal for casting cannon because it had a much higher bursting threshold than iron. It was, however, not only a more expensive metal than iron, but also harder to cast, and for these reasons the foundries of the South, including the remarkable Tredegar Ironworks in Richmond, were mostly restricted to making cannon out of iron. This required Confederate artillerymen to reduce their powder loads, which, in turn, reduced the muzzle velocity, range, and kinetic impact of CSA artillery.

The advantage of smoothbores was the speed with which they could be loaded and reloaded as well as their durability. But, like all smoothbore firearms, the Napoleons were not terribly accurate. USA artillery engineers therefore created two major categories of rifled cannon for field use.

The Parrott gun (or Parrott Rifle) was made of cast iron that was reinforced with a wrought-iron band (wrought iron is stronger than cast iron) around its breech. This gave the gun a distinctive bloated-breech appearance. The cast-iron barrel was easier to rifle than the brass barrel—and it was much cheaper to manufacture. It was delivered mainly in 10-pound and 20-pound models. (Very large Parrott guns were also used as heavy artillery. Those used for sieges could fire a 300-pound projectile!) The Parrott Rifle was capable of greater accuracy and range than the Napoleons.

Superior to the Parrott Rifle was the Ordnance Rifle invented by John Griffen in 1855. This weapon was fashioned completely out of wrought iron and so had a far higher bursting threshold than the Parrott. Its range, however, was somewhat less than that of the Parrott Rifle—1,835 yards versus about 2,000 yards (both outdistancing the Napoleons)—but it was also 100 pounds lighter, which meant that it could be moved forward much faster.

Field artillery: The most commonly encountered Union heavy artillery were the seacoast cannon, of which the most numerous were the columbiads. These weapons had a distinctive bottle shape because their breeches were very heavily reinforced to resist catastrophic bursting. They were mostly mounted in fixed coastal fortifications and were, beginning during the War of 1812, the backbone of America's seaward-facing defense system. By the time of the Civil War, three models of columbiad were in use:

- Model 1844, in eight-inch and ten-inch versions

- Model 1858, also in eight-inch and ten-inch versions

- The Model 1861 was called a Rodman gun, after US ordnance engineer Thomas J. Rodman, who developed a method of casting large guns by cooling them from the inside out, which prevented the metal

This fifteen-inch Rodman gun was part of Battery Rodgers, an artillery emplacement defending a portion of Washington, DC. NATIONAL ARCHIVES AND RECORDS ADMINISTRATION

Union photographer David Knox photographed the massive "Dictator" siege mortar at Petersburg, Virginia, in October 1864. NATIONAL ARCHIVES AND RECORDS ADMINISTRATION

from becoming brittle and thereby greatly increased the weapon's resistance to bursting. The Rodman, cable of firing up to a fifteen-inch shell, had a range of 4,680 yards, compared to 1,800 yards for the Model 1844.

Of these weapons, the Confederacy managed to copy eight-inch and ten-inch versions of the Rodman, which were produced in limited quantities.

The "Dictator," a 17,000-pound seacoast mortar that fired a thirteen-inch projectile, was mounted on a special railroad flatcar so that it could be transported close to the front. It fired its 200-pound shells more than two miles (3,600 yards). Being mounted on a flatcar not only meant that the Dictator could be transported over distances, but also made it easy to change the gun's direction of fire, provided the piece was positioned on a curved section of track. This enabled the Dictator to pound a fortification from a variety of directions, something no fixed heavy gun could do.

Heavy Parrott guns (such as the 200-pounder "Swamp Angel," which laid siege to Charleston, South Carolina) and mortars brought to mid-nineteenth-century warfare a foretaste of the destructive power that would be unleashed in the two world wars of the twentieth century. These weapons were the very embodiment of war waged on an industrial scale.

Chapter 13

THE AFRICAN-AMERICAN CIVIL WAR

EFFECTIVE USE OF AFRICAN-AMERICAN TROOPS IN THE CONFEDERATE FORCES: ✶

EFFECTIVE USE OF AFRICAN-AMERICAN TROOPS IN THE UNION FORCES: ✶ ✶ ✶

Most of the 186,097 African Americans who served in the Union army were admitted following the implementation of the final Emancipation Proclamation on January 1, 1863.[1] As for the Confederacy, it is estimated that between 3,000 and 10,000 African Americans "shouldered arms" for the Confederate cause and an additional 20,000 to 50,000 provided war-related labor.[2]

The issue of *slavery* had divided the nation, South from North, politically and morally, from its very beginning. In 1861 slavery at long last divided it existentially and violently. Within the South and the North, the issue of *race* created further divisions. The force of the racial issue is evident in the fact that, despite a desperate need for military manpower that compelled both the Confederacy and the Union to conscript soldiers, popular resistance to enrolling black men into the armies was intense, strident, and bitter.

AFRICAN AMERICANS IN THE US ARMY BEFORE THE CIVIL WAR

Except for some forty years preceding the Civil War, during which federal policy barred their enlistment, African Americans served in the United States Army (USA) and its antecedents since colonial times. In the North, pre-Revolutionary militia companies enlisted free black troops, and even militia companies in the South enlisted slaves in times of emergency; however, after the Stono (South Carolina) slave revolt of 1739,[3] most Southern jurisdictions explicitly outlawed the arming of slaves under any circumstances.

Although African Americans served extensively in Northern militia companies during the American Revolution, they were initially barred from the Continental army—the first national army—by a resolution of the Continental Congress. This was in response to ongoing Southern fears concerning the arming of slaves or, indeed, any African Americans, free or slave. In contrast, the British army serving in North America had no such qualms and made it a practice to recruit local blacks.[4] In 1776, George Washington, a slave-owning Southerner himself, defied the congressional resolution and began to recruit African Americans into the Continental army of which he was general-in-chief. Such was Washington's stature that the Continental Congress made no challenge, and by the end of the war, approximately 5,000 African Americans had served in the Continental force. Many more served in the various state militias.

After the American Revolution both the USA and US Navy (USN) were almost totally demobilized—though soon reestablished. Black troops were not only recruited into both service branches, but were fully integrated with white soldiers and sailors. They served, in combat, in various wars and skirmishes against the Indians as well as in the War of 1812 (1812–15), but in 1820 they were once again legally banned from federal service. In that year President James Monroe's secretary of war, John C. Calhoun, a native of South Carolina, officially brought an end to African-American enlistments in the USA. Currently serving African Americans were not summarily discharged from the service, but at the expiration of their terms of enlistment, they were not permitted to reenlist, and so, quite quickly, the USA became an all-white force. This situation prevailed unchallenged until the Civil War.

THE STRUGGLE TO SERVE

From the beginning of the Civil War, Northern abolitionists and black activists such as Frederick Douglass called for recruitment of "colored troops" in the Union army. President Lincoln and Congress resisted, but some individual black men and a handful of Union generals acted on their own initiative.

Despite the ban on black troops, a few managed to enlist in all-white Union regiments very early in the war. Indeed, on April 18, 1861, Nicholas Biddle, an African American from Pennsylvania, was struck in the face by a stone hurled by a Southern sympathizer as his regiment, the Washington Artillerists, marched through Baltimore en route to garrison Washington, DC. He was therefore the first Union soldier to shed blood in the Civil War.[5] A few Union volunteer regiments offered a category of quasi-official enlistment for so-called independent men. Some African Americans used this as means of evading the ban. In this way, for instance, William Henry Johnson was accepted into the 2nd Connecticut Volunteer Infantry in a ninety-day enlistment. After its expiration he was enrolled in the 8th Connecticut Regiment and fought in the First Battle of Bull Run and other early engagements.[6]

Johnson wrote for an "emigration society" (an organization advocating African-American nationalism outside of the United States) newspaper and reported that "many" blacks had formed "defensive associations" to train themselves as soldiers in anticipation of a time when the United States would finally call upon them to fight. These organizations were also known as "drill companies" and were a means by which African Americans who wanted to fight but were refused admission into the USA could express their willingness. In some cases African Americans who could not secure enlistment accompanied white officers as their servants or orderlies.

In May 1862, Major General David Hunter, whose Union troops occupied the Sea Islands of Georgia and South Carolina, acted without federal authorization to raise a black regiment. In Kansas at this time, a militia commander, Major General James H. Lane, recruited two black regiments, consisting of fugitive slaves and free blacks. Congress and President Lincoln more or less backed into a policy of recruiting African Americans. Section 11 of the Confiscation Act of July 17, 1862, authorized the president "to employ persons of African descent as he may deem necessary and proper for the suppression of this rebellion." It additionally authorized him to "organize and use them in such manner as he may judge best for the public welfare."[7] On August 25 the War Department accordingly authorized Brigadier General Rufus Saxton, the military governor of the Sea Islands, to raise five black regiments. The authorization specified that the troops were to receive the "same pay and rations as are allowed by law to volunteers in the service."[8]

On September 27, 1862, Major General Benjamin F. Butler, commanding the Union forces occupying New Orleans, formed the 1st Regiment of the Louisiana Native Guards, composed of free blacks and ex-slaves. These men became the first African Americans officially mustered into the USA; they were followed in October and November by the 2nd and 3rd Regiments of the Louisiana Native Guards. Creating these regiments was in itself a bold action, but even bolder was Butler's appointment of seventy-five black captains and lieutenants in addition to

An African-American burial party collects bones of soldiers killed in battle at Cold Harbor, Virginia. LIBRARY OF CONGRESS

a single major. The appointments, however, were short lived. Major General Nathaniel Banks, who replaced Butler as commander in New Orleans in December 1862, rescinded the commissions, arguing that the "appointment of colored officers is detrimental to the service."[9]

THE EFFECT OF THE EMANCIPATION PROCLAMATION

In August 1861 President Abraham Lincoln prevailed on Congress to declare slaves in the rebellious states "contraband" property. As such, they were liable to military seizure by the federal government, which could then refuse to return them. In March 1862 Congress passed a law *forbidding* army officers from returning fugitive slaves. In July 1862 Congress passed legislation freeing slaves confiscated from owners "engaged in rebellion." In addition, a militia act authorized the president to use freed slaves in the army; the intention was to assign them to labor details, but, at the president's discretion, they could also be used in combat.

As Lincoln's government edged closer to outright emancipation early in the war and amid a string of Union military defeats, Secretary of State William H. Seward warned that any official emancipation proclamation would ring hollow with desperation unless Union forces could first claim a significant victory. It was not until the Battle of Antietam (September 17, 1862), a narrow and costly Union strategic victory, that Lincoln felt sufficiently confident to issue the preliminary Emancipation Proclamation of September 23, 1862. It did not free the slaves, but, rather, warned slave owners living in states "still in rebellion on January 1, 1863" that their slaves would at that time be declared "forever free." Only on that deadline day did Lincoln issue the final Emancipation Proclamation, which gave freedom only to those slaves living in areas of the Confederacy that were not under the control of the Union army. Slaves in the border states (slave states that had not seceded from the Union) were not emancipated. However, on the strength of the enactment of the final Emancipation Proclamation, President Lincoln personally called for four black regiments to be raised.

The Louisiana Native Guards set a precedent for equal pay and rations for black troops in such regiments. Ultimately, this precedent was honored in neither letter nor spirit; however, another precedent, set by General Banks, barring the appointment of black officers was overwhelmingly observed throughout the war. African-American soldiers were strictly segregated into "colored" regiments—166 of them by 1865[10]—commanded by white officers. Most histories record that, during the entire course of the Civil War, only thirty-two black officers were commissioned, thirteen of whom were chaplains and eight (possibly more) physicians.[11] In fact, at least 120 African Americans were commissioned

Two soldiers of the US Colored Troops pose here on picket duty at Dutch Gap, Virginia. LIBRARY OF CONGRESS

through the War Department's Bureau of Colored Troops (established on May 22, 1863), but more than seventy of these were so relentlessly harassed by their white superior officers that they quickly resigned.[12]

Typically, black troops were less well clothed and fed than white soldiers, and they were armed with weapons often deemed too old or obsolescent to be issued to white units. For most of the war, black troops were also paid at a lower rate than their white counterparts. African Americans were assigned to serve mainly as laborers; nevertheless, "colored" regiments fought in 41 major battles and 449 smaller engagements.[13] A total of seventeen African American soldiers received the Medal of Honor.

On the whole, treated shabbily by the country they served, African-American soldiers faced even greater combat danger than whites. On May 1, 1863, the Confederate Congress authorized President Davis to "put to death or . . . otherwise [punish]" any black soldiers captured as prisoners of war. The same fate was promised to white officers found in command of black troops. This law prompted President Lincoln to respond on July 30 with an executive order warning that "for every soldier of the United States killed in violation of the laws of war, a Rebel soldier shall be executed; and for every one enslaved by the enemy or sold into Slavery, a Rebel soldier shall be placed at hard labor on public works."[14]

THE UGLY IRONY OF NORTHERN RACISM

While an important white minority in the North not only advocated the abolition of slavery but also believed in the racial and legal equality of African Americans, the prevailing view throughout the "free" North was distinctly racist. In an 1863 letter to his family, Enoch T. Baker, a Union army sergeant, wrote: "Thair is a great controversy out hear about the nigger Question. . . . If they go to Sending them out hear to fight they will get Enough of it for it Will raise a rebellion in the army that all the abolitionists this side of Hell could not stop. The Southern People are rebels to government but they are White and God never intended a nigger to put White People down."[15] This expressed the sentiments, more or less, of many, perhaps most, Northern whites of the era.

The ugly force of racism exploded in the so-called draft riots that began in New York City on July 13, 1863 (see chapter 6). Not only were the city's draft office and an armory attacked and ransacked, but a mob turned its wrath on whatever African Americans were unfortunate enough to cross their path. Some were beaten. Some were strung up from lampposts. By the afternoon of July 13, rioters set fire to Manhattan's Colored Orphan Asylum, cheering as the blaze destroyed the building. Many of those rioting were recent immigrants, including refugees from the catastrophic poverty of Ireland. They objected to the draft as not only unfair and corrupt, but also as an attempt to force them to fight and die to free black slaves, who would, in turn, immigrate to the North and snatch their means of livelihood. A slave, after all, would work for the lowest of wages. Despite such violent protest against risking their white lives to liberate black men, many Northern whites felt as Sergeant Baker did and vehemently opposed allowing African Americans to fight—and die—to secure their own liberty.

THE 54TH MASSACHUSETTS

In March 1863, while Lincoln's government continued to wrestle with the issue of how to bring African Americans into the military, John A. Andrew, governor of Massachusetts, a hotbed of abolitionism before the war, authorized raising a "colored" regiment, which became the 54th Massachusetts. The unit instantly drew national attention as the first African-American regiment raised in the North; all previous black units had been recruited from Union-occupied Southern states. Since Secretary of War Edwin M. Stanton followed the precedent, set by Major General Nathaniel Banks, of assigning white officers to command black troops, Governor Andrew appointed as colonel the charismatic, earnest, and dashing twenty-five-year-old Robert Gould Shaw, son of a prominent Boston abolitionist family. In contrast to most regiments on either side, which were undersize, the 54th mustered on May 13, 1863, with its full authorized complement of 1,000 men—and then some—for a total strength of 1,100.

The regiment was sent off from Boston amid great fanfare. Shortly after it arrived in Union-occupied Beaufort, South Carolina, however, its personnel, who had been promised pay and allowances equal to those of white troops—subsistence and fourteen dollars a month—were notified that they would receive only seven dollars per month (ten dollars less three withheld for clothing—something white soldiers were not obliged to pay for). The state of Massachusetts offered to make up the difference, but the enlisted men, together with their white officers, boycotted their paydays and refused to accept pay on the army's terms. Pay discrimination was not rescinded until March 3, 1865.[16]

Nevertheless, the regiment continued to serve and quickly established a reputation within the army for gallantry. It was thrust into full national prominence by its performance on July 18, 1863, in a desperate assault on Fort (Battery) Wagner, a Confederate fort protecting the entrance to Charleston Harbor. Spearheading the two-brigade attack, the 54th took on the essentially suicidal assignment of making a frontal assault on the fort via a narrow beach passing below and in front of it. The assault was from low ground, there was little space in which to deploy and maneuver, and the column of men was obliged to pass parallel to the fort, flank

exposed, before turning to attack. Although the troops managed to breach a portion of the fort's wall in the initial assault, the brigades engaged were ultimately repulsed. Of the 600 men of the 54th who charged the fort, 272 were killed, wounded, or captured. Shaw was killed in the initial assault along with 29 of his men. Another 24 later died of their wounds, 149 others were wounded and recovered, 52 went missing and were never accounted for, and 15 were captured. The defenders of Fort Wagner sought to dishonor Shaw by throwing him into a common grave with the bodies of the black soldiers he had led. Hearing of this, Shaw's father spoke for his family: "We can imagine no holier place than in which he is."[17] Years later, William H. Carney, a sergeant in the 54th, received the Medal of Honor for seizing the flag from its fallen bearer and preventing its capture. Sixteen other black soldiers and four sailors would receive the medal during the war, but Carney's action is the earliest for which a black soldier was recognized.[18]

UNITED STATES COLORED TROOPS

On May 22, 1863, the War Department created the Bureau of Colored Troops to direct recruitment and to establish examining boards and screen applicants for officer commissions in what was officially called the United States Colored Troops (USCT). Although the USCT was officially a part of the USA, its personnel were universally and routinely subjected to discrimination, not only in matters of command and pay, but in disproportionate assignment to labor duties (some generals believed that labor was the only appropriate assignment for "colored" troops), issuance of obsolete or inferior weapons, and inadequate or virtually nonexistent medical care—far inferior even to the scandalously low level of care provided to white soldiers. Black regiments lost 29,000 dead to disease, nine times the number of those who died of combat wounds

A total of 186,097 African Americans served in the Union Army, making up about 10 percent of the force. Yet photographs of African-American troops are few. These are men of the 4th United States Colored Infantry.
LIBRARY OF CONGRESS

and a far higher proportion that the number of white troops who died in Union hospitals.[19]

The USCT was disbanded almost immediately after the war, in the fall of 1865, and in 1867 the regular army was authorized to raise two regiments of black cavalry and four of black infantry. Although the USCT no longer existed as a racially segregated part of the USA, all of the postbellum black regiments were segregated, commanded exclusively by white officers, and invariably distinguished by the word *Colored*: the 9th (Colored) and 10th (Colored) Cavalry and the 38th (Colored), 39th (Colored), 40th (Colored), and 41st (Colored) Infantry. All of these

regiments were overwhelmingly composed of veterans of the USCT.[20]

IN THE CONFEDERATE SERVICE

The Conscription Acts of 1862 and 1863 passed by the Confederate Congress did not allow for the recruitment of African-American combat troops, but did authorize measures to conscript both free and enslaved blacks for use in building fortifications, expanding river defenses, repairing rail networks, and even assisting in the manufacture of arms. Additionally, such legislation as the Regimental Cooks Bills (1862 and 1863) and the Negro Musicians Bill (1863) authorized free and enslaved black men to be attached to regiments and assigned to laboring and support roles in order to free up white troops for combat. Some Confederate states enlisted or drafted blacks as well as whites into home guards and militia units that were entirely separate from the CSA. Intended to provide for the defense of the state, these arrangements led to frequent friction between some states and the Confederate central government.[21]

Throughout most of the war, the Richmond government was unwilling to go beyond the military employment of African Americans in any role other than as servants, laborers, and musicians. Until nearly the very end of the conflict, the Confederate Congress refused even to discuss authorizing frontline or combat service. Perhaps surprisingly, however, slaves and free blacks did offer their services as soldiers, and some commanders took them up on their offers. General Nathan Bedford Forrest (who would become infamous during the war for his alleged role in the Fort Pillow Massacre of April 12, 1864, which targeted Union "colored" troops for slaughter, and, after the war, for his early involvement in the founding of the Ku Klux Klan) accepted blacks into Harvey's Scouts. The 3rd Georgia Infantry Regiment included black soldiers, and a number of free New Orleans black men offered their services to the Confederate cause. Louisiana governors Thomas O. Moore

(1861) and Henry W. Allen (1864) issued proclamations authorizing the use of African Americans as soldiers, and, at the very outbreak of the war, South Carolina governor Francis Pickens granted a request from free black citizens' groups in Columbia and Charleston to allow them "to render service where we can be most useful." Pickens assigned one group of these volunteers to assist in the artillery barrage against Fort Sumter (April 12–14, 1861).

In January 1864, Major General Patrick Cleburne, who commanded a division in the Army of Tennessee, circulated a document urgently calling for the enlistment of slaves. Jefferson Davis rejected this proposal, but, late in 1864, his secretary of war, Judah P. Benjamin, made a similar proposal, which was supported in January 1865 by no less a figure than Robert E. Lee, who wrote, "We must decide whether slavery shall be extinguished by our enemies and the slave used against us, or use them ourselves at the risk of the effects which may be produced upon our social institutions."[22] A tipping point had been reached, and on March 13, 1865, the Confederate Congress authorized recruitment of "Negro Soldiers," the slaves among them to be rewarded by a vaguely defined form of emancipation—*after* the Union had been defeated. Although several African-American companies were mustered in Richmond, there is no record of any of these participating in combat.

Chapter 14

MEDICS SOUTH, MEDICS NORTH

CONFEDERATE MILITARY MEDICINE: ✭

UNION MILITARY MEDICINE: ✭ ✭

Mid-nineteenth-century medical science was barely on the verge of revolutionary discoveries concerning the causes of disease and posttraumatic infection. The French chemist and microbiologist Louis Pasteur was beginning to explore the role of microorganisms in disease processes, and the British physician Joseph Lister was experimenting with antisepsis during this period. The work of both men, however, was slow to gain acceptance in both the European and American medical communities. Indeed, one of the physicians who served as US Army surgeon general during the Civil War, William A. Hammond, observed in later years that "the Civil War was fought at the end of the medical Middle Ages."[1] Where general civilian medical practice was concerned, Hammond's assessment was eloquent and accurate. As for the specific practice of military medicine, it was probably too generous.

In the years leading up to the Civil War, the military devoted little attention to medicine, and the best and brightest physicians did not seek military careers. As a result, military medicine lagged behind even the most conservative American civilian practitioners. The work of Pasteur, Lister, and others received some academic attention, but little notice from most physicians. Whereas the technology of inflicting devastating wounds on a mass scale was greatly advanced by the ongoing Industrial Revolution, medical science remained mired in an earlier time. For this reason, a soldier's chances of dying from his wounds were eight times greater

during the Civil War than they would be some fifty years later, in World War I, when the technology of destruction was even more terrible but medicine had advanced. Moreover, although the mass production of weapons created casualties on an unprecedented scale during the Civil War, disease killed twice as many soldiers as combat. A soldier's odds of succumbing to disease while in the military service in 1861–65 were ten times what they would be during 1914–18—even though the close of World War I saw the onset of a great global influenza pandemic.[2]

MEDICAL LEADERSHIP AND PERSONNEL

At the outbreak of the war, the Medical Department of the US Army (USA) was presided over by its superannuated surgeon general, Colonel Thomas Lawson, who had held his position as a sinecure for more than forty years. Year after year, his highest priority and greatest source of pride was conducting the USA's medical operations without ever spending all of the budget allotted it. Inert and incompetent, Lawson died in May 1861, which might have been a boon for Union forces were it not for the fact that his successor, Dr. Clement A. Finley, was even worse. Finley confronted the Medical Department's first challenge, examining recruits for basic fitness, by prescribing only the most cursory of examinations. Indeed, many recruits were not accorded even that much. In consequence, a large number of young men were inducted only to be invalided out of the service within weeks.

Thanks to the enlightened activism of a civilian relief organization, the US Sanitary Commission (see "Civilian Relief Organizations" in this chapter), Finley was replaced by Dr. William

In a carefully staged photograph, members of a Union Zouave ambulance crew collect "wounded" for transportation.
LIBRARY OF CONGRESS

Alexander Hammond on April 25, 1862. He led vigorous reforms, instituted a medical inspection system, expanded military hospital facilities, built government pharmaceutical laboratories to produce much-needed medicines and drugs, and promoted the creation of an ambulance service—whose personnel were the precursors of the modern military medic. His change leadership brought him into conflict with the Union military establishment—all the way up to Secretary of War Edwin M. Stanton—which led to his court-martial and replacement as surgeon general by Dr. Joseph K. Barnes in August 1864. If Stanton and others expected Barnes to be quietly complacent, they were mistaken. Barnes picked up where Hammond had left off, continuing his reforms and stepping outside of the military to recruit civilian doctors to provide additional care for the sick and wounded.

At the outbreak of the war, the Medical Department surgeon general headed a staff of thirty surgeons and eighty-three assistant surgeons. (Of this number, three surgeons and twenty-one assistant surgeons resigned to join the Confederate service.) At the height of the war, this modest cadre grew to a force of approximately 12,000 physicians, apportioned into seven classifications:

1. Regular USA surgeons and assistant surgeons who passed the required USA qualifying examinations and served in the regular army

2. Surgeons and assistant surgeons who were commissioned in the United States Volunteers (USV)

3. Regimental surgeons and assistant surgeons (in theory, commissioned by the governor

of the state that raised the regiment, they were more usually commissioned by the regiment's commanding colonel)

4. "Contract" surgeons, officially called "acting assistant surgeons," commissioned in neither the regular nor volunteer armies; they served for the most part in general hospitals rather than in the field

5. Medical officers of the Veteran Reserve Corps; created on April 28, 1863, as the Invalid Corps and later renamed the Veteran Reserve Corps, this unit was intended to allow soldiers rendered by wounds or illness unfit for full service to be of use in garrison and light duty functions

6. Acting staff surgeons, contract surgeons who served many of the functions of senior surgeons, but who did not hold commissions

7. Surgeons and assistant surgeons for the US Colored Troops

On both sides surgeons were the best-educated and most experienced medical personnel available. They provided the most advanced treatment (such as it was) and also handled administrative tasks. Assistant surgeons were less experienced—often new to the practice of medicine. The acting assistant surgeons, civilians contracted by both sides, were used during periods of heavy casualties. These men were sometimes too old for regular service or lacked the educational credentials to receive regular commissions.

In both the USA and CSA, every regiment was supposed to have one surgeon and one or two assistant surgeons attached to it. As the war continued, each army was supposed to have medical directors on the level of brigade, division, corps, and army.[3] Often, this was not the case in practice, especially in the understaffed CSA.

As with much else in the Civil War, the Confederacy created its Medical Department from scratch, beginning with the three surgeons and twenty-one assistant surgeons who resigned from the USA to offer their services to the South. The organization of the Confederate department imitated that of the USA's Medical Department and was initially led by Dr. David C. DeLeon, who was appointed in May 1861. In June he was replaced, briefly, by Dr. Charles Smith, who stepped down after just two weeks on the job and was succeeded in July by Dr. Samuel Preston Moore. Moore commanded the Confederate States Army Medical Department for the rest of the war, and it was he who built the service into a body of 3,200 surgeons and assistant surgeons. He recruited physicians, he examined them, and he did his best to develop autonomous Southern sources of medicines and drugs. Moore built, from scratch, a modest system of military medical evacuations and hospitals. He personally recruited nurses and instructed them as well as physicians in the latest available methods of treating wounds.

The CSA Medical Department differed significantly from its Union counterpart in that it did not directly commission military surgeons. Instead, it recruited them from wherever they were in the CSA. This meant that many Confederate surgeons were not officers but enlisted men who, once chosen, were promoted from the ranks.

FEMALE NURSES

Both the Union and Confederate armies had male nurses (usually called hospital stewards), who were supplemented by male civilian volunteer nurses (such as the poet Walt Whitman, who served the Union in this role). In both the North and the South, women began volunteering to nurse wounded troops, and between 3,000 and 8,000 may have served, most of them with Union forces. They often met with moral objections, mostly from members of a civilian public

Photographer James F. Gibson recorded these Union wounded gathered in a "field hospital" after the Battle of Savage's Station, an inconclusive engagement fought in Henrico County, Virginia, on June 29, 1862. LIBRARY OF CONGRESS

that believed the practice of medicine in any capacity was the exclusive sphere of men and that, in any case, the horrors of war were beyond a woman's capacity to bear.

Dorothea Lynde Dix, who had already become well known before the war as a tireless crusader for the humane treatment of prison inmates and the mentally ill, volunteered to lead the brand-new nursing corps of the US Army and was duly appointed superintendent of female nurses. In an era when nursing by women was often thought of as a form of prostitution, Dix set about recruiting women of impeccable moral character, strength of mind, and strength of will. Stern and overbearing, Dix ruled the nursing corps with an iron hand, earning the

sobriquet "Dragon Dix." Her nurses, however, were intensely loyal to her and doubtless saved many lives and relieved much suffering.

Another woman, Clara Barton, who had been a schoolteacher in Massachusetts and New Jersey and then a clerk in the US Patent Office in Washington, DC, applied for official military service as a nurse. Rejected, she responded by almost single-handedly organizing a private civilian agency to obtain and distribute supplies for wounded soldiers. She personally visited the battlefields and field hospitals, carrying supplies in a wagon she drove herself. Her kindly demeanor, the opposite of Dix's steely sternness, won her the soldiers' grateful affection, who dubbed her the "Angel of the Battlefield."

If female nurses were resisted and finally accepted only grudgingly by the military medical establishment—both in the North and the South—female physicians were all but unheard of. Mary Edwards Walker, born in Oswego, New York, on November 26, 1832, bucked the male-dominated medical establishment first by winning admission to and then succeeding in graduating from Syracuse Medical College. During the prewar 1840s and 1850s, she struggled to survive in her Cincinnati, Ohio, practice and, at the outbreak of the war, volunteered her medical services to the Union army. Rejected as a physician, she was able to find some work as a nurse, but it was not until 1863 that the Army of the Cumberland at last hired her as a "Contract Acting Assistant Surgeon (civilian)" for six months. Remarkably, in October 1864, the 52nd Ohio Infantry appointed her a regimental assistant surgeon. During her tour of duty, she saw service not only as a physician, but also as a spy. Known for looking after wounded on both sides, including civilians, Walker was captured by Confederate troops when she stopped to treat a wounded rebel. She spent four months in a Southern prison camp.

Walker became the first woman to be awarded the Medal of Honor. In 1919, however, the Board of Medals revoked the award because Walker was not a sworn member of the armed forces. Six days before she died, the eighty-seven-year-old Walker refused to relinquish the medal. It was officially restored to her by President Jimmy Carter in 1977.

HOSPITALS AND AMBULANCE CORPS

In mid-nineteenth-century America, the sick and the injured were generally treated at home. In consequence, the nation had relatively few hospitals and almost none outside of the cities. Both the USA and CSA recognized that the situation of prolonged warfare required the establishment of dedicated military hospitals. They were of four major types:

1. **Field hospitals** were established by regiments and staffed by the regimental surgeon with one or two assistant surgeons, a hospital steward, and soldiers assigned as nurses. The facility might be housed in tents or whatever appropriate building could be found—a house, an inn, or another public facility. Field hospitals were temporary and were intended to treat sick or wounded troops without removing them from the front. During battles, field hospitals were located as close to the fighting as possible but beyond artillery range. Since combat is fluid, however, field hospitals often came under fire and had to relocate quickly.

2. **General hospitals** were used to treat troops whose condition could not be satisfactorily addressed in a field hospital. Established in cities and larger towns well behind the frontlines, general hospitals were not restricted to a particular army, corps, or regiment, but were open to all army personnel. In the North, Washington, DC, and Philadelphia were the sites of the largest hospitals. In the South, the central hospital was at Richmond, Virginia. Other Confederate general hospitals were in Nashville, Tennessee; Atlanta, Georgia; and Lynchburg, Virginia. Smaller facilities were found in numerous other towns in the North and the South. The first military general hospitals occupied such existing structures as hotels, churches, schools, and courthouses. Later, purpose-built military hospitals were constructed.

   Typically, each general hospital was staffed by a chief surgeon and a variable number of surgeons, assistant surgeons, and nurses. As their name implied, general hospitals treated all wounds and sicknesses.

3. **Wayside hospitals** were established, often by civilian relief organizations, in the North and, even more numerously, in the South,

A ward in Carver General Hospital, Washington, DC. NATIONAL ARCHIVES AND RECORDS ADMINISTRATION

mainly to provide food and rest for troops in transit to or from the front. Accordingly, they were located at depots along rail lines or at transfer points between trains and boats.

On May 1, 1863, the Confederate Congress passed a law directing the surgeon general to establish "way hospitals." Seventeen were eventually located in Virginia and North Carolina, in addition to others in Georgia, South Carolina, Alabama, and Mississippi. Northern wayside hospitals were established and run by members of the US Sanitary Commission or the US Christian Commission; while they provided rudimentary medical treatment, they were primarily feeding stations.[4]

4. **Receiving and distributing hospitals** were also known (in the North) as depot hospitals or clearing hospitals. Located in large cities or at transportation transfer points, they functioned as what would today be called triage centers to evaluate patients and determine where they should be sent for extended treatment. Turnaround was intended to be rapid. After receiving food, water, medication, and wound attention, patients were triaged and sent on their way.

The clearing hospital at City Point, Virginia, a major depot for the Army of the Potomac, was the largest, with 8,000 beds. More than 65,000 soldiers passed through the Union's three Virginia-based clearing hospitals during the summer of 1864.[5]

There were also three types of specialized hospitals:

1. **Officers' hospitals:** Although officers were often given general hospital accommodations separate from enlisted soldiers, the USA established separate officers' hospitals in Philadelphia and Memphis, Tennessee (when it came under Union control). The CSA operated two officers' hospitals in Richmond. In March 1864 the USA established officers' hospitals for every military department, for a total of ten. Union officers paid a fee of one dollar per day for hospitalization—in addition to a thirty-cent "servant's fee," if the officer had a servant.[6]

2. **Pest (smallpox) hospitals:** Both the CSA and USA established special hospitals to isolate highly contagious patients with so-called eruptive diseases, especially smallpox and measles. Such facilities ranged from separate tents to commandeered or purpose-built permanent structures. The USA built a 750-bed smallpox hospital in Memphis in 1864, and the CSA built Howard's Grove in what had been a popular picnic spot outside of Richmond, Virginia.[7]

3. **Hospital ships:** Used by both sides, these were vessels of various sizes either pressed into emergency service, thoroughly modified as genuine floating hospitals, or used as waterborne ambulances to transport the sick and wounded from field hospitals to general hospitals. The CSA operated the very first hospital ship used in the Civil War, at Charleston, South Carolina. It was a barge whose cabin held eight to ten beds. Staffed by a single physician, it was moored to a floating battery during the attack on Fort Sumter in April 1861. The CSA subsequently operated hospital ships on the western rivers, as did the USA. On April 1, 1862, the USA purchased the *D. A. January*, a side-wheel steamer, which was immediately used to treat and transport those wounded at the Battle of Shiloh (April 6–7, 1862). During its first three months of service, the *D. A. January* carried 3,000 patients, and in September 1862 it was completely remodeled as a hospital ship. By war's end it had carried a total of 23,738 patients.[8]

FEDERAL AMBULANCE CORPS

The medical director of the Army of the Potomac, Dr. Jonathan W. Letterman, established an Ambulance Corps, which subsequently served as a prototype for all Union armies. Officers and men assigned to the Ambulance Corps were trained for medical duty and provided life-saving first aid in the field in addition to transporting wounded men in ambulances specifically dedicated to ambulance service. The Ambulance Corps proved so successful that, on March 11, 1864, Congress passed the Ambulance Corps Act, appropriating funds for Letterman's system to be adopted universally throughout the USA.

WOUNDS AND THEIR TREATMENT

Most combat wounds were gunshot wounds, but all wounds were treated essentially in the same way. The patient was examined to determine the nature and extent of his injuries. Minor wounds were given first aid and, if needed, the patient was sent to the field hospital. In the case of more serious gunshot wounds, the surgeon first looked for an exit wound. If there was none, he probed for the bullet, usually with his finger and then with a ceramic-tipped Nélaton probe. Once the bullet was located, the surgeon attempted to remove it. If he judged that it could not be removed, it remained in place—often for the rest of the soldier's life.

Wounds were debrided (cleaned of visible dirt, clothing scraps, grass, bone fragments, and so on). Many surgeons followed the precepts of Joseph Lister to the extent of using bromine or another antiseptic to clean the wound; however, sterilization of instruments and even basic hand washing were not practiced. It was common for surgeons to move from patient to patient without washing and with the same set of instruments. Wounds and incisions were sewn with silk or horsehair, treated with an ointment made of beeswax, and usually bandaged (some serious wounds were left open). Virtually all wounds became infected, and some were soon infested with flies and their maggots. Wounds to the extremities were, more often than not, treated by amputation. Since no effective anesthetics were available, speed was the primary skill looked for in a surgeon, especially in the case of amputation.

Based on 29,980 cases treated by USA surgeons, these are the available statistics on amputation:[9]

Extremity	Number of Cases/ Deaths	Percentage of Deaths
Fingers	7,902/198	2.5%
Forearms	1,761/245	13.9%
Upper Arms	5,540/1,273	23.0%
Toes	1,519/81	5.3%
Shins	5,523/1,790	32.4%
Thighs	6,369/3,411	53.6%
Knee Joints	195/111	56.9%
Hip Joints	66/55	83.3%
Ankle Joints	161/119	73.9%

DISEASES AND THEIR TREATMENT

Infectious disease was a leading cause of death in the mid-nineteenth century, and the conditions in which Civil War soldiers lived and fought (poor sanitation, inadequate nutrition, and prolonged exposure to the elements) exacerbated both the incidence and severity of diseases. The following statistics are for white USA troops from 1861 to 1866:[10]

Disease	Number of Cases	Number of Deaths
Typhoid Fever	75,368	27,056
Typhus Fever	2,501	850
Diarrhea (acute and chronic)	1,325,714	30,481
Dysentery (acute and chronic)	259,482	7,313
Yellow Fever	49,871	4,059
Erysipelas	23,276	1,860
Smallpox and Varioloid	12,236	4,717
Measles	67,763	4,246
Scarlet Fever	578	70
Diphtheria	7,277	716
Mumps	48,128	72
Epidemic Catarrh	134,397	33
Syphilis	73,382	123
Gonorrhea	95,833	6
Scurvy	30,714	383
Rheumatism (acute and chronic)	254,738	475
Itch	32,080	0
Insanity	2,410	80
Inflammation of Brain	1,232	1,269[sic]
Inflammation of Membranes of Brain	805	741
Inflammation of Spinal Cord	1,479	235
Nostalgia	5,213	58
Neuralgia	58,774	18

Ophthalmia	8,904	1
Inflammation of Conjuctiva	65,739	1
Asthma	9,365	75
Bronchitis (acute and chronic)	195,627	1,179
Inflammation of Lungs	61,202	14,738
Cholera morbus	25,215	275
Dyspepsia	37,514	31
Inflammation of Liver (acute and chronic)	11,120	243
Jaundice	71,691	341
Inflammation of Kidneys	9,464	154

Of the 186,097 African Americans who served in the Union army, mostly in the US Colored Troops (USCT), more than 29,000 died from disease, nine times the number of African American troops killed in combat and two and a half times the number of white soldiers who succumbed to disease.[11] Medical care for African-American soldiers was markedly inferior to that provided to white troops. They were treated in segregated facilities, white medical personnel were often reluctant to offer them care, and of the eight African American surgeons who served in the Union army, only three were assigned to the USCT. The following statistics were compiled for sickness and mortality among USCT troops from 1864 to 1866:[12]

Disease	Number of Cases	Number of Deaths
Typhoid Fever	4,094	2,280
Typhus Fever	123	108
Diarrhea (acute and chronic)	125,899	4,646
Dysentery (acute and chronic)	28,040	2,118
Yellow Fever	190	27
Erysipelas	1,536	247

Smallpox and Varioloid	6,716	2,341
Measles	8,555	931
Scarlet Fever	118	2
Diphtheria	776	61
Mumps	12,186	12
Epidemic Catarrh	9,869	5
Syphilis	6,207	28
Gonorrhea	7,060	1
Scurvy	16,217	388
Rheumatism (acute and chronic)	32,125	235
Itch	3,156	0
Insanity	193	10
Inflammation of Brain	249	262 [sic]
Inflammation of Membranes of Brain	166	108
Inflammation of Spinal Cord	68	45
Nostalgia	334	16
Neuralgia	6,018	5
Ophthalmia	–	–
Inflammation of Conjuctiva	5,153	–
Asthma	762	18
Bronchitis (acute and chronic)	25,381	404
Inflammation of Lungs	16,133	5,233
Cholera morbus	1,151	30
Dyspepsia	2,607	5
Inflammation of Liver (acute and chronic)	1,949	135
Jaundice	15,545	73
Inflammation of Kidneys	778	24

CIVILIAN RELIEF ORGANIZATIONS

On both sides, organizations of civic-minded and charitable civilians, mostly women, supplemented the almost always inadequate efforts of the two governments to provide medical care. The relief organizations chiefly provided food, medical supplies, and nursing assistance.

The principal Confederate organizations were:[13]

- **Association for the Relief of Maimed Soldiers:** The only relief organization that existed in all states of the Confederacy, the association furnished prosthetics to CSA and CSN amputees.

- **Georgia Relief and Hospital Association:** This was typical of organizations created in specific states, including Alabama, Louisiana, and South Carolina in addition to Georgia. The organization furnished medicines, bandages, and other supplies to military hospitals and even subsidized the services of civilian physicians. The Georgia organization provided clothing to wounded soldiers, fully equipped four CSA hospitals in Richmond, and established several wayside hospitals.

- **Richmond Ambulance Committee:** Staffed by men exempt from military duty, this organization was dedicated to supporting, feeding, and transporting wounded Confederate soldiers from the frontlines to hospitals in the rear.

- **Women's Relief Organizations:** In contrast to the North, where the United States Sanitary Commission aggregated many local efforts, the Confederacy maintained hundreds of much smaller women's societies. These organizations collected clothing, food, and medical supplies; established wayside hospitals; and provided volunteer female nursing services.

The principal Union organizations were:[14]

- **The United States Sanitary Commission:** Coordinated the efforts of thousands of local groups on a national scale. The commission was established very early in the war, in June 1861, and had the official sanction and cooperation of the federal government. With the government's blessing it inspected Union camps and hospitals for the purpose of improving sanitary conditions. The commission collected clothing, food, medicines, and medical supplies and subsidized nursing care for the sick and wounded. The commission became virtually integral with the USA Medical Department.

  Initially financed by wealthy Northerners, the commission later staged "Sanitary Fairs," elaborate public fund-raising events that succeeded in collecting some $20 million, all of which was contributed to the federal war effort.

- **United States Christian Commission:** Founded in 1861 by the Young Men's Christian Association (YMCA) of New York, this group raised approximately $6 million for the war effort and financed food and coffee wagons, which traveled to the front.

- **Western Sanitary Commission:** Established in St. Louis in 1861 under the direction of Major General John C. Frémont, the Western Sanitary Commission set up hospital kitchens, furnished medical supplies, and outfitted the *City of Louisiana* as a hospital ship.

Chapter 15

POWs South, POWs North

CONFEDERATE TREATMENT OF POWS: *

UNION TREATMENT OF POWS: *

Both sides in the broken United States entered the Civil War in every way wholly unprepared for a long contest involving hundreds of thousands of troops. Low on the list of priorities in the South as well as the North was the issue of prisoners of war: what to do with them, how to care for them, and where to house them. The United States had never fought a war in which significant numbers of prisoners had been taken. As it turned out, between 1861 and 1865, 462,634 Confederate soldiers would be captured,

including those who surrendered at war's end. Of this total, 247,769 were paroled in the field and never went to a POW camp. Confederates captured 211,411 Union troops, of whom 16,668 were paroled without going to prison camps. Together, South and North, an estimated total of 409,608 Americans spent time in one or more of the 150 military prisons established on American soil. Of this number, 30,218 Union soldiers died in Confederate POW camps, and 25,976 Confederate troops died in Union captivity. This makes for an overall 15.5 percent mortality rate in Confederate prison facilities and a 12 percent rate in Northern camps and prisons. It is sobering to consider that the more than 56,000 who

Confederate prisoners at Belle Plain Landing, Virginia, captured on May 12, 1864. Library of Congress

died as POWs in the four-year Civil War is very nearly the same fatality count as Americans who were killed in action during the decade-long Vietnam War.[1]

PAROLE AND CARTEL

The American Civil War erupted in an era of what Europeans liked to think of as "civilized warfare." The armies of the Western nations made credible shows of treating prisoners of war humanely. American officers, South and North, were inclined to emulate this example and, early in the war, followed the European convention of parole and exchange of prisoners. The concept of parole is rooted in the Old French *parole*, meaning "word" in the sense of making a formal promise or giving one's word. A POW was paroled when he gave his word not to take up arms against the side that had captured him until such time as he was formally exchanged for an enemy captive of equal rank. Ideally, a POW was held very briefly, perhaps for a week or ten days, and then sent home to await formal notice of exchange. In some cases paroled prisoners were released to encampments located near their own commands, there to await official word of their exchange. In the meantime, they were on their honor not to fight.

Early in the war, the convention of parole and exchange was agreed to ad hoc by commanders of opposing forces in the field. When US Army major general David E. Twiggs, commanding the Department of Texas, surrendered his entire command to Confederate-aligned state forces in February 1861, all of his USA troops were paroled on February 18. On May 10 some 700 Confederate-aligned Missouri militiamen were captured by Union forces in St. Louis and duly paroled. The first formal exchange agreement came on August 30, 1861, between Union colonel W. H. L. Wallace (headquartered at Bird's Point, Missouri) and Confederate general

Gideon Pillow (headquartered at Columbus, Kentucky). On December 11, 1861, Congress passed resolutions authorizing an exchange agreement with the Confederacy, but President Abraham Lincoln resisted concluding anything resembling an international treaty with the Confederacy, arguing that to do so would be a per se recognition of its sovereignty and right to exist.

On February 16, 1862, Confederate general Benjamin Huger and Union general John Wool began discussing formal prisoner parole and exchange. Brigadier General Howell Cobb soon took Huger's place for the next meeting with Wool, on February 23. An agreement was hammered out, but on February 26 Union secretary of war Edwin Stanton rejected the agreement, and negotiations broke down. At last, on July 12, 1862, President Lincoln authorized Union major general John Dix to negotiate with Confederate major general Daniel Harvey Hill a prisoner exchange "cartel" for the exchange, parole, and humane treatment of prisoners. The resulting document, the Dix-Hill Cartel, signed on July 22, 1862, was concluded not between one government and another, but between the opposing armies. This way, Lincoln was not obliged to recognize the Confederacy as a sovereign foreign power. The aim of the cartel was to establish a system whereby prisoners would be both paroled and exchanged within ten days of capture according to a table that precisely spelled out the exchange "rates":

- Soldiers of equivalent ranks were to be exchanged one for one.

- Corporals and sergeants were worth two privates.

- Lieutenants were worth four privates.

- A captain was worth six privates.

- A major was worth eight privates.

- A lieutenant-colonel was worth ten privates.

- A colonel was worth fifteen privates.

- A brigadier general was worth twenty privates.

- A major general was worth forty privates.

- A commanding general was worth sixty privates.

Under the direction of appointed "agents of exchange"—Judge Robert Ould for the Confederacy and Colonel William H. Ludlow for the Union—the Dix-Hill Cartel was a noble undertaking. Indeed, by August 1862 it had substantially reduced the number of prisoners held in makeshift camps and commandeered civilian jails, but it also increasingly revealed itself to be impractical, especially as the volume of prisoners each side took grew. Despite the efforts of the two agents of exchange, hundreds and then thousands of prisoners accumulated in detention camps, all awaiting exchange. In an effort to expedite the process, the temporary detention requirement was largely dropped, and, as was the case in earlier exchanges, prisoners were paroled, set free after giving their word not to fight until officially exchanged. Under Dix-Hill they were not sent home, however, but, rather, were entrusted to the care of their units.

New complications soon surfaced. When it became clear that the prospect of being sent home encouraged a good many weary and frightened men to allow themselves to be captured in battle, both the North and the South established additional parolee detention camps, where those awaiting release on parole were miserably housed until appropriate exchanges could be concluded. Soldiers assigned to detention camps often suffered from shortages of food and clothing as well as poor sanitation. They often became pawns of the two governments, with high-value prisoners (such as field-grade officers) held until highly favorable exchanges were negotiated.

BREAKDOWN OF THE CARTEL

The final breakdown in the parole and exchange cartel began in July 1863, following Ulysses S. Grant's victory in the long Vicksburg Campaign. The Union took more than 31,000 Confederate POWs. Faced with the daunting prospect of transporting and guarding them all, Grant decided instead to parole them per the cartel. This done, he moved on to the Chattanooga Campaign (September 21–November 25, 1863). As at Vicksburg, his forces took a good many prisoners—and what alarmed Grant was that so many of these prisoners were the very men he had paroled at Vicksburg.

This fact stuck in Grant's craw. Following his successes at Vicksburg and Chattanooga, he was promoted to lieutenant general and, in March 1864, assigned to command the Union armies under the direct supervision of President Lincoln. The very next month, on April 17, reasoning that the parole of POWs had become the chief means by which the CSA was making up its personnel losses, General Grant effectively canceled the Dix-Hill Cartel by calling a halt to all prisoner exchanges.

Publicly, Grant and Lincoln justified the cancellation of exchange by citing Confederate violations of parole and the refusal of the Confederacy to exchange black POWs and the white officers commanding black regiments. Privately, both Grant and Lincoln had come to understand that prisoner exchange was far more strategically beneficial to a Confederacy that was increasingly starved for manpower than it was to the Union, with its larger population and still-untapped reserves of recruits and conscripts. It was a cruel calculus. The North could afford to lose soldiers to captivity; the South could not. Additionally, Grant reasoned that the presence of Union prisoners in Southern POW camps was a tremendous burden to an overstrained Confederate economy, which could not even clothe, supply, and feed its own army properly.

The victims in this strategic equation were, of course, the POWs. Those consigned to Confederate POW camps found themselves, for the most part, lodged in overcrowded, filthy, and unhealthy conditions. Starvation rations and rampant disease were the norm. This was due in large measure to the poverty of the Confederacy. In the North, however, conditions for POWs were not much better. While it is true that Northern authorities were simply unwilling to expend scarce (but available) assets on the POW camps, it is also the case that harsh and even inhumane treatment of prisoners was motivated in some considerable measure by a desire for vengeance and punishment.

CONFEDERATE PRISONS AND PRISON CAMPS

The principal Confederate prisons included the following.[2]

ALABAMA

CAHAWBA PRISON

Active from 1864 to 1865, the prison was housed in an old cotton warehouse ten miles south of Selma. Intended as a temporary facility, it was only partly roofed. Bunks were supplied for 500 POWs, but by October 1864 there were more than 2,000 men incarcerated here.

ARKANSAS

MILITARY PRISON, LITTLE ROCK

This facility began operation in 1863 and continued throughout the war. It was notorious for rampant smallpox.

GEORGIA

ANDERSONVILLE (OFFICIALLY CAMP SUMTER)

Set in the sweltering heart of Georgia, on twenty-six acres (at its largest) northeast of Americus, the Andersonville stockade was built

to accommodate 10,000 POWs. Tents provided the only shelter, medical care was nonexistent, food was next to nil, and water came from Stockade Creek, which also served as the prison latrine and sewer. "The stench polluted and pervaded the whole atmosphere of the prison," attested Union captive Warren Lee Goss. "When the prisoner was fortunate enough to get a breath of air outside the prison, it seemed like a new development of creation, so different was it from the poisonous vapors inhaled from this cesspool with which the prison air was reeking. During the day the sun drank up the most noxious of these vapors, but in the night the terrible miasma and stench pervaded the atmosphere almost to suffocation."[3] Infection was endemic and there was a very high death rate from disease.

At the height of its operations, prisoners (exclusively enlisted men) poured in at the rate of 400 a day. By August 1864 Andersonville harbored 33,000 POWs. Some 12,912 graves are in the Andersonville National Cemetery.

The camp was first run by Brigadier General John Henry Winder, provost marshal general of the Confederate army. After Winder was transferred to Richmond (where he collapsed and died from fatigue in February 1865), Captain Henry Wirz was put in charge of the prison. He instituted the infamous "Dead Line," which, as Goss wrote in an 1867 memoir,

consisted of a row of stakes driven into the ground, with narrow board strips nailed down upon the top, at the distance of about fifteen feet from the stockade, on the interior side. This line was closely guarded by sentinels, stationed above on the stockade, and any person who approached it, as many unconsciously did, and as in the crowd was often unavoidable, was shot dead, with no warning whatever to admonish him that death was near. . . . A poor one-legged cripple placed one hand on the dead line to support him while he got his crutch,

A photographer identified as A. J. Riddle made this image of Union POWs awaiting distribution of rations at Andersonville, the infamous Confederate POW compound in Georgia. NATIONAL ARCHIVES AND RECORDS ADMINISTRATION

which had fallen from his feeble grasp to the ground. In this position he was shot through the lungs, and laid near the dead line writhing in torments during most of the forenoon, until at last death came to his relief. None dared approach him to relieve his sufferings through fear of the same fate.[4]

After the war Wirz was tried by a Union tribunal, which found him guilty of unjustly causing at least 10,000 deaths, mostly from neglect and starvation. He was the only Confederate soldier executed by the United States for his actions during the war. The Daughters of the Confederacy, maintaining that all prisoner deaths were caused by unavoidable food shortages, declared Wirz a victim of "judicial murder" and erected a memorial to the captain at the town of Andersonville in 1909. It still stands.

CAMP DAVIDSON

A prison stockade adjacent to the Savannah city hospital, Camp Davidson was an exemplary facility in which POWs were reasonably well fed (thanks to the generosity of local civilians) and built their own brick ovens for cooking.

CAMP OGLETHORPE

Built in Macon in 1862 to accommodate the overflow from converted-warehouse prisons at Montgomery, Alabama, Camp Oglethorpe closed in the fall of 1863 when POWs who had survived captivity were exchanged. The facility was reopened in 1864 to house officer POWs.

OGLETHORPE STOCKADE

Erected on a fairgrounds just outside of Oglethorpe, the stockade POW camp held 1,500 officer prisoners. Field-grade officers were provided with large private quarters, but officers of lower rank lived in the open. The stockade was evacuated in July 1864 in advance of Sherman's March to the Sea.

SOUTH CAROLINA

CHARLESTON STOCKADE

Set up in the yard of the Charleston city jail, this facility held some 600 officers and 300 white and black enlisted men in addition to captured deserters from both sides.

CASTLE PINCKNEY

Located in Charleston, Castle Pinckney was a former USA fort converted to hold POWs, both enlisted men and officers.

TEXAS

CAMP FORD

This stockade, operational from 1863 to 1865, was sited some four miles northwest of Tyler and was the largest POW camp in Texas. Union prisoners were permitted to construct their own log cabins, and, thanks to a freshwater stream, were supplied with adequate water and sanitation. After the great Union defeat in the Red River Campaign (March 10–May 22, 1864), Camp Ford became catastrophically overcrowded, its population exploding from 100 men to nearly 5,000 by July 1864. Disease became a serious issue.

VIRGINIA

BELLE ISLE PRISON

Located in the James River at Richmond, the camp was notorious for starving its prisoners. Walt Whitman wrote of Belle Isle survivors released at the end of the war, 90 percent of whom weighed less than 100 pounds:

Can those be men—those little livid brown, ash-streak'd, monkey-looking dwarfs?—are they really not mummied, dwindled corpses? They lay there, most of them, quite still, but with a horrible look in their eyes and skinny lips (often with not enough flesh on the lips to cover their teeth). Probably no more appalling sight was ever seen on this earth. (There are deeds, crimes, that may be forgiven; but this is not among them. It steeps its perpetrators in blackest, escapeless, endless damnation. Over 50,000 have been compell'd to die the death of starvation—reader, did you ever try to realize what starvation actually is?—in those prisons—and in a land of plenty.) An indescribable meanness, tyranny, aggravating course of insults, almost incredible—was evidently the rule of treatment through all the southern military prisons. The dead there are not to be pitied as much as some of the living that come from there—if they can be call'd living—many of them are mentally imbecile, and will never recuperate.[5]

CASTLE THUNDER #1

Located in Petersburg City, in a converted tobacco warehouse, Castle Thunder's name came from Union prisoners held there while Petersburg was under prolonged artillery siege.

CASTLE THUNDER #2

This Castle Thunder was located in Richmond and was a converted tobacco warehouse. It held political prisoners, spies, and persons charged with treason. When the Union occupied Richmond, Confederates charged with war crimes were incarcerated here.

LIBBY PRISON

Located in the three-story Richmond warehouse of Libby & Sons, ships' chandlers, the prison held officers exclusively, becoming overcrowded after the decline and cancellation of the Dix-Hill Cartel. The floor plan of the building was just 100 by 150 feet, but it eventually held

1,200 prisoners. The officers organized numerous escapes, most of them successful. In an effort to stem the outflow, however, jailer Dick Turner gave his guards leave to shoot anyone who dared even to venture toward a window.

UNION PRISONS AND PRISON CAMPS

Andersonville may have been the most notorious of Civil War prison camps, but it was hardly the only scene of inhumane prisoner treatment. The North, which, unlike the South, had plenty of food and other supplies to go around, also treated its POWs with little charity and less conscience. At the POW camp in Elmira, New York, for example, the death rate among some 12,000 prisoners ran to 24 percent—the result of poor rations, disease, and perhaps most of all, exposure to the Upstate New York winter. Eventually, Secretary of War Edwin Stanton ordered the already inadequate rations *cut* to the levels Confederates reportedly supplied Union prisoners. The secretary declared this to be fair play. Others, both North and South, saw it as raw revenge.

The major Union prisons included the following.[6]

DELAWARE

FORT DELAWARE

Built in 1846 as a harbor fort on Pea Patch Island in the Delaware River, Fort Delaware began operating as a military prison in 1862; by August 1863 it held more than 11,000 prisoners, including most of the POWs taken at the Battle of Gettysburg (July 1–3, 1863). Although Fort Delaware was much feared by Confederate troops, it was actually among the less lethal of large Civil War prisons. Some 2,500 out of a total of 33,000 men held there died in the course of the war, a comparatively modest mortality rate of 7.6 percent.[7]

ILLINOIS

CAMP ALTON

Established as the first Illinois state prison during the 1850s, the facility was denounced as unhygienic by no less a figure than Dorothea Dix, an activist for the humane treatment of convicts, asylum inmates, and, during the war, wounded troops and POWs. The decrepit facility was abandoned for the newly built penitentiary at Joliet, but was reopened in early 1862 as a "military detention camp." Quickly overcrowded, it was swept by a smallpox epidemic that killed scores of POWs daily. Citizens of Alton demanded that the sick be evacuated to a deserted island in the Mississippi River. On this island thousands died and were buried. The prison was active until the end of the war, after which it was never reused and was soon demolished.

CAMP DOUGLAS

Opened in 1862 on what is today the South Side of Chicago, this POW camp covered sixty acres and held about 30,000 prisoners in the course of the war. The peak population, recorded in December 1864, was more than 12,000 men. It is believed that at least 4,450 prisoners died and some 500 escaped before the end of the conflict.

ROCK ISLAND BARRACKS

Built in 1863 on a Mississippi River island between Rock Island, Illinois, and Davenport, Iowa, the Barracks was still under construction when it accepted 5,000 POWs in December. Its prisoner population varied between 5,000 and 8,000 throughout the rest of the war. Eighty-four barracks buildings were enclosed within a high fence. Although the prisoners were adequately clothed and fed, water was always in short supply, sometimes acutely. There was no hospital and virtually no medical care, and smallpox was endemic throughout the prison.

Tintype photograph of five unidentified Confederate POWs in front of their barracks at Camp Douglas, Chicago.

INDIANA

CAMP MORTON

Erected on the Indianapolis state fairgrounds and opened as a POW camp in 1861, Camp Morton was furnished with crude, dirt-floor barracks surrounded by a stockade. Conditions were dirty and, in winter, frigid. Nevertheless, it is often cited as one of the best-run camps on either side. A total of 1,700 POWs died here during 1861–65.

MARYLAND

FORT MCHENRY

Located in Baltimore Harbor, Fort McHenry earned fame during the War of 1812 as the subject of Francis Scott Key's "The Star-Spangled Banner." In 1861 it was converted into a military prison and a hospital for Union and Confederate wounded. Suspected Confederate spies and dissidents were also held here.

POINT LOOKOUT

From 1863 to 1865 this facility operated as an all-tent POW camp sited where the Potomac River empties into Chesapeake Bay. It held some 20,000 POWs in harsh conditions. When its shallow wells became polluted, fresh water had to be shipped in—and was therefore a chronically scarce, strictly rationed commodity.

MASSACHUSETTS

FORT WARREN

This military prison on George's Island in Boston Harbor was originally a fortress forming part of Boston's coastal defenses. It was used early in the war as a training base for Massachusetts regiments. When they complained about inadequate shelter and food, it became a POW camp.

MISSOURI

PRISON AT GRATIOT AND MYRTLE STREETS, ST. LOUIS

Originally a medical college, the facility was used as a military prison from 1862 to 1865. It had a capacity of 500 but held twice that number.

NEW YORK

ELMIRA PRISON CAMP

This thirty-acre facility operated from 1864 to 1865, during which time it earned the sobriquet "Hell-mira." Its thirty-five two-story barracks held half of the 10,000 prisoners. The rest lived in tents or slept in the open—even in the depths of weather. Southern relief societies sent clothing and supplies to Elmira, but these

Defiant and proud, three Confederate POWs, captured at Gettysburg, pose for a photograph in the field.
National Archives and Records Administration

were warehoused by the camp commandant for some six months before being distributed. Local churches donated food, which was seized by corrupt Union officers, who then sold it to prisoners.

POWs were guarded mainly by specially recruited ex-slaves, who treated the prisoners cruelly. Elmira's mortality rate of 24 percent was the highest of any Civil War prison, including the infamous Andersonville.

HART ISLAND

Located at the western end of Long Island Sound in New York City, Hart Island was the site of a public workhouse, a hospital, and a prison before the Civil War. It became a POW camp in 1865, holding 3,413 Confederate soldiers.

FORT LAFAYETTE

Built in the Narrows of New York as a coastal fortification at the southern tip of the modern Brooklyn neighborhood of Bay Ridge, Fort Lafayette became a military prison in 1861 and housed Confederate officers as well as United States citizens accused of disloyalty.

OHIO

CAMP CHASE

Originally a USA training camp west of Columbus, Camp Chase became a military prison in 1861 and had an inmate population of some 8,000 by 1863. A Confederate officer POW pronounced it so filthy that no self-respecting Tennessee farmer would house his pigs there.

JOHNSON'S ISLAND

This military prison in Sandusky Bay, on Lake Erie, opened in 1862 and closed at the end of the war. Some 12,000 CSA officers were held here during that period. Out of this total, 221 died.

OHIO STATE PENITENTIARY

Between 1862 and 1865 this large prison was used to hold POWs as well as civilian criminal prisoners. Its most famous "guests" during the Civil War were the Confederate raider General John Hunt Morgan and six of his men. After the war the prison reverted to its civilian correctional role until it was demolished in 1984.

WASHINGTON, DC

OLD CAPITOL PRISON

Constructed in 1815 to temporarily house Congress after the British burned the original US Capitol in the War of 1812, the building later became a hotel. Purchased by the government, it was used to hold POWs, Union deserters, and suspected spies, including the notorious "Rebel Rose," Rose O'Neal Greenhow, who was imprisoned here with her young daughter in 1862.

TURNING PRISONERS

In both Confederate and Union prison camps, officials attempted to "turn" prisoners. The Confederates focused their efforts on foreign-born Union POWs, offering them release in exchange for joining the CSA. About 4,500 accepted the offer and were employed mostly as military laborers rather than combat troops. The Union offered selected Confederate POWs freedom as well as amnesty in exchange for their volunteering to fight in the ongoing warfare against the Sioux and other "hostile" Plains tribes. Before the end of the war, six regiments of these so-called Galvanized Yankees were formed. Their recruitment for combat duty on the far western frontier avoided pitting them against fellow Southerners while it freed up western-based Union soldiers for service against the Confederacy.

Part Three
The Principal Armies

Chapter 16

ARMY OF NORTHERN VIRGINIA

OVERALL PERFORMANCE: ★ ★ ★ ★

Both the primary and the premier fighting force of the Confederate States Army (CSA), the Army of Northern Virginia (ANV) was above all the army of Robert E. Lee. It dominated Confederate operations in the Eastern Theater and was the principal opponent of the Union's flagship Army of the Potomac, with which it contested some of the greatest battles of the war against the most important of the Union's generals, from Seven Pines (May 31–June 1, 1862), pitting Joseph E. Johnston (and G. W. Smith) against George B. McClellan, to Appomattox Court House (April 9, 1865), in which Lee surrendered the ANV to Ulysses S. Grant, precipitating the end of the Civil War.[1]

ESTABLISHMENT

By coincidence, the ANV came into being on June 20, 1861, bearing the name of the Union army destined to be its chief antagonist, the Army of the Potomac. At the time, it aggregated all Confederate fighting units in northern Virginia. The following month, on July 20–21, the Army of the Shenandoah and units making up the District of Harpers Ferry were added to the army. During March–May 1862 a force originally designated as the Army of the Northwest was added, and on April 12 the Army of the Peninsula was folded into the Army of the Potomac, which had been renamed (on March 14, 1862) the Army of Northern Virginia. Some histories assert that the army was actually renamed on June 1, 1862, by Lee himself when he assumed command; however, Lee referred to it as the Army of Northern Virginia before then.

It is possible that Lee was merely conflating the name of the Confederate military department—Department of Northern Virginia—with the name of the army.

The final name of the army, like most names applied to Confederate armies, referred to the area in which the Army of Northern Virginia chiefly operated—though Lee would take it elsewhere, too, most notably invading Maryland and Pennsylvania. The composition of the army was not exclusively Virginian, let alone northern Virginian. Regiments and other units from all over the Confederacy were included. In this sense the Army of Northern Virginia was broadly representative of the Confederate States of America, even as the general with whom it is most closely identified was the most universally respected commander in the Confederacy and, perhaps, in the Civil War itself.

COMMANDING GENERALS

The first commanding general of the Army of Northern Virginia (as the Army of the Potomac) was Pierre Gustave Toutant Beauregard (June 20–July 20, 1861), who, having resigned his USA commission, became the Confederacy's very first general on March 1, 1861. Assigned to command the defenses of Charleston, South Carolina, he directed the bombardment of Fort Sumter (April 12–14, 1861), which began the Civil War. On the eve (July 20, 1861) of the First Battle of Bull Run, Joseph E. Johnston replaced Beauregard as commanding officer of the army (six infantry brigades, plus militia, a total of some 23,000 men), and Beauregard led I Corps into battle. He created a battle flag for the (Confederate) Army of the Potomac, which became the

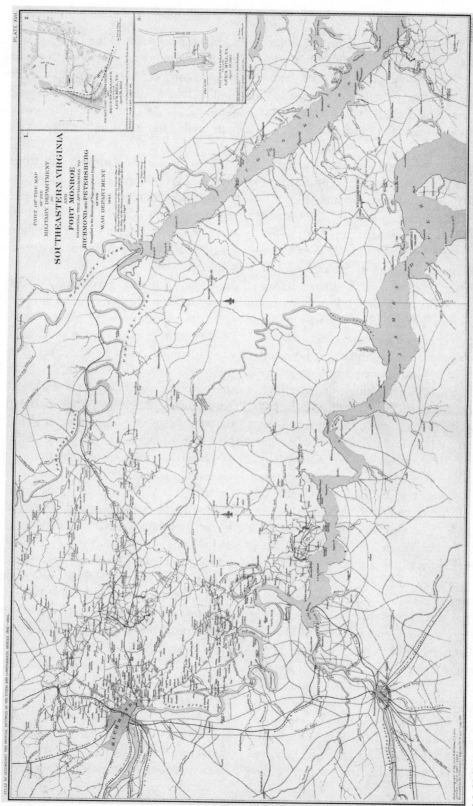

McClellan's Peninsula Campaign was supposed to end in the capture of Richmond. It did not. UNITED STATES MILITARY ACADEMY

Confederate battle flag for the entire CSA and was ultimately more closely identified with the Confederate States of America than the "Stars and Bars" national flag (which, Beauregard felt, too closely resembled the US flag and might therefore cause confusion on the battlefield).

Joseph Eggleston Johnston assumed command of the ANV (as the Army of the Potomac) on July 20, 1861, and continued through May 31, 1862. Like Beauregard, Johnston had served with the USA in the US-Mexican War (1846–48) and, also like him, was trained at West Point as an engineer. At the time of the outbreak of the Civil War, Johnston was quartermaster general of the USA, with the rank of brigadier general. He thus became the highest-ranking USA officer to resign his commission and join the CSA. A methodical commander, Johnston often ran afoul of Confederate president Jefferson Davis, who considered him overly cautious, but his leadership at the First Battle of Bull Run was highly effective. He came to command the (Confederate) Army of the Potomac when his Army of the Shenandoah was merged with it. After First Bull Run he led the enlarged army against Union general George B. McClellan at the Siege of Yorktown (April 5–May 4, 1862) and the Battle of Seven Pines (May 31–June 1, 1862), both during McClellan's Peninsula Campaign (March–July 1862). The result of both of these battles was inconclusive.

At Seven Pines, Johnston was seriously wounded and was temporarily replaced as army commander by Major General Gustavus Woodson Smith on May 31, 1862. Another West Point alumnus and engineer, Smith had fought gallantly in the US-Mexican War, resigning his commission at the end of 1854 to become a civil engineer in New York City, where he served as street commissioner from 1858 until 1861, when he traveled to Richmond to offer his services to the CSA. He was a wing commander in the

(Confederate) Army of the Potomac and stepped in for the wounded Johnston, only to suffer what appeared to be a nervous collapse the next day, June 1. This is when President Davis appointed Robert E. Lee to command what was now formally called the Army of Northern Virginia.

Born at Strafford, Virginia, the third son of Henry "Light-Horse Harry," one of the heroes of the American Revolution, Robert E. Lee graduated from West Point, second in the Class of 1829, and was commissioned in the Corps of Engineers. While posted to service along the southeast coast, he met and married another descendent of the revolution, Mary Custis, great-granddaughter of Martha Washington.

Like so many of his fellow West Pointers who went on to command in the Civil War, Lee was an engineer. But he was a standout among the others, not only for his work on the Mississippi River defenses at St. Louis and the New York Harbor defenses during 1836–46, but in the field during the US-Mexican War, in which he built bridges and performed daring topographical reconnaissance. Appointed West Point superintendent in 1852, he became a colonel of cavalry in 1855, serving out of St. Louis and in Texas and the Southwest. In 1857 he returned to Virginia on family business following the death of his father-in-law and was in the state when he was ordered to Harpers Ferry to crush John Brown's raid on the federal arsenal there. He captured Brown on October 18, 1859, and from February 1860 until he was recalled to Washington on February 4, 1861, he commanded the Department of Texas.

On April 20, 1861, Union general-in-chief Winfield Scott offered Lee command of Union forces, but, unwilling to draw his sword against his home state, Lee resigned his USA commission when Virginia seceded. He accepted command of Virginia's military and naval forces. Lee's first forays in the field in western Virginia were not successful. The western locals were hostile to Tidewater Virginia and would (in 1862) break with the rest of the state and (in 1863) unite with the Union as West Virginia. Defeated at the Battle of Cheat Mountain (September 12–13, 1861), Lee was ordered to withdraw from western Virginia to apply his engineering expertise to strengthening the defenses of the southeast coast at Charleston, Port Royal, and Savannah (October 1861–March 1862). He was then recalled to Richmond as President Jefferson Davis's personal military advisor.

After General Johnston's wounding, Lee took command of the ANV and led it through the battles and campaigns enumerated at the end of this chapter. From the battles of the Seven Days (June 25–July 1, 1862) through

Appomattox Court House (April 9, 1865), Robert E. Lee created his military legacy, which was also that of the Army of Northern Virginia and, to a great extent, of the Confederacy itself.

SIZE AND ORGANIZATION

Both the size and organization of the Army of Northern Virginia were fluid during the course of the war. Under P. G. T. Beauregard (June 20–July 20, 1861), the army was simply organized into six brigades, with assorted militia units attached, and numbered about 23,000 men. Under Joseph E. Johnston and G. W. Smith (July 20, 1861—June 1, 1862), the army was first organized into I and II Corps, commanded by Beauregard and Smith, respectively. In 1862 the

These Confederate fortifications at Manassas, Virginia, were photographed by George N. Barnard in March 1862, about six months before the Second Battle of Bull Run (August 28–30, 1862). The photograph appeared in Alexander Gardner's Photographic Sketch Book of the Civil War, *published in 1865 and 1866.* NATIONAL ARCHIVES AND RECORDS ADMINISTRATION

corps were replaced by "wings" and a Reserve: the Left Wing (Major General Daniel Harvey Hill), the Center Wing (Major General James Longstreet), the Right Wing (Major General John B. Magruder), and the Reserve (Major General G. W. Smith).

Under Lee's command (June 1, 1862–April 9, 1865), the army varied in strength from 55,633 men (at the time of Seven Pines, May 31–June 1, 1862), to a high of some 92,000 (Seven Days Battles, June 25–July 1, 1862), and afterward varied from 54,000 (Second Bull Run, August 28–30, 1862) to 75,000 (Fredericksburg, Chancellorsville, and Gettysburg, December 11, 1862–July 3, 1863). Strength fell to a low of 50,000 at the end of 1863, rising to 62,230 as it contested Grant's Overland Campaign (May 4–June 24, 1863). The ANV was built up to 82,633 men during the desperate Richmond-Petersburg Campaign (June 9, 1864–March 25, 1865), by the end of which it dwindled to about 50,000 and, at the very end of the war, half that number.

As with the army's strength under Lee, the organization also varied; however, from May 30, 1863, until Lee's surrender on April 9, 1865, the Army of Northern Virginia consisted of three corps in addition to a cavalry division, reserve artillery, and "Imboden's Command," a brigade-strength unit that served variously as a raiding force, a rearguard, and a logistical unit. At their height the three corps consisted of the following:

I CORPS:

Called Longstreet's Corps, after commanding officer James Longstreet.

- Pickett's Division
  (Major General George E. Pickett)
  Three brigades and one artillery battalion

- McLaw's Division
  (Major General Lafayette McLaw)
  Four brigades and one artillery battalion

- Hood's Division
  (Major General John Bell Hood)
  Four brigades and one artillery battalion

II CORPS:

Called Jackson's Corps during 1862–63, after commanding officer Thomas "Stonewall" Jackson. Following Jackson's death on May 10, 1863, Lieutenant General Richard S. Ewell assumed command.

- Early's Division
  (Major General Jubal A. Early)
  Four brigades and one artillery battalion

- Johnson's Division
  (Major General Edward Johnson)
  Four brigades and one artillery battalion

- Rodes's Division
  (Major General Robert E. Rodes)
  Five brigades and one artillery battalion

III CORPS:

Called A. P. Hill's Corps, after commanding officer Lieutenant General Ambrose Powell Hill.

- Anderson's Division
  (Major General Richard H. Anderson)
  Five brigades and one artillery battalion

- Heth's Division
  (Major General Henry Heth)
  Four brigades and one artillery battalion

- Pender's Division
  (Major General W. Dorsey Pender)
  Four brigades and one artillery battalion

At various times the Army of Northern Virginia included units (regiments, battalions, and companies) from Alabama, Arkansas, Florida, Georgia, Kentucky, Louisiana, Maryland (formed at Richmond and Winchester, Virginia), Mississippi, North Carolina, South Carolina, Tennessee, and Texas in addition to Virginia.

LEE'S GENERALS

Lee's Army of Northern Virginia corps commanders were his principal commanders.

LIEUTENANT GENERAL JAMES P. LONGSTREET

Born in 1821 and raised in Edgefield District, South Carolina, Longstreet graduated from West Point in 1842 and served in the US-Mexican War, during which he was promoted to first lieutenant and then brevetted to captain after distinguishing himself at Churubusco on August 20, 1847. He was brevetted again, to major, at the Battle of Molino del Rey on September 8, but was severely wounded on September 13, at Chapultepec.

After the war Longstreet reverted to his regular rank, first lieutenant. He was promoted to captain in December 1852 and to major in July 1858. Longstreet resigned his commission in June 1861, after the secession of South Carolina, and accepted a Confederate commission as brigadier general. Commanding the advance guard at Blackburn's Ford (near Centreville, Virginia) on July 18, he repulsed Union general Irvin McDowell shortly before the First Battle of Bull Run and fought well at Williamsburg on May 5, 1862, but was dilatory at Fair Oaks on May 31, drawing much criticism. His first service under Lee was at the Second Battle of Bull Run (August 28–30, 1862), when he commanded five divisions well-coordinated in support of Stonewall Jackson.

Lee and Longstreet developed a close working relationship, even though Longstreet fundamentally disagreed with Lee's decision to invade Maryland (September 4–20, 1862). Nevertheless, he acquitted himself well at South Mountain (September 14) and at Antietam (September 17), a month after which, promoted to lieutenant general, he took command of ANV I Corps. At Fredericksburg (December 11–15,

1862) he successfully defended Marye's Heights, but because his units were detached from the main army for campaigning in Suffolk, Virginia, during April 1863, he missed Chancellorsville (April 30–May 6, 1863).

When Lee decided to invade Pennsylvania, Longstreet again disagreed and would later publicly criticize Lee's tactical plan at Gettysburg (July 1–3, 1863). Longstreet himself was criticized for being overly cautious during that turning-point battle. Following the hard Gettysburg defeat, Longstreet was dispatched to reinforce Braxton Bragg's Army of Tennessee. He fought at Chickamauga (September 19–20, 1863) and in the Chattanooga Campaign (September 21–November 25, 1863) before returning to the ANV in April 1864. Longstreet fought at the Wilderness (May 5–7, 1864), where he was severely wounded by friendly fire, his right arm permanently paralyzed. Returning to duty in October, he fought throughout the rest of the war, distinguishing himself at Petersburg and Richmond, before surrendering with Lee at Appomattox Court House on April 9, 1865.

LIEUTENANT GENERAL THOMAS J. "STONEWALL" JACKSON

A native of Clarksburg, Virginia (now West Virginia), Jackson was born in 1824. He graduated from West Point in 1846, was commissioned a second lieutenant of artillery, and fought in the US-Mexican War, where he immediately distinguished himself for his steely gallantry at the Siege of Veracruz (March 9–29, 1847), Cerro Gordo (April 18), and Chapultepec (September 13). At the last battle he was brevetted major.

Jackson resigned from the army in February 1851 and accepted a position as professor of artillery tactics and natural philosophy at the Virginia Military Institute, teaching there until April 1861, when he was commissioned as a colonel of Confederate volunteers. Promoted to brigadier general on June 17, he fought

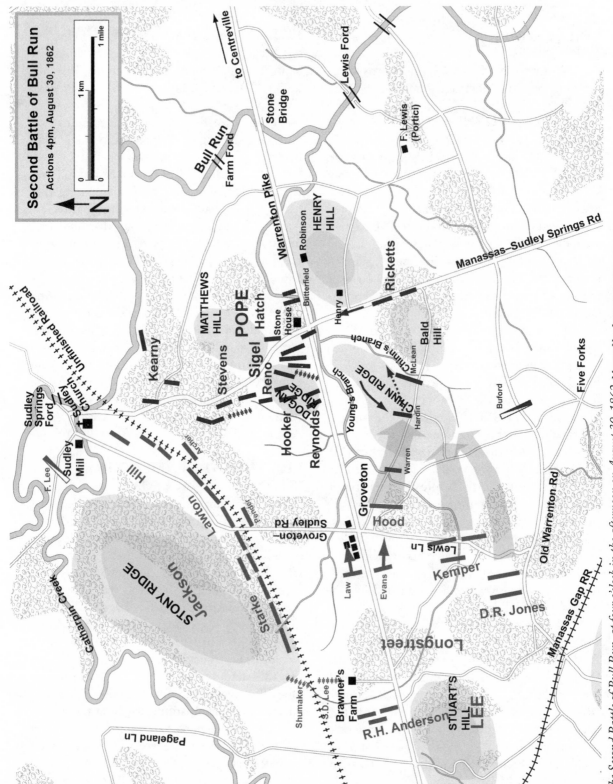

Second Battle of Bull Run

Actions 4pm, August 30, 1862

1 mile

1 km

N

to Centreville

Bull Run

Stone Bridge

Farm Ford

Lewis Ford

F. Lewis (Portici)

Warrenton Pike

Robinson

HENRY HILL

Manassas–Sudley Springs Rd

MATTHEWS HILL

POPE

Sigel

Hatch

Stone House

Butterfield

Ricketts

Kearny

Stevens

Reno

Henry

Bald Hill

Sudley Springs Ford

Sudley Church

Unfinished Railroad

DOGAN RIDGE

Hooker

Reynolds

Chinn's Branch

CHINN RIDGE

McLean

Buford

Five Forks

F. Lee

Sudley Mill

Hill

Archer

Young's Branch

Hardin

Pender

Lawton

Groveton–Sudley Rd

Groveton

Warren

STONY RIDGE

Jackson

Starke

Hood

Law

Lewis Ln

Longstreet

Evans

Kemper

Old Warrenton Rd

Catharpin Creek

Shumaker

S.D. Lee

Brawner's Farm

R.H. Anderson

D.R. Jones

STUART'S HILL

LEE

Manassas Gap RR

Pageland Ln

brilliantly at the First Battle Bull Run (July 21), earning the nickname "Stonewall" for his steadfast reinforcement of critical high ground at Henry House Hill. After promotion to major general in October 1861, Jackson was appointed commander of all forces in the Shenandoah Valley. In this capacity he executed an extraordinary campaign against substantially superior Union forces, effectively foiling Union general George B. McClellan's advance on Richmond during 1862. Although he was repulsed at the Battle of Kernstown (March 23, 1862), Jackson nevertheless went on to outmaneuver and defeat Union forces at Front Royal (May 23). This positioned him for victories at Winchester (May 24–25), Cross Keys (June 8), and Port Republic (June 9). Having driven Union forces out of the Shenandoah Valley, Jackson was then ordered to support Lee's efforts to drive McClellan from the Yorktown Peninsula during the series of battles known as the Seven Days (June 25–July 1, 1862).

On August 27, 1862, Jackson engaged Union general John Pope's Army of Virginia at Manassas Junction and then beat back Pope's attack at Groveton (August 28). During the next two days, Jackson was instrumental in the Confederate victory at the Second Battle of Bull Run and played a central role in the invasion of Maryland, winning special distinction at Antietam (September 17).

In October 1862 Jackson was promoted to lieutenant general and was made commander of II Corps. He commanded the right flank at the Battle of Fredericksburg (December 11–15) and at Chancellorsville (April 30–May 6, 1863) led a devastating flanking maneuver against Major General Joseph Hooker's Army of the Potomac. During this battle Jackson fell victim to friendly fire, shot by one of his own pickets. When his badly mangled left arm was amputated, Lee told Jackson, "You have lost your left. I have lost my right arm." Jackson developed pneumonia and died within a week of his wounding.

George W. Minnes photographed Confederate lieutenant general Thomas J. "Stonewall" Jackson in April 1863, less than a month before Jackson succumbed to wounds suffered as a result of friendly fire at the Battle of Chancellorsville on May 2, 1863. NATIONAL ARCHIVES AND RECORDS ADMINISTRATION

LIEUTENANT GENERAL RICHARD S. EWELL

Ewell was born in 1817 in Georgetown (now part of Washington, DC) but grew up in Prince William County, Virginia. He graduated from West Point in 1840 and was commissioned in the dragoons, with which he served in Kansas, Oklahoma, and along the Oregon and Santa Fe trails. He served in the US-Mexican War, fighting at Veracruz (March 9–29, 1847) and Contreras-Churubusco (August 19–20), which earned him a brevet to captain. After the war Ewell served as a recruiter and then returned to the southwestern frontier—now with the permanent rank of captain—in 1850. He fought against Apache raiders, sustaining a serious wound during an 1859 engagement.

Like a significant number of his fellow Southern officers, Ewell opposed secession, but he felt allegiance to his native state, and when the Civil War erupted, he resigned his commission in April 1861 to offer his services to Virginia. In May he was commissioned a colonel in the Confederate provisional army, and on June 1 he sustained a wound in a sharp exchange at the Fairfax Court House. He was promoted to brigade command on June 17 and led 2nd Brigade at the First Battle of Bull Run on July 21. Promoted to major general on January 24, 1862, Ewell served under Stonewall Jackson in the Shenandoah Valley, where he was instrumental in the defeat of Union general Nathaniel Banks at the Battle of Winchester (May 25). Following this, he took part in the Confederate victories at Cross Keys (June 8) and Port Republic (June 9), and then marched to Richmond, where he fought at the Battle of Gaines's Mill (June 27) and Malvern Hill (July 1) during the bloody series of fights known as the Seven Days.

Ewell was gravely wounded at Groveton on August 28. His left leg was amputated, and he languished for nine months during a painfully slow convalescence. When Stonewall Jackson was mortally wounded at Chancellorsville on May 2, 1863, Ewell was promoted to lieutenant general and assigned command of II Corps on May 29, 1863. On the first day of the Battle of Gettysburg (July 1, 1863), Ewell captured the town, but on subsequent days, July 2 and 3, he repeatedly failed in his attacks against the Union lines. Ewell remained at the head of II Corps at the Battle of the Wilderness (May 5–7, 1864) and Spotsylvania (May 8–21); however, never having fully recovered from his Groveton wound, his health deteriorated. On May 31 he relinquished II Corps to Jubal Early.

The ailing Ewell accepted reassignment to the minimally demanding post of commander of the Department of Richmond. When Robert E. Lee withdrew the ANV from the Richmond-Petersburg defenses during April 2–3, 1865, Ewell attempted to join him with his own forces but was surrounded and captured at Sayler's Creek on April 6 and imprisoned for several months at Fort Warren, Massachusetts. In August 1865 he was released to the solace of Spring Hill, his Maury County, Tennessee, estate.

LIEUTENANT GENERAL AMBROSE POWELL HILL

Lee called Hill "the best soldier of his grade with me." Born in 1825 at Culpepper, Virginia, Hill graduated from West Point in 1847 and was commissioned a second lieutenant in the artillery—just in time to see service in the US-Mexican War. When it was over he was posted in Texas and then fought in policing actions against the Seminoles during 1855. From that year to 1860, as captain, he participated in the US Coastal Survey, Washington, DC.

Hill resigned his commission in March 1861 and was made a colonel in the Provisional Army of the Confederacy. He was assigned to command the 13th Virginia Regiment at the First Battle of Bull Run (July 21, 1861). In February 1862 he was promoted to brigadier general, and on May 5 he distinguished himself at Williamsburg. By the end of the month, on May 26, Hill was promoted to major general and, five days later, fought valiantly at Fair Oaks.

During the so-called Seven Days Battles (June 25–July 1, 1862), Hill led his division in very heavy fighting. On August 8 he supported Stonewall Jackson at the Battle of Cedar Mountain, and he fought at the Second Battle of Bull Run (August 28–30). Hill was the spoiler at Antietam (September 17), leading a forced march to reinforce Confederate lines so as to deprive the Union army of what would have been its first truly decisive victory. At the Battle of Fredericksburg (December 11–15), Hill had charge of the right flank. Wounded at Chancellorsville (April

This 1867 lithograph is titled "The Room in the McLean House, at Appomattox C. H., in which Gen. Lee surrendered to Gen. Grant." It was commissioned by Wilmer McLean, the owner of the house in which Grant and Lee negotiated the terms of the surrender of the Army of Northern Virginia. McLean hoped that profits from sale of the lithograph would help him recoup losses from the furniture Union soldiers carried off as mementos of the historic surrender. Pictured from left to right are John Gibbon, George Armstrong Custer, Cyrus B. Comstock, Orville E. Babcock, Charles Marshall, Walter H. Taylor, Robert E. Lee, Philip Sheridan, Ulysses S. Grant, John Aaron Rawlins, Charles Griffin, unidentified, George Meade, Ely S. Parker, James W. Forsyth, Wesley Merritt, Theodore Shelton Bowers, and Edward Ord. The man not identified in the legend at the bottom of the lithograph is believed to be Joshua Chamberlain, one of the Union heroes of Gettysburg, who officiated at the formal surrender of arms by the Army of Northern Virginia on April 12, 1865.

NATIONAL ARCHIVES AND RECORDS ADMINISTRATION

30–May 6, 1863), he was promoted to lieutenant general and assigned command of the newly formed III Corps on May 24. He led the corps into battle at Gettysburg (July 1–3, 1863) and at Bristoe Station (October 14). Ewell was also a key commander at the Battle of the Wilderness (May 5–7, 1864) and the Battle of Spotsylvania Court House (May 8–21).

Always leading from the front, Hill was cut down while rallying his troops during the defense against the Union assault on Petersburg, April 2, 1865, becoming the last important Confederate commander killed in battle.

Combat Chronology

- Peninsula Campaign: Battle of the
  Seven Pines
  (May 31–June 1, 1862)
  —Inconclusive

- Seven Days Battles: Gaines's Mill
  (June 27, 1862)
  —Confederate victory

- Seven Days Battles: Malvern Hill
  (July 1, 1862)
  —Confederate tactical defeat

- Northern Virginia Campaign:
  Second Bull Run
  (August 28–30, 1862)
  —Confederate victory

- Maryland Campaign: Antietam
  (September 17, 1862)
  —Tactically inconclusive, but Confederate
  strategic defeat

- Fredericksburg Campaign: Fredericksburg
  (December 11–15, 1862)
  —Confederate victory

- Chancellorsville Campaign:
  Chancellorsville
  (April 30–May 6, 1863)
  —Confederate victory

- Gettysburg Campaign: Gettysburg
  (July 1–3, 1863)
  —Confederate defeat

- Bristoe Campaign:
  (October 13–November 7, 1863)
  —Confederate defeat

- Mine Run Campaign:
  (November 27–December 2, 1863)
  —Inconclusive

- Overland Campaign: Wilderness
  (May 5–7, 1864)
  —Inconclusive

- Overland Campaign: Spotsylvania
  Court House
  (May 8–21, 1864)
  —Inconclusive

- Overland Campaign: Cold Harbor
  (May 31–June 12, 1864)
  —Confederate victory

- Richmond-Petersburg Campaign:
  Siege of Petersburg
  (June 9, 1864–March 25, 1865)
  —Confederate defeat

- Richmond-Petersburg Campaign:
  Battle of the Crater
  (July 30, 1864)
  —Confederate victory

- Appomattox Campaign:
  Battle of Five Forks
  (April 1, 1865)
  —Confederate defeat

- Appomattox Campaign:
  Battle of Appomattox Court House
  (April 9, 1865)
  —Confederate defeat

Chapter 17

ARMY OF THE TRANS-MISSISSIPPI

OVERALL PERFORMANCE: ★ ★

The Army of the Trans-Mississippi was the army of the Confederate Trans-Mississippi Department (originally District). The department encompassed approximately a third of the territory of the Confederate States of America and included Missouri, Arkansas, Texas, Indian Territory (mostly modern Oklahoma), and the portion of Louisiana west of the Mississippi River. After the fall of Vicksburg, Mississippi, to Ulysses S. Grant on July 4, 1863, a Union victory that put the Mississippi River under USA control and split the Confederacy along its north-south axis, both the Trans-Mississippi Department and its army operated almost independently from the rest of the CSA. Indeed, the commander of the army, General Kirby Smith, acted with such autonomy that the Trans-Mississippi Department was universally referred to as "Kirby Smithdom." The general and his force had the distinction of being the last Confederate army to surrender, on May 26, 1865. Terms were concluded at Galveston, Texas, on June 2, but the 1st Cherokee Mounted Rifles, a part of the Army of the Trans-Mississippi, under the command of Brigadier General Stand Watie, himself a Cherokee, remained in the field until June 23, 1865. Watie thus became the last Confederate general to surrender.

ESTABLISHMENT

The Department of the Trans-Mississippi was formed with the separation of the District of the Trans-Mississippi from the Western Department of the Confederacy on May 26, 1862. Its army was called the Army of the Southwest until February 9, 1863, when it was renamed the Army of the Trans-Mississippi. The only principal Confederate army west of the Mississippi River, it mustered between 40,000 and 50,000 soldiers in units of varying permanence that were widely broadcast across the vast territory of the department. The enormous area covered promoted the development of cavalry; however, with most manpower and supplies concentrated in the Eastern Theater of the Civil War, the Army of the Trans-Mississippi was chronically undermanned, underfed, and underequipped.

COMMANDING GENERALS

The District of the Trans-Mississippi was commanded by Earl Van Dorn from January 10 to May 23, 1862, when it was part of the Western Department (Department No. 2) of the CSA. A great-nephew of Andrew Jackson, Van Dorn was born in Mississippi, educated at West Point (graduating fifty-second out of the fifty-six members of the Class of 1842) and saw peacetime duty in the South before participating in the US-Mexican War (1846–48). Van Dorn fought with distinction, earning two brevets and sustaining two wounds, near Mexico City on September 3, 1847, and little more than a week later, on September 13, during the storming of Belén Gate. After the war he saw action against the Seminoles and, in Texas, against the Comanches. At the Battle of Wichita Village (October 1, 1858) in Indian Territory, he was severely wounded. Given up for dead, the resilient Van Dorn surprised all by recovering and returning to action. Promoted to major on June 28, 1860, Van Dorn took a leave of absence from the USA until he resigned his commission on January 21, 1861, and became a brigadier general in the

Mississippi Militia later that month. In February, promoted to major general, he replaced Jefferson Davis, who was now the Confederate president, as commander of all Mississippi state forces.

Van Dorn fought at the Battle of Pea Ridge (March 6–8, 1862, Arkansas; defeated), the Second Battle of Corinth (October 3–4, 1862, Mississippi; defeated), Thompson's Station (March 5, 1863, Tennessee; victorious), and the (first) Battle of Franklin (April 10, 1863, Tennessee; defeated). A brave and vigorous commander of cavalry units, Van Dorn was out of his depth commanding larger forces.

From May 26 to June 20, 1862, the District of the Trans-Mississippi was commanded by Brigadier General Paul Octave Hébert, who graduated from West Point at the top of the Class of 1840, resigned from the USA in 1845 to become Louisiana state engineer, but resigned that post to accept a USA commission as lieutenant colonel and commanded the 14th Infantry Regiment in the US-Mexican War (1846–48). He fought at Contreras, Churubusco, Molino del Rey, Chapultepec, and Mexico City, receiving a brevet to colonel for his gallantry. In 1853 he was elected governor of Louisiana and served until 1856.

In the run-up to the Civil War, Hébert was instrumental in reorganizing the Louisiana militia and preparing the defenses of New Orleans. After his state seceded on April 1, 1861, he was commissioned as a brigadier general, but was not activated until 1862, when he was sent to Texas and briefly assumed command of the District of the Trans-Mississippi.

After Hébert, what was now the *Department* of the Trans-Mississippi was briefly commanded by Major General Thomas C. Hindman (June 20–July 16, 1862) and then by Major General Theophilus H. Holmes (July 30, 1862–February 9, 1863). A North Carolinian, Holmes graduated from West Point in 1829, second from the bottom of his class, and fought in the Second Seminole War (1835–42) and the US-Mexican War. He was effectively exiled to command of the Department of the Trans-Mississippi after his undistinguished performance at the Battle of Malvern Hill (July 1, 1862, Virginia; Confederate defeat). While commanding the Trans-Mississippi Department, Holmes refused to send troops to the aid of Vicksburg, which was under siege by Ulysses S. Grant. This prompted Jefferson Davis to remove Holmes from command of the department.

Lieutenant General Edmund Kirby Smith took over the department and the Army of the Trans-Mississippi on March 7, 1863, and held command of both throughout the rest of the war. His combat record in this position is covered in "Trans-Mississippi Army Combat Chronology" at the end of the chapter.

SIZE AND ORGANIZATION

The Army of the Trans-Mississippi varied in strength from about 40,000 to 50,000 soldiers. At the very end of the war, desertion reduced its rolls considerably below 40,000. The army was organized into three numbered corps in addition to a cavalry corps and a reserve corps. Because of the large area assigned to the army, the corps were headquartered in widely dispersed locations.

Headquartered at Shreveport, Department of Louisiana, I Corps was organized under Simon Bolivar Buckner. Headquartered variously in locations within the Department of Arkansas and Missouri, II Corps was organized on August 4, 1864, under the command of John B. Magruder. Headquartered at Galveston, Department of Texas, III Corps was organized on August 4, 1864, under John George Walker. The Cavalry Corps was organized on August 4, 1864, under Sterling Price, and the Reserve Corps was created on September 10, 1864.

CORPS COMMANDERS

SIMON BOLIVAR BUCKNER, I CORPS

Buckner was born in 1823 at Glen Lily, near Munfordville, Kentucky, and was named in honor of Simón Bolívar, the "Great Liberator" of Spanish South America. An 1844 graduate of the US Military Academy at West Point, Buckner was commissioned a brevet second lieutenant in the 2nd US Infantry Regiment and served in a Lake Ontario fortress garrison until he was appointed assistant professor of geography, history, and ethics at his alma mater.

In May 1846 Buckner joined the 6th US Infantry, initially as a recruiter during the US-Mexican War (1846–48) and then in the field, at Vera Cruz and nearby Amazoque. While serving as quartermaster of the 6th Infantry, Buckner fought at San Antonio and Churubusco, receiving a minor wound at the latter battle. Brevetted to first lieutenant for gallantry at Churubusco and Contreras, Buckner declined the honor because reports of his having participated at Contreras were mistaken; he had not fought at that battle. When subsequently offered the brevet for Churubusco, he accepted—and then was again brevetted, this time to captain, for gallantry at Molino del Rey. Buckner fought in the culminating battles of the war: Chapultepec, Belen Gate, and the storming of Mexico City.

Following the war, Buckner returned to West Point, this time as an instructor of infantry tactics. In protest of West Point's policy of compulsory chapel attendance, Buckner resigned in 1849 and was assigned as a recruiter at Fort Columbus, Ohio. After serving in the West and as captain of the commissary department of the 6th US Infantry in New York City, Buckner resigned his commission to join his father-in-law's real estate firm in Chicago. He joined the Illinois State Militia and, in 1857, was appointed adjutant general of Illinois by the state's governor. Resigning that post shortly after

his appointment, he was promoted to colonel and assigned to lead an Illinois volunteer regiment during the so-called Utah (or Mormon) War of 1857–58. The conflict was settled before he marched, and Buckner moved his family to Louisville, where he became captain of the local militia. When his unit was mustered into the 2nd Regiment of the Kentucky State Guard, Buckner was appointed inspector general of Kentucky in 1860. The following year, Kentucky governor Beriah Magoffin appointed him adjutant general and promoted him to major general. When Kentucky declared itself neutral at the outbreak of the Civil War, Buckner mustered sixty-one companies to defend its neutrality.

After state officials condemned the militia as pro-secessionist, Buckner resigned on July 20, 1861. He twice declined the offer of a brigadier general's commission in the Union army and, following the Confederate occupation of Columbus, Kentucky, accepted a commission as a brigadier general in the Confederate States Army on September 14, 1861. He was assigned command of a division in the Army of Central Kentucky under Brigadier General William J. Hardee.

Buckner fought at the Battle of Fort Donelson (February 11–16, 1862; Confederate defeat) on the Cumberland River. Buckner's delay in supporting an attack in defense of the fort contributed to its capture by Union forces. To Buckner fell the unwelcome assignment of surrendering to General Grant. Held as a POW at Fort Warren in Boston, he was exchanged after five months for Union brigadier general George A. McCall. On his release Buckner was promoted to major general and ordered to join the Army of Mississippi (under General Braxton Bragg) at Chattanooga.

On October 8, 1862, Buckner fought at Perryville, Kentucky, a battle that ended in strategic defeat. After serving in the District of the Gulf, building up the defenses of Mobile, Alabama, he was assigned (on May 11, 1863) to command the Army of East Tennessee. Soon, his army became III Corps in the Army of Tennessee. He led his corps against Ulysses S. Grant at Chickamauga (September 19–20, 1863, Tennessee; narrow Confederate victory). Disgusted by Bragg's leadership, Buckner collaborated with other generals in writing an anti-Bragg protest to President Davis, who retaliated for what he deemed disloyalty and insubordination by reducing Buckner to division command. On April 28, 1864, however, Buckner was assigned to the Army of the Trans-Mississippi as commander of I Corps. He did not arrive until August 4 and was promoted the following month to lieutenant general, on September 20.

Following Lee's surrender to Grant on April 9, 1865, the Army of the Trans-Mississippi rapidly disintegrated as soldiers simply walked away. Ten days after Appomattox, the Confederate District of Arkansas was consolidated with the District of West Louisiana, and Buckner assumed command of the combined district. On May 9 Kirby Smith appointed him his chief of staff. It was rumored that Smith and Buckner intended to lead Confederate loyalists into Mexico; however, Buckner surrendered at New Orleans on May 26.

Buckner entered politics after the war and was elected governor of Kentucky in 1887. His term ended in 1891, and he continued to be politically active, living to the age of ninety.

JOHN BANKHEAD MAGRUDER, II CORPS

Magruder was born in 1810 at Winchester, Virginia, and graduated from West Point in 1830, where his imperious flamboyance earned him the sobriquet "Prince John." He entered the army as a second lieutenant of infantry but soon transferred to the artillery. He saw service in the West, as well as on the East Coast, including in Florida during the Second Seminole War (1835–42). Magruder was promoted to first lieutenant in 1836 and

made captain a decade later, shortly before the outbreak of the US-Mexican War (1846–48). He fought at the Battle of Palo Alto (May 8, 1846) and commanded an artillery battery at the Battle of Cerro Gordo (April 18, 1847), receiving a brevet to major. Another brevet, to lieutenant colonel, was forthcoming after the assault on Chapultepec (September 13, 1847).

After the war with Mexico, Magruder was assigned to garrison duty in Maryland, Rhode Island, and California. He resigned his USA commission on the eve of the Civil War and joined the Confederate forces as an infantry colonel on March 16, 1861. In June he saw his first action, at Big Bethel (June 10, 1861, Virginia; Confederate victory), successfully repulsing Major General Benjamin Butler's attempt to advance from Fortress Monroe. Magruder was rewarded with a promotion to brigadier general in July, which was followed by a step up to major general in October.

Magruder had charge of Confederate forces on Virginia's Yorktown Peninsula, where he went head to head with Union general George B. McClellan during the Peninsula Campaign (March–July 1862). He maneuvered his 12,000 troops so skillfully that he succeeded in deceiving McClellan into vastly overestimating his strength. This tied down the Union general in what was an unnecessary siege of Yorktown during April 5–May 4, 1862.

Magruder fought gallantly in the Seven Days Battles (June 25–July 1), but his tardiness in executing Robert E. Lee's orders at Malvern Hill (July 1, 1862; Confederate defeat) drew Lee's ire. Lee exiled Magruder to service in Texas in October, where he assumed command of II Corps, Army of the Trans-Mississippi. His responsibilities were extended to include Arizona and New Mexico.

Magruder excelled as the head of II Corps, taking Galveston, Texas, seizing the Union gunboat *Harriet Lane*, and driving off the

Galveston blockading squadron on January 1, 1863. He also participated in General Richard Taylor's operations against General Nathaniel Banks's Red River Campaign (March 10–May 22, 1864; Confederate victory). At the conclusion of the Civil War, Magruder fled to Mexico, where he accepted a commission as major general in the service of the doomed Mexican emperor Maximilian I. He did not return to the United States until 1869, two years before his death in 1871.

JOHN GEORGE WALKER, III CORPS

Walker was born in Jefferson City, Missouri, in 1821 and was educated at Washington Institute (today Washington University) in St. Louis. Two years after graduating in 1844, he joined the USA as a first lieutenant in the Regiment of Mounted Rifles. He served with this unit in the US-Mexican War (1846–48), receiving a brevet to captain after the Battle of San Juan de los Llanos, and was wounded at the Battle of Molino del Rey (September 8, 1847).

After the war, in June 1851, Walker was promoted to the regular rank of captain and, seven years later, married Sophie Baylor, of the family for whom Baylor University is named. Walker remained in the USA until July 1861, when he resigned his commission to join the CSA as a major in the cavalry. Rapidly promoted to lieutenant colonel of the 8th Texas Cavalry Regiment in August 1861, he was sent to North Carolina and promoted to colonel in September 1861, and, in January 1862, to brigadier general. He fought in the Peninsula Campaign (March–July 1862) under Brigadier General Theophilus H. Holmes and was wounded at the Battle of Malvern Hill (July 1, 1862; Confederate defeat). He fought under Major General James Longstreet at the Battles of South Mountain (September 14, 1862, Maryland; Confederate defeat) and Antietam (September 17, 1862, Maryland; Confederate strategic defeat).

Promoted to major general two months after Antietam, Walker was assigned to command a dozen Texas regiments—a total of 12,000 men—in the Trans-Mississippi Army. He organized his regiments into what was initially termed a division and subsequently designated as III Corps. His command was given the sobriquet of "Walker's Greyhounds" because of the great speed and marching endurance of its personnel. The Greyhounds fought with the Army of the Trans-Mississippi from November 1862 until war's end.

In March 1863 Lieutenant General Edmund Kirby Smith assigned Walker's Greyhounds to the Western Louisiana Command under Major General Richard Taylor. Walker was tasked with disrupting General Grant's supply line, which initially ran along the west bank of the Mississippi River to the shore opposite Vicksburg, the fortress town to which Grant was laying siege. Unobserved by the Confederates, Grant had quietly moved his supply lines to the east bank of the river. Walker's attack therefore proved fruitless. One of his units, Hawes's Brigade, was engaged in combat against the Federals at the Battle of Young's Point (June 7, 1863, Louisiana; Confederate defeat). Another, McCullough's Brigade, engaged US Colored Troops at the Battle of Milliken's Bend (June 7, 1863, Louisiana; Confederate defeat). The raw Union African Brigade, poorly trained, was badly mauled, but Union gunboats fired on McCullough's men, driving his brigade back and snatching victory from the jaws of defeat.

Following the defeat at Milliken's Bend, Taylor requested General Smith to assign Walker's Greyhounds to support his attack on New Orleans. Smith refused, however, and III Corps did nothing for the rest of the summer except to patrol northeastern Louisiana without engaging the enemy. In the meantime, Grant took Vicksburg on July 4, 1863.

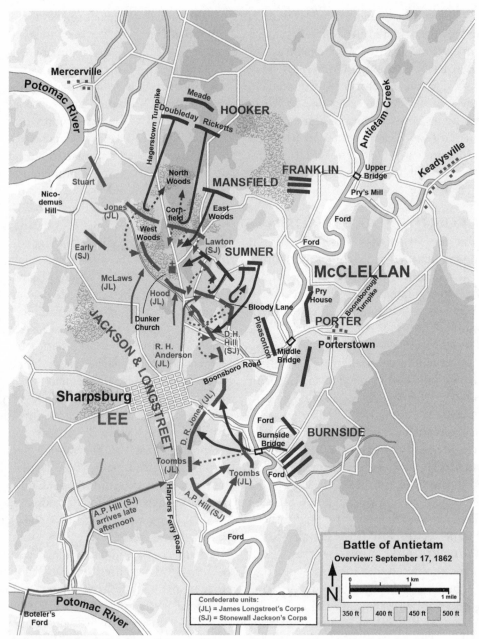

The Battle of Antietam, September 17, 1862. Map by Hal Jespersen, www.cwmaps.com

Late in 1863, Walker led III Corps back to Arkansas, where it was headquartered. In March 1864 his corps was dispatched to assist Taylor in opposing Union general Nathaniel P. Banks's Red River Campaign. The corps was instrumental in winning the Battle of Mansfield (April 8, 1864, Louisiana; Confederate victory), which brought Banks's miserably failed Red River Campaign to an end.

From Mansfield, Smith ordered Walker's corps north to engage Major General Frederick Steele at the Battle of Jenkins' Ferry (April 30, 1864, Arkansas; narrow Confederate defeat). Although forced into retreat, Steele preserved his command intact and frustrated what had seemed a certain victory for Walker.

In August 1864 Walker was assigned command of the Department of Alabama, Mississippi, and Eastern Louisiana. Before war's end he was transferred yet again, to command of the District of Texas, New Mexico, and Arizona. Like Magruder, Walker crossed into Mexico at the end of the Civil War and did not return to the United States until several years later. Fluent in Spanish, he served the US government as consul in Bogotá, Colombia, and as special commissioner to the Pan-American Conference held in Washington, DC, during 1889–90.

STERLING PRICE, CAVALRY CORPS (AMONG OTHER COMMANDS)

Born in Prince Edward County, Virginia, in 1809, Price spent a year at Hampton-Sydney College (Virginia) and then studied law. In 1831 he followed his parents in a move to Missouri, where Price set up as a tobacco farmer in Chariton County. He became active in politics and served for six years in the Missouri legislature, four of them as speaker. He was elected to the US House of Representatives in 1844, resigning in August 1846 to command a Missouri regiment in the US-Mexican War (1846–48). Headquartered in Santa Fe, New Mexico,

Price was ultimately assigned to command all US forces in the area. He suppressed the Taos Revolt (an uprising by local Pueblo Indians, January 19–July 9, 1847) and then led an invasion into Mexico itself, capturing Chihuahua, of which he was appointed military governor in July 1847 and promoted to brigadier general of US Volunteers.

Price returned to Missouri a military hero, which helped him to win the governorship in 1853. After leaving office in 1857, he resumed tobacco farming and served as the Missouri state bank commissioner until 1861.

Opposed to the secession of Missouri, Price was elected to preside over the state's 1861 Secession Convention, which voted on February 28, 1861, against seceding. But when US Army forces seized Camp Jackson, the Missouri state militia headquarters in St. Louis, Price took the action as a declaration of war against his home state, threw in his lot with the secessionists, and accepted appointment as commanding officer of the Missouri State Guard in May.

He led the state guard at the Battle of Wilson's Creek (August 10, 1861, Missouri; Confederate victory) and pushed Union forces back into southwestern Missouri. With the onset of winter, many of Price's guardsmen joined the CSA, to which Missouri contributed two brigades. In the meantime, Price and CSA Brigadier General Benjamin McCulloch fell to disputing over strategy, whereupon Confederate president Jefferson Davis appointed Major General Earl Van Dorn to command of the Trans-Mississippi District. Van Dorn resolved the Price-McCulloch dispute by ordering Price's units to unite with those under McCulloch as the Army of the West, and Price was commissioned a major general in the CSA on March 6, 1862.

Van Dorn engaged Union forces at the Battle of Pea Ridge (March 6–8, 1862, Arkansas; Confederate defeat), in which Price participated. Following defeat in this battle, Price crossed the Mississippi River to reinforce P. G. T. Beauregard at Corinth, Mississippi. En route he engaged Union Major General William S. Rosecrans in the Battle of Iuka (September 19, 1862, Mississippi; Confederate defeat). Defeated, Price could not advance and was forced to withdraw. Fortunately for him, Rosecrans declined to give chase, but it was not until October 3–4 that Price finally fought at Corinth, at the *Second* Battle of Corinth, under the command of Van Dorn. The result of that engagement was a heavy Confederate defeat, which sent Price to Richmond, Virginia, early in 1863, where he demanded and received an audience with President Jefferson Davis. He asked that both he and the Missouri troops he led be transferred west of the Mississippi. Davis regarded Price as supremely arrogant and responded to his request by sending him back to Missouri—without his command.

Price returned to fighting in Arkansas during the summer of 1863. Early in 1864, General Edmund Kirby Smith, as commanding officer of the Army of the Trans-Mississippi, sent Price to Arkansas, where he engaged Union forces under Major General Frederick Steele at the Battle of Prairie D'Ane (Camden, April 9–13, 1864, Arkansas; Confederate defeat).

Despite his failures in Arkansas, Price was assigned command of the Confederate District of Arkansas on March 16, 1864, and invaded Missouri in a raid that commenced with a loss at the Battle of Fort Davidson (September 27, 1864, Missouri). Price scored victories at the Battle of Glasgow (October 15), Little Blue River (October 21), and the Second Battle of Independence (October 21–22). These were succeeded by the Battle of Westport (October 23; Confederate defeat), in which Price was outnumbered more than two to one. It was the largest battle in the Trans-Mississippi Theater and was followed two days later by the Battle of Mine Creek (October 25, Kansas), another loss.

Numerous small engagements came after Mine Creek, steadily wearing away Price's force, including the Cavalry Corps. Price returned to Arkansas, where he established a headquarters at Laynesport, but he never returned to the field. At war's end Sterling Price refused to surrender, instead leading some of his men into Mexico. When Emperor Maximilian declined his offer of military service, Price founded a Confederate exile colony in Carlota, Veracruz. The colony soon faltered, Price fell ill, and he returned to Missouri, where he died in 1867 in St. Louis.

COMBAT CHRONOLOGY

Confederate military formations west of the Mississippi River often came into being quickly, only to vanish even more rapidly. The Army of the Trans-Mississippi was loosely organized, and its constituent units were flung far across an enormous area. This chronology lists only the major battles.

- Battle of Wilson's Creek
  (August 10, 1861)
  —Confederate victory

- Battle of Chustenahlah
  (December 26, 1861)
  —Confederate victory

- Battle of Pea Ridge
  (or Elkhorn Tavern, March 6–8, 1862)
  —Confederate defeat

- Battle of Galveston
  (January 1, 1863)
  —Confederate defeat

- Battle of Honey Springs
  (July 17, 1863)
  —Confederate defeat

- Second Battle of Sabine Pass
  (September 8, 1863)
  —Confederate victory

- Battle of Little Rock
  (September 10, 1863)
  —Confederate defeat

- Battle of Mansfield
  (April 8, 1864)
  —Confederate victory

- Battle of Prairie D'Ane
  (Camden, April 9-13, 1864)
  —Confederate defeat

- Battle of Poison Spring
  (April 16, 1864)
  —Confederate victory

- Battle of Marks' Mill
  (April 25, 1864)
  —Confederate victory

- Battle of Yellow Bayou
  (May 18, 1864)
  —Confederate defeat

- Battle of Pilot Knob
  (September 27, 1864)
  —Confederate defeat

- Battle of Westport
  (October 23, 1864)
  —Confederate defeat

- Battle of Mine Creek
  (October 25, 1864)
  —Confederate defeat

- Battle of Palmito Ranch
  (May 12–13, 1865)
  —Confederate victory, and the final battle
  of the Civil War

Chapter 18

ARMY OF TENNESSEE

OVERALL PERFORMANCE: ★ ★ ⸓

The Army of Tennessee was the Confederacy's primary force in the Western Theater, demarcated by the Appalachian Mountains on the east and the Mississippi River on the west. (The theater west of the Mississippi was referred to as the Trans-Mississippi Theater and was the responsibility of the Army of the Trans-Mississippi; see chapter 17.) Formed in November 1862, the Army of Tennessee endured through the end of the war and fought in most of the major battles in this theater. It was something of a hard-luck force, with gallant soldiers but mediocre to poor leadership at the top. Of the four biggest battles in which it was engaged (Murfreesboro, July 13, 1862; Chickamauga, September 19–20, 1863; Atlanta, July 22, 1864; and Nashville, December 15–16, 1864), only Chickamauga was a clear Confederate victory. (The Army of Tennessee is an example of the CSA tendency to name its armies after states or geographical areas, versus the USA's tendency to name them after prominent rivers. Thus the CSA Army of Tennessee is not to be confused with the USA Army of the Tennessee, covered in chapter 22.)[1]

ESTABLISHMENT

The defeat of Braxton Bragg, commanding a formation designated the Army of Mississippi, and Edmund Kirby Smith, commanding what was at the time called the Army of East Tennessee, at the bloody Battle of Perryville (October 8, 1862) brought the collapse of the Confederate invasion of Kentucky and motivated the merger of Bragg's and Smith's armies as the Army of Tennessee, under the command of Bragg, on November 20, 1862. Initially, the new army was divided into three corps, I Corps under Leonidas Polk, II Corps under William J. Hardee, and III Corps under Smith. The latter was disbanded, however, in December when Smith returned to east Tennessee. Early the next year, in March 1863, he would assume command of the Army of the Trans-Mississippi.

COMMANDING GENERALS

Braxton Bragg commanded the Army of Tennessee from its establishment on November 20, 1862, until December 2, 1863. A passionate but deeply flawed commander, Bragg was born in 1817 in Warrenton, North Carolina, and graduated from West Point in 1837. The new second lieutenant was assigned to the 3rd Artillery. Throughout his career, it was as an artilleryman that Bragg proved most adept. His first combat service was in the Second Seminole War (1835–42), and his next was in the US-Mexican War (1846–48). Serving under Major General Zachary Taylor, Bragg was initially stationed at Fort Brown (near present-day Brownsville, Texas) during May 3–9, 1846, and was brevetted to the rank of captain. At the Battle of Monterrey (September 21–24, 1846), he performed with distinction and was brevetted major. Likewise at Buena Vista (February 22–23, 1847), he showed great courage and competence. The skill with which he deployed his artillery battery played a key role in Taylor's victory.

Emerging a hero from the war with Mexico, Bragg plodded through the peacetime army until his penchant for dispute erupted in December 1855 against his friend Jefferson Davis, who was at the time secretary of war in the cabinet of Franklin Pierce. When Davis proposed stationing artillery batteries in various western frontier posts, Bragg lashed out at what he termed the absurdity of "chas[ing] Indians with six-pounders." He then went out of his way to travel to Washington and tell Davis in person. Davis dug in and refused to back down. Bragg immediately tendered his resignation—and Davis accepted it without protest. Bragg resigned his commission in January 1856 and purchased a sugar plantation outside of Thibodaux, Louisiana.[2] As a planter he displayed great ability in civil engineering, designing not only a drainage and levee system for his property, but for the entire state.

In February 1861 Bragg answered the call to service in the Louisiana militia, and then entered the Confederate States Army as a brigadier general on March 7. In September he was promoted to major general and took command of II Corps in the newly formed Army of Mississippi under General Albert S. Johnston. After leading the Confederate right flank at the Battle of Shiloh (April 6–7, 1862, Tennessee; Confederate defeat), he was promoted to full general on April 12, 1862. Assigned in June to command what was then designated the Army of Mississippi, Bragg invaded Kentucky from August through October of 1862. His intention was to bring this border state into the Confederate fold, but, though reinforced by Smith's Army of Eastern Tennessee, Bragg was defeated at the Battle of Perryville (October 8, 1862) and withdrew from the state. He fought against General William Rosecrans at the Battle of Stones River (Murfreesboro; December 31, 1862–January 2, 1863, Tennessee; Confederate defeat), but was once again compelled to withdraw. He nevertheless managed to maneuver out of Chattanooga early in September 1863 and defeat Rosecrans at the chaotic Battle of Chickamauga (September 19–20, 1863, Georgia). This time it was the Union forces that withdrew, to Chattanooga, where Bragg held them under siege until Ulysses Grant came to Rosecrans's relief,

Lieutenant General Joseph E. Johnston, CSA.
National Archives and Records Administration

defeating Bragg in the Battles for Chattanooga (November 23–25, 1863, Tennessee).

In the wake of this defeat, Bragg was relieved of command of the Army of Tennessee on December 2, 1863, and replaced by a temporary commander, William J. Hardee (December 2–16, 1863). On December 16 General Joseph E. Johnston assumed command. Recalled from the field, Bragg was appointed as one of Jefferson Davis's military advisers. Early in 1865, however, he personally raised a small force in North Carolina to defend against the advance of William T. Sherman's March to the Sea. With General Johnston, Bragg surrendered to Sherman on April 26, 1865. The war over, he returned to civil engineering, practicing his profession in Texas.

Joseph E. Johnston was a native of Farmville, Virginia, born in 1807. He graduated from West

Point in 1829 and was commissioned a second lieutenant in the artillery. During service in the Second Seminole War (1835–42), he was promoted to first lieutenant (July 1836), but, the promotion notwithstanding, Johnston was discouraged by the paucity of prospects for advancement in the military. He resigned his commission in May 1837 to enter civil engineering, only to return a year later, once again fighting the Seminoles—this time as a member of the Corps of Topographical Engineers rather than the artillery.

During the US-Mexican War, Johnston served under General Winfield Scott and distinguished himself at Cerro Gordo on April 18, 1847, after which he was brevetted to colonel. After serving in the Utah (or Mormon) War (1857–58), Johnston was promoted to brigadier general and appointed quartermaster general of the army in June 1860. Less than a year later, in April 1861, he resigned his commission to join the Provisional Army of the Confederate States of America as a brigadier general in command of the (Confederate) Army of Shenandoah (not to be confused with the [Union] Army of the Shenandoah, discussed in chapter 26). At the First Battle of Bull Run (July 21, 1861, Virginia), Johnston was the ranking Confederate officer and was instrumental in giving the South its first major victory.

In August 1861 Johnston was promoted to general and made commander of the (Confederate) Army of the Potomac, predecessor of the Army of Northern Virginia (Chapter 16). He faced Union general George B. McClellan in the Peninsula Campaign (March–July 1862), during which he was wounded at the Battle of Fair Oaks (May 31–June 1, 1862, Virginia; inconclusive). He was replaced by Robert E. Lee as commander of what was now called the Army of Northern Virginia.

After Johnston's convalescence and return to duty, he was named commander of the Department of the West in November 1862

and directed the first phase of a heroic defense of Vicksburg, Mississippi, against an attack and siege by Ulysses S. Grant. In command of dwindling forces, Johnston was driven from his base of operations at Jackson, Mississippi, by Major General William T. Sherman on May 14, 1863, and could do nothing to prevent the fall of Vicksburg on July 4.

After Vicksburg, Johnston became commander of the Army of Tennessee (December 16, 1863), and was able to extract a measure of revenge against Sherman by capitalizing on the Union general's ill-judged offensive at the Battle of Kennesaw Mountain (June 27, 1864, Georgia; Confederate victory), near Atlanta. Johnston next defended Atlanta itself, but did so through a series of strategic retreats. Confederate president Jefferson Davis, appalled by Johnston's inability to drive back the attack on the South's key rail hub, relieved him of command of the Army of Tennessee.

Johnston's successor, John Bell Hood, was born in Owingsville, Kentucky, in 1831, the son of a respected physician and his socially prominent wife. They lived on a 600-acre plantation, owned slaves, and conducted themselves as aristocrats. Although his father wanted him to become a physician, Hood enrolled at West Point in 1849 and, despite a poor disciplinary record, graduated forty-fourth out of the fifty-two-member Class of 1853.

As new second lieutenant, Hood was assigned to the 4th US Infantry in California and was transferred to the 2nd US Cavalry at Fort Mason, Texas. Hood was thrilled with patrolling in Comanche country and received his first combat wound—an arrow through his left hand—in an 1857 skirmish. Promoted to first lieutenant, he turned down an offer to serve as chief instructor of cavalry at West Point in 1860, likely because, with civil war in the offing, he preferred the company of fellow

Confederate defenses on the perimeter of Atlanta. NATIONAL ARCHIVES AND RECORDS ADMINISTRATION

Southerners in Texas to a teaching post on the Hudson. With the fall of Fort Sumter in April 1861, Hood resigned his commission, intending to volunteer for service in the Kentucky militia. When the state voted not to secede, he secured a commission as first lieutenant in the Provisional Army of the Confederate States and reported to Robert E. Lee in Richmond, Virginia. Lee sent him to Yorktown under the command of Colonel John Magruder, who assigned Hood command of all his cavalry companies, promoting him to captain and almost immediately thereafter to major.

On September 30, 1861, Hood was promoted to colonel and given command of 4th Texas Infantry Regiment, which had been sent to the Eastern Theater. Upgraded to brigade strength, the unit became Hood's Texas Brigade,

which was attached to the Army of Northern Virginia. On March 3, 1862, Hood was promoted to brigadier general.

Hood's first battle was at Eltham's Landing (May 7, 1862, Virginia; inconclusive). During the Seven Days, Hood fought at the Battle of Gaines's Mill (June 27, 1862, Virginia; Confederate victory). He led his brigade at the Second Battle of Bull Run (August 28–30, 1862; Confederate victory) and was promoted to division commander. At Antietam (September 17, 1862, Maryland; Confederate strategic defeat), Hood sacrificed much of his division to protect Stonewall Jackson's corps. Next came the Battle of Fredericksburg (December 11–15, 1862, Virginia; Confederate victory) and then Gettysburg (July 1–3, 1863, Pennsylvania; Confederate defeat). Hood protested Lee and Longstreet's

An incongruously pictorial view of the "Destruction of General Hood's Ordnance Train," photographed by George N. Barnard and included in his Photographic Views of Sherman's Campaign, *published in 1864.* NATIONAL ARCHIVES AND RECORDS ADMINISTRATION

order to assault Little Round Top frontally, proposing instead to attack from the rear. It was a good tactical idea, but Longstreet spurned it. Hood suffered serious wounds at Gettysburg and was out of action until the Battle of Chickamauga (September 19–20, 1863, Georgia; Confederate victory).

It was during the Atlanta Campaign (May 7–September 2, 1864, Georgia) that Jefferson Davis chose Hood to replace Joseph E. Johnston as commanding officer of the Army of Tennessee. Abandoning Johnston's policy of tactical defense, Hood launched four reckless, futile, and costly counterattacks on the Union's William T. Sherman. After losing Atlanta and suffering heavy casualties, Hood marched west to link up with Nathan Bedford Forrest,

intending to defeat the Union's Army of the Ohio under James M. Schofield and the Army of the Cumberland under George H. Thomas and draw Sherman out of Georgia. Instead, he was defeated by Schofield at Franklin and by Thomas at Nashville. These losses decimated the Army of Tennessee. Hood asked President Davis to relieve him of command. The Confederate president obliged, replacing him in February 1865 with (at Lee's request) Johnston, the commander Hood had earlier replaced. Johnston led the Army of Tennessee in a valiant effort to check Sherman's March to the Sea (November 15–December 21, 1864, Georgia; Confederate defeat) and at the Battle of Bentonville (March 19–21, 1865, North Carolina; Confederate defeat). Vastly outnumbered in North Carolina,

Johnston surrendered to Sherman at Durham Station on April 26, effectively ending the Civil War.

SIZE AND ORGANIZATION

As with most Confederate armies, the organization of the Army of Tennessee varied. At the height of its strength prior to Chickamauga, in September 1863, it numbered 48,000 infantry and 15,000 cavalry. The army consisted of three infantry corps and one of cavalry.

In November 1862 I Corps was created under the command of Lieutenant General Leonidas Polk. He was succeeded by Major General B. F. Cheatham, Lieutenant General William J. Hardee, and Major General Patrick Cleburne. A part of III Corps was added to I Corps on October 31, 1863; the Reserve Corps was added to it on November 4, 1863; and on April 10, 1865, as the war was rapidly winding down, all forces remaining in Georgia were added.

April 1862 brought the creation of II Corps at Corinth, Mississippi, consisting of two divisions, one under Jones Withers, the other commanded by Daniel Ruggles. This corps had the distinction of being the largest in the CSA at the time of its formation, at 22,000 men. It was initially commanded by Braxton Bragg. When Bragg was promoted to commanding officer of the Army of Mississippi effective May 7, 1862, William J. Hardee assumed command of the Army of Tennessee, followed by John Breckenridge. Breckinridge was relieved after the struggle for Chattanooga, and John Bell Hood became commanding officer. After Hood was elevated to command of the Army of Tennessee during the Atlanta Campaign, John C. Breckinridge and then Alexander P. Stewart assumed command of II Corps.

Five commanders had a turn leading III Corps: William J. Hardee, Edmund Kirby Smith, Simon Bolivar Buckner, Leonidas Polk, and Alexander P. Stewart. It was formed when Major General Hardee's division, originally part of the Central Army of Kentucky, was consolidated with other Confederate forces prior to the Battle of Shiloh (April 6–7, 1862). With only 6,789 men, it was the smallest of the corps in the Army of Tennessee at that point but grew to 26,500 men late in 1862. Not fighting in a major battle, the corps was soon broken up, only to be reconstituted during the Siege of Vicksburg (May 18–July 4, 1863), when it became 33,000 strong. Disbanded in the course of the siege, it was reassembled for operations designed to lift the siege, reaching a strength of 42,000 before it was again dissolved after the fall of Vicksburg on July 4, 1863, with portions going to II Corps. In the campaign culminating in the Battle of Chickamauga (September 19–20, 1863), III Corps was reconstituted under Stewart, only to be broken up after the battle. Under Polk, III Corps was assembled a final time following the Battles for Chattanooga (November 23–25, 1863).

Although Forrest's Cavalry Corps is the cavalry formation most closely associated with the Army of Tennessee, it was not the only cavalry unit to fight as part of it. On January 22, 1863, Major General Joseph Wheeler was given command of all the cavalry in Middle Tennessee, and in March the cavalry divisions in the Army of Tennessee were designated as two corps, one under Wheeler and the other under Earl Van Dorn. Wheeler's Corps, at its height, consisted of 12,000 men and was active (often in diminished numbers) throughout the war. Van Dorn's Corps was activated on March 16, 1863, numbering 8,000. When Van Dorn was murdered on May 7 of that year by a physician who claimed the general was sleeping with his wife, command of his cavalry was assumed by Nathan Bedford Forrest. It served with the Army of Tennessee until early in the Chattanooga Campaign, when army commander Braxton Bragg ordered Forrest to transfer most of his corps to Wheeler's

Corps. Forrest essentially mutinied, threatening to kill Bragg if he dared give him further orders. At this, President Davis transferred Forrest to Mississippi to form a new cavalry corps.

MAJOR CAMPAIGNS AND BATTLES

KENTUCKY CAMPAIGN (JUNE–OCTOBER 1862)

In August 1862 Braxton Bragg invaded Kentucky with his Army of Mississippi (predecessor to the Army of Tennessee). His objective was to rally Southern supporters in the border state to join the Confederacy, thereby drawing the Union's Army of the Ohio (Don Carlos Buell) away from the Eastern Theater. He concentrated in Chattanooga, Tennessee, whence he moved north into Kentucky, coordinating his advance with that of Edmund Kirby Smith, who was starting out from Knoxville.

At the Battle of Munfordville (September 14–17, 1862, Kentucky; Confederate victory), Bragg captured some 4,000 Union soldiers, then advanced to Bardstown and participated in the inauguration of a provisional Confederate governor (October 4, 1862). The Army of Mississippi engaged the Army of the Ohio at the Battle of Perryville (October 8, 1862, Kentucky; Confederate strategic defeat). Had Bragg pressed the fight, he might have achieved victory, but he vacillated and then retreated through the Cumberland Gap to Knoxville.

The Kentucky Campaign collapsed but did succeed in pushing Union forces out of northern Alabama and much of Middle Tennessee. Bragg's unsure leadership provoked protest and near-mutiny among his subordinates.

BATTLE OF STONES RIVER (DECEMBER 31, 1862–JANUARY 2, 1863)

Bragg's Army of Tennessee engaged William Rosecrans's Army of the Cumberland just outside of Murfreesboro, Tennessee. Bragg took the initiative, mauling Rosecrans's right flank. Unfortunately for Bragg, the false report of Rosecrans's withdrawal kept Bragg from moving to exploit his gains. By January 2 it became apparent that Rosecrans was holding his ground. Bragg therefore ordered Breckinridge to attack the Union left late in the afternoon. The Confederates came close to a breakthrough, but Union artillery disrupted the assault, resulting in a tactical draw—until Union reinforcements forced Bragg to retreat. Rosecrans thus gained a strategic victory.

CHICKAMAUGA CAMPAIGN (AUGUST 21–SEPTEMBER 20, 1863)

After the successful Tullahoma Campaign, Rosecrans continued the Union offensive, aiming to force Bragg's Confederate army out of Chattanooga. Through a series of skillful marches toward the Confederate-held city, Rosecrans forced Bragg out of Chattanooga and into Georgia. Determined to reoccupy the city, Bragg followed the Federals north, brushing with Rosecrans's army at Davis's Cross Roads. While they marched on September 18, Bragg's cavalry and infantry skirmished with Union mounted infantry, who were armed with state-of-the-art Spencer repeating rifles. Fighting began in earnest on the morning of the 19th near Chickamauga Creek. Bragg's men heavily assaulted Rosecrans's line, but the Union line held. Fighting resumed the following day. That afternoon, eight fresh brigades from the Army of Northern Virginia under General James Longstreet exploited a gap in the Federal line, driving one-third of Rosecrans's army, including Rosecrans himself, from the field. Only a portion of the Federal army, under General George Thomas, staved off disaster by holding Horseshoe Ridge against repeated assaults, allowing the Yankees to withdraw after nightfall. For this action Thomas earned the nickname the "Rock of Chickamauga." The defeated Union troops retreated to Chattanooga, where they remained until late November.

CHATTANOOGA CAMPAIGN (SEPTEMBER 21–NOVEMBER 25, 1863)

Grant's first priority after he was assigned to command the Union's western armies in October 1863 was to lift the Confederate siege of Chattanooga and the Army of the Cumberland that was holding the city. He brought in Sherman's Army of *the* Tennessee, and Bragg now found his Army of Tennessee fighting a heavily reinforced Union army. The Battles for Chattanooga began on November 23 when Union forces overran Orchard Knob and continued with Lookout Mountain (November 24–25) and Missionary Ridge (November 25). The breakthrough sent Bragg's army into a withdrawal that threw the door open to a Union invasion of the Deep South. It was the Army of Tennessee's most consequential defeat.

ATLANTA CAMPAIGN (MAY 7–SEPTEMBER 2, 1864)

The Army of Tennessee was under the command of Joseph E. Johnston during the Atlanta Campaign and consisted of three corps—I Corps, designated Hardee's Corps; II Corps, designated Hood's Corps; and III Corps, designated Polk's Corps—in addition to a cavalry corps, designated Wheeler's Corps, and an artillery reserve under Brigadier General Francis A. Shoup. Throughout the first phase of the campaign, Johnston responded to Sherman's attacks by steadily falling back on the city. After the Battle of Pace's Ferry (July 5, 1864), President Jefferson Davis replaced Johnston with the aggressive Hood, whose attempts at counterattack, from the Battle of Peachtree Creek (July 20, 1864) through the Battle of Jonesborough (August 31–September 1, 1864), failed to prevent the fall of Atlanta and the surrounding area.

BATTLE OF FRANKLIN (NOVEMBER 30, 1864)

Defeated at Atlanta, Hood and the Army of Tennessee marched west while Sherman, leaving an occupying force in Atlanta, commenced his March to the Sea. While Sherman marched east, he assigned the Army of the Ohio (John M. Schofield) and the Army of the Cumberland (George H. Thomas) to deal with Hood in Tennessee. On November 29, 1864, Hood engaged Schofield at Spring Valley, intending to destroy his outnumbered forces. He failed, and Schofield advanced to Franklin, not far from Nashville. On November 30 Hood made a reckless assault against Schofield's well-entrenched army and was repulsed with the loss of more than 6,000 men killed and wounded. Six Confederate generals died in the battle.

BATTLE OF NASHVILLE (DECEMBER 15–16, 1864)

Bloodied but unbowed, the Army of Tennessee (numbering about 30,000 at this point) advanced on Nashville, which was defended by some 55,000 men of Thomas's Army of the Cumberland. Despite the odds, Hood positioned his army south of the city on December 2. After a delay caused by winter weather, Thomas attacked on December 15, shattering the Army of Tennessee by the next day.

CAROLINAS CAMPAIGN (FEBRUARY–MARCH 21, 1865)

The Battles of Franklin and Nashville decimated the Army of Tennessee, but, once again under the command of Joseph E. Johnston, it marched toward the Carolinas. Johnston's objective was to consolidate with the remaining forces under Beauregard, Hardee, and Bragg to arrest Sherman's devastating advance through the Carolinas. The Army of Tennessee fought at Aiken (February 11, South Carolina; Confederate victory),

Monroe's Crossroads (March 10, North Carolina; inconclusive), and Averasborough (March 16, North Carolina; inconclusive) before the final showdown at Bentonville (March 19-21, North Carolina; Union victory). Johnston's battered army fought gallantly, doing great damage to Union general O. O. Howard's XIV Corps before Union counterattacks arrested Johnston's offensive thrust. The Army of Tennessee and units consolidated with it retreated toward Raleigh. Sherman failed to pursue. For his part, however, Johnston believed the Army of Tennessee and the rest of the CSA were finished. He held a grand review of his forces on April 6 at Selma, North Carolina, and surrendered to Sherman on April 26.

Chapter 19

ARMY OF THE POTOMAC

OVERALL PERFORMANCE: ★ ★ ★

At the height of its strength at the time of the Battle of Chancellorsville (April 30–May 6, 1863), the Army of the Potomac numbered 133,868 men classified as fit and ready for duty. It was, beyond question, the largest force in the Union army and far larger than its Confederate counterpart, the great Army of Northern Virginia (which fielded at Chancellorsville 60,298 men).[1] More than this, it was the largest military formation the United States Army had fielded up to that time and would not be surpassed in size until the two world wars of the twentieth century. It also suffered more casualties, proportionately, than any other American army before or since. Its most famous battle—of many famous battles—was Gettysburg (July 1–3, 1863), which was also the bloodiest battle of America's bloodiest war. Of the 104,256 Union troops engaged at Gettysburg, 23,049 became casualties (3,155 killed, 14,529 wounded, 5,365 captured or missing).[2] A 22 percent casualty rate, it was all too typical of Army of the Potomac losses. Yet this valiant army, more than any other, was responsible for the Union victory in the Civil War.

ESTABLISHMENT

Humble indeed was the precursor of an army larger than any previously imagined by the American military. It was the Army of Northeastern Virginia (sometimes called the Army of Northern Virginia), commanded by Brigadier General Irvin McDowell, which numbered between 32,000 and 35,000 men—the size of a single corps at the height of the Civil War. The ignominious defeat McDowell suffered in the first major engagement of the war, the

First Battle of Bull Run (July 21, 1861), persuaded President Lincoln and his generals that the nation required a larger and better flagship fighting force. At this point only one general had delivered victories—albeit minor ones—for the Union. George Brinton McClellan was recalled from his command in western Virginia to organize military forces in and around Washington, DC. As recruits answered the president's call for volunteers and regiments flowed into Washington, McClellan, who had been in civilian life chief engineer and vice president of the Illinois Central Railroad, exercised his considerable managerial prowess to process the incoming recruits. He organized them into provisional brigades for purposes of training—training in a program of his own design. Simultaneously, he built esprit de corps, beginning with the majestic name of the army into which the men would be inducted: the Army of the Potomac.

By October 15, 1861, McClellan had organized the army into a dozen divisions and paraded his creation in a grand review just outside of the capital. But at this moment of the promise of triumph to come, McClellan demonstrated the excess of caution that would mark his generalship of the Army of the Potomac. He delayed deploying the army in the field until the spring of 1862. This provoked a congressional investigation into what came to seem an interminable delay. Worse, Congress, not McClellan or other senior officers, appointed the army's subordinate generals, choosing from among candidates who shared the view that action, even premature action, was preferable to delay.

At this point generals lobbying Congress for corps commands entered the dispute between Congress and McClellan. He favored using divisions as the largest formation within the army and delaying the creation of corps until the divisional commanders proved themselves in battle. The most successful officers could then be promoted to corps command. As Congress relentlessly pushed the corps upon McClellan, so its Joint Committee on the Conduct of the War rejected his time-consuming plan for operations against the Confederate capital at Richmond and demanded immediate action. President Lincoln, acting as commander in chief, officially established the corps as the major organizational unit of the Army of the Potomac in March 1862. Born in hope, the new army was soon roiled by internecine dispute and military careerism.

COMMANDING GENERALS

Brigadier General Irvin McDowell, as commanding officer of the Army and Department of Northeastern Virginia (May 27–July 25, 1861), was the first commander of the army from which the Army of the Potomac was created. He was born in 1818 in Columbus, Ohio, and was educated abroad, in France, before returning to the United States to enroll at West Point. After graduating in 1838, he was assigned to duty along the Canadian border with the 1st Artillery Regiment during 1838–41 and then returned to West Point as an instructor, serving in this capacity to 1845. In October of that year, McDowell was appointed aide-de-camp to Major General John E. Wool, under whom he served during the US-Mexican War (1846–48). McDowell distinguished himself at the Battle of Buena Vista (February 22–23, 1847) and was brevetted to captain, a promotion that became permanent in 1848, when he was assigned to the adjutant general's corps. From 1848 until the outbreak of the Civil War, McDowell served in a variety of staff posts, receiving promotion to major in 1856. During 1858–59, he was posted in Europe, to study military administration.

At the outbreak of the Civil War, McDowell was jumped to brigadier general and made field commander of the Washington area in May 1861. The formation he organized as the Army of Northeastern Virginia consisted of roughly 35,000 men. He deployed them in and around Washington, DC, although he believed they required more training before they could be declared ready for battle. Pushed by Congress to strike a preemptive blow against the "rebels," however, McDowell drew up a plan to outflank the army of Confederate general P. G. T. Beauregard at Centreville, Virginia, so as to cut it off from its base of supply at Richmond. Accordingly, McDowell led five divisions toward Manassas, Virginia, and occupied Centreville on July 18. He took three days to prepare his troops as best he could for battle—a delay that gave Beauregard ample opportunity to redeploy his forces advantageously. Worse, the delay gave Confederate general Joseph E. Johnston time to receive reinforcements (and the soon-to-be-legendary Thomas J. Jackson) from the Shenandoah Valley and link up with Beauregard. The result was the defeat of the Army of Northeastern Virginia at the First Battle of Bull Run (July 21, 1861), which prompted McDowell's replacement in August by George B. McClellan, who was given the task of building a new army.

As for McDowell, he was assigned command of III Corps in General John Pope's Army of the Rappahannock and fought in the Second Battle of Bull Run (August 28–30, 1862), which again resulted in defeat. Relieved of command, he was brought before a court of inquiry, which exonerated him of wrongdoing. Nevertheless, the unlucky general was exiled to distant commands: the Department of the Pacific and, subsequently, the Department of California. After the war he was given command of the Department of the East (July 1868) and, in November 1872, promoted to major general, he was named commander of the Department of the South.

From June 1876 until his retirement in October 1882, McDowell returned to command of the Department of the Pacific.

George B. McClellan, hailed by the press as the "Young Napoleon," was born in 1826 in Philadelphia. Always precocious, he graduated, second in his class, from West Point in 1846, just in time to serve in the US-Mexican War (1846–48). He distinguished himself at Contreras and Churubusco (August 19–20, 1847), for which he was brevetted to first lieutenant. He next fought with conspicuous gallantry at Chapultepec (September 13, 1847), for which he was brevetted captain. Following the war, McClellan returned to West Point as an instructor in engineering (1848–51) and then was assigned as chief engineer in the construction of Fort Delaware (near Delaware City, Delaware) during 1851–54. Promoted to the regular rank of captain, he was assigned to the cavalry in March 1855 and was dispatched to the Crimea as a US observer of the ongoing Crimean War.

McClellan resigned his commission in January 1857 to become chief engineer and vice president of the expanding Illinois Central Railroad. He then left that position in 1860 to become president of the Ohio & Mississippi Railroad. With the outbreak of the Civil War, McClellan accepted appointment as major general of Ohio Volunteers in April 1861. The next month he was commissioned a major general of regulars and given command of the Department of the Ohio. His first engagement, at Rich Mountain on July 11, resulted in a victory that secured for the Union what subsequently became West Virginia. This and other minor triumphs prompted McClellan's recall to the Eastern Theater to organize the defenses around the capital and create a new principal army to put down the rebellion. Not only was he named to command the new Army of the Potomac in July, he also was chosen by Abraham Lincoln to replace the aging Winfield Scott as general-in-chief of the United States Army in November 1861.

Although McClellan worked miracles in organizing the Army of the Potomac, he soon proved himself chronically overcautious as a field commander. He led his army on the Peninsula Campaign (March–July 1862) with the objective of taking the Confederate capital, Richmond, but he repeatedly hesitated, insisting on more time and resources to build an army that he judged capable of defeating the Confederate forces whose strength he vastly overestimated. At last, in March 1862, President Lincoln began to give up on the "Young Napoleon," relieving McClellan as Union general-in-chief, but retaining him in command of the Army of the Potomac.

During April 5–May 4, McClellan used the army to lay siege to Yorktown, which fell to him after inordinate delay due to yet another gross overestimation of Confederate strength there. He successfully repulsed an attack by Joseph E. Johnston at Fair Oaks (May 31) and then fought Robert E. Lee to a draw at Mechanicsville (June 26), but withdrew instead of pressing his advantage. Mechanicsville was one of the bloody series of battles known as the Seven Days (June 25–July 1, 1862). Although McClellan drove Lee back at the Battle of Malvern Hill (July 1, 1862, Virginia; Union tactical victory), he suffered a critical strategic defeat in the Seven Days, withdrawing with the Army of the Potomac and aborting his campaign against Richmond.

McClellan checked Robert E. Lee's ill-conceived invasion of Maryland in the fall of 1862, defeating the Army of Northern Virginia at South Mountain (September 14) and earning a slim, costly, but significantly strategic victory at Antietam (September 17). President Lincoln used the win as a platform from which to launch his preliminary Emancipation Proclamation. Nevertheless, as usual, McClellan failed to capitalize on what he had gained by declining

President Lincoln visits Major General George B. McClellan (the short man seen in profile facing Lincoln) at his camp on the Antietam battlefield. The 1862 photograph is by Alexander Gardner. NATIONAL ARCHIVES AND RECORDS ADMINISTRATION

to pursue the retreating Army of Northern Virginia. Deeply discouraged, President Lincoln at last replaced McClellan as commanding officer of the Army of the Potomac with Ambrose E. Burnside on November 9, 1862.

Sidelined after Antietam, McClellan remained in the army but, in 1864, became the Democratic nominee for president of the United States, challenging Lincoln's bid for reelection. McClellan resigned his commission just before election day and, after losing by a wide margin, he took a protracted European grand tour, ceasing to play any further role in the Civil War. In 1870 he became chief engineer for New York City's Department of Docks while also serving as trustee, then president, of the Atlantic & Great Western Railroad. McClellan was elected governor of New Jersey in 1877, serving until 1881. He succumbed to a heart attack in 1885.

Major General Ambrose E. Burnside twice declined President Lincoln's urging that he assume command of the Army of the Potomac, accepting only after being pressed and pressured a third time. He entered upon the assignment quite unsure that he was equal to it. As it turned out, his self-doubts were well justified. "General Burnside was an officer who was generally liked and respected," U. S. Grant wrote in his great *Personal Memoirs*. "He was not, however, fitted to command an army. No one knew this better than himself."[3]

Born in 1824 in Liberty, Indiana, Burnside graduated from West Point in 1847 and was commissioned a second lieutenant in the artillery. Quickly finding the army unrewarding, he resigned his commission in 1853 to take up management of a gun factory in Bristol, Rhode Island. He personally designed an innovative breech-loading carbine in 1856, but was unable to persuade the USA to adopt and purchase it. This led to his bankruptcy in 1857, after which he became an executive with the Illinois Central Railroad until the Civil War commenced in 1861. He assumed command of the 1st Rhode Island Volunteer Regiment in April, and by the First Battle of Bull Run (July 21, 1861), he was elevated to brigade command. On August 6 Burnside was promoted to brigadier general of volunteers, and in January 1862 he successfully led an amphibious expeditionary force against Confederate positions along the North Carolina coast. Burnside took Roanoke Island (February 7) and New Bern (March 14). His unit also sank Confederate blockade-runner vessels riding at anchor in the Albemarle and Pamlico Sounds. In recognition of these accomplishments, Burnside was promoted to major general of volunteers in March and, after his unit was redesignated IX Corps, he and his troops were transferred to regular federal service in the Army of the Potomac.

Burnside commanded the right wing (I and IX Corps) at the Battle of South Mountain (September 14, 1862, Maryland; Union victory) and three days later was in command of the left wing at Antietam (September 17, 1862, Maryland; Union strategic victory). Disappointed by McClellan's failure to capitalize on what was a narrow victory in an extremely bloody battle, President Lincoln replaced him with a reluctant Burnside as commander of the Army of the

Of Major General Ambrose Burnside, Grant wrote that he was not "fitted to command an army. No one knew this better than himself." NATIONAL ARCHIVES AND RECORDS ADMINISTRATION

Potomac in November. Immediately on taking command, Burnside unwisely reorganized the army into huge "Grand Divisions" (his term) containing two corps each. These gave the Army of the Potomac an impressively streamlined appearance on paper, but proved quite unwieldy in the field. Burnside led the Army of the Potomac to catastrophic defeat against an outnumbered Army of Northern Virginia at Fredericksburg (December 11–15, 1862, Virginia). In January 1863 Burnside attempted to mount a winter offensive but became bogged down in a January thaw, resulting in the so-called Mud March. On January 26, 1863, he was replaced by Major General Joseph Hooker as commander of the army.

Burnside was transferred to the Department of the Ohio in March but rejoined the Army of the Potomac in spring 1864 as commanding officer of IX Corps. At the siege of Petersburg (June 9, 1864–March 25, 1865), he suffered a grim defeat at the Battle of the Crater (July 30, 1864) and, following an adverse judgment by a court of inquiry, resigned his commission in April 1865. He was elected governor of Rhode Island in 1866, served to 1869, and then entered the US Senate in 1874. He died in office in 1881.

Major General Joseph Hooker assumed command of the Army and Department of the Potomac on January 26, 1863. Born in 1814 at Hadley, Massachusetts, Hooker graduated from West Point in 1837 and was commissioned a second lieutenant of artillery. His first combat assignment was in the Second Seminole War (1835–42). He was promoted to first lieutenant in November 1838. During the US-Mexican War (1846–48), Hooker was assigned as a staff officer, under first Zachary Taylor and then Winfield Scott. In combat Hooker demonstrated conspicuous gallantry, for which he received three brevet promotions, ending the war as a brevet lieutenant colonel. After the war, from 1849 to 1851, Hooker served in the Division of the Pacific, taking a leave of absence at the end of this period, then resigning in 1853 to take up farming in Sonoma, California.

In 1858 Hooker left farm life to become superintendent of military roads in Oregon until 1859, when he was appointed colonel of the California militia. In May 1861, at the outbreak of the Civil War, he became brigadier general of volunteers and moved to the Eastern Theater as a division commander in III Corps of the Army of the Potomac during McClellan's Peninsula Campaign (March–July 1862). He fought at the siege of Yorktown (April 5–May 4, 1862, Virginia; Union victory) and at the Battle of Williamsburg (May 5, Virginia; inconclusive).

Promoted to major general of volunteers, Hooker transferred to the short-lived Army of Virginia and led a division at the Second Battle of Bull Run (August 28–30, 1862, Virginia; Union defeat). In September he became commander of I Corps, Army of the Potomac, and fought at South Mountain (September 14, 1862, Maryland; Union victory), but he was wounded three days later at Antietam (September 17, Maryland; Union strategic victory). He recovered in time to command the Center Grand Division (a combination of III and V Corps) at the Battle of Fredericksburg (December 11–15, 1862, Virginia; Union defeat).

After replacing Burnside as commanding general of the Army of the Potomac, Hooker extensively reorganized the force along more conventional corps lines. This improved the maneuverability of the army greatly. Nevertheless, he was catastrophically defeated by Robert E. Lee at Chancellorsville (April 30–May 6, 1863) and asked to be relieved as commanding officer of the Army of the Potomac. Hooker was transferred with XI and XII Corps of the Army of the Potomac to reinforce the Army of the Cumberland in the Chattanooga Campaign (September 21–November 25, 1863). In this he redeemed himself as an excellent field commander at the Battle of Lookout Mountain (November 24, 1863, Tennessee; Union victory). For his action in this engagement, he was brevetted to major general of regulars, and, as commander of what was now designated XX Corps, he served well with William Tecumseh Sherman in the Atlanta Campaign (May 7–September 2, 1864).

Passed over for command of the Army of the Tennessee, Hooker again asked to be relieved of command of his corps, but was instead given command of the Northern Department (1864–65). At the end of the war, he commanded the Department of the East and in 1866 took command of the Department of the Lakes. Hooker retired in 1868 with the permanent rank of major general.

After Chancellorsville, Hooker was replaced as Army of the Potomac commanding general by Major General George G. Meade on June 28, 1863. Meade was born in 1815, into the family of an American naval agent in Cadiz, Spain. He grew up in Philadelphia and attended West Point, graduating in 1835, and was commissioned a second lieutenant in artillery. Posted to Florida, he served during the opening of the Second Seminole War (1835–42) but fell ill with fever and was invalided back north. Meade was so debilitated from this illness that he resigned his commission in 1836 and became a civil engineer; however, he rejoined the army in 1842, this time with the engineers. Four years later, with the outbreak of the US-Mexican War, he served under Zachary Taylor and fought at Palo Alto (May 8, 1846) and Resaca de la Palma (May 9). He performed with distinction at Monterrey (September 21–24), for which he was brevetted to first lieutenant.

When the war was over, Meade did survey work for the army in the Great Lakes region, in Philadelphia, and in Florida. In August 1851 his promotion to first lieutenant was made permanent, and in May 1856 he was promoted to captain. At the start of the Civil War, Meade was jumped to brigadier general of the Pennsylvania volunteers and was rushed to an assignment as part of the forces defending Washington. He next served under George McClellan in the Peninsula Campaign (March–July 1862) and was seriously wounded at the Battle of Frayser's Farm (June 30, 1862, Virginia; inconclusive).

Meade recovered by late summer and was present at the Second Battle of Bull Run (August 28–30, 1862, Virginia; Union defeat), after which he was promoted to command a division. He fought at South Mountain (September 14, 1862, Maryland; Union victory). Following this,

he took command of I Corps in the Army of the Potomac at the Battle of Antietam (September 17, 1862, Maryland; Union strategic victory) after Joseph Hooker was disabled by wounds. In November Meade was promoted to major general of volunteers and given command of 3rd Division, I Corps, at the Battle of Fredericksburg, where his troops eked out a temporary success on the Union left (December 11–15, 1862, Virginia; Union defeat).

Following Fredericksburg, Meade was given command of V Corps, then commanded the Center Grand Division (III and VI Corps) of the Army of the Potomac in December. With the recovery of Hooker, Meade reverted to command of V Corps only. He was present at the Battle of Chancellorsville (April 30–May 6, 1863, Virginia; Union defeat) but was not heavily engaged. Nevertheless, after Hooker's terrible performance there, Meade was named to replace him as commander of the Army of the Potomac. In the meantime, Lee once again invaded Maryland, on June 28, 1863, and then moved into Pennsylvania. At Gettysburg, Meade commenced an entirely unplanned battle (July 1–3, 1863, Pennsylvania; Union victory) with Lee. As Lee seized the initiative, Meade assumed the defensive. The first day gave the aggressively positioned Army of Northern Virginia the advantage, but the second day turned the tide toward the Union. On the third day, Lee ordered a massive infantry charge (remembered as Pickett's Charge) against Union positions in the high ground east of town. The charge was repulsed with heavy Confederate losses, but instead of pursuing Lee's retreat, Meade failed to press a counterattack. President Lincoln was disappointed, but Meade was promoted to regular army brigadier general nonetheless and remained in command the Army of the Potomac.

When Ulysses S. Grant was promoted to lieutenant general and given command of all Union armies on March 3, 1864, the Army of

"Battle of the Wilderness—Desperate fight on the Orange C. H. Plank Road, near Todd's Tavern, May 6th, 1864," a chromolithograph published by Kurz & Allison in 1887. LIBRARY OF CONGRESS

the Potomac became his personal instrument of war. Although Meade retained command, he functioned, in effect, as Grant's executive officer. Meade had a reputation for irritability, but he worked very well with Grant, taking direction from him at the Battles of the Wilderness (May 5–7, 1864, Virginia; Union tactical defeat), Spotsylvania Court House (May 8–21, Virginia; inconclusive), and Cold Harbor (May 31–June 12, Virginia; Union defeat). It was at Cold Harbor that Meade persuaded Grant to refrain from further frontal attacks, which were proving both costly and unproductive.

Meade commanded the Army of the Potomac during the Siege of Petersburg (June 9, 1864–March 25, 1865) and, with Grant, directed final operations during the Battle of Five Forks (April 1, 1865, Virginia; Union victory) and the Appomattox Campaign (March 29–April 9, Virginia; Union victory). Meade remained with the army after the war as commander of the Third Military District (encompassing Alabama, Georgia, and Florida), and was one of very few Northern military governors who attempted to discharge their duty with fairness and humanity. In 1869 Meade became commander of the Military Division of the East. Unfortunately, he never fully recovered from the wound he received early in the war. As a result of his lingering injury, he developed pneumonia in 1872 and succumbed to it. He had been the final commander of the Army of the Potomac.

Some historians believe this photograph depicts Union troops waiting to attack in the trenches at Petersburg, Virginia, in 1864. Others believe it shows Union troops entrenched along the Rappahannock River at Fredericksburg, Virginia, a year earlier. In either case, they are soldiers of the Army of the Potomac. LIBRARY OF CONGRESS

SIZE AND ORGANIZATION

The size of the Army of the Potomac varied throughout the course of the war:

- First Battle of Bull Run (fought as Army of Northeastern Virginia), July 21, 1861: 35,732[4]

- Peninsula Campaign (with the Seven Days Battles), March–July 1862: 115,350–106,466[5]

- Battle of Antietam, September 17, 1862: 87,164[6]

- Battle of Fredericksburg (December 11–15, 1862): 122,009[7]

- Battle of Chancellorsville (April 30–May 6, 1863): 133,868[8]

- Battle of Gettysburg (July 1–3, 1863): 104,256[9]

- Overland Campaign (May 4–June 24, 1864): 103,875–124,232[10]

- Battle of Appomattox Court House (April 9, 1865): 100,000[11]

As with other major armies in the Civil War, the organization of the Army of the Potomac varied. A representative picture of the great army's overall organization can be gathered from its order of battle at Gettysburg:[12]

GENERAL STAFF AND HEADQUARTERS

Major General George G. Meade, commanding

GENERAL STAFF

Chief of Staff: Major General Daniel Butterfield

GENERAL HEADQUARTERS

Provost Marshal General: Brigadier General Marsena R. Patrick

Guards and Orderlies

Engineer Brigade

I CORPS

Major General John F. Reynolds (killed July 1, 1863)

Major General Abner Doubleday (July 1–2, 1863)

Major General John Newton

1ST DIVISION

Brigadier General James S. Wadsworth

2ND DIVISION

Brigadier General John C. Robinson

3RD DIVISION

Brigadier (then Major) General Abner Doubleday

II CORPS

Major General Winfield Scott Hancock

Brigadier General John Gibbon

Brigadier General William Hays

1ST DIVISION

Brigadier General John C. Caldwell

2ND DIVISION

Brigadier General John Gibbon

Brigadier General William Harrow

3RD DIVISION

Brigadier General Alexander Hays

III CORPS

Major General Daniel E. Sickles

Major General David B. Birney

1ST DIVISION

Major General David B. Birney

Brigadier General J. H. Hobart Ward

2ND DIVISION

Brigadier General Andrew A. Humphreys

V CORPS

Major General George Sykes

1ST DIVISION

Brigadier General James Barnes

2ND DIVISION

Brigadier General Romeyn B. Ayres

3RD DIVISION

Brigadier General Samuel W. Crawford

VI CORPS

Major General John Sedgwick

1ST DIVISION

Brigadier General Horatio G. Wright

2ND DIVISION

Brigadier General Albion P. Howe

3RD DIVISION

Major General John Newton

Brigadier General Frank Wheaton

XI CORPS

Major General Oliver O. Howard

Major General Cark Schurz

1ST DIVISION

Brigadier General Francis C. Barlow

Brigadier General Adelbert Ames

2ND DIVISION

Brigadier General Adolph von Steinwehr

3RD DIVISION
Major General Carl Schurz
Brigadier General Alexander Schimmelfennig
Major General Carl Schurz

XII CORPS
Major General Henry W. Slocum
Brigadier General Alpheus S. Williams

1ST DIVISION
Brigadier General Alpheus S. Williams
Brigadier General Thomas H. Ruger

2ND DIVISION
Brigadier General John W. Geary

CAVALRY CORPS
Major General Alfred Pleasonton

1ST DIVISION
Brigadier General John Buford

2ND DIVISION
Brigadier General David McMurtrie Gregg

3RD DIVISION
Brigadier General Judson Kilpatrick

HORSE ARTILLERY
Captain James M. Robertson, 1st Brigade
Captain John C. Tidball, 2nd Brigade

ARTILLERY RESERVE
Brigadier General Robert O. Tyler
1st Regular Brigade
1st Volunteer Brigade
2nd Volunteer Brigade
3rd Volunteer Brigade
4th Volunteer Brigade
[Artillery] Train Guard

MAJOR CAMPAIGNS AND BATTLES

As the Union's principal military organization in the principal theater of the Civil War, the Army of the Potomac carried the North's hope for victory over the Confederacy and restoration of the Union. Most of the weight of this burden rested on the shoulders of the army's commanding officers, and after each heartbreaking failure the Army of the Potomac suffered, President Lincoln tried a new commander. Through the Army of the Potomac, the president and the nation desperately searched for their military savior. The history of the army's principal battles and campaigns is largely the history of this search, which culminated in the elevation of Ulysses S. Grant as the US Army's general-in-chief. He rode the Army of the Potomac—commanded by George G. Meade—to final victory.

The army's maiden battle, fought as the Army of Northeastern Virginia, was the First Battle of Bull Run (July 21, 1861, Virginia). Brigadier General Irvin McDowell faced Confederate generals Joseph E. Johnston and P. G. T. Beauregard. The Union and Confederate forces were evenly matched by the numbers. The Army of Northeastern Virginia had 35,732 troops available, of which about 18,000 were engaged in the battle, and the Confederates had perhaps 34,000 available, engaging 18,000, give or take. McDowell marched out of Washington on July 16, intent on taking the fight to the Confederates, whose forces were positioned behind Bull Run near Centreville, Virginia. McDowell crossed the run at Sudely Ford on July 21 and attacked the Confederate left flank on Matthews Hill. He drove the Confederates back upon Henry Hill, but, late in the afternoon, Confederate reinforcements arrived, including a brigade from the Shenandoah Valley under Thomas J. Jackson. This enabled a stand followed by a counterattack, which drove the green Union troops into a panicked retreat that quickly became a rout. For their part, the Confederates were also disorganized and therefore could not capitalize on their victory by pursuing the disordered Union forces. Union casualties were 2,708, including 481 killed.[13]

The catastrophe of First Bull Run persuaded the Lincoln administration to transform the Army of Northeastern Virginia into a major fighting force capable of suppressing the rebellion and winning the war. McDowell was relieved, and Major General George B. McClellan was summoned not merely to take his place, but to create the army the nation needed.

After much delay, which outraged both president and Congress, McClellan led the Army of the Potomac on the Peninsula Campaign, an operation on which he bestowed a deliberately Napoleonic name. The central feature of this operation was the series of battles called the Seven Days. McClellan embarked on the Peninsula Campaign with numbers far superior to those of Lee's Army of Northern Virginia, which opposed him. Yet he grossly overestimated his enemy's strength, and, as a result, was overly cautious in conducting his offensive. While McClellan hesitated, James Ewell Brown "Jeb" Stuart, commanding Lee's cavalry, performed a daring reconnaissance of the Army of the Potomac that completely circled it (June 12–15, 1862).

The humiliation of having been ridden around convinced McClellan to stop delaying and begin his drive to Richmond in earnest. On June 25 he marched through Oak Grove along the Chickahominy River, where Confederate forces drove him back until he was able to summon reinforcements, repel the Confederates, and occupy positions around Oak Grove. Lee, seeing that 25,000 of McClellan's troops were on the left bank of the Chickahominy, separated from the rest of the Army of the Potomac, which was on the right, and decided to use the bulk of his Army of Northern Virginia—about 65,000 troops available—to attack this isolated force. The resulting Battle of Mechanicsville (also called the Battle of Beaver Dam Creek, June 26) failed, however, because of a lack of coordination between "Stonewall Jackson's cavalry and one of Lee's division commanders, A. P. Hill. In the end, Mechanicsville resulted in a bloody repulse

for the Confederates. Believing, however, that Lee was about to attack him with overwhelmingly superior numbers, McClellan not only failed to exploit the repulse, but withdrew away from Richmond, prompting futile protests by his astonished subordinates.

For his part, Lee continued to harass the thoroughly intimidated McClellan, giving battle at Gaines's Mill on June 27. The delayed arrival of Jackson gave McClellan's corps commander, Fitz-John Porter, time to reinforce his position, so that the fighting here was bloody. Nevertheless, once the Confederates fully coordinated their operations, the Union line broke and was forced into a costly retreat. Of 34,214 Army of the Potomac troops engaged, 894 died, 3,107 were wounded, and 2,836 were reported missing. Lee, though victorious—having forced McClellan to depart the field—suffered even heavier casualties, nearly 8,000 killed and wounded.

On June 29 Lee attacked McClellan's retreating forces again, at Savage's Station, hitting Edwin Sumner's II Corps. Poor Confederate coordination resulted in an inconclusive battle that nevertheless caused heavy Union casualties. Moreover, the Army of the Potomac abandoned a large quantity of supplies to the Confederates—as well as some 2,500 wounded men in a field hospital. Helpless as they were, they became prisoners of war.

After withdrawing from Savage's Station, McClellan concentrated behind White Oak Swamp, deploying his forces in a line to Malvern Hill to protect the Union supply trains on their way to Harrison's Landing on the James River. Lee again mounted an attack—which, again, was hobbled by the poor coordination of its various components. While Lee pushed McClellan farther from Richmond, he also sustained losses equal to McClellan's—something his much smaller force could ill afford. The Battle of Frayser's Farm (Battle of Glendale, June 30) ended inconclusively, with 3,797 Union casualties and 3,673 on the Confederate side.[14]

After Frayser's Farm, McClellan withdrew his entire army to Malvern Hill, a low ridge along the James River. The withdrawal marked the collapse of the Peninsula Campaign and what was supposed to be the decisive advance against Richmond. Unwilling to let McClellan get away, Lee attacked his high-ground position on July 1. The challenging terrain combined with poor execution to foil the attack, and McClellan's artillery wreaked havoc on Lee, who suffered more than 5,600 casualties compared to about 3,000 for the Army of the Potomac. McClellan's subordinates urged a counterattack on the battered Army of Northern Virginia, but McClellan instead withdrew to his base at Harrison's Landing. It was one in a tragic series of command failures in the use of a great military force.

Lee invaded Maryland for the first time in September 1862, and on September 16 McClellan confronted his Army of Northern Virginia at Sharpsburg. At daybreak on September 17, "Fighting Joe" Hooker's corps of the Army of the Potomac hit Lee's left flank, the first blow in what would be the single bloodiest day in American military history. It was a seesaw battle of assault and counterblow, but when his army finally broke through Lee's center, McClellan, as usual, failed to capitalize in timely fashion on what he had gained. Ambrose Burnside's corps entered the battle late, crossing the stone bridge over Antietam Creek and smashing the Confederate right. But it was too late. A Confederate division under A. P. Hill arrived from Harpers Ferry, counterattacked, and drove Burnside back. Ultimately, the issue was that Lee, outnumbered two to one, threw everything he had into the battle, whereas McClellan sent in somewhat less than three-fourths of his available troops. The result was a tactical draw and a narrow strategic victory for the Union—barely enough of a victory to create a platform from which Lincoln launched the preliminary Emancipation Proclamation. Of 87,164 men available, McClellan lost 12,410 killed, wounded, or captured. Of Lee's

much smaller deployed force—about 38,000—10,000 to 13,000 became casualties.[15]

Deeply disappointed in the high cost of a victory that gained precious little, President Lincoln replaced McClellan with Ambrose Burnside as commanding general of the Army of the Potomac. On November 14 the new commander sent a corps to Falmouth, Virginia, near Fredericksburg. With this position secured, the rest of the Army of the Potomac followed. Lee responded to this advance toward Richmond by digging into the hills behind Fredericksburg on the opposite bank of the Rappahannock. Trained as an engineer, Lee had chosen his ground brilliantly.

On December 11, Burnside's engineers, working under fire from the heights, threw five pontoon bridges across the Rappahannock, and, on the following day, the Army of the Potomac crossed. On December 13 Burnside launched one frontal attack after another against Fredericksburg. The slaughter was tragic. Burnside responded to each bloody repulse by repeating the attempt. On the verge of personally leading a fourteenth advance into the fire, he allowed himself to be dissuaded by his officers. On December 15 Burnside officially called off the offensive and withdrew. He sought to redeem his effort in January by launching a new offensive, but was bogged down in the mud of a January thaw. His horrific defeat, combined with the ignominy of the so-called Mud March, prompted Lincoln to replace him with Major General Joseph Hooker in January 1863.

This latest commander mounted a new offensive along the Rappahannock River. Hooker concentrated the Army of the Potomac near Chancellorsville, Virginia, during April 30 and May 1. Leaving a covering force under Major General Jubal Early in Fredericksburg, Lee marched the rest of the Army of Northern Virginia to fight Hooker. The Union commander intended to take Fredericksburg, but, facing increasing resistance from gathering Confederate

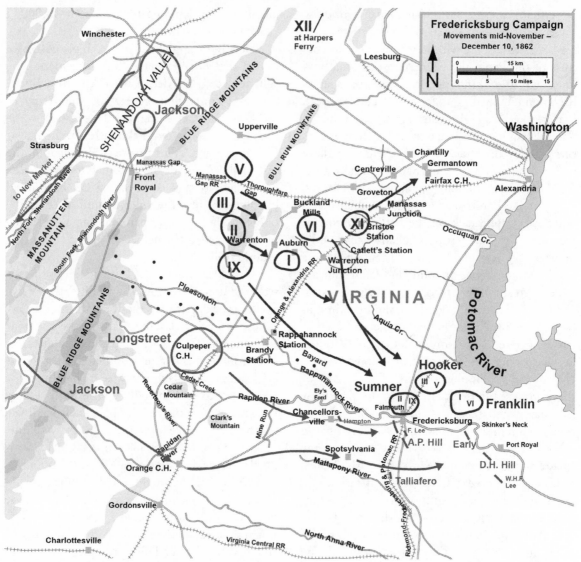

The Battle of Fredericksburg, maneuvering from November to December 10, 1862. MAP BY HAL JESPERSEN, CWMAPS.COM

forces, and acting on faulty intelligence of the overwhelming superiority of Lee's numbers (in fact, Lee was outnumbered nearly two to one), Hooker halted his advance on Fredericksburg and turned again to Chancellorsville. Worse, Hooker shifted from offense to defense, yielding the initiative to Lee. In a masterpiece of daring tactics, Lee struck, breaking the Union line at Chancellorsville, forcing Hooker to hunker down with the

back of his army to the Rappahannock. Army of the Potomac losses were 17,287 killed, wounded, and captured, with another 4,700 casualties suffered in action at Salem Church on May 3.[16] Losses to the Army of Northern Virginia were 13,303 killed, wounded, and captured.[17]

Hooker remained in command of the Army of the Potomac in what amounted to the run-up to the Battle of Gettysburg, as he pursued

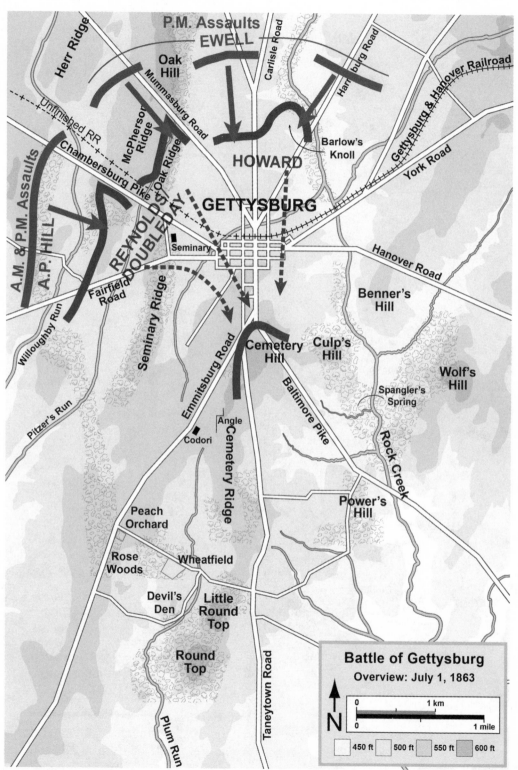

The Battle of Gettysburg, July 1. Map by Hal Jespersen, cwmaps.com

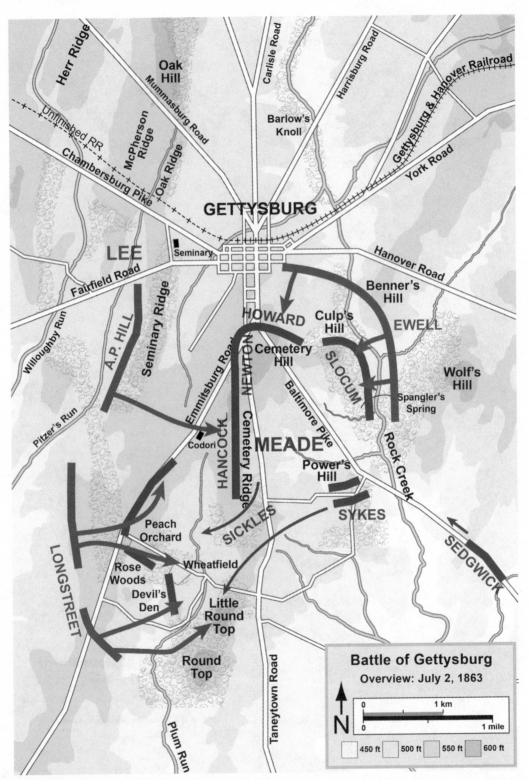

The Battle of Gettysburg, July 2. Map by Hal Jespersen, cwmaps.com

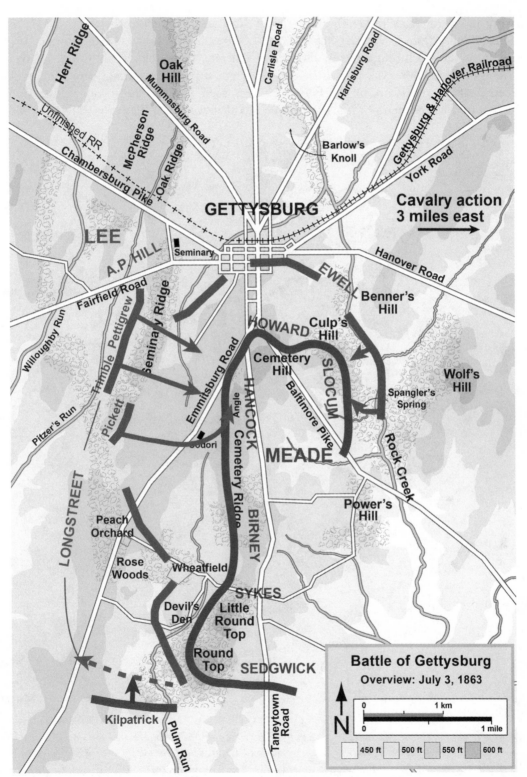

The Battle of Gettysburg, July 3. Map by Hal Jespersen, cwmaps.com

the Army of Northern Virginia through the
Shenandoah Valley, from which Lee prepared to
invade Pennsylvania. Lincoln replaced Hooker
with George Meade, however, just three days
before elements of the Army of the Potomac
stumbled into advance units of the Army of

Northern Virginia in the Pennsylvania town of
Gettysburg on July 1, 1863. On that day, Confederate forces closed in from the west and
north, driving the outnumbered Union defenders back through the town itself to Cemetery
Hill above it. On the night of July 1, Union and

*This remarkably candid Timothy O'Sullivan photograph of an Army of the Potomac council of war was taken at Mas-
saponax Church on May 21, 1864, during Grant's Overland Campaign. Grant looks over Major General George
Meade's shoulder at the map Meade holds.* NATIONAL ARCHIVES AND RECORDS ADMINISTRATION

Confederate reinforcements arrived, and on July 2 Lee sought to achieve rapid victory by enveloping Union forces on the left flank and the right. But by nightfall, the Army of the Potomac still held Little Round Top, having driven off most of the attempted envelopment. Determined to recover and win, Lee attacked the Union center on Cemetery Ridge with a massive infantry charge (popularly known as Pickett's Charge), a portion of which briefly pierced the Union line before the whole charge was driven back with extremely heavy casualties. On July 4 Lee withdrew, and Meade, noting the exhaustion of his army, declined to pursue.

Lincoln saw Gettysburg as the turning point of the war—proof that the Union army was up to the task of defending the United States and that the Confederacy could not successfully invade the North. On March 9, 1864, President Lincoln summoned Ulysses S. Grant to Washington and there promoted him to lieutenant general and named him general-in-chief of the US Army. While Meade remained in command of the Army of the Potomac, Grant used it as the vehicle by which he meant to end the war.

Beginning with the Overland Campaign (May 4–June 24, 1864), Grant's push to finally take Richmond and bring the war to an end, Meade and Grant were effectively co-commanders of the Union's principal army. The main battles of the Overland Campaign were the Wilderness (May 5–7), Spotsylvania Court House (May 8–21), Yellow Tavern (May 11),

and Cold Harbor (May 31–June 12). Of these, the first and second were inconclusive, the third a Union victory, and the fourth a Union tactical defeat. All were extremely bloody—with total losses to the Army of the Potomac amounting to 54,926 killed, wounded, or captured, and to the Army of Northern Virginia, as many as 35,000 killed, wounded, or captured.[18] Heedless of the tactical outcome of each battle, however, Grant never withdrew. Instead, he side-slipped and, after each engagement, unwaveringly advanced closer to Richmond. Yet instead of making a direct assault on the Confederate capital, Grant changed course and commenced the Richmond-Petersburg Campaign (June 9, 1864–March 25, 1865), laying siege to the industrial and transportation center of Petersburg, which he saw as the gateway to Richmond. After Grant failed to make a breakthrough early in the siege, the situation developed into one of prolonged trench warfare, and thus the Army of the Potomac became the first American army to fight the kind of static war that would engulf western Europe in World War I early in the twentieth century.

The Army of the Potomac had its showdown battle with the Army of Northern Virginia at Appomattox Court House on April 9, 1865, which culminated in Lee's surrender of the Confederacy's premier military formation to Lieutenant General Grant on April 12. This did not immediately end the war, but it was the first of a series of surrenders that did bring it to an end.

Chapter 20

ARMY OF THE SOUTHWEST
(ARMY OF SOUTHWEST MISSOURI)

OVERALL PERFORMANCE: ★ ★ ⁊

The Army of the Southwest was short-lived but played a key role in occupying Missouri, a Union state that was also claimed by the Confederacy. The Army of the Southwest fought the Battle of Pea Ridge (March 6–8, 1862, Arkansas; Union victory), which secured Union control of Missouri and northern Arkansas. Beyond this, the army is significant as an unusual instance in the nineteenth-century USA of an military formation whose mission was principally territorial occupation.

ESTABLISHMENT

The Army of the Southwest (which was also called the Army of Southwest Missouri) was formed on December 25, 1861, under the command of Brigadier General Samuel R. Curtis, using troops from the Department of Missouri. At its formation the army consisted of three divisions, commanded by Brigadier General Franz Sigel, Brigadier General Alexander Asboth, and Colonel Jefferson Columbus Davis (no relation to the Confederate president). By March 1862 a fourth division, under Colonel Eugene A. Carr, was formed. The army was unique in its preponderance of immigrant commanders, officers, and enlisted personnel. Sigel was from Germany and Asboth from Hungary, and more than half of the army's soldiers were first-generation German immigrants.

COMMANDING GENERALS

Samuel R. Curtis took command of the army upon its creation. He was born near Champlain, New York, graduated from West Point in 1831, and entered the Engineer Corps, serving only briefly before resigning his commission in 1832 to practice law in Ohio. He rejoined the army at the outbreak of the US-Mexican War (1846–48), held the rank of colonel, and served as military governor of a number of occupied cities.

After the war Curtis entered politics, becoming mayor of Keokuk, Iowa, in 1856, and US representative from Iowa's 1st Congressional District. A supporter of fellow Republican Abraham Lincoln, Curtis nevertheless turned down a possible cabinet post in the Lincoln administration and later resigned from Congress to fight in the Civil War. He was appointed colonel of the 2nd Iowa Infantry on June 1, 1861, and was subsequently promoted to brigadier general. After winning the Battle of Pea Ridge (March 6–8, 1862, Arkansas; Union victory), Curtis was promoted to major general.

Brigadier General Franz Sigel, originally a divisional commander in the new army, resented Curtis's appointment over him and threatened to resign. Appreciating the great value of the German-born Sigel in an army whose soldiery consisted of more than 50 percent German immigrants, Curtis mollified the unhappy brigadier by naming him his second-in-command. He then gave Sigel overall command of the 1st and 2nd Divisions, both of which were predominantly

German. Sigel was, in fact, a mediocre commander, but his presence provided a strong boost to esprit de corps, his soldiers proudly proclaiming "I fight mit Sigel."

On August 29, 1862, Curtis was replaced as commanding general of the Army of the Southwest by Frederick Steele. A native of Delhi, New York (born 1819), Steele graduated from West Point in 1843 and served in the US-Mexican War (1846–48) and in the Yuma War (1850–53). He was then posted variously in Minnesota, Kansas, and Nebraska Territory until the outbreak of the Civil War.

Promoted to major and assigned on May 14, 1861, to the 11th US Infantry, Steele fought at the Battle of Wilson's Creek (August 10, 1861, Missouri; Union defeat). He was appointed colonel of the 8th Iowa Infantry on September 23, 1861, and quickly rose to brigadier general of US Volunteers, assigned to command the District of Southeast Missouri. After the Battle of Pea Ridge (March 6–8, 1862, Arkansas; Union victory) he assumed command of the 1st Division of the Army of the Southwest and briefly commanded the entire army (August 29–October 7, 1862). After his promotion to major general of volunteers on March 17, 1863, Steele and his division were transferred to the Army of the Tennessee as the 11th Division, XIII Corps. With that army he fought at the Battle of Chickasaw Bayou (December 26–29, 1862; Union defeat) and the Battle of Arkansas Post (January 9–11, 1863, Arkansas; Union victory). He and his division (as the 1st Division, XV Corps) fought in the Siege of Vicksburg (May 18–July 4, 1863, Mississippi; Union victory).

Brevetted to colonel in the US Army, Steele assumed command of the Army of Arkansas and then command of VII Corps in the Department of Arkansas, which involved him in the failed Red River Campaign (March 10–May 22, 1864). From February 18 to May 18, 1865, Steele commanded the "Column from Pensacola," an African-American unit in Major General Edward R. S. Canby's Army of West Mississippi. Steele's "colored" troops fought at the battles of Spanish Fort and Fort Blakely.

Frederick Steele continued to serve in the army after the war, until his death in 1868, but his brief command of the Army of the Southwest ended on October 7, 1862, when he was replaced by Eugene A. Carr. Born in Hamburg, New York, Carr graduated from West Point in 1850. As a brevet second lieutenant in the Regiment of Mounted Riflemen, he fought in the Indian Wars until the outbreak of the Civil War in 1861. He first saw combat in the war at the Battle of Wilson's Creek (August 10, 1861, Missouri; Union defeat) and was subsequently appointed colonel of the 3rd Illinois Cavalry, six days later receiving a brevet to lieutenant colonel in the regular army (he had been promoted to captain in 1858). Carr led the 4th Division of the Army of the Southwest at the Battle of Pea Ridge (March 6–8, 1862, Arkansas; Union victory) in combat at Elkhorn Tavern, suffered multiple wounds, and was later decorated with the Medal of Honor.

Promoted on April 30, 1862, to brigadier general of volunteers, Carr commanded the Army of the Southwest from October 7 to November 12, 1862, and then went on to command the 2nd Division of the Army of Southeast Missouri before he and that division were transferred to the Army of the Tennessee as the 14th Division in XIII Corps. After fighting in the Siege of Vicksburg (May 18–July 4, 1863), Carr returned to Arkansas as commanding officer of a division in the Army of Arkansas. He commanded the Cavalry Division in VII Corps during Frederick Steele's Camden Expedition (March 23–May 2, 1864, Arkansas) as part of the disastrous Red River Campaign (March 10–May 22, 1864). Near the end of the war, Carr commanded 3rd Division, XVI Corps at the Battle of Fort Blakely (April 2–9, 1865, Alabama; Union victory). After the Civil War he returned to service in the Indian Wars.

The final commander of the Army of the Southwest, Willis A. Gorman, took over from Carr on November 12, 1863. A native of Flemingsburg, Kentucky, Gorman was born in 1816, studied at Indiana University's law school, earned his degree in 1835, and opened a practice in Bloomington, Indiana. He also entered state politics, and in 1846 enlisted as a private in the army to fight in the US-Mexican War (1846–48). He was soon appointed major in the 3rd Indiana Volunteer Infantry and was seriously wounded at the Battle of Buena Vista (February 22–23, 1847). After recovering, he rejoined and was appointed colonel of the 4th Indiana. At the end of the war, he served as both civil and military governor of Puebla, Mexico. After returning to Indiana, Gorman was elected to the US House of Representatives, serving from 1849 to 1853.

Gorman was appointed colonel of the 1st Minnesota Infantry early in the Civil War and fought at the First Battle of Bull Run (July 21, 1861, Virginia; Union defeat). He subsequently fought at the Battle of Antietam (September 17, 1862, Maryland; Union strategic victory) and was then assigned to command the District of Eastern Arkansas, assuming command of the Army of the Southwest, as a brigadier general, during its final month of existence.

Size and Organization

The Army of the Southwest numbered about 15,000 men, of whom only 10,500 fought at Pea Ridge. Still, all of its units were represented there, so the order of battle at Pea Ridge provides a useful picture of the organization of this small Union army.[1] Its largest unit was the division; there were no corps.

As explained under "Commanding Generals," Brigadier General Franz Sigel resented being passed over (as he thought) for command of the army. To prevent Sigel's resignation, Brigadier General Samuel R. Curtis made him his second-in-command. Thus Sigel was assigned overall command of the 1st and 2nd Divisions.

Curtis's headquarters units consisted of five companies of the 24th Missouri, four of the 3rd Iowa Cavalry, and five of Bowen's Missouri Cavalry Battalion.

1ST AND 2ND DIVISIONS
Combined command under Brigadier General
     Franz Sigel
1st Division: Colonel Peter J. Osterhaus
2nd Division: Brigadier General
     Alexander Asboth

3RD DIVISION
Colonel Jefferson C. Davis

4TH DIVISION
Colonel Eugene A. Carr

Major Campaigns and Battles

The army fought two major battles, the Battle of Pea Ridge and the Battle of Cotton Plant.

The Battle of Pea Ridge (also called the Battle of Elkhorn Tavern) was fought March 6–8, 1862, near Leetown, Arkansas. It was one of a minority of Civil War battles in which Confederate forces (16,500 engaged) outnumbered Union forces (10,500 engaged).[2] On the night of March 6, Confederate major general Earl Van Dorn, commanding the Army of the West, took up a position near Pea Ridge. Intending to flank the Army of the Southwest (under Curtis), he divided his forces into two divisions. Curtis, however, learned of the approach of

Van Dorn and advanced on March 7 to intercept him. In a skirmish prior to the main battle, two Confederate generals, Brigadier General Ben McCulloch and Brigadier General James McQueen McIntosh, were killed and a Confederate colonel captured. This near-decapitation arrested the attack at Pea Ridge, but Van Dorn led his other division to make an attack at Elkhorn Tavern. The resulting engagement gave him control of Elkhorn Tavern and Telegraph Road leading out of it.

On March 8 Brigadier General Curtis consolidated his forces and counterattacked at Elkhorn Tavern, supporting his infantry with his artillery. Although he was outnumbered, this combined arms tactic succeeded in driving Van Horn back. Short of ammunition, he had no choice but to depart the field, and, with that, the Union effectively seized control of Missouri and held it for the rest of the war.

On July 7, 1862, 400 soldiers from three brigades of the Army of the Southwest were in search of supplies to support a planned move to establish an operational headquarters at Helena, Arkansas. They advanced toward the White River, where the US Navy had a supply flotilla standing off Clarendon. Three Confederate regiments of Texas Cavalry (12th, 16th, and 17th)—5,000 men—descended on the small Union detachment. The attack, however, was made piecemeal, and the Union colonel in charge, Charles E. Hovey, drove back each sortie. The timely arrival of Army of the Southwest reinforcements dispersed the Confederate cavalrymen. The Union lost 63 men, killed or wounded, the Confederates, 245, in what was called the Battle of Cotton Plant.[3]

DISSOLUTION

Shortly after the Battle of Cotton Plant, the 1st Division (now commanded by Major General Frederick Steele) was transferred to the Army of the Tennessee (chapter 22) and the 2nd and 3rd Divisions were transferred to the Army of the Mississippi (chapter 21). The remaining division, the 4th, was briefly redesignated the Army of Southeast Missouri, but it, too, was soon disbanded and its personnel transferred to the Army of the Tennessee, under which they participated in the Vicksburg Campaign (March 29–July 4, 1863).

Chapter 21

ARMY OF THE MISSISSIPPI

OVERALL PERFORMANCE: ✷ ✷ ✷

Two short-lived but important Union armies were designated Army of the Mississippi, the first in 1862, the second in 1863. The mission of both was to bring the Mississippi River under Union control. Although most of the significant battles of the war were fought in the Eastern Theater—and most of those between the Confederacy's Army of Northern Virginia and the Union's Army of the Potomac—President Lincoln, Secretary of War Edwin P. Stanton, and the USA's top command recognized that victory in the war could not be achieved without gaining control of the Mississippi River. Not only was it the heartland's principal transportation artery, both for supplies and for troop transport, it also bisected the Confederacy. Seize the river, and the government and military resources emanating from Richmond would be entirely cut off from the Confederate states adjacent to the Mississippi or west of it. Corinth, the railroad junction town for which the Army of the Mississippi would fight most fiercely, was known as the "Crossroads of the Confederacy."[1] Ulysses S. Grant called it "the great strategic position at the West between the Tennessee and Mississippi rivers and between Nashville and Vicksburg."[2]

ESTABLISHMENT

The first incarnation of the Army of the Mississippi was created on February 23, 1862, under Brigadier General John Pope. As initially established, the army consisted of two divisions, about 7,600 men. Within days, by the end of February, the army was enlarged to five divisions, about 19,000 soldiers, in addition to a river transportation flotilla. It was with this force that Pope began the New Madrid Campaign preparatory to the Battle of Island No. 10 (February 28, 1862–April 8, 1862).

COMMANDING GENERALS

Brigadier General John Pope was the first commanding officer of the Army of the Mississippi, assuming that post on February 23, 1862. He had been born in Louisville, Kentucky, in 1822, the son of a federal judge assigned to Illinois Territory who became a close friend of Abraham Lincoln, when Lincoln was practicing law there. Pope's father was also distantly related to Lincoln's sister-in-law. Although John Pope was a West Point graduate (Class of 1842), the connections to the president would effectively make him one of Lincoln's political generals, a category of field-grade commander appointed more on account of connections than proven military prowess.

After graduating from the United States Military Academy, Pope served in the Corps of Topographical Engineers, mapping portions of Florida and subsequently participating in the survey of the northeastern US-Canadian border. At the outbreak of the US-Mexican War (1846–48), he fought under Zachary Taylor and was at the Battles of Monterrey (September 21–24, 1846) and Buena Vista (February 22–23, 1847). Action in the battle resulted in brevets to first lieutenant and, in the second battle, to captain.

After the war with Mexico, Pope worked as a military surveyor in Minnesota and in 1850 demonstrated that the Red River was navigable. In 1851 he was promoted to chief engineer for the military's Department of New Mexico, serving until 1853, when he was assigned (still in uniform) to survey a route for the planned transcontinental railroad. On the eve of the Civil War, Pope was serving as a lighthouse keeper and was assigned as one of four army officers escorting President-elect Lincoln to Washington, DC, for his inauguration in March 1861. Pope volunteered his services as Lincoln's military aide, but Lincoln saw instead to his appointment, on June 14, 1861, as brigadier general of volunteers. He was dispatched to Illinois as a recruiter of volunteers.

Pope's first combat assignment in the Civil War was as commanding officer of the District of North and Central Missouri. Early success in this command resulted in his appointment, by Major General Henry W. Halleck, as commanding general of the newly formed Army of the Mississippi. His mission was straightforward: to secure the Mississippi River as far as possible for Union navigation.

Pope led the Army of the Mississippi in the capture of New Madrid, Missouri (March 14, 1862), which was followed by the capture of Island No. 10 (April 7, 1862), occupied by the Confederates. These victories were highly significant, making available to the Union army large portions of the Mississippi, and Pope was promoted from brigadier general to major general.

Pope commanded the left wing of Halleck's army during the Siege of Corinth (April 29–May 30, 1862), but was called to the Eastern Theater by President Lincoln and assigned command of the Army of Virginia on June 26, 1862. In that role Pope was disastrously outgeneraled by Robert E. Lee at the Second Battle of Bull Run (August 28–30, 1862). In September, relieved of command, he was transferred to the Department of the Northwest, effectively removed from the Civil War for its remainder.

Brigadier General William S. Rosecrans assumed command of the Army of the Mississippi on

June 26, 1862. Born in 1819 at Delaware City, Ohio, he was the great-grandson of Stephen Hopkins, colonial governor of Rhode Island and a signer of the Declaration of Independence. Graduating in 1842 from West Point, Rosecrans served mainly as an engineer and, at West Point, an instructor in engineering, until he left the army in 1854 to practice architecture and civil engineering.

Unlike many of the top commanders who would fight the Civil War, Rosecrans had not fought in the US-Mexican War (1846–48) or in the conflicts with the Indians. He was, however, an extraordinary engineer and businessman, specializing in the coal-mining industry. Not only did he map the richest coal veins in western Virginia (present-day West Virginia), he led a navigation company specializing in coal transport, and he invented improvements in mining and other industries. A miner safety lamp of his own design exploded while he was testing it in his laboratory, resulting in severe burns that confined him to bed for a year and a half. He volunteered for Civil War military service even before he had fully recovered.

Rosecrans's initial assignment was as drillmaster of Ohio's "Marion Rifles" regiment. He was next assigned to lay out the plan for Camp Dennison, Ohio, after which he was promoted to colonel and made commanding officer of the 23rd Ohio Volunteer Infantry. Promoted to brigadier general in the regular army (effective May 16, 1861), Rosecrans served under George B. McClellan and was largely responsible for the Union victory at the Battle of Rich Mountain (July 11, 1861, Virginia). Nevertheless, McClellan both claimed and received full credit, an action that prompted Rosecrans to secure a transfer to the Western Theater and out of McClellan's command.

Rosecrans took command of the left wing of the Army of the Mississippi at the Battle of Iuka (September 19, 1862, Mississippi; Union victory) and the Siege of Corinth (April 29–May 30, 1862, Mississippi; Union victory). Despite this success in siege and battle, Major General Ulysses S. Grant complained that Rosecrans was negligent for having failed to pursue Confederate forces after the battle. Rosecrans responded, in turn, by blaming Grant for failing to reinforce him. Regardless of the dispute, Rosecrans assumed command of the Army of the Mississippi from June 26, 1862, until October 24, 1862, when it was dissolved (temporarily, as it turned out).

From command of the Army of the Mississippi, Rosecrans, promoted to major general in the regular army, was assigned command of XIV Corps. He led the fight at the Battle of Stones River (December 31, 1862–January 2, 1863, Tennessee; Union victory). Following this, he reorganized his corps into the Army of the Cumberland and went on to conduct the Tullahoma Campaign (June 24–July 3, 1863, Tennessee; Union victory), driving the Confederates away from Chattanooga.

Rosecrans sullied his record of competence and success by his faulty conduct at the Battle of Chickamauga (September 19–20, 1863, Georgia; Union defeat) when, in the confusion of a chaotic battle, he created a gap in his own lines and, under intense attack, prematurely withdrew from the engagement. (The Army of the Cumberland was saved only by the steadfastness of Major General George H. Thomas, the "Rock of Chickamauga.") Relieved of command of the Army of the Cumberland, Rosecrans was later assigned command of the Department of Missouri, which he held through the end of the war. Rosecrans resigned his commission in 1867, resumed his business career, and was later appointed US minister to Mexico (1868–69). Elected to Congress as representative from California's 1st District in 1881, he served until 1885 and was then appointed register of the US Treasury. He died in 1898.

Major General John A. McClernand assumed command of the Army of the Mississippi when it was very briefly reconstituted during January 4–12, 1863, for an expedition down the river. McClernand led the army in the capture of Fort Hindman, Arkansas, at the Battle of Arkansas Post (January 9–11, 1863, Arkansas; Union victory), but, receiving reports from Admiral David Dixon Porter and Major General William T. Sherman pronouncing McClernand unfit for command, Major General Grant effectively dissolved the Army of the Mississippi and personally assumed command of its troops. A subsequent dispute with Grant following McClernand's performance at the Battle of Champion's Hill (May 16, 1863, Mississippi; Union victory) resulted in his formal relief of command on June 18. Out of political expediency, President Lincoln restored him to command, of VIII Corps in January 1864. McClernand participated in the calamitous Red River Campaign (March 10, 1864–May 22, 1864, Louisiana; Union defeat) and resigned on November 30 due to malaria.

John Alexander McClernand had been born in 1812 in Breckinridge County, Kentucky. He studied law and was admitted to the Illinois bar in 1832, also serving that year as a volunteer militiaman in the Blackhawk War. He was elected to the Illinois House of Representatives in 1836 and also served during 1840–43. During 1843–51 and 1859–61, he served in the US House of Representatives as a Democrat and a Unionist. He resigned from Congress in 1861 to raise the McClernand Brigade from Illinois and was commissioned (May 17, 1861) a brigadier general of volunteers. He fought at the Battle of Belmont (November 7, 1861, Missouri; Union victory) and commanded the right wing at the Battle of Fort Donelson (February 11–16, 1862, Tennessee; Union victory). Promoted to major general of volunteers in March, he commanded a division at the Battle of Shiloh (April 6–7, 1862, Tennessee; Union victory). On orders of Secretary of War Edwin Stanton, he raised troops for the expedition against Vicksburg, and it was in January of 1863 that he combined two corps of the Army of the Tennessee into the reconstituted Army of the Mississippi. After the war McClernand returned to the practice of law, served during 1870–73 as judge in the circuit court, and remained active in politics, although he held no further elective offices before his death in 1900.

SIZE AND ORGANIZATION

At its maximum strength in 1862, the Army of the Mississippi numbered 19,000 soldiers in five divisions. The order of battle during the assault against Island No. 10 reveals the organization of the army at its height:[3]

1ST DIVISION
Brigadier General David S. Stanley
1st Brigade: Colonel John Groesbeck
2nd Brigade: Colonel J. L. Kirby Smith

2ND DIVISION
Brigadier General Schuyler Hamilton
1st Brigade: Colonel William H. Worthington
2nd Brigade: Colonel Miklós Perczel
Artillery: Captain Frank C. Sands

3RD DIVISION
Brigadier General John M. Palmer
1st Brigade: Colonel James R. Slack
2nd Brigade: Colonel Graham N. Fitch
Cavalry: Colonel William P. Kellogg

4TH DIVISION
Brigadier General Eleazar A. Paine
1st Brigade: Colonel James D. Morgan
2nd Brigade: Colonel Gilbert W. Cumming
Cavalry: Major D. P. Jenkins
Sharpshooters: Major F. W. Matteson

5TH DIVISION
Brigadier General Joseph B. Plummer
1st Brigade: Colonel John Bryner
2nd Brigade: Colonel John M. Loomis
Artillery: Captain Albert M. Powell

REPORTING DIRECTLY TO ARMY COMMAND
Cavalry Division: Brigadier General Gordon Granger
Artillery Division: Major Warren L. Lothrop
Unattached units:
Engineer Regiment of the West: Colonel Josiah Bissell
22nd Missouri Infantry Regiment: Lieutenant Colonel John D. Foster
2nd Iowa Cavalry Regiment: Colonel Washington L. Elliott
Four companies, 2nd Illinois Cavalry: Lieutenant Colonel Harvey Hogg
Three companies, 4th US Cavalry: Lieutenant Colonel M. J. Kelly
Six companies, 1st US Infantry: Captain George A. Williams

FLOTILLA BRIGADE
Colonel Napoleon B. Buford
27th Illinois: Lieutenant Colonel Fazilo A. Harrington
42nd Illinois: Colonel George W. Roberts
15th Wisconsin: Colonel Hans C. Heg
Battery I, 2nd Illinois Light Artillery: Captain Arthur O'Leary
Battery G, 1st Missouri Light Artillery: Captain Frederick Sparrestrom

In the New Madrid Campaign and the Battle of Island No. 10, the Army of the Mississippi operated in close coordination with the Union Navy Western Flotilla. This was an early US military example of a combined arms operation.

UNION NAVY WESTERN FLOTILLA
Flag Officer Andrew H. Foote
USS *Benton:* Lieutenant Commander Seth L. Phelps
USS *Mound City:* Commander Augustus H. Kilty
USS *Carondelet:* Commander Henry Walke

USS *Cincinnati:* Commander R. N. Stembel

USS *St. Louis* (later USS *Baron De Kalb*):
Lieutenant Leonard Paulding

USS *Pittsburg:* Lieutenant Egbert Thompson

The organization of the Army of the Mississippi during January 1863 can be gathered from the order of battle during the Battle of Arkansas Post:[4]

XIII CORPS
Brigadier General George W. Morgan

1ST DIVISION
Brigadier General Andrew Jackson Smith

1st Brigade: Brigadier General Stephen Gano Burbridge

2nd Brigade: Colonel William J. Landram

Artillery:

Chicago Mercantile Light Artillery: Captain Charles G. Cooley

17th Ohio Light Artillery: Captain Ambrose A. Blount

Cavalry:

6th Missouri (squadron): Colonel Clark Wright

2ND DIVISION
Brigadier General Peter J. Osterhaus

1st Brigade: Colonel Lionel A. Sheldon

2nd Brigade: Colonel Daniel W. Lindsey

3rd Brigade: Colonel John F. DeCourcy

Artillery:

Battery G, 1st Michigan Light Artillery: Captain Charles H. Lanphere

1st Wisconsin Light Artillery: Captain Jacob T. Foster

Engineers:

Patterson's Kentucky Engineers & Mechanics: Captain William F. Patterson

XV CORPS
Major General William T. Sherman

4TH DIVISION
Brigadier General Frederick Steele

1st Brigade: Brigadier General Francis Preston Blair Jr.

2nd Brigade: Brigadier General Charles E. Hovey

3rd Brigade: Brigadier General John Milton Thayer

Cavalry:

3rd Illinois Cavalry: Colonel Lafayette McCrillis

2ND DIVISION
Brigadier General David Stuart

1st Brigade: Colonel Giles A. Smith

2nd Brigade: Colonel Thomas Kilby Smith

Artillery:

Battery A, 1st Illinois Light Artillery: Captain Peter P. Wood

Battery B, 1st Illinois Light Artillery: Captain Samuel E. Barrett

Battery H, 1st Illinois Light Artillery: Lieutenant Levi W. Hart

8th Ohio Light Artillery: Lieutenant James F. Putnam

Cavalry:

Company A & B, Thielman's Battalion (Illinois): Captain Bertold Marschner

Company C, 6th Missouri Cavalry: Lieutenant Daniel W. Ballou

NAVAL FORCES COORDINATING WITH THE ARMY OF THE MISSISSIPPI
Rear Admiral David D. Porter

Fifty transport ships in addition to the following combat vessels:

USS *Baron DeKalb*: Lieutenant Commander William Gwin

USS *Cincinnati:* Lieutenant George M. Bache

USS *Louisville:* Lieutenant Commander Elias K. Owen

USS *Glide:* Acting Lieutenant Selim E. Woodworth

USS *Rattler:* Lieutenant Commander Watson Smith

USS *Black Hawk:* Lieutenant Commander K. R. Breese

USS *Lexington:* Lieutenant James W. Shirk
USS *Monarch:* Colonel C. R. Ellet
USS *New Era:* Acting Master F. W. Flanner
  (or Acting Master J. C. Bunner)

MAJOR CAMPAIGNS AND BATTLES

In its initial incarnation, the Army of the Mississippi fought four important actions, all of which were key to the Union's gaining and maintaining control of the Mississippi River.

The army was formed explicitly to seize the Confederate fortifications on Island No. 10 and the associated garrison at New Madrid, Missouri. After Ulysses S. Grant (Army of the Tennessee) and Flag Officer Andrew Foote (Western Flotilla) took Fort Henry on the Tennessee River (February 6, 1862) and Fort Donelson on the Cumberland River (February 11–16, 1862), the Confederates withdrew from their stronghold at Columbus, Kentucky, and General P. G. T. Beauregard, commanding the Confederate Army of Mississippi, fortified Island No. 10, some sixty miles below Columbus. From this new position he sought to defend the Confederate hold on the Mississippi River and the adjacent valley. In response, Brigadier General John Pope led the Union Army of *the* Mississippi against New Madrid, which Beauregard had garrisoned. He set out from Commerce, Missouri, on February 28 and made a slow and difficult advance through swampy river land—particularly tortuous with field artillery in tow—reaching the outskirts of New Madrid on March 3. Pope set up a siege, which was met by Confederate Brigadier General M. Jeff Thompson, commanding the Missouri State Guard, who bombarded Pope's army. Pope, however, held fast and continued the siege, whereupon Thompson withdrew his garrison from New Madrid to Island No. 10 and Tiptonville.

On March 14, discovering that New Madrid had been abandoned, Pope and his Army of the Mississippi occupied it. The next day, March 15, ironclads of the Western Flotilla commanded by Foote took up positions off New Madrid. Their guns suppressed Confederate fire from Island No. 10 while Pope's forces crossed the river and blocked the Confederate route of retreat. On April 8 the defenders of Island No. 10 surrendered, and the Mississippi fell under Union control as far down as Fort Pillow, Tennessee, key to the Confederate defense of Memphis.

The next major actions for the Army of the Mississippi were the Siege of Corinth and the Battle of Iuka, both in Mississippi. Called the "Crossroads of the Confederacy" because it was the junction of the Mobile and Ohio Railroad and the Memphis and Charleston Railroad, Corinth came under Union siege beginning on April 29, 1862. The operation, which culminated in a multi-objective battle (or series of engagements) that spanned May 3–30, is sometimes called the First Battle of Corinth to distinguish it from the Second Battle of Corinth, which the Army of the Mississippi fought under William Rosecrans on October 3–4, 1862.

The April 29–May 30 operation involved the Union Army of the Mississippi (Pope) as well as the Army of the Tennessee (George H. Thomas) and the Army of the Ohio (Don Carlos Buell) and was under the overall direction of Major General Henry Halleck as commander of the Union's Department of the Missouri. The initial engagement was Pope's capture of Farmington, Mississippi, on May 3. Over the next three weeks, under Halleck's overly cautious direction, the other two armies took additional objectives that finally, by May 25, positioned them advantageously to capture their objective. Following a preliminary bombardment, the armies closed in, and, on the night of May 29–30, General Beauregard quietly evacuated the city and withdrew to Tupelo. This delivered Corinth into Union hands, but the Confederate army had been allowed to escape intact.

In September the Confederate Army of the West, under Major General Sterling Price, advanced into Iuka, Mississippi, on orders from General Braxton Bragg (commanding the Confederate Army of Mississippi) to block the advance into Middle Tennessee of the Union Army of the Mississippi, now commanded by Major General William S. Rosecrans. Rosecrans's objective was to tie into and reinforce Major General Don Carlos Buell's Army of the Ohio, which was occupying Nashville.

With just 14,000 men, Price knew he could not interdict Rosecrans, and he relied, therefore, on obtaining reinforcements from Major General Earl Van Dorn, commanding the District of the Mississippi. Major General Ulysses S. Grant, who was commanding the Army of the Tennessee, sent his left wing to advance on Iuka from the west while Rosecrans marched from the southwest. The plan was to link up on September 18 and attack Price, together, on September 19. Rosecrans was delayed, however, and the coordination collapsed. Nevertheless, Price was compelled to relinquish Iuka. Rosecrans gave chase, but Price was able to escape with his army intact and joined Van Dorn in what would be the Second Battle of Corinth. Price suffered 1,516 killed, wounded, or captured, and Rosecrans lost 790 killed, wounded, or captured. Because Iuka fell to the Union, the battle was officially a victory, but Grant blamed Rosecrans for having lost the opportunity to destroy Price's army.

The Second Battle of Corinth was fought on October 3–4, by the Army of the Mississippi (Rosecrans) and the Confederate Army of the West Tennessee commanded by Van Dorn, who was joined by elements of the Army of the West under Price. The combined Confederate force numbered about 22,000 men versus some 23,000 in the Union's Army of the Mississippi.

Van Dorn's plan was to march southeast from Pocahontas to retake Corinth, from which the army would advance into Middle Tennessee.

Rosecrans, however, had fortified Corinth, and his army was positioned behind a well-prepared outer line of fortifications, with units also positioned in front of this line. The fighting began about three miles outside of town on the morning of October 3. At first Van Dorn pushed the Union troops out of their advanced positions, and a gap was opened up between two of Rosecrans's brigades. The Confederates successfully exploited this by about one o'clock in the afternoon and beat back a Union attempt to close the gap. By evening Van Dorn had forced Rosecrans back to his inner lines; however, instead of bringing the battle to an immediate decision, the Confederate commander decided to rest his troops, so that they could finish the battle the next morning. It proved to be a critical error.

During the night Rosecrans regrouped within the town's fortifications. When Van Dorn attacked at about nine in the morning, Rosecrans opened up with his artillery, thinning Van Dorn's ranks. Nevertheless, elements of his army penetrated the Union fortifications and some Confederates even fought their way into the heart of the city. There, however, they were repulsed, and, ultimately, a battered Van Dorn was forced into full retreat. Yet, just as Van Dorn had unwisely postponed his final attack on Rosecrans, so Rosecrans now postponed his pursuit of Van Dorn. Although defeated, Van Dorn was nevertheless able to retreat intact, and yet another opportunity to neutralize a Confederate army was lost. The Confederates had suffered 4,233 casualties (killed, wounded, or captured), nearly twice the Union forces' total of 2,520.

The final battle of the Army of the Mississippi, the Battle of Arkansas Post (January 9–11, 1863; Union victory), was fought by the unit as reconstituted under Major General John A. McClernand. It was an operation to capture Fort Hindman, a strong point located at Arkansas Post, from which Confederates had been harassing Union shipping on the Mississippi.

Union transports under Rear Admiral David Dixon Porter landed troops near Arkansas Post during the night of January 9, 1863. The soldiers advanced toward Fort Hindman, and XV Corps, under Major General William T. Sherman, overran the Confederate trenches defending the fort, forcing the troops to withdraw into the fort itself. Porter, on the next day, began bombarding Fort Hindman as McClernand's troops fired on it from artillery positions across the river. In the meantime, McClernand moved his infantry into position for an attack, which was superbly coordinated with a renewed round of shelling from Porter's ironclads. The naval bombardment not only hit the fort itself, but cut off avenues of retreat, forcing a Confederate surrender on January 11. Union losses out of a combined land and naval force of some 33,000 were 1,061 killed, wounded, or missing, versus 709 out of a much smaller Confederate force of some 5,500.

Chapter 22

ARMY OF THE TENNESSEE

OVERALL PERFORMANCE: ✭ ✭ ✭ ✭

For some three years, the Army of the Tennessee took the lead in most of the Union's western campaigns—in Tennessee and at Vicksburg, before going on to the Atlanta Campaign and then to the Carolinas, the final campaign of the Civil War. Except for the Army of the Potomac, no force was more important to the Union war effort. It was the first army Ulysses S. Grant and William Tecumseh Sherman, successively, commanded. Its victories were major Union breakthroughs and turning points in the war.

ESTABLISHMENT

Brigadier General Ulysses S. Grant commanded predecessor units to the Department and Army of the Tennessee—the District of Southeast Missouri, District of Cairo, and District of West Tennessee—from September 1, 1861, to October 16, 1862. With Grant commanding, the Department of the Tennessee was created on the latter date, encompassing Cairo, Illinois (at the confluence of the Mississippi and Ohio Rivers), Forts Henry and Donelson, northern Mississippi, and those parts of Tennessee and Kentucky west of the Tennessee River. At first all troops in the new military department were lumped into a single corps, the XIII. It quickly became apparent, however, that the XIII Corps was the size of an army and therefore required more commanders and more flexibility. It was therefore divided into four corps—XIII, XV, XVI, and XVII—and designated the Army of the Tennessee on December 18, 1862, with Grant commanding both the department and the army. By April 30, 1863, the new army was a huge force of about 150,000 men—although its constituents were frequently attached to other armies as needed and so it was rarely fielded at anything approaching its maximum strength.[1]

COMMANDING GENERALS

Grant, the army's first commanding officer, led the organization from its creation as an army, October 16, 1862, to October 24, 1863, when Major General William Tecumseh Sherman took over. During Grant's command, the Battles of Belmont, Forts Henry and Donelson, and Shiloh were fought, as were the Siege and Battle of Corinth and the Vicksburg Campaign and Siege.

When Grant was born in 1822, at Point Pleasant, Ohio, it was as Hiram Ulysses Grant, a farmer's son. Enrolled at West Point in 1839, he learned that he was listed on the rolls as "Ulysses Simpson Grant." The first was a name he sometimes went by, and the second was his mother's maiden name. If that's who the army wanted him to be, he had no objections, and he was Ulysses Simpson Grant from that day forward.

A mediocre cadet, Grant graduated in 1843, twenty-first of out of a class of thirty-nine. In September 1845 Second Lieutenant Grant was attached to Zachary Taylor's command on the Texas-Mexico border, awaiting the outbreak of war. He fought with distinction during the US-Mexican War (1846–48) at Palo Alto (May 8, 1846), Resaca de la Palma (May 9), and Monterrey (September 21–24). When Winfield Scott replaced Taylor in March 1847, Grant, transferred to his command, fought at the capture of Veracruz (March 9–29, 1847) and in the battles of Cerro Gordo (April 18), Churubusco (August 20), and Molino del Rey (September 8).

In the latter battle he earned a brevet promotion to first lieutenant for gallantry. He distinguished himself further at Chapultepec (September 13), for which he was brevetted captain. On September 16 he was formally commissioned first lieutenant.

After the war Grant was posted variously in New York, Michigan, California, and Oregon during 1848–54. Promoted to captain (August 1853), he grew impatient with the army's glacial system of advancement and resigned—only to discover that he had little talent for anything other than soldiering. In 1860 he moved to Galena, Illinois, where he joined his father and brothers in the family tannery, and he was working in the business as a clerk when the Civil War began in April 1861. Grant was chosen to train the Galena militia company and then worked in the state adjutant general's office until June 1861, when he was appointed colonel of the 21st Illinois Volunteer Infantry regiment. In August he was promoted to brigadier general of volunteers and took command of the District of Southeast Missouri, headquartered at Cairo.

Acting on his own initiative, Grant seized Paducah, Kentucky, on September 6, 1861, but, despite winning the Battle of Belmont (November 7, 1861, Missouri), had insufficient numbers to hold it and was forced to withdraw. The aggressive Grant found himself repeatedly at odds with his overly cautious superior, Major General Henry Wager Halleck. At length he nevertheless managed to persuade Halleck to allow him to move against Fort Henry on the Tennessee River, which he captured on February 6, 1862. This was followed by the Battle of Fort Donelson (February 11–16, 1862, Tennessee; Union victory). With these wins, Union forces seized the initiative in the Western Theater. When the commander of the Confederate garrison at Donelson presented his surrender terms, Grant replied that nothing less than unconditional surrender was acceptable. This

gave him yet another name, and "Ulysses Simpson" became "Unconditional Surrender" Grant. Halleck, far from unconditionally satisfied with Grant's victories, temporarily relieved him of command for insubordination—only to restore him late in March.

In a lapse of judgment, Grant allowed himself to be surprised at the Battle of Shiloh (April 6–7, 1862), but recovered and drove the Confederates back, albeit with heavy losses. This prompted Halleck to take direct command of western forces until he was elevated to general-in-chief of all Union armies, and Grant was returned to absolute command of the Army of the Tennessee. Under Halleck the army had fought the Siege of Corinth (April 29–May 30, 1862, Mississippi; Union victory), which positioned Grant to conduct the long siege against heavily fortified Vicksburg, key to the Mississippi River.

From December 1862 through March 1863, Grant tried various tactics to lay effective siege against the fortress town. After all of them failed, he marched his forces south of Vicksburg and, under covering fire furnished by Rear Admiral David Dixon Porter's gunboats, led the Army of the Tennessee back to the east bank of the Mississippi during April 30–May 1. He took Grand Gulf, Mississippi, just below Vicksburg, on May 3, then captured Jackson on May 14. This split the armies of Confederate generals John C. Pemberton and Joseph E. Johnston. Defeating Pemberton at the Battle of Champion's Hill (May 16, 1863), Grant at last laid siege to Vicksburg itself, which did not fall to him until July 4, 1863. With the Union victory at Gettysburg, which came on the day before, Vicksburg was a turning point of the Civil War and a triumph for the Army of the Tennessee.

Grant was promoted to major general in the regular army and was assigned command of the Military Division of the Mississippi on October 4, with command of the Army of the

Tennessee transferred to Major General William T. Sherman on October 24. The first task Grant assigned to Division of the Mississippi forces was to break the Confederate siege of the Union's Army of the Cumberland at Chattanooga. This was accomplished in two battles, Lookout Mountain (November 24, 1863) and Missionary Ridge (November 25, 1863), the second of which involved the Army of the Tennessee (Sherman) as well as the Army of the Cumberland (now commanded by Major General George H. Thomas).

The performance of Grant and his two principal army commanders moved President Lincoln to promote Grant to lieutenant general on March 3, 1864, and give him command of all Union armies. Grant now focused on the Eastern Theater and, using the Army of the Potomac (commanded by Major General George Meade) as his primary weapon, conducted the Overland Campaign (May 4–June 24, 1864), which culminated in the campaigns and battles that led to the surrender of Robert E. Lee's Army of Northern Virginia, at Appomattox Court House on April 9, 1865. With the flagship army of the Confederacy lost, the war itself came to an end before the close of the following month.

Grant's prosecution of the war's endgame was extremely costly, but the victory it produced was decisive. After the war Grant returned to Washington, where he was put in charge of the massive military demobilization and the army's role in postwar Reconstruction. In recognition of his services to the nation, he was promoted to the newly created rank of general of the army in July 1866. He served briefly as interim secretary of war under President Andrew Johnson during 1867–68, but his insistence on measures to protect the army of occupation in the South caused a permanent rift with Johnson, who, as a Tennessean, was sympathetic to the South. Grant then embraced the strong—often punitive— Reconstruction policies of the radical wing of the Republican Party and easily achieved the Republican nomination for president in 1868. He was elected to two terms, 1869–1877, both plagued by corruption and scandal, though none of it traceable to him. He unsuccessfully sought nomination to a third term in 1880, suffered ruinous financial reversals, and completed his masterful *Personal Memoirs* just days before his death, from throat cancer, on July 23, 1885. The proceeds of the tremendously successful book made Julia Dent Grant a wealthy widow.

Under the command of Major General William Tecumseh Sherman, which spanned October 24, 1863, to March 26, 1864, the Army of the Tennessee fought in the Chattanooga Campaign, including at the Battle of Missionary Ridge and the Battle of Meridian.

He was born in 1820, in Lancaster, Ohio, the son of an Ohio Supreme Court judge. After graduating from West Point in 1840, Sherman was commissioned in the artillery and saw action in the Second Seminole War (1835–42), gaining promotion to first lieutenant (November 1841). At the outbreak of the US-Mexican War (1846–48), Sherman was assigned to the staff of Brigadier General Stephen Watts Kearny, but was disappointed that he saw no combat, serving most of the war as an administrative officer in California until that territory joined the Union in 1848. Sherman became a commissary captain in September 1850 but, feeling profound dissatisfaction with what amounted to a desk career, resigned his commission and embarked on thoroughly unsuccessful careers in banking and in law during 1853–58. In 1859 he was appointed superintendent of the newly established Louisiana State Seminary of Learning & Military Academy, a position he relished—but resigned in January 1861, when it became clear that the country was about to fight a civil war.

After a brief interval as president of the St. Louis Railroad streetcar company, Sherman was

The Union's William Tecumseh Sherman—an intelligent, high-strung man who proved to be among the Union's most ferocious warriors. NATIONAL ARCHIVES AND RECORDS ADMINISTRATION

commissioned colonel of the 13th US Infantry on May 14, 1861—a regiment yet to be raised by the time he assumed command of a volunteer brigade at the First Battle of Bull Run (July 21, 1861; Union defeat). In August Sherman was promoted to brigadier general of US Volunteers and subsequently commanded the Department of the Cumberland in Louisville, Kentucky. Overcome by deep pessimism, he suffered a nervous collapse and asked to be relieved of command. By the end of the year, he returned to service under Henry W. Halleck in the Department of the Missouri (in March 1862 enlarged into the Department of the Mississippi). After Sherman successfully supported operations against Fort Donelson (February 11–16, 1862), Grant assigned him to command the 5th Division in the Army of

West Tennessee. The fighting retreat Sherman led at the Battle of Shiloh (April 6–7, 1862) was instrumental both in averting a Union rout and in making Grant's counterattack on April 7 a success. Twice wounded, Sherman showed himself heroic and steadfast under fire. He was promoted to major general of volunteers on May 1, 1862.

Sherman fought under Grant at the Siege of Corinth and the Second Battle of Corinth (April 29–May 30, 1862, and October 3–4, 1862, respectively) and during the Vicksburg Campaign (March 29–July 4, 1863). He was transferred to command of XV Corps, Army of the Mississippi, and successfully took Arkansas Post (January 9–11, 1863), after which he transferred with XV Corps to the Army of the Tennessee and resumed his support of Grant's siege of Vicksburg. Sherman and his corps were instrumental in Grant's capture of Jackson, Mississippi (May 14, 1863).

Promoted to brigadier general in the regular army in July, Sherman rushed to the relief of William Rosecrans and the Army of the Cumberland at Chattanooga (September 21–November 25, 1863), succeeding Grant as commander of the Army of the Tennessee on October 24, 1863. Leading that army, he played a strong supporting role in coordinating with the Army of the Cumberland (command of which George H. Thomas had assumed from Rosecrans) and commanded the Union left at Chattanooga in the Battle of Lookout Mountain (November 24, 1863) and the Battle of Missionary Ridge (November 25, 1863).

During February 14–20, 1864, Sherman led the Army of the Tennessee in the Meridian Campaign, which culminated in the capture—and heavy destruction—of that Mississippi town, a railroad hub and the site of a Confederate arsenal, POW camp, and hospital. The following month, after Grant was elevated to Union general-in-chief, Sherman took his place as commander of the Military Division of the Mississippi, with control of the Armies of the Tennessee, the Cumberland, and the Ohio. He consolidated these forces—more than 100,000 men at this point—in a spectacular drive toward Atlanta, which he coordinated with Grant's advance (using the Army of the Potomac) on Richmond. Sherman marched 100 miles in seventy-four days, pushing the Confederate Army of Tennessee (then commanded by Joseph E. Johnston) before him, fighting battles across Georgia at Rocky Face Ridge (May 7–13; Union victory), Resaca (May 13–15; inconclusive), New Hope Church (May 25–26; Union defeat), and Dallas (May 26–June 1; Union victory), always closing inexorably on Atlanta. Although he suffered a sharp defeat at the Battle of Kennesaw Mountain (June 27), he beat John Bell Hood (now in command of the Confederate Army of Tennessee) at the Battles of Peachtree Creek (July 20), Atlanta (July 22), Ezra Church (July 28), Dalton (August 14–15), and Jonesborough (August 31–September 1). On September 2 Sherman and his armies occupied Atlanta.

From Atlanta—which he left ablaze—Sherman set out on his March to the Sea (November 15–December 21, 1864) with the Army of the Tennessee and the newly constituted Army of Georgia (consisting of the XIV and XX Corps of the Army of the Cumberland). The march culminated in the occupation of Savannah, Georgia (December 21, 1864). From here Sherman led the Armies of the Tennessee, the Ohio, and Georgia on the Carolinas Campaign, which culminated in the capture and burning of Columbia, South Carolina (February 17),

This engraving, "The burning of Columbia, South Carolina, February 17, 1865, by General Sherman's troops," appeared in Harper's Weekly *(April 8, 1865).* LIBRARY OF CONGRESS

the Battle of Bentonville (March 19–21, 1865, North Carolina; Union victory), the capture of Raleigh, North Carolina (April 13), and Joseph E. Johnston's surrender to Sherman on April 26, near Durham Station, North Carolina. With this, the last substantial Confederate force (the so-called Army of the South) had been defeated.

Sherman was appointed commander of the Division of the Missouri in June 1865 and was promoted to lieutenant general of regulars in July 1866. From his headquarters in Chicago, he directed much of the strategy and policy during the Indian Wars—although he participated on the field in no battles. In November 1869 he became commanding general of the army and was promoted to general. He held this largely ceremonial post until his retirement in 1884. Sherman died on February 14, 1891.

Major General James B. McPherson assumed command of the Army of the Tennessee on March 26, 1864, and led it through half of the Atlanta Campaign (May 7–September 2, 1864), until he was killed in action on July 22 of that year. McPherson was born in 1828 and graduated from West Point in 1853, a class that included both the future Union general Philip Sheridan and the future Confederate commander of the army defending Atlanta, John Bell Hood. Commissioned into the Corps of Engineers, McPherson was involved in such civil engineering projects as improving New York Harbor, building Fort Delaware, and building the fortifications on Alcatraz Island in San Francisco Bay.

At the start of the Civil War, McPherson briefly served on the staff of Major General Henry Halleck before being transferred to the District of Cairo as chief engineer during Brigadier General Grant's assaults on Forts Henry (February 6, 1862, Tennessee and Kentucky; Union victory) and Donelson (February 11–16, Tennessee; Union victory). McPherson fought at the Battle of Shiloh (April 6–7) and, promoted

to brigadier general on August 19, 1862, fought at the Second Battle of Corinth (October 3–4), emerging with a promotion to major general of volunteers, effective October 8, 1862. Given command of XVII Corps in the Army of the Tennessee under Ulysses S. Grant, he served in the Vicksburg Campaign (March 29–July 4, 1863) and was promoted to brigadier general in the regular army on August 1, 1863. He took command of the Army of the Tennessee on March 26, 1864, after Sherman was elevated to command all armies in the West.

Under McPherson, the Army of the Tennessee was the right wing of Sherman's combined forces in the Atlanta Campaign. At the Battle of Rocky Face Ridge (May 7–13, 1864), McPherson's move to flank Joseph E. Johnston's Army of Tennessee failed because he was blocked by a much smaller Confederate force. He met another defeat at the Battle of Kennesaw Mountain (June 27, 1864).

On July 22, 1864, the Confederate Army of Tennessee, now under James Bell Hood, launched a sharp attack against Union forces and nearly captured McPherson, who was shot by skirmishers when he attempted to get away.

After McPherson's death, Major General John A. Logan was given temporary command, from July 22 to July 27, 1864, as the army continued to fight the Atlanta Campaign. He was replaced by Major General Oliver O. Howard, who led the army from July 27, 1864, to May 19, 1865.

Howard was born in 1830 in Leeds, Maine, and graduated from Bowdoin College in 1850, after which he enrolled at West Point, from which he graduated with the Class of 1854. Commissioned a second lieutenant, he was assigned as an artillerist, and then returned to West Point as a mathematics instructor. With the outbreak of the Civil War, he was appointed colonel of the 3rd Maine Volunteers in June of 1861. By the time of the First Battle of Bull Run

(July 21, 1861, Virginia; Union defeat), he was a brigade commander, and, in September 1861, a brigadier general of volunteers.

Howard served under George B. McClellan in the Peninsula Campaign (March–July 1862, Virginia; Confederate victory), fighting at Fair Oaks (May 31–June 1, 1862, Virginia; Union defeat), where he lost his right arm. Later returning to combat, Howard fought at South Mountain (September 14, 1862, Maryland; Union victory) and at Antietam (September 17, Maryland; Union strategic victory). In November 1862 he was promoted to major general of volunteers and divisional commander. He led II Corps of the Army of the Potomac at the Battle of Fredericksburg (December 11–15, 1862, Virginia; Union defeat) and on April 2, 1863, was assigned command of XI Corps.

At the Battle of Chancellorsville (April 30–May 6, 1863; Union defeat), Thomas "Stonewall" Jackson routed XI Corps, but Howard redeemed himself amply at Gettysburg (July 1–3, 1863; Union victory), when his corps performed with such distinction as to merit the special thanks of Congress.

In September 1863 Howard transferred to the Army of the Cumberland, where he won distinction in the Chattanooga Campaign (September 21–November 25, 1863, Tennessee; Union victory) at the Battle of Lookout Mountain (November 24–25, Tennessee; Union victory). In command of IV Corps, Army of the Tennessee (April 2, 1864), he served under William Tecumseh Sherman in the Atlanta Campaign (May 7–September 2, 1864, Georgia; Union victory) and was elevated to command of the Army of the Tennessee on July 27, 1864. He led the army at the Battles of Ezra Church (July 28, 1864, Georgia; Union victory) and Jonesborough (August 31–September 1, 1864, Georgia; Union victory) and in Sherman's March to the Sea (November 15–December 21, 1864, Georgia; Union victory) and his Carolinas Campaign

(February–March 21, 1865, South and North Carolina; Union victory). In December 1864 Howard was promoted to brigadier general of regulars and in March 1865 brevetted to major general.

Following the war, Howard was appointed commissioner of the Freedman's Bureau, the agency charged with assisting freed slaves, serving in this capacity from May 1865 through June 1872. In 1867 he founded (and later became president of) Howard University in Washington, DC. The institution remains the most prestigious historically black university in the nation.

During the 1870s Howard was closely involved in Indian affairs and also served as military commander of the Department of the Columbia. In this capacity he unsuccessfully negotiated with a faction of the Nez Percé for their removal from lands desired by the government and led a military campaign against the faction and its leader, Chief Joseph the Younger. During 1878 Howard campaigned against the Bannock Indians, who were raiding in the Northwest. In January 1881 Howard was named superintendent of the US Military Academy at West Point, serving until September 1882, when he was appointed commander of the Department of the Platte (1882–86) and then the Division of the East (March 1886–November 1894). Belatedly, in 1893, Howard was honored with the Medal of Honor for action at the Battle of Fair Oaks during the Civil War. He retired the following year and founded Lincoln Memorial University in Tennessee in 1895. He then returned to New England to write military history and an autobiography. Howard died on October 26, 1909.

The Army of the Tennessee ended its existence on August 1, 1865, with Major General John A. Logan returned to command beginning on May 19 of that year. He had been born in 1826 in rural Murphysboro, Illinois, and was largely self-educated before volunteering for service in the US Army as a second lieutenant in the US-Mexican War (1846–48). After the war he entered the University of Louisville (Kentucky), graduating with a law degree in 1851, and in 1858 he was elected Democratic congressman from Illinois. He resigned his seat in 1861 to join the Union Army as a private in a Michigan regiment. After fighting in the First Battle of Bull Run (July 21, 1861, Virginia; Union defeat), he returned to Illinois to form the 31st Illinois Regiment and was appointed its colonel in September.

Colonel Logan served under Brigadier General Ulysses S. Grant (then commanding the District of Southeast Missouri) at the Battle of Belmont (November 7, 1861, Missouri; Union victory) and in the assaults on Fort Henry (February 6, 1862, Tennessee and Kentucky; Union victory) and Fort Donelson (February 11–16, 1862, Tennessee; Union victory). Promoted to brigadier general in March 1862, Logan fought in the Vicksburg Campaign during January–July 4, 1863, commanding a division in General James B. McPherson's XVII Corps, Army of the Tennessee. In November 1863 Logan was promoted to major general and given command of XV Corps in that army. When McPherson was killed during the Atlanta Campaign (May 7–September 2, 1864, Georgia; Union victory), Logan assumed temporary command of the army on July 22, but was relieved on July 27 by Major General William T. Sherman, who lacked confidence in his experience, claiming in particular that he paid insufficient attention to logistics. Sherman returned him to corps command and turned over the Army of the Tennessee to O. O. Howard.

After the war Logan was reelected to the House of Representatives (now as a Republican) and served from 1867 to 1871. He was then elected to the Senate and played a key role in the impeachment of President Andrew Johnson.

SIZE AND ORGANIZATION

At its height the Army of the Tennessee mustered as many as 150,000 men, although Major General Sherman, as commander of the Military Division of the Mississippi (effectively, commander of the Western Theater), frequently detached divisions and corps from the army and attached them to others. A good idea of the organization of the Army of the Tennessee can be gathered by its structure during the Atlanta Campaign:[2]

GENERAL STAFF
Major General James B. McPherson, commanding
Escort: 4th Company Ohio Cavalry, B Company, 1st Ohio Cavalry

XV CORPS
Major General John A. Logan

1ST DIVISION
Brigadier General Peter J. Osterhaus, Brigadier General Charles R. Woods

2ND DIVISION
Brigadier General Morgan L. Smith

3RD DIVISION
Brigadier General John E. Smith

XVI CORPS
Major General Grenville M. Dodge
Escort: 1st Alabama Cavalry; Company A, 52nd Illinois

2ND DIVISION
Brigadier General Thomas W. Sweeny

4TH DIVISION
Brigadier General James C. Veatch

XVII CORPS
Major General Francis P. Blair Jr.
Escort: Company M, 1st Ohio Cavalry; Company G, 9th Illinois Mounted Infantry

3RD DIVISION
Brigadier General Mortimer D. Leggett

4TH DIVISION
Brigadier General Walter Q. Gresham

MAJOR CAMPAIGNS AND BATTLES

BATTLE OF BELMONT
(NOVEMBER 7, 1861)

On November 6, 1861, Grant transported 3,114 troops of the District of Southeast Missouri by steamboats from Cairo, Illinois, intending to attack Columbus, Kentucky. On the next morning, he was told that Confederate troops had crossed the Mississippi River from Columbus to Belmont, Missouri. Grant responded by landing his troops on the Missouri shore and advanced on Belmont. The battle began at nine o'clock on the morning of November 7, and before the end of the day, Grant had driven Gideon Pillow's Confederate forces out of their encampment in the town. Although routed, the Confederates were reinforced from Columbus, on the Kentucky side of the Mississippi River. Pillow counterattacked Grant, forcing his withdrawal to Cairo, Illinois. Strategically inconclusive, the battle did result in nearly twice as many Confederate casualties as Union losses: 966 Confederate killed, wounded, or captured versus 498 Union casualties.

BATTLE OF FORT HENRY
(FEBRUARY 6, 1862)

During February 4–5, Grant landed troops on the east bank of the Tennessee River and on the high ground on the Kentucky bank. His objective was to capture Fort Henry on the Tennessee River. His troops on the Kentucky bank blocked any attempt Fort Henry's Confederate garrison might make to withdraw in that direction, and Grant prepared an assault force on the west bank, where the fort stood. Once the troops were in place, Union navy flag officer Andrew

H. Foote began bombarding the fort from his flotilla of seven gunboats on February 6. Brigadier General Lloyd Tilghman, commanding the Confederate garrison, knew he could not long withstand the amphibious assault. While his artillery fired back against the gunboats, he removed the remainder of his garrison to Fort Donelson, ten miles away. This done, Tilghman returned to Fort Henry and surrendered. Casualties numbered forty for the Union and seventy-nine for the Confederate army.

BATTLE OF FORT DONELSON
(FEBRUARY 11–16, 1862)

With Fort Henry taken, the way was clear for an assault on Fort Donelson, the other Confederate river strongpoint, this one on the Cumberland. Grant advanced against the fort and began a siege on February 11. The Confederate garrison responded with an all-out counterattack intended to break the siege lines. This failed, and on February 16 Confederate Brigadier General Simon Bolivar Buckner asked Grant for terms. The Union commander replied that the only acceptable terms were unconditional surrender—and thus he earned the wartime sobriquet of "Unconditional Surrender" Grant.

The Confederate loss of Forts Henry and Donelson not only opened up the Mississippi, Cumberland, and Tennessee Rivers to Union traffic in this region, but ensured that Kentucky would not join the Confederacy. The Union suffered 2,331 casualties, killed or wounded, and the Confederate army lost 15,067 men, most of them becoming POWs.

BATTLE OF SHILOH
(APRIL 6–7, 1862)

The bloodiest battle in which the Army of the Tennessee (with the Army of the Ohio, chapter 24) engaged during the war, Shiloh pitted Grant and Major General Don Carlos Buell (commanding the Army of the Ohio) against the

Confederate Army of Mississippi, under General Albert Sidney Johnston. Combined, the two Union armies fielded 65,085 men in this battle. The Confederate Army of the Mississippi mustered 44,968.

With Forts Henry and Donelson lost, General Johnston fell back, ceding to Grant Kentucky and a large part of western and Middle Tennessee. Intending to mount a counterattack, Johnston used Corinth, Mississippi, as a staging area. He was determined to make a preemptive attack on the Army of the Tennessee *before* it could link up with the Army of the Ohio. He retrenched his position, and Grant, at this point with some 40,000 men available in the Army of the Tennessee, prepared to attack along the Tennessee River, toward Pittsburg Landing. Major General Halleck, however, ordered him to await the arrival of the Army of the Ohio at Pittsburg Landing. Grant complied but declined to fortify his position as he waited. On April 6 Johnston made a surprise attack, nearly routing the Army of the Tennessee.

Union forces dug into a battle line at a sunken road. As Confederates made attack after attack against this position, only to be repulsed each time, they dubbed it the "Hornet's Nest." Finally, when infantry failed them, the Confederates unleashed their artillery, causing many Union casualties. Albert S. Johnston, however, fell mortally wounded in the combat, and General P. G. T. Beauregard assumed command. The Union troops withdrew closer to Pittsburg Landing and established a new battle line there, which was now reinforced by Buell's Army of the Ohio. Fighting was extremely fierce, continuing even through part of the night. Come morning, Beauregard, unaware that Buell had reinforced Grant, counterattacked. Outnumbered and surprised, Beauregard ultimately withdrew from the field. The Union suffered 13,047, the Confederates, 10,699, killed, wounded, or captured.

SIEGE OF CORINTH (APRIL 29–MAY 30, 1862)

From April 29 to May 30, 1862, Major General Halleck led the three armies he controlled—Army of the Tennessee, Army of the Ohio, and Army of the Mississippi—in a siege against Corinth, a Mississippi town known as the "Crossroads of the Confederacy" because of the key rail junction there. Thanks to Halleck's excessive caution, the operation was unduly prolonged, but the city nevertheless finally fell to the Union on May 30.

BATTLE OF IUKA (SEPTEMBER 19, 1862)

William S. Rosecrans's Army of the Mississippi (chapter 21) defeated Sterling Price's Army of the West at Iuka, Mississippi, on September 19, after which Price withdrew and linked up with Major General Earl Van Dorn's Army of West Tennessee. The combined force attacked what was now Union-held Corinth. Although the Confederates were repulsed, they withdrew intact.

VICKSBURG CAMPAIGN (MARCH 29–JULY 4, 1863)

Perhaps the most ambitious role the Army of the Tennessee played was in the Vicksburg Campaign, in which the army invested the Confederacy's "Gibraltar of the West" beginning on May 18, 1863, forcing Vicksburg's surrender on July 4. The Confederate Army of Mississippi, under Lieutenant General John Pemberton, bottled up in Vicksburg and was neutralized, and the fortress city fell, yielding control of the Mississippi River to the Union.

CHATTANOOGA CAMPAIGN (SEPTEMBER 21–NOVEMBER 25, 1863)

The western end of the Western Theater having been largely secured by the capture of Vicksburg, the Army of the Tennessee spearheaded the

Chattanooga Campaign, the objective of which was to relieve the Army of the Cumberland, most of which was being held under siege in Chattanooga by General Braxton Bragg's Confederate Army of Tennessee. Grant (commanding the Military Division of the Mississippi) established a line of supply to the besieged army (celebrated as the "cracker line") and awaited the arrival of Sherman and the Army of the Tennessee. That came in November, and during November 23–24 Union forces took Orchard Knob and Lookout Mountain. On November 25 "Fighting Joe" Hooker waged the Battle of Missionary Ridge, routing the Confederates, liberating the Army of the Cumberland, and seizing Chattanooga, the so-called Gateway to the Lower South. From here Sherman would mount his 1864 Atlanta Campaign.

BATTLE OF MERIDIAN (FEBRUARY 14–20, 1864) AND THE ATLANTA CAMPAIGN (MAY 7–SEPTEMBER 2, 1864)

Before the drive to Atlanta could commence, however, Sherman's Army of the Tennessee fought the Battle of Meridian (February 14–20, 1864, Mississippi; Union victory), taking this important railroad hub. The Atlanta Campaign then got under way on May 7, 1864, and was not concluded until September 2. Now commanding the Military Division of the Mississippi, Sherman had control of the Army of the Tennessee, the Army of the Cumberland, and the Army of the Ohio, all three of which were involved in the campaign against the Confederate Army of Tennessee, first under Joseph E.

This ruined roundhouse in Atlanta was photographed in 1866 by George N. Barnard. NATIONAL ARCHIVES AND RECORDS ADMINISTRATION

Johnston and then under John Bell Hood. The campaign is described in detail in chapter 18.

THE MARCH TO THE SEA (NOVEMBER 15–DECEMBER 21, 1864)

On November 15, 1864, Sherman and the Army of the Tennessee and the Army of Georgia divided into two columns and commenced a march from Atlanta southeast to Savannah, Georgia, with the purpose of demonstrating the vulnerability of the South and the incapacity of the Confederate government and Confederate military to protect its citizens. The 62,000 men Sherman led on the march tore a broad swath of destruction across the state, taking particular care to destroy railroad track and equipment. The march culminated in the capture of Savannah on December 21.

CAROLINAS CAMPAIGN (FEBRUARY–MARCH 21, 1865)

In January 1865 Sherman led the Army of the Tennessee and the Army of Georgia, now joined by the Army of the Ohio, in a campaign against the Confederate Army of Tennessee, which was once again commanded by Joseph E. Johnston. The campaign, discussed in chapter 18, led to Johnston's surrender on April 26, 1865—and, effectively, the end of the Civil War.

Chapter 23

ARMY OF THE CUMBERLAND

OVERALL PERFORMANCE: ★ ★ ⸱

With the Army of the Tennessee, the Army of the Mississippi, and the Army of the Ohio, the Army of the Cumberland was one of the four major Union military forces of the Civil War's Western Theater. Its area of responsibility was all of Tennessee east of the Tennessee River in addition to the northern portions of Georgia and Alabama. The army's maiden battle, Stones River (December 31, 1862–January 2, 1863, Tennessee; Union victory), brought a victory that greatly lifted Union morale after the Army of the Potomac had been dealt a severe defeat at the Battle of Fredericksburg (December 11–15, 1862, Virginia; Union defeat) in the Eastern Theater.

ESTABLISHMENT

The immediate predecessor of the Army of the Cumberland was the Army of the Ohio created in November 1861 under the Department of the Ohio (which had been formed in May 1861). The army was commanded by Brigadier General Robert Anderson, the commandant of Fort Sumter at the outbreak of the Civil War. This organization is sometimes called the 1st Army of the Ohio to distinguish it from the Army of the Ohio created on March 25, 1863, and treated in chapter 24. Early in 1862, all of the forces in the department were combined into the Army of the Ohio, and Major General Don Carlos Buell was appointed to replace Anderson as commanding general.

On October 8, 1862, Buell and the (1st) Army of the Ohio fought the Battle of Perryville (Kentucky) against Braxton Bragg commanding

the Confederate Army of Mississippi. Although the result was a strategic victory for the Union, the losses of the Army of the Ohio were considerably greater than those of the Army of Mississippi. Later in October, William S. Rosecrans was given command of XIV Corps, created out of the Army of the Ohio. At the same time, Rosecrans was given command of the newly established Department of the Cumberland. Rosecrans was then ordered to replace Buell—who was discredited by his performance at the Battle of Perryville—and the Army of the Ohio, which consisted mostly of the men of XIV Corps, was renamed the Army of the Cumberland on October 24, 1862, with Rosecrans commanding.

COMMANDING GENERALS

The Army of the Cumberland had just two commanding officers: Rosecrans, from October 24, 1862, to October 19, 1863, and Major General George H. Thomas, from October 19, 1863, to August 1, 1865—the date on which the army was disbanded.

Major General William S. Rosecrans led the Army of the Cumberland at the Battle of Stones River (December 31, 1862–January 2, 1863, Tennessee; Union victory), in the Tullahoma Campaign (June 24–July 3, 1863, Tennessee; Union victory), and at Chickamauga (September 19–20, 1863, Georgia; Union defeat). Notoriously harsh with his officers, Rosecrans was very popular with enlisted soldiers, who were intensely loyal to him. He had, however, a fatal flaw as a commander. Excitable in combat, he developed a crippling stutter under fire and had difficulty making his orders understood. This

The fatally flawed Major General William S. "Rosy" Rosecrans commanded the Army of the Cumberland when it was held under siege in Chattanooga after the catastrophe of Chickamauga (September 19–20, 1863).

that resulted in a Confederate victory. This occasioned Rosecrans's relief as commanding general of the Army of the Cumberland and his replacement by George H. Thomas. (See chapter 21 for a more detailed biography of Rosecrans.)

Like Robert E. Lee, George Henry Thomas was a Virginian, born in 1816 at Newsom's Depot, the son of a prosperous plantation owner with twenty-four slaves. Unlike Lee, he remained loyal to the Union. Thomas's father was killed in a farm accident in 1829, leaving the thirteen-year-old George to look after his mother and sisters, all of whom were forced to flee for their lives during Nat Turner's slave rebellion of 1831. Instead of turning Thomas toward repression against slaves, the event turned him against slavery. Nine years later, in 1840, he graduated from West Point. He fought in the Second Seminole War; served garrison duty in New Orleans, at Fort Moultrie (in Charleston Harbor), and at Fort McHenry (in Baltimore); and then fought in the US-Mexican War (at Fort Brown, Resaca de la Palma, Monterrey, and Buena Vista), earning a reputation for calmness, bravery, and acute skill as an artillerist.

After the war he served in Florida during 1849–50 and then was assigned as an artillery and cavalry instructor at West Point (where he earned the particular admiration of the academy's superintendent, Robert E. Lee) until 1854, when he was transferred to duty in the far West. During the 1850s it was widely suspected that Jefferson Davis, US secretary of war during 1853–57, was covertly assembling an elite cadre of Southern officers in anticipation of civil war and that Thomas, whom Davis had promoted to major, was among them. From 1857 until 1860 Thomas commanded a cavalry regiment, and he was wounded by a Comanche arrow in a skirmish at Clear River, Texas.

The Civil War broke out during a yearlong leave of absence Thomas had taken from the

impediment was compounded by his tendency to violate the chain of command by issuing direct orders to junior officers. The combination of poor communication and distinctly unmilitary micromanagement exacerbated the confusion that prevailed during the Battle of Chickamauga. His ambiguous order to Major General Thomas John Wood "to close in and support his left"—that is, to pull his division out of the line in order to support another division farther to his left—should have been questioned because it opened a gap in the Union line precisely opposite the Confederate troops of James Longstreet. Instead, Wood simply obeyed, giving Longstreet an opening

army. Most of his fellow officers assumed that he would resign to fight for the Confederacy. Although he struggled with the decision—which alienated members of his family—he resolved to remain with the Union. He held various commands until January 19, 1862, when as commanding officer of 1st Division in the (1st) Army of the Ohio (predecessor of the Army of the Cumberland), he fought his first major battle, at Mill Springs (Kentucky; Union victory).

Thomas was at Shiloh (April 6–7, 1862) by the second day of battle, but arrived after the fighting had ended. When Major General Henry W. Halleck, appalled by the heavy losses at that battle, maneuvered to push Grant out of command of the Army of the Tennessee, he redesignated four divisions of that army and one from the (1st) Army of the Ohio as the Right Wing of the Department of the Mississippi and assigned Thomas (now a brigadier general) to command it. Thomas led his new command at the Siege of Corinth (April 29–May 30, 1862). When Grant returned to the helm of the restored Army of the Tennessee, Thomas returned to divisional command in the (1st) Army of the Ohio, which became the Army of the Cumberland when Major General William S. Rosecrans replaced Buell on October 24, 1862.

Thomas's next major battles were Perryville (October 8, 1862, Kentucky; Union strategic victory), Stones River (December 31, 1862–January 2, 1863, Tennessee; Union victory), and Chickamauga (September 19–20, 1863, Georgia; Union defeat). After Rosecrans's blundering gave Confederate commander James Longstreet an opening that touched off a Union rout and the flight of Rosecrans himself, Thomas stubbornly held out at Snodgrass Hill throughout the battle's second day. For this heroism he was dubbed the "Rock of Chickamauga." It was the saving grace of an otherwise catastrophic battle.

The bulk of the Army of the Cumberland having withdrawn to Chattanooga, where it was laid under siege by Braxton Bragg and the Confederate Army of Tennessee, Grant (now in overall command in the West) sent the Army of the Tennessee and that portion of the Army of the Cumberland Thomas had held at Chickamauga to lift the siege. Grant named the "Rock of Chickamauga" as the new commanding general of the Army of the Cumberland on October 19, 1863, and Thomas broke through the Confederate lines at the Battle of Missionary Ridge (November 25, 1863, Tennessee; Union victory), routing Bragg and liberating the main portion of the Army of the Cumberland.

Thomas and what was now his army fought in the Atlanta Campaign (May 7–September 2, 1864), and when Confederate general John Bell Hood and his Army of Tennessee withdrew from Atlanta in September 1864 and made for Tennessee, hoping Sherman would follow him out of Georgia, Sherman instead commenced his March to the Sea (November 15–December 21, 1864), detaching part of the Army of the Cumberland to accompany him and leaving Thomas with just two corps with which to advance west in pursuit of Hood. Although the Army of the Cumberland would continue to exist officially until August 1, 1865, it was, in effect, no longer a field army.

Thomas was subordinate to Major General John M. Schofield, who commanded the newly formed Army of the Ohio (chapter 24). Reinforced with a large portion of Thomas's men, Schofield defeated Hood at the Battle of Franklin (November 30, 1864, Tennessee; Union victory). In the meantime, Thomas was assembling forces at Nashville to attack Hood. He refused to attack prematurely, however, and was on the verge of being relieved of command by Grant, when, on December 15–16, 1864, he launched his attack with 55,000 men against Hood's roughly 30,000, winning a massively decisive victory and inflicting some 6,000 casualties on Hood while suffering approximately half that number. Hood's Army of Tennessee had been neutralized, and the Western Theater was now secured to the Union.

George H. Thomas received the thanks of Congress, but the combat constituents of the Army of the Cumberland were dispersed to other theaters of operations, leaving him with a small force to occupy Tennessee, which he did through the end of the war and into Reconstruction. In 1867 Thomas was transferred to command on the Pacific coast. He held that post until his death, from a stroke, on March 28, 1870. He was fifty-three.

SIZE AND ORGANIZATION

At its maximum field strength, the Army of the Cumberland numbered about 60,000 men. Its organization at the Battle of Chickamauga (September 19–20, 1863) reflects its mature configuration under Major General William Rosecrans.[1]

GENERAL STAFF AND HEADQUARTERS

Major General William Rosecrans, commanding
General Staff:
Chief of Staff: Brigadier General
    James A. Garfield
Chief of Ordnance: Captain Horace Porter
General Headquarters
1st Battalion, Ohio Sharpshooters: Captain
    Gershom M. Barber
10th Ohio Infantry: Lieutenant Colonel
    William M. Ward
15th Pennsylvania Cavalry: Colonel
    William J. Palmer

XIV CORPS

Major General George Henry Thomas
Headquarters:
Provost Guard, 9th Michigan Infantry:
    Colonel John Gibson Parkhurst

Escort, 1st Ohio Cavalry, Company L: Captain
    John D. Barker

1ST DIVISION

Brigadier General Absalom Baird
1st Brigade: Colonel Benjamin F. Scribner
2nd Brigade: Brigadier General John C.
    Starkweather
3rd Brigade: Brigadier General John H. King
Artillery:
4th Battery, Indiana Light: Lieutenant David
    Flansburg, Lieutenant Henry J. Willits

2ND DIVISION

Major General James S. Negley
1st Brigade: Brigadier General John Beatty
2nd Brigade: Colonel Timothy R. Stanley,
    Colonel William L. Stoughton
3rd Brigade: Colonel William Sirwell
Artillery:
Bridges' Battery, Illinois Light: Captain
    Lyman Bridges
Battery G, 1st Ohio Light: Captain
    Alexander Marshall
Battery M, 1st Ohio Light: Captain
    Frederick Schulz

3RD DIVISION

Brigadier General John Milton Brannan
1st Brigade: Colonel John M. Connell
2nd Brigade: Colonel John T. Croxton,
    Colonel William H. Hays
3rd Brigade: Colonel Ferdinand
    Van Derveer
Artillery:
Battery D, 1st Michigan Light: Captain
    Josiah W. Church
Battery C, 1st Ohio Light: Lieutenant
    Marco B. Gary
Battery I, 4th United States: Lieutenant
    Frank G. Smith

4TH DIVISION

Major General Joseph J. Reynolds
1st Brigade: Colonel John T. Wilder

2nd Brigade: Colonel Edward A. King,
    Colonel Milton S. Robinson
3rd Brigade: Brigadier General
    John B. Turchin
Artillery:
18th Battery, Indiana Light: Captain Eli Lilly
19th Battery, Indiana Light:
    Captain Samuel J. Harris,
    Lieutenant Robert S. Lackey
21st Battery, Indiana Light: Captain William
    W. Andrew

XX CORPS

Major General Alexander McDowell McCook
Headquarters:
Provost Guard, 81st Indiana Infantry,
    Company H: Captain William J. Richards
Escort, 2nd Kentucky Cavalry, Company I:
    Lieutenant George W. L. Batman

1ST DIVISION

Brigadier General Jefferson C. Davis
1st Brigade: Colonel P. Sidney Post
2nd Brigade: Brigadier General William P.
    Carlin
3rd Brigade: Colonel Hans C. Heg, Colonel
    John A. Martin

2ND DIVISION

Brigadier General Richard W. Johnson
1st Brigade: Brigadier General August Willich
2nd Brigade: Colonel Joseph B. Dodge
3rd Brigade: Colonel Philemon P. Baldwin,
    Colonel William W. Berry

3RD DIVISION

Major General Philip Sheridan
1st Brigade: Brigadier General William Haines
    Lytle, Colonel Silas Miller
2nd Brigade: Colonel Bernard Laiboldt
3rd Brigade: Colonel Luther Prentice Bradley,
    Colonel Nathan H. Walworth

XXI CORPS

Major General Thomas Leonidas Crittenden

Headquarters:
Escort, 15th Illinois Cavalry, Company K:
    Captain Samuel B. Sherer

1ST DIVISION

Brigadier General Thomas J. Wood
1st Brigade: Colonel George P. Buell
2nd Brigade: Brigadier General
    George D. Wagner
3rd Brigade: Colonel Charles G. Harker
Artillery:
8th Battery, Indiana Light: Captain
    George Estep
10th Battery, Indiana Light: Lieutenant
    William A. Naylor
6th Battery, Ohio Light: Captain
    Cullen Bradley

2ND DIVISION

Major General John M. Palmer
1st Brigade: Brigadier General Charles Cruft
2nd Brigade: Brigadier General William
    Babcock Hazen
3rd Brigade: Colonel William Grose
Artillery: Captain William E. Standart
Battery B, 1st Ohio Light: Lieutenant
    Norman A. Baldwin
Battery F, 1st Ohio Light: Lieutenant
    Giles J. Cockerill
Battery H, 4th United States: Lieutenant
    Harry C. Cushing
Battery M, 4th United States: Lieutenant
    Francis L. D. Russell
Unattached:
110th Illinois (battalion): Lieutenant Colonel
    Ebenezer Hibbard Topping

3RD DIVISION

Brigadier General Horatio P. Van Cleve
1st Brigade: Brigadier General Samuel Beatty
2nd Brigade: Colonel George F. Dick
3rd Brigade: Colonel Sidney M. Barnes
Artillery:
7th Battery, Indiana Light: Captain George R.
    Swallow

Battery B, Pennsylvania Light: Captain
Alanson J. Stevens, Lieutenant
Samuel M. McDowell
3rd Battery, Wisconsin Light: Lieutenant
Cortland Livingston

RESERVE CORPS
Major General Gordon Granger

1ST DIVISION
Brigadier General James B. Steedman
1st Brigade: Brigadier General
Walter C. Whitaker
2nd Brigade: Colonel John G. Mitchell
2nd Division: At Chickamauga, the division
consisted only of the 2nd Brigade and had
no division-level commander.
2nd Brigade: Colonel Daniel McCook Jr.

CAVALRY CORPS
Brigadier General Robert B. Mitchell

1ST DIVISION
Colonel Edward M. McCook
1st Brigade: Colonel Archibald P. Campbell
2nd Brigade: Colonel Daniel M. Ray
3rd Brigade: Colonel Louis D. Watkins

2ND DIVISION
Brigadier General George Crook
1st Brigade: Colonel Robert H. G. Minty
2nd Brigade: Colonel Eli Long
Artillery:
Chicago (Illinois) Board of Trade Battery:
Captain James H. Stokes

MAJOR CAMPAIGNS AND BATTLES

BATTLE OF STONES RIVER
(DECEMBER 31, 1862–JANUARY 2, 1863)
See chapter 18.

TULLAHOMA CAMPAIGN
(JUNE 24–JULY 3, 1863)
Following his defeat at the Battle of Stones River
(December 31, 1862–January 2, 1863), Confederate Braxton Bragg led his Army of Tennessee
in a thirty-five-mile retreat to Tullahoma, Tennessee, to establish a new defensive line there.
His objective was to block Rosecrans's Army of
the Cumberland from advancing against Chattanooga. For his part, however, Rosecrans consolidated his position at Murfreesboro, Tennessee,
and, month after month, did not advance against
the Confederates. The morale of the idled Army
of Tennessee steadily eroded, as did the physical
condition of the poorly supplied troops at Tullahoma. Indeed, as the Confederates were compelled to forage, they depleted available food in
the area and were forced to extend their supply
lines, which made the Army of Tennessee frag-
mented and highly vulnerable. In the meantime,
infighting among Confederate high command
further undermined Bragg, who was already an
unpopular officer.

Union high command, including President
Lincoln, Secretary of War Edwin Stanton, and
Union general-in-chief Henry W. Halleck, was
also at odds with its commander in the field,
Rosecrans, whose delay was becoming intoler-
able. Instead of coordinating an offensive with
Grant in the Western Theater and Joseph Hooker
in the Eastern Theater, Rosecrans persisted in
building up the Army of the Cumberland, which
was already twice the size of the forces opposing
it. At last, on June 24, 1863, the Army of the
Cumberland marched out of Murfreesboro and
forced those elements of Bragg's Army of Tennessee that were not in Tullahoma to fall back on
their stronghold. By the time Rosecrans's troops
reached Tullahoma on July 1, however, Bragg
had withdrawn from it and was retreating south
toward Chattanooga. For all of Rosecrans's delay
and caution, his advance against Tullahoma had,
in the space of two weeks, inflicted some 2,000

casualties (killed, wounded, or captured) on the Confederate Army of Tennessee and had driven Bragg out of Middle Tennessee entirely. Union losses were under 600 killed or wounded.

CHICKAMAUGA CAMPAIGN (AUGUST 21–SEPTEMBER 20, 1863)

See chapter 18.

CHATTANOOGA CAMPAIGN (SEPTEMBER 21–NOVEMBER 25, 1863)

See chapter 18.

ATLANTA CAMPAIGN (MAY 7–SEPTEMBER 2, 1864)

See chapter 18.

FRANKLIN-NASHVILLE CAMPAIGN (SEPTEMBER 18–DECEMBER 27, 1864)

The principal engagements in this campaign were the Battle of Franklin (November 30, 1864, Tennessee; Union victory) and the Battle of Nashville (December 15–16, 1864, Tennessee; Union victory). Although the Battle of Franklin was fought by units of the Army of the Cumberland, these fought as part of the Army of the Ohio under the command of Major General John M. Schofield (see chapter 24).

The Battle of Nashville, which followed, was fought by two corps (IV and XXIII) of the Army of the Cumberland, along with a detachment from the Army of the Tennessee and other smaller units, which Army of the Cumberland

The ruins of central Charleston, South Carolina, as photographed by George N. Barnard from the Circular Church.

NATIONAL ARCHIVES AND RECORDS ADMINISTRATION

commanding officer George H. Thomas had patiently assembled before launching his attack.

Confederate general John Bell Hood had led the Army of Tennessee west from Atlanta with the intention of drawing Sherman out of Atlanta and the state of Georgia. Instead, the Union commander divided his forces, detaching the IV and XXIII Corps of the Army of the Cumberland and sending them west under Thomas while he led the rest of his command southeastward on his infamous March to the Sea.

After suffering a heavy defeat at Franklin on November 30, Hood continued to advance toward Nashville, where Thomas was busily augmenting his two corps. Hood, with about 30,000 men, reached the outskirts of the city on December 2 and deployed his troops on hills parallel to the Union's high-ground positions. Instead of immediately responding to Hood, however, Thomas spent two weeks, from December 1 through December 14, building up his forces and preparing for what he intended to be an overwhelming offensive that would not merely hurt but kill the Army of Tennessee, taking it out of the war once and for all. Grant, however, lost patience and was on the verge of relieving Thomas. This was averted by Thomas's telegram on December 14, announcing that he intended to attack on December 15.

The Army of the Cumberland commander's plan was to hit both of Hood's flanks nearly simultaneously. Troops under Major General James Steedman set out before daybreak on December 15, targeting Hood's right.

Steedman's attack succeeded in pinning down one entire Confederate corps. The Union attack on the left, however, was delayed and did not begin until after noon. Nevertheless, when it did finally step off, its effect was stunning—a classic charge against Hood's position on Montgomery Hill. As the defenders melted away there, Thomas unleashed more attacks on the left.

By nightfall, fighting halted. Hood, although badly battered, refused to believe that the battle was lost. He formed a new line of defense some two miles south of his starting position. During the morning, Union forces assumed assault positions opposite the new line. Thomas began by attacking Hood's right flank on Overton's Hill. This time, however, the attempt to take it by a frontal main force charge failed. Still, another attack, against Hood's position on Shy's Hill, was successful. Inspired by this, Thomas's troops made a fresh assault on Overton's Hill and, this time, captured it, sending the Army of Tennessee into full flight.

Thomas had failed to block one escape route. Unwilling to let Hood escape intact, he gave chase in a pursuit that stretched over ten days. The remnants of the Army of Tennessee recrossed the Tennessee River and withdrew to Tupelo, Mississippi, where a beaten Hood resigned his command. Thomas had neutralized the Army of Tennessee, which was no longer a force in the Western Theater. Hood lost 4,462 men, killed, wounded, or captured; Thomas, 2,140 casualties.

Chapter 24

ARMY OF THE OHIO

OVERALL PERFORMANCE: ★ ★

The Union had two formations called the Army of the Ohio, the first of which became the Army of the Cumberland (chapter 23) and the second of which, variously configured, played a major role in east Tennessee, a supporting role in the Atlanta Campaign (May 7–September 2, 1864), and, near the war's end, a critical role in the capture of Wilmington, North Carolina (February 11–22, 1865), a vital Confederate base of supply.

The careers of the Confederate Army of Northern Virginia and the Union's Army of the Potomac lend color to the historical impression that the Civil War was fought by great, quasi-permanent military institutions. In fact, the United States Army, from which both the Union and Confederate forces were developed, had never before been big enough to warrant military formations larger than regiments, let alone corps and armies. Like the corps, the armies were created in the Civil War as an organizational means of commanding unprecedentedly large numbers of men and equipment. They were, in a very real sense, military experiments and, as such, always retained an ad hoc quality.

ESTABLISHMENT

There were two distinct Armies of the Ohio, and while the first to be formed was the direct predecessor of the Army of the Cumberland (chapter 23), neither it nor the Army of the Cumberland had a direct relation to the *second* Army of the Ohio. For this reason, it is most useful historically to distinguish the two Armies of the Ohio with unofficial labels, (1st) Army of the Ohio and (2nd) Army of the Ohio, two unique organizations.

The (1st) Army of the Ohio was created on November 8, 1861, under the command of Major General Don Carlos Buell, an officer battle tested in fighting against the Seminoles in Florida as well as in the US-Mexican War (1846–48). As for the Army of the Ohio, it did not see action until the Battle of Mill Springs (January 19, 1862, Kentucky; Union victory), in which only the 1st Division (under Brigadier General George H. Thomas) was engaged. The Battle of Shiloh (April 6–7, 1862, Tennessee; Union victory) and the Battle of Perryville (October 8, 1862, Kentucky; Union strategic victory) were the only major engagements in which the (1st) Army of the Ohio fought—and Buell's performance was deemed so insufficiently aggressive at Perryville (a strategic victory but a costly tactical defeat against numerically inferior numbers) that he was relieved of command and replaced by Major General William S. Rosecrans on October 24, 1862. Rosecrans received command of the army simultaneously with being named commanding officer of the Department of the Cumberland. This moved him to rename his field army the Army of the Cumberland (chapter 23), and, from this point, the (1st) Army of the Ohio ceased to exist.

Major General Ambrose Burnside was named to command the Department of the Ohio on March 25, 1863. This, in fact, was the *second* Department of the Ohio. It had been formed on August 19, 1862, under Major General Horatio G. Wright, and covered Ohio, Michigan, Indiana, Illinois, Wisconsin, and that part of Kentucky east of the Tennessee River. Western Virginia was added to the department's territory in September. The *first* Department of the Ohio had been created very early in the war, on May 3, 1861, to cover only Ohio, Indiana, and Illinois, with Major General George B. McClellan in command. When McClellan resigned to assume command of the Army of the Potomac in August 1861 (chapter 19), Brigadier General Ormsby M. Mitchel briefly took over until Buell was named to command the department and the (1st) Army of the Ohio on November 8, 1861. The *first* Department of the Ohio was dissolved on March 11, 1862, when it, together with the (1st) Army of the Ohio, was merged into the Department of the Mississippi and the Department of the Mountains. Six months later, on August 19, 1862, the *second* Department of the Ohio was created, first under Major General Horatio G. Wright and then, after the Senate declined to confirm Wright's promotion, assigned to Burnside.

Initially, Burnside gathered all field forces in the department into a new corps, XXIII Corps, which was alternatively—even interchangeably—called the Army of the Ohio. This (2nd) Army of the Ohio remained a single-corps army until IX Corps was added on March 19, 1863. Even then, the (2nd) Army of the Ohio was still often referred to simply as XXIII Corps. On May 26, 1864, IX Corps, having been detached to serve in the Overland Campaign (May 4–June 24, 1864), was formally attached to the Army of the Potomac, and the (2nd) Army of the Ohio once again became a single-corps army.

COMMANDING GENERALS

Major General Don Carlos Buell commanded the (1st) Army of the Ohio from November 15, 1861, to October 24, 1862, when he was replaced by Major General Rosecrans. Buell was born in 1818 at Lowell, Ohio, and graduated from West Point below the middle of the Class of 1841. He first saw action against the Seminoles in Florida and then served with distinction in the US-Mexican War (1846–48), receiving three brevet promotions (the last to brevet major) for

gallantry and sustaining a wound at the Battle of Churubusco.

Between the war with Mexico and the outbreak of the Civil War, Buell served in the US Army Adjutant General's Office in several different postings, receiving a promotion to captain in the regular army in 1851. In 1861, at the outbreak of the Civil War, he was a lieutenant colonel serving in California as adjutant of the Department of the Pacific. In May he was promoted to brigadier general and was transferred to Washington, DC, to begin training Union recruits. Major General George B. McClellan, then serving as commander of the Department of the Ohio, chose Buell to command the (1st) Army of the Ohio in Kentucky.

On assuming army command, Buell proposed that Union forces immediately begin moving along the Tennessee and Cumberland Rivers toward Nashville, but he was overruled both by McClellan and President Lincoln. In fact, this very plan would be adopted by Ulysses S. Grant in his spectacularly successful campaign to capture Forts Henry and Donelson (February 6 and February 11–16, 1862, respectively). Following Grant's victories, Buell moved his (1st) Army of the Ohio into Nashville, occupying it with virtually no opposition. This earned him promotion to major general of volunteers on March 22, 1862. The following month, he and his army fought at the Battle of Shiloh (April 6–7, 1862, Tennessee; Union victory) and were instrumental in snatching victory from the jaws of defeat in that most desperate of battles. Buell next led the (1st) Army of the Ohio in Henry Halleck's Siege of Corinth (April 29–May 30, 1862, Mississippi; Union victory).

In June 1862 Buell started four of his divisions marching toward Chattanooga with the objective of taking and occupying the city and its key railroad lines. Highly effective harassment from Confederate cavalry led by General Nathan Bedford Forrest and a raid against his supply lines led by John Hunt Morgan forced

Buell to halt. In September Buell diverted to Kentucky to interdict an invasion by Confederate forces under Braxton Bragg and Edmund Kirby Smith. Occupying Louisville unopposed, Buell fought the Battle of Perryville (October 8, 1862, Kentucky), achieving a strategic victory—in that he forced Bragg's Army of Mississippi into retreat—but suffering substantially heavier casualties than Bragg, who commanded a far smaller force than he. Because he allowed Bragg and his army to escape, Buell was hauled before a military commission, relieved of command of the army on October 24, 1862, and replaced by Major General Rosecrans.

Buell was sidelined, and for more than a year he awaited a new assignment before he finally resigned his commission on May 23, 1864. No less a figure than Ulysses S. Grant, now general-in-chief, recommended that Buell be recalled and restored to duty. Buell, however, declined and took up a career in the coal and iron industries before accepting a position as a US government pension agent. He died on November 19, 1898.

Major General William S. Rosecrans commanded the (1st) Army of the Ohio from October 24, 1862, until October 30, 1863, when he officially renamed it the Army of the Cumberland. A full biography of Rosecrans is given in chapter 23.

Major General Ambrose Burnside, as explained above in the history of the establishment of the (2nd) Army of the Ohio, was appointed to command both the Department of the Ohio and the reconstituted Army of the Ohio on March 25, 1863. He served in these capacities until December 9, 1863, when he left to take command of the Army of the Potomac. A full biography is given in chapter 19.

Major General John Gray Foster held command of the (2nd) Army of the Ohio briefly, from December 9, 1863, when Burnside left for the Army of the Potomac, to February 9, 1864.

He was born in Whitefield, New Hampshire, in 1823 and graduated from West Point in 1846. In the US-Mexican War, he served as an engineer and was wounded at the Battle of Molino del Rey. When the Civil War began, Captain Foster commanded the garrison at Fort Moultrie, Charleston Harbor, South Carolina. He evacuated the garrison to Fort Sumter, where he served as second-in-command under Major Robert Anderson during the Battle of Fort Sumter (April 12–14, 1861), which began the Civil War.

Appointed brigadier general of volunteers on October 23, 1861, Foster commanded the 1st Brigade in Burnside's North Carolina expedition (February–June 1862, North Carolina; Union victories). Foster assumed command of the Department of North Carolina and was promoted to major general of volunteers on July 18, 1862. He won the Battle of Goldsborough Bridge (December 17, 1862, North Carolina; Union victory). A year later, he was transferred to Tennessee, where he assumed command of the Department of the Ohio and (2nd) Army of the Ohio on December 9, 1863. His command, however, was ended prematurely by severe injuries sustained in a riding accident. Recovering, he was assigned command of the Department of the South and played a role in forcing Savannah to surrender, without resistance, to William T. Sherman on December 20, 1864, at the conclusion of the March to the Sea (November 15–December 21, 1864, Georgia; Union victory). Foster served out the rest of the war as commanding officer of the Department of Florida and spent the postwar years as a US Army engineer until his death on September 2, 1874.

Major General John McAllister Schofield took over command of the (2nd) Army of the Ohio from the injured John G. Foster on February 9, 1864. He served in the command until March 31, 1865. Born in Gerry, New York, in 1831, Schofield graduated from the United States Military Academy at West Point in 1853 and served two years as an artillery officer. He then returned to West Point as assistant professor of natural and experimental philosophy. He took a leave from the academy in 1860 to teach physics at Washington University in St. Louis, returning to active duty at the outbreak of the Civil War.

Schofield was appointed chief of staff to Brigadier General Nathaniel Lyon, under whom he fought at the Battle of Wilson's Creek (August 10, 1861, Missouri; Union defeat), performing with "conspicuous gallantry" that merited a Medal of Honor. In November 1862 he was promoted to major general of volunteers and named in 1863 to command the Department of Missouri. He assumed command of the (2nd) Army of the Ohio on February 9, 1864, and led it through three of the four last major actions of the war: the Atlanta Campaign (May 7–September 2, 1864, Georgia; Union victory), the Battle of Franklin (November 30, 1864, Tennessee; Union victory)—in which he led the repulse of John Bell Hood's Army of Tennessee—and the Battle of Nashville (December 15–16, 1864, Tennessee; Union victory), in which he played a key supporting role to Major General George H. Thomas, commanding officer of the Army of the Tennessee.

In the years after the war, Schofield served as the military governor of Virginia (1867–68), US secretary of war (1868–69), superintendent of West Point (1876–81), and commanding general of the United States Army (1888–95). He died on March 4, 1906.

When Schofield was appointed to command the Department of North Carolina on February 2, 1865, Major General Jacob D. Cox temporarily assumed command of the (2nd) Army of the Ohio from February 2 to February 9, 1865, while Schofield was in the process of taking over the department to which he had been assigned. Although Schofield returned to the (2nd) Army of the Ohio on February 9 and held command until it was dissolved on March 31, 1865, it was Cox's 3rd Division of the army that bore the brunt of the Battle of Wilmington (February 11–22, 1865, North Carolina; Union victory). Schofield and the rest of the army occupied the captured Confederate port city.

Cox had been born in 1828, in Montreal, to American parents. He was raised and educated in New York City, and he worked as a law office clerk and then as a brokerage bookkeeper before studying to become a minister. He graduated from Oberlin College in 1850 and, instead of seeking ordination, served as superintendent of the Warren (Ohio) school system while studying law. He was admitted to the Ohio bar in 1853, and was instrumental in establishing the Republican Party in that state. Elected to the Ohio State Senate in 1860, he accepted a commission as a brigadier general in the state militia. When the war broke out, Cox commanded a state recruiting station and then took command of the Kanawha Brigade, which, in 1862, was reorganized as the Kanawha Division, IX Corps, Army of the Potomac. Cox led the division in fighting at the Battles of South Mountain (September 14, 1862, Maryland; Union victory) and Antietam (September 17, 1862, Maryland; Union strategic victory).

In 1863 Cox was named to command the District of Ohio and, later, the District of Michigan. The following year, he commanded the 3rd Division, XXIII Corps, (2nd) Army of the Ohio. He and the 3rd Division fought in the Atlanta Campaign (May 7–September 2, 1864) and the Battles of Franklin (November 30, 1864, Tennessee; Union victory) and Nashville (December 15–16, 1864, Tennessee; Union victory). Promoted to major general on December 7, 1864, he fought at the Battle of Wilmington (February 11–22, 1865, North Carolina; Union victory) and then at the Battle of Wyse Fork (March 8–10, 1865, North Carolina; tactical Union victory but strategic Union defeat).

After the war Cox served as governor of Ohio (1866–68), accepted appointment as secretary of the interior in 1869 by President Grant, but resigned the following year due to political differences with the president. He was president of the Toledo and Wabash Railroad (1873–78) and served a single term in the US Congress (1877–79). Cox was dean the University of Cincinnati Law School (1881–97) and also president of that university (1885–89). He died on August 4, 1900.

SIZE AND ORGANIZATION

The organization of the (1st) Army of the Ohio can be ascertained from its structure at the Battle of Shiloh (April 6–7, 1862).[1] The maximum strength of the (1st) Army of the Ohio was about 55,000 men just before it was renamed the Army of the Cumberland on October 24, 1862. Its strength at the Battle of Shiloh was about 18,000 men.

(1ST) ARMY OF THE OHIO

GENERAL STAFF
Major General Don Carlos Buell, commanding
Chief of Staff: Colonel James B. Fry

2ND DIVISION
Brigadier General Alexander M. McCook
4th Brigade: Brigadier General Lovell H. Rousseau
5th Brigade: Edward N. Kirk
6th Brigade: Colonel William H. Gibson

4TH DIVISION
Brigadier General William Nelson
10th Brigade: Colonel Jacob Ammen
19th Brigade: Colonel William B. Hazen
22nd Brigade: Colonel Sanders D. Bruce

5TH DIVISION
Brigadier General Thomas L. Crittenden
11th Brigade: Brigadier General Jeremiah T. Boyle
14th Brigade: Colonel William S. Smith
Units not brigaded:
3rd Kentucky Cavalry: Colonel James S. Jackson
Battery G, 1st Ohio Light Artillery: Joseph Bartlett

Batteries H and M, 4th US Artillery: Captain John Mendenhall

6TH DIVISION
Brigadier General Thomas J. Wood
20th Brigade: Brigadier General James A. Garfield
21st Brigade: Colonel George D. Wagner

The following is the organization of the (2nd) Army of the Ohio, when it was also known as XXIII Corps, in the Atlanta Campaign (May 7–September 2, 1864). Its maximum strength was 15,564 men as of June 30, 1864.[2]

(2ND) ARMY OF THE OHIO

GENERAL STAFF
Major General John M. Schofield
Brigadier General Jacob Cox
Escort: Company G, 7th Ohio Cavalry

1ST DIVISION
Brigadier General Alvin P. Hovey
1st Brigade: Colonel Richard F. Barter
2nd Brigade: Colonel John McQuiston, Colonel Peter T. Swaine
Artillery:
23rd Indiana Light Battery
24th Indiana Light Battery

2ND DIVISION
Brigadier General Henry M. Judah, Brigadier General Milo S. Hascall
1st Brigade: Brigadier General Nathaniel C. McLean, Brigadier General Joseph A. Cooper
2nd Brigade: Brigadier General Milo S. Hascall, Colonel John R. Bond, Colonel William E. Hobson
3rd Brigade: Colonel Silas A. Strickland
Artillery: Captain Joseph C. Shields
22nd Indiana Light Battery
Battery F, 1st Michigan Light
19th Ohio Light Battery

3RD DIVISION

Brigadier General Jacob D. Cox

1st Brigade: Colonel James W. Reilly, Colonel
   James W. Gault

2nd Brigade: Brigadier General Mahlon D.
   Manson, Colonel John S. Hurt, Brigadier
   General Milo S. Hascall, Colonel John
   Casement, Colonel Daniel Cameron

3rd Brigade: Brigadier General Nathaniel
   McLean, Colonel Robert K. Byrd, Colonel
   Israel Stiles

Dismounted Cavalry: Colonel Eugene
   Crittenden

Artillery: Major Henry W. Wells

15th Indiana Light Battery

Battery D, 1st Ohio Light

STONEMAN'S CAVALRY DIVISION

Major General George Stoneman

1st Brigade: Colonel James Biddle

2nd Brigade: Colonel Horace Capron

Independent Brigade: Colonel Alexander
   Holeman

Artillery: 24th Indiana Light Battery (from July 6)

MAJOR CAMPAIGNS AND BATTLES: (1ST) ARMY OF THE OHIO

BATTLE OF SHILOH (APRIL 6–7, 1862)

The action of the (1st) Army of the Ohio was
key to the Union recovery from an engagement
that began disastrously for Union forces. The
battle is summarized in chapter 22.

*The firm of L. Prang & Co. produced some of the finest chromolithographs of the nineteenth century, including this 1888
depiction by the artist Thure de Thulstrup of the Battle of Shiloh (April 6–7, 1862).*

BATTLE OF PERRYVILLE (OCTOBER 8, 1862)

During the fall of 1862, Confederate General Braxton Bragg invaded Kentucky with his Army of Mississippi, getting as far as the outskirts of Louisville and Cincinnati before he was forced to fall back on the Kentucky hamlet of Perryville. At this point the strength of Buell's (1st) Army of the Ohio was at its maximum—about 55,000 men. Dividing his forces into three columns, Buell converged on Perryville, skirmishing on October 7, 1862, with Confederate cavalry on the Springfield Pike outside of town. Before the end of the day, Bragg's infantry arrived and took up positions on Peters Hill. The battle proper did not begin, however, until dawn of the next day, October 8. After a lull shortly before noon, more of Bragg's infantry arrived, and a new Confederate attack was mounted against Buell's left flank, which fell back. When yet more Confederate troops joined in, Buell's men rallied, stiffening their defense and then counterattacking—only to be forced to fall back yet again.

Unaware of the critical situation on his left, Buell failed to reinforce his line. Bragg had only 16,000 men to Buell's 55,000—of which Buell engaged 22,000. Fortunately for the Union, the battered left flank was finally reinforced and thus able to stabilize its line, repulsing two new Confederate attacks and sending an entire brigade back into Perryville. Buell pursued, taking the fight into the streets of the town while additional, albeit belated, Union reinforcements threatened Bragg's left. Recognizing that he could not hold Perryville, Bragg withdrew. The battle thus ended as a strategic victory for the Union, effectively closing Bragg's offensive in Kentucky, which came under Union control, where it remained for the rest of the war. Nevertheless, in tactical terms, the battle was a Union loss. Despite overwhelming superiority of numbers, Buell had lost 4,241 men killed, wounded, captured, or missing, to Bragg's 3,396 casualties. Buell was relieved of command and would never hold another.

MAJOR CAMPAIGNS AND BATTLES: (2ND) ARMY OF THE OHIO

MORGAN'S RAID (JUNE 11–JULY 26, 1863)

Confederate Brigadier General John Hunt Morgan led some 2,460 men out of Tennessee with the object of harassing Major General William S. Rosecrans's Army of the Cumberland (chapter 23) as it advanced toward Chattanooga. Along the way his forces raided Union encampments and supply depots as well as towns in Kentucky and Indiana. These the raiders looted—but notably, on Morgan's orders, refrained from harming civilians.

Home guards—loosely organized citizen militias—offered resistance, which was largely ineffective. On July 13 the raiders crossed into Ohio, avoiding Cincinnati and instead attacking the small towns of Williamsburg and Pomeroy (July 18). Outside of Pomeroy, Morgan's men were suddenly confronted not just by home guards but by Union cavalry of the (2nd) Army of the Ohio, which was commanded by Ambrose Burnside. Union forces pursued Morgan's raiders relentlessly, killing or wounding more than 800 and capturing 700. Morgan led the rest in an effort to evade the pursuing cavalry, but, on July 26, unable to ford the rising Ohio River, he and most of his remaining command surrendered.

KNOXVILLE CAMPAIGN (SEPTEMBER–DECEMBER 1863)

Ambrose Burnside, commanding the (2nd) Army of the Ohio (except for a brief period at the end of the campaign, when Major General John Gray Foster assumed command of the army), engaged Longstreet's Command, an independent force (not connected with any larger Confederate army) under Confederate lieutenant general James Longstreet, in a series of maneuvers and battles aimed at securing control of Knoxville, Tennessee. The Battle of Blountville (September 22, Tennessee; Union victory) forced a Confederate withdrawal. The Battle of Blue Springs (October 10, Tennessee; Union victory) forced a partial Confederate withdrawal from all of east Tennessee. Nevertheless, Longstreet continued his advance toward Knoxville, a movement that resulted in three more battles.

The Battle of Campbell's Station (November 16, Tennessee; Union victory) checked Longstreet's attempt to beat Burnside to Knoxville. At the Battle of Fort Sanders (November 29, Tennessee; Union victory), Longstreet laid siege to the Union-held fort, which defended the outskirts of Knoxville. The siege failed. Longstreet's next move, however, was a successful attempt to capture Bean's Station (December 14, Tennessee; Union defeat), which, however, gained the Confederates little. After this small victory Longstreet decided that Union forces were too well entrenched in and around Knoxville and would not be ejected. Both Burnside and Longstreet retired into winter quarters, bringing the Knoxville Campaign to an anticlimactic close.

ATLANTA CAMPAIGN (MAY 7–SEPTEMBER 2, 1864)

Under Major General John M. Schofield, the 2nd Army of the Ohio supported the other two armies of Sherman's Military Division of the Mississippi—the Army of the Cumberland and the Army of the Tennessee—in the long campaign to capture the South's central transportation hub, Atlanta. The campaign is discussed in chapter 18.

FRANKLIN-NASHVILLE CAMPAIGN (SEPTEMBER 18–DECEMBER 27, 1864)

A portion of the (2nd) Army of the Ohio, under Major General Schofield, supported two corps Sherman had detached from the Army of the Tennessee under Major General George H.

William Tecumseh Sherman's troops destroy Confederate railroad tracks in Atlanta, 1864. NATIONAL ARCHIVES AND RECORDS ADMINISTRATION

Thomas to pursue John Bell Hood after he withdrew his Army of Tennessee from Atlanta. The Army of the Ohio repulsed Hood at the Battle of Franklin (November 30, 1864, Tennessee; Union victory) and supported Thomas in the decisive Battle of Nashville (December 15–16, 1864, Tennessee; Union victory). The campaign is discussed at greater length in chapter 23.

CAROLINAS CAMPAIGN (FEBRUARY–MARCH 21, 1865)

With the Army of the Tennessee and the specially constituted Army of Georgia, the (2nd) Army of the Ohio fought in the Carolinas Campaign, the culminating action of the Civil War in the Eastern Theater. The campaign is discussed in chapter 18.

Chapter 25

ARMY OF THE JAMES

OVERALL PERFORMANCE: ✶

The Army of the James, operating along the James River in Virginia, was supposed to support the Army of the Potomac in the Overland Campaign (chapter 19). Instead, under the incompetent leadership of its commanding general, Benjamin F. Butler—one of President Lincoln's infamous political generals—the army of some 30,000 men was "bottled up" at the most critical phase of the campaign by Confederate forces on the Bermuda Hundred neck between the James and Appomattox Rivers.

ESTABLISHMENT

The Army of the James was created by the merger of the Department of Virginia and the Department of North Carolina in 1863. The field forces of the combined departments were designated as XVIII Corps, and when X Corps was transferred from the Department of the South in April 1864, the two corps became the Army of the James on April 28, 1864, under the command of Major General Butler. Its authorized strength was 50,000 men, although its total fielded strength was closer to 30,000.

COMMANDING GENERALS

The mostly ill-fated Army of the James had just two commanding generals, Major General Benjamin Franklin Butler, who assumed command on April 28, 1864, and his replacement, as of January 8, 1865, Major General Edward Ord, who commanded the army until its dissolution on August 1, 1865.

Born in 1818 in Deerfield, New Hampshire, Butler was a lawyer in civilian life, working out of Lowell, Massachusetts. He served twice in the Massachusetts legislature, in 1853 and 1859, earning a reputation as a champion of labor rights and the rights of immigrants (naturalized American citizens). In the general election of 1860, Butler affiliated himself with the Southern wing of the Democratic Party, yet he never advocated secession or slavery and was, in fact, an enthusiastic and outspoken Unionist once the war began. Butler was anxious to be given a high-ranking military appointment, and President Lincoln, eager for his support, obliged with a commission as a major general.

Butler proved to be among the more notorious of the civil war's political generals—men accorded military rank on the basis of political expediency rather than military training or qualifications. It should be noted, however, that Butler was not entirely without military experience. He had served as a private in the Lowell militia in 1840 and was elected colonel of militia regiment composed of Irish immigrants. In 1855 he was elected brigadier general of the Massachusetts militia, and in 1857, Jefferson Davis—at the time secretary of war in the cabinet of Franklin Pierce—appointed Butler to the West Point Board of Visitors. None of these positions gave him combat experience or a true military education, however.

Butler's first Civil War assignment was commanding troops in Baltimore, which had been put under martial law after secessionist riots in April 1861. In May he was promoted to major general of volunteers and put in command of the garrison at Fort Monroe, Virginia. Acting on his

One of Abraham Lincoln's political generals, Major General Benjamin F. Butler proved his essential military incompetence as the hapless commanding officer of the Army of the James. NATIONAL ARCHIVES AND RECORDS ADMINISTRATION

own initiative and without consulting President Lincoln or anyone else in the government, Butler refused to return fugitive slaves to the Confederacy, arguing that they were "contraband of war." This questionable argument was subsequently upheld by the government and later used as the legal basis for the Emancipation Proclamation (January 1, 1863).

Butler's maiden battle was at Big Bethel (June 10, 1861, Virginia), where he was defeated by a Confederate force under John B. Magruder with less than half the strength of his own (1,400 versus 3,500 men). He did, however, capture the Hatteras Inlet Batteries near Cape Hatteras in the Outer Banks of North Carolina (August 28–29, 1861). The timing was propitious for Butler, since the victory came hard on the heels

of the shocking Union defeat at the First Battle of Bull Run (July 21, 1861). Early in 1862, he was assigned to command the land component of the mostly naval Battle of New Orleans (April 25–May 1, 1862, Louisiana; Union victory), which resulted in the Union occupation of the most important of the Confederacy's Mississippi River and Gulf ports. After the capture of the city, Butler was appointed its military governor. He treated its residents with a deliberate and punitive disrespect that not only alienated them—they called him "Beast Butler"—but also drew criticism even from his own government. Fearing a local insurrection on top of a civil war, President Lincoln removed Butler as military governor by the end of the year.

Butler's next major military assignment was as commanding general of the Army of the James beginning on April 28, 1864. In May he fought the first of the five battles of the Bermuda Hundred Campaign with the objective of threatening the Confederate capital of Richmond, thereby supporting the ongoing Overland Campaign of U. S. Grant and the Army of the Potomac under Major General George Meade. All Butler succeeded in doing, however, was to get his army bottled up on the Bermuda Hundred Peninsula, a 30,000-man army pinned down by a Confederate force of perhaps 18,000 men, mostly underage or superannuated.

Butler attempted to redeem himself by supporting Rear Admiral David Dixon Porter's naval siege against Fort Fisher (December 23–27, 1864, North Carolina; Union defeat), but aborted the mission because he judged the fort impregnable. Little more than a week later, on January 8, 1865, Butler was removed from command of the Army of the James and was replaced by Major General Edward Ord. A week after this, another Union commander, Major General Alfred Terry, captured Fort Fisher.

After the war Butler left the Democratic Party and embraced the Radical Republicans, repeatedly winning election to the US House of Representatives (1867–75, 1877–79). He favored a stringently punitive Reconstruction policy and was a leading figure in the impeachment of President Andrew Johnson. Following a disagreement over Republican fiscal policy, Butler returned to the Democrats and, in 1882, was elected Democratic governor of Massachusetts. In 1884 he ran for president on the combined Greenback-Labor Party and Anti-Monopoly Party tickets. He failed to win any electoral votes. Butler died on January 11, 1893.

Major General Edward Otho Cresap Ord replaced Butler as commanding officer of the Army of the James on January 8, 1865. Born in Cumberland, Maryland, in 1818, Ord grew up in Washington, DC, and graduated from West Point in 1839. As a young artillery officer, he saw his first action during the Second Seminole War (1835–42) and was promoted, for gallantry, from second to first lieutenant in 1841. At the outbreak of the US-Mexican War (1846–48), he was sent to California as military governor of Monterey, the post at which he spent the war years. Promoted to captain in 1850, he fought in the Indian Wars of the Northwest during 1855–59.

Transferred back to the East in 1859, he was posted to the Artillery School at Fort Monroe. In October 1859 he served under Colonel Robert E. Lee, USA, who led a mixed contingent of Virginia militia, US Army troops, and US Marines on a mission to end abolitionist John Brown's seizure of the federal arsenal at Harpers Ferry, Virginia (today West Virginia). Shortly after this, Ord was transferred back to the far West. The outbreak of the Civil War found him posted in San Francisco. Recalled to the Eastern Theater, Ord was promoted to brigadier general of volunteers and given command of a brigade in the Army of the Potomac in September 1861. In November of that year, he was promoted to major of regulars and scored a brilliant defensive

victory against Confederate general J. E. B. Stuart at the Battle of Dranesville (December 20, 1861, Virginia). For this action, he was brevetted to lieutenant colonel of regulars.

In May 1862 Ord was promoted to major general of volunteers and assigned to the Department of the Mississippi, where he commanded the left wing of the Army of the Tennessee (under Ulysses S. Grant) during August and September. Following his performance at the Battle of Iuka (September 19, 1862, Mississippi; Union victory), Ord was once again brevetted, this time to colonel of regulars. In the aftermath of the Second Battle of Corinth (October 3–4, 1862, Mississippi; Union victory), Ord displayed valiant aggressiveness in a thrust against Confederate troops withdrawing from Corinth under Earl Van Dorn. The October 5 action mauled Van Dorn's command but cost Ord a serious wound, which kept him out of action until June 1863, when he took command of XIII Corps in the Army of the Tennessee. He played a major role in the siege and capture of Vicksburg during May 19–July 4, 1863.

In August, Ord transferred to the Army of Western Louisiana, but he was felled by illness in October and did not return to active duty until March 1864. He was assigned to command VIII Corps in the Shenandoah Valley in July, and then took command of XVIII Corps during the Petersburg Campaign (June 9, 1864–March 25, 1865). On September 29, 1864, Ord led the capture of Fort Harrison, south of Richmond, but was again badly wounded and out of action until January 8, 1865, when he replaced Butler as commanding officer of the Army of the James. In March he received a brevet to major general of regulars and, as commanding officer of the Army of the James, fought alongside Grant in the final operations against Lee.

After the war, in December 1865, Ord was promoted to lieutenant colonel of regulars and, in July of the following year, to brigadier general. After leaving volunteer service in December

1866, he assumed command, as a regular army officer, of the Department of Arkansas. In his later career, he commanded the Departments of California, the Platte, and Texas, retiring from the latter post in December 1880. Ord was promoted to major general on the retired list in January 1881.

SIZE AND ORGANIZATION

The order of battle at the Battle of Chaffin's Farm (September 29–30, 1864, Virginia), a rare victory for Benjamin Butler, reveals the Army of the James at its field strength of about 30,000. Note the large contingent of black (US Colored Troops) in the Army of the James.[1]

GENERAL STAFF
Major General Benjamin F. Butler, commanding
Chief of Engineers: Major General Godfrey Weitzel

X CORPS
Major General David B. Birney

1ST DIVISION
Brigadier General Alfred H. Terry
1st Brigade: Colonel Francis B. Pond, Colonel Thomas Mulcahy
2nd Brigade: Colonel Joseph C. Abbott
3rd Brigade: Colonel Harris M. Plaisted

2ND DIVISION
Brigadier General Robert Sanford Foster
1st Brigade: Colonel Rufus Daggett, Lieutenant Colonel Albert M. Barney
2nd Brigade: Colonel Galusha Pennypacker
3rd Brigade: Colonel Louis Bell

3RD DIVISION
(incomplete)
1st Brigade: Brigadier General William Birney
29th Connecticut
7th US Colored Troops
8th US Colored Troops

9th US Colored Troops
45th US Colored Troops
Artillery:
Artillery Brigade: Colonel Richard H. Jackson
1st Battery, Connecticut Light
4th Battery, New Jersey Light
5th Battery, New Jersey Light
Battery E, 1st Pennsylvania Light
Battery C, 3rd Rhode Island Heavy
Batteries C and D, 1st US Artillery Artillery
Battery M, 1st US Artillery
Battery E, 3rd US Artillery
Battery D, 4th US Artillery

XVIII CORPS
Major General Edward O. C. Ord, Brigadier General Charles A. Heckman, Brevet Major General Godfrey Weitzel

1ST DIVISION
Brigadier General George J. Stannard, Colonel James Jourdan, Brigadier General Gilman Marston
1st Brigade: Colonel Aaron Fletcher Stevens, Lieutenant Colonel John B. Raulston
2nd Brigade: Brigadier General Hiram Burnham, Colonel Michael Donohoe, Lieutenant Colonel Stephen Moffitt, Colonel Edgar M. Cullen
3rd Brigade: Colonel Samuel H. Roberts, Colonel Edgar M. Cullen, Lieutenant Colonel Stephen H. Moffitt

2ND DIVISION
Brigadier General Charles A. Heckman, Colonel Harrison S. Fairchild, Brigadier General Charles A. Heckman
1st Brigade: Colonel James Stewart Jr., Colonel George M. Guion
2nd Brigade: Colonel Edward H. Ripley
3rd Brigade: Colonel Harrison S. Fairchild

3RD DIVISION
Brigadier General Charles J. Paine
1st Brigade: Colonel John Henry Holman

1st US Colored Troops
22nd US Colored Troops
37th US Colored Troops
2nd Brigade: Colonel Alonzo G. Draper
5th US Colored Troops
36th US Colored Troops
38th US Colored Troops
3rd Brigade: Colonel Samuel A. Duncan,
    Colonel John W. Ames
4th US Colored Troops
6th US Colored Troops

UNATTACHED

US Sharpshooters
Artillery Brigade: Major George B. Cook
Battery E, 3rd New York Light Artillery
Battery H, 2nd New York Light Artillery
Battery K, 3rd New York Light Artillery
Battery M, 3rd New York Light Artillery
7th Battery, New York Light Artillery
16th Battery, New York Light Artillery
17th Battery, New York Light Artillery
Battery A, 1st Pennsylvania Light Artillery
Battery F, 1st Rhode Island Light Artillery
Battery B, 1st US Artillery
Battery L, 4th US Artillery
Battery A, 5th US Artillery
Battery F, 5th US Artillery

CAVALRY

Brigadier General August V. Kautz
1st Brigade: Colonel Robert M. West
2nd Brigade: Colonel Samuel P. Spear
Artillery: 4th Battery, Wisconsin Light

MAJOR CAMPAIGNS AND BATTLES

BERMUDA HUNDRED CAMPAIGN (MAY 1864)

Founded in 1613, just six years after Jamestown, Bermuda Hundred was the first town formally incorporated in the colony of Virginia. It was sited on a broad neck of land at the confluence of the James and Appomattox Rivers, which made it an ideal port. By the time of the Civil War, Bermuda Hundred was also the site of the right-of-way of the Richmond & Petersburg Railroad, the capital's link to all points south. Moreover, the town was just fifteen miles south of Richmond. Given the strategic location of Bermuda Hundred, Grant arranged for the Army of the James to be landed there and tasked with conducting operations against Richmond while the Army of the Potomac began the Battle of the Wilderness (May 5–7, 1864, Virginia; inconclusive) in the Overland Campaign (May 4–June 24, 1864, Virginia; Union strategic victory). By menacing the Confederate capital, Butler's army was intended to draw a portion of the Army of Northern Virginia away from the fight against the Army of the Potomac.

Pursuant to Grant's orders, Butler marched west—but did so slowly, very slowly, precisely when speed was of the essence. Although Confederate forces in the area were significantly outnumbered, they fought a series of battles that thwarted the mission of the Army of the James. At Port Walthall Junction (May 6–7, 1864, Virginia; Union victory), a Confederate brigade under Brigadier General Johnson Hagood blocked Butler's cautious patrols probing the rail junction at Port Walthall. The next day, it took an entire division of the Army of the James to break through and cut the rail line. On May 9, at Swift Creek, Confederate general P. G. T. Beauregard deployed just 4,200 men against the 14,000 Butler had on the march—a force supported by five gunboats—and fought Butler to an inconclusive standstill. On May 10, 2,000 of Beauregard's command attacked some 3,400 troops of the Army of the James at the Battle of Chester Station (Virginia; inconclusive). Although Butler destroyed Confederate rail lines there, he was forced back to his entrenchments at Bermuda Hundred. He then tried moving against the Confederates at Drewry's Bluff, but assumed a defensive posture when a strong offense was called for. The resulting Battle of Proctor's Creek

(May 12–16, 1864, Virginia; Union defeat) pitted 18,000 Confederates under Beauregard against most of the Army of the James committed to the campaign—about 30,000 men. The timid Butler was thoroughly outgeneraled and, once again, withdrew to his Bermuda Hundred entrenchments.

The Confederate victory at Proctor's Creek arrested Butler's abortive offensive against Richmond. On May 20 Beauregard hit Butler at the Battle of Ware Bottom Church (Virginia; Union defeat). While Butler and his army yet again languished in their defenses, Beauregard directed the building of his own defensive earthworks, dubbed the Howlett Line, which bottled up the Army of the James on the Bermuda Hundred neck. Butler's army was virtually immune from attack at Bermuda Hundred, but it was also neutralized at the time that it was most needed. With Butler's force held at bay, Beauregard sent Lee reinforcements that proved critically important against Grant at the Battle of Cold Harbor.

BATTLE OF COLD HARBOR (MAY 31–JUNE 12, 1864)

The bloodiest battle of Grant's Overland Campaign (see chapter 19), Cold Harbor resulted in nearly 13,000 Union casualties (versus about 5,300 for the Confederates), even though the Army of the Potomac outnumbered the Army of Northern Virginia in this engagement by as many as 60,000 men. It was one of the most lopsided Union defeats of the war. During the battle half of the Army of the James was idled—"bottled up"—at Bermuda Hundred. The XVIII Corps, under William Farrar "Baldy" Smith, was available to reinforce the Army of the Potomac and made a brave assault on the Confederate entrenchments at Cold Harbor, but to no avail.

SIEGE OF PETERSBURG (JUNE 9, 1864–MARCH 25, 1865)

Blocked at Bermuda Hundred from directly menacing Richmond, Butler attempted to make a breakthrough attack on the vulnerable city of Petersburg on June 9, only to be defeated at the First Battle of Petersburg. From Cold Harbor, however, Grant ordered XVIII Corps to march to Petersburg to make a second attempt at seizing the city before its highly vulnerable defenses could be reinforced. Grant's intention was to take this important Confederate strongpoint and use it as a staging area from which to complete a rapid advance against Richmond.

"Baldy" Smith had about 13,700 men in his corps, exhausted from the fighting at Cold Harbor. Nevertheless, on June 15 the Second Battle of Petersburg (June 15–18, 1864, Virginia; Union defeat) began with Smith's attacks on Beauregard's outnumbered defensive lines. The battle commenced promisingly as Smith forced the Confederates out of their outer-perimeter entrenchments. Unaccountably, however, the general lost his nerve. Fearing an imminent counterattack (despite an evident lack of sufficient Confederate forces to make such an attack), he declined to press his assault and instead awaited reinforcements. By the time of their arrival, it was too late. Beauregard had received reinforcements, and what could have been the rapid, triumphal capture of Petersburg became instead a grinding and costly siege that lasted through March of 1865.

BATTLE OF CHAFFIN'S FARM (SEPTEMBER 29–30, 1864)

Richmond, capital of the Confederacy, was defended by an elaborate permanent system of fortifications and entrenchments, of which Chaffin's Farm, on Chaffin's Bluff south of the James River, was an anchor point. On the night of September 28–29, Butler's Army of the James crossed the river to attack Chaffin's Farm and captured two strongpoints, New Market Heights and Fort Harrison. Although Lee responded by reinforcing his lines and, on September 30, launching a counterattack, Butler held firm, forcing the Confederates to set up a new defensive line behind the captured forts. More importantly, Lee was compelled to shift troops from the defense of Petersburg to protect Richmond. The victory at Chaffin's Farm was a rare success for Benjamin Butler, but it was an important one.

EXPEDITION AGAINST FORT FISHER (DECEMBER 7–27, 1864)

Grant tasked Butler and the Army of the James with leading an amphibious assault against Fort Fisher, a Confederate strongpoint defending Wilmington, North Carolina, the South's sole remaining Atlantic coast port. Receiving intelligence that Union troops had embarked from Hampton Roads on December 13, Robert E. Lee correctly surmised that an assault on Fort Fisher was imminent. He dispatched Hoke's Division (Major General Robert Frederick Hoke, commanding) to defend the fort against the anticipated attack.

On Christmas Eve a Union fleet commanded by Rear Admiral David D. Porter began shelling Fort Fisher as an infantry division from the Army of the James disembarked from its transport vessels and began probing the fort's defenses. With Hoke's approach, however, Butler suddenly broke off the assault and hurriedly withdrew, re-embarking his troops on a return to Fortress Monroe, announcing that Fort Fisher was impregnable. This final failure moved General Grant to relieve Butler of command of the Army of the James and to replace him with Major General Edward Ord on January 8, 1865. A week after this, on January 15, an expedition led by Major General Alfred Terry quickly captured the "impregnable" Fort Fisher.

FALL OF PETERSBURG AND RICHMOND (JANUARY–APRIL 1865)

On January 3, 1865, just before Major General Ord assumed command, the Army of the James was reorganized. The XVIII and X Corps were disbanded, and all the US Colored Troops in the army were formed into a new, racially segregated XXV Corps, while the white troops were assigned to XXIV Corps. Under Ord the XXIV Corps of the Army of the James participated in the final assaults that ended the long siege of Petersburg on March 25, 1865. On April 3, 1865, the all-black XXV Corps, commanded by Major General Godfrey Weitzel, became the first Union corps to enter and occupy Richmond, which the Confederate army and government had evacuated.

BATTLE OF APPOMATTOX COURT HOUSE (APRIL 9, 1865)

Major General Ord, commanding XXIV Corps of the Army of the James, followed Robert E. Lee and his much-reduced Army of Northern Virginia as it marched to its final battle at Appomattox Court House. While that battle was being fought by elements of the Army of the Potomac, Ord's command took up positions intended to cut off Lee's avenue of escape. Instead, of course, Lee sought terms from Grant and proposed to surrender to him the Army of Northern Virginia. In this way, the Army of the James (represented by Ord and XXIV Corps) found itself present at one of the most momentous events in the Civil War.

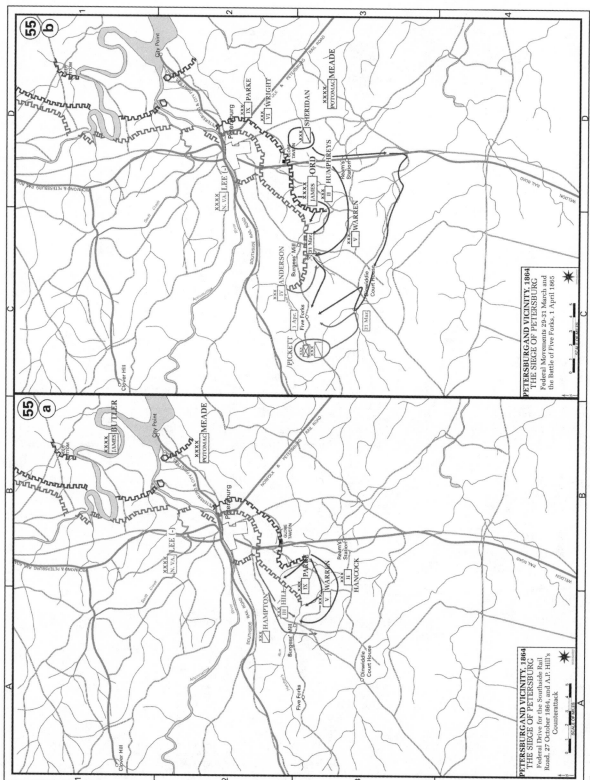

55 **a**

BUTLER
XXXX
JAMES

MEADE
XXXX
POTOMAC

LEE (-)
XXXX
N. VA.

Petersburg

HAMPTON
XXX

HILL
III

PARKE
IX

WARREN
V

HANCOCK
II

Globe Tavern

Ream's Station

Burgess' Mill

Dinwiddie Court House

Five Forks

Clover Hill

City Point

PETERSBURG AND VICINITY, 1864
THE SIEGE OF PETERSBURG
Federal Drive for the Southside Rail
Road, 27 October 1864, and A.P. Hill's
Counterattack

SCALE OF MILES

55 **b**

PARKE
IX

WRIGHT
VI

SHERIDAN
XXX

MEADE
XXXX
POTOMAC

LEE (-)
XXXX
N. VA.

ORD
XXXX
JAMES

HUMPHREYS
II

WARREN
V

ANDERSON
IV
XXX

PICKETT
XXXX

Petersburg

Globe Tavern

Ream's Station

Burgess' Mill

1 Apr.
Five Forks

31 Mar.

Dinwiddie
Court House

Clover Hill

City Point

PETERSBURG AND VICINITY, 1864
THE SIEGE OF PETERSBURG
Federal Movements 29-31 March and
the Battle of Five Forks, 1 April 1865

SCALE OF MILES

The Siege of Petersburg, situations as of October 27, 1864, and March 29–31, 1865.

UNITED STATES MILITARY ACADEMY

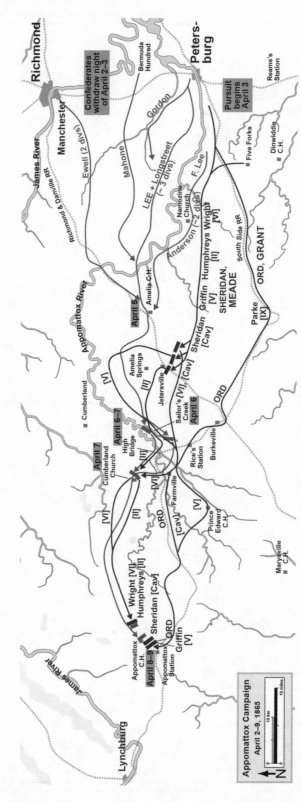

The Appomattox Campaign, movement and engagements during April 2–9, 1865. UNITED STATES MILITARY ACADEMY

Chapter 26

ARMY OF THE SHENANDOAH

OVERALL PERFORMANCE: ★ ★ ★

As with the Army of the Ohio (chapter 24), there was more than one Union military organization designated the Army of the Shenandoah. The first was established on April 27, 1861, and disbanded less than a year later, on March 18, 1862. The second existed briefly, from May 21 to July 3, 1864. Neither of these was officially designated the Army of the Shenandoah. The third, however, was. Ulysses S. Grant established it on August 7, 1864, as a weapon to be wielded by his great cavalry general Philip H. Sheridan against two enemies. Enemy number one was Confederate general Jubal Early, who had staged a daring raid on the defenses of Washington, DC, on July 11–12, 1864 (Battle of Fort Stevens; Union victory) and then rode away with his force of 15,000. Sheridan was ordered to "pursue Early to the death."[1] Enemy number two was nothing less than the entire Shenandoah Valley, the endlessly fertile breadbasket of the South. The Shenandoah fed the regular Confederate army as well the guerillas who operated throughout the valley. Thus the army was founded with the dual purposes of quasi-personal vengeance and the waging of warfare as total as that which William T. Sherman would wage later in the year against Georgia with his March to the Sea.

ESTABLISHMENT

The Army of the Shenandoah of 1861–62 was the field army of the Department of Pennsylvania, which existed from April 27 to July 25, 1861, and the Department of the Shenandoah, which replaced the Department of Pennsylvania on July 25, 1861, and was itself disbanded on March 18, 1862. Major General Robert Patterson commanded the Department of Pennsylvania, and Major General Nathaniel P. Banks commanded the Department of the Shenandoah, but neither general officially called the single field army associated with their department the Army of the Shenandoah. Nevertheless, that is how its soldiers referred to it until, on March 18, 1862, its constituent elements were designated V Corps and attached to the Army of the Potomac. With that, the Army of the Shenandoah ceased to exist for the next two years.

On May 21, 1864, General Grant assigned Major General David H. Hunter to command the Department of West Virginia, whose field army was unofficially styled the Army of the Shenandoah. Grant's orders to Hunter were to rake the valley with scorched-earth tactics, living off the country, destroying what the army did not eat, and wrecking every railroad track they could find. This second Army of the Shenandoah ceased to exist on July 3, 1864, but was reborn, this time officially, on August 7 of that year, under Major General Philip Sheridan's command. Two days after this, the Army of West Virginia was created out of what had been the Army of the Kanawha. It became the field army of the Department of West Virginia. In practice, however, the Army of West Virginia functioned as a corps in Sheridan's new Army of the Shenandoah. The final incarnation of the Army of the Shenandoah was disbanded on June 27, 1865.

COMMANDING GENERALS

Major General Robert Patterson commanded the Department of Pennsylvania and its field army, loosely and unofficially referred to as the Army of the Shenandoah, from April 27 to July

25, 1861. He was an Irish immigrant, born in 1792 in City Tyrone, the son of a father banished by the English for insurrection. The family immigrated in 1798.

Young Patterson went into banking in Philadelphia and fought in the War of 1812 (1812–15). After the war he returned to Philadelphia and became a wholesale merchant. A partisan of President Andrew Jackson, Patterson dabbled in Pennsylvania politics and enlarged his mercantile interests to the West and the South. When the US-Mexican War broke out in 1846, he volunteered his services and was commissioned a major general of volunteers. He served as a staff officer to General Winfield Scott.

Between the war with Mexico and the Civil War, Patterson returned to business, which included ownership of a Louisiana sugar plantation and thirty cotton mills in Pennsylvania. It was Scott who recruited Patterson back into the volunteer service at the outbreak of the Civil War. He was commissioned a major general of Pennsylvania volunteers and given command of the Department of Pennsylvania. His command debut was far from successful. Ordered by Scott in May 1861 to retake the federal arsenal at Harpers Ferry, which was in Confederate hands, he dithered and delayed. This gave the Confederate troops at Harpers Ferry ample time to evacuate the arsenal, destroy its buildings, and then march to join the Confederate army mustering at Manassas in advance of what would be the First Battle of Bull Run (July 21, 1861, Virginia; Union defeat). Patterson did, however, successfully lead two brigades of his field army against Jackson's Brigade (Thomas J. Jackson) at the Battle of Hoke's Run (July 2, 1861, Virginia [present-day West Virginia]; Union victory), in which Patterson outnumbered Jackson 8,000 to 4,000. Nevertheless, on July 25, three months after he had commissioned him, Scott relieved Patterson of command. He died in Philadelphia on August 7, 1881.

On July 25, 1861, Major General Nathaniel P. Banks replaced Patterson as commanding general of what was now renamed the Department of the Shenandoah. Born in 1816 in Waltham, Massachusetts, Banks was the son of a textile mill worker and, at the age of fourteen, joined his father in the mills. His first job was as a "bobbin boy," running from loom to loom to replace spent bobbins with full ones. In his scant free time, he educated himself and generally improved his lot, entering politics and eventually becoming speaker of the lower house of the Massachusetts legislature, a US representative from his home state, Speaker of the US House of Representatives (1856–57), and, just before the outbreak of the Civil War, governor of Massachusetts. Politically popular, he was proud of the nickname that had followed him since he left the mills: "Bobbin Boy" Banks.

President Lincoln considered Banks for a cabinet post but instead chose him as a major general of volunteers on May 16, 1861. Lacking any military experience, Banks was a blatant example of a political general. His appointment was intended to do nothing more or less than drum up support for the war effort. Banks was initially assigned to command the Department of Annapolis and, afterward, the Department of the Shenandoah. His command of the latter department ended on March 18, 1862, when its field army was attached to the Army of the Potomac as V Corps—with Banks commanding it. Major General George B. McClellan ordered Banks to pursue Stonewall Jackson up the Shenandoah Valley. At the First Battle of Winchester (May 25, 1862, Virginia; Union defeat), however, Jackson drubbed Banks. This was partly a matter of numbers—Jackson outnumbered Banks 16,000 to 6,500—but mostly a case of military genius confronting military ignorance. The defeat disrupted Major General George B. McClellan's advance on Richmond, his Peninsula Campaign (March–July 1862, Virginia; Union defeat).

On June 26, 1862, Banks was assigned to command II Corps in Major General John A. Pope's short-lived Army of Virginia. He once again fought Stonewall Jackson, this time at the Battle of Cedar Mountain (August 9, 1862, Virginia) and was once again outnumbered and defeated—with very heavy losses. On September 4 Banks was relieved of command of II Corps and assigned to command the Military District of Washington, DC (September 7– October 27, 1862). President Lincoln next gave him command of the Department of the Gulf, replacing another notorious political general, Benjamin "Beast" Butler, as military governor of New Orleans.

From his new base in New Orleans, Banks set out on the Red River Campaign (March 10– May 22, 1864, Louisiana; Union defeat). Planned largely by Major General Henry W. Halleck, the objective was to neutralize the Confederate army under Lieutenant General Richard Taylor, capture Shreveport, confiscate as much Confederate cotton as possible, and plant pro-Union governments throughout the state. Unrealistically ambitious and incompetently led, the Red River Campaign was an unmitigated disaster. Although Banks's force outnumbered Taylor's two to one and sometimes even five to one, the Union general was finally forced into retreat, the campaign having achieved nothing—except to create bloodshed and bring Banks's military career to an end.

After the war Banks returned to politics, serving in Congress and in the Massachusetts State Senate. He died on September 1, 1894.

From May 21 to July 3, 1864, Major General David Hunter briefly commanded a force familiarly referred to as the Army of the Shenandoah. Ulysses S. Grant had ordered him to conduct a scorched-earth campaign through the fertile Shenandoah Valley in an effort to disrupt supply for Confederate regulars and guerrillas in the region.

Hunter was born in 1802 in Troy, New York (some sources report his birthplace as Princeton, New Jersey), graduated from West Point in 1822, and served from 1828 to 1831 on the Old Northwest frontier, operating out of Fort Dearborn (present-day Chicago), Illinois. He resigned from the army in July 1836 to become a real estate agent in Illinois. In 1841 he rejoined the army as a paymaster, achieving promotion to major in March 1842. He fought in the Second Seminole War (1835–42) and the US-Mexican War (1846–48).

In 1860, with civil war looming, Hunter began a correspondence with Abraham Lincoln, presenting himself as a committed abolitionist. Hunter became a Lincoln favorite and, after the fall of Fort Sumter (April 12–14, 1861), he was promoted to colonel of the 3rd US Cavalry and then brigadier general of volunteers. Wounded at the First Battle of Bull Run (July 21, 1861, Virginia; Union defeat), he was promoted to major general of volunteers in August, named to command the Western Department on November 2, 1861, transferred to command the Department of Kansas in March 1862, and then transferred again to command the Department of the South. In this posting he issued General Order No. 11, emancipating (on his own authority) slaves in Georgia, South Carolina, and Florida. He then recruited black soldiers from the occupied areas of South Carolina, creating what he called the 1st South Carolina Regiment (African Descent). President Lincoln rescinded General Order No. 11, but it had already made Hunter famous.

Hunter fought the Battle of Fort Pulaski (April 10–11, 1862, Georgia; Union victory), Battle of Piedmont (June 5, 1864, Virginia; Union victory), and Battle of Lynchburg (June 17–18, 1864, Virginia; Union defeat)—the last two as part of his brief scorched-earth Shenandoah campaign. He served in the honor guard at the funeral of Abraham Lincoln in 1865 and was subsequently named president of the military commission that tried the assassination conspirators. He retired from military service in 1866 and died on February 2, 1886.

Major General Philip Sheridan led the formally constituted Army of the Shenandoah in its principal actions from August 7, 1864, through April 22, 1865 (except for October 16–19, 1864). Born in 1831 in Albany, New York, he graduated from West Point in 1853 and first saw service with the 1st Infantry Regiment in Texas and the 4th Infantry in Oregon, fighting the Indians. Promoted to first lieutenant in March 1861, he rose to captain in May and fought in the Siege of Corinth (April 29–May 30, 1862, Mississippi; Union victory). He was appointed colonel of the 2nd Michigan Cavalry after Corinth and, following his daring raid in the Battle of Booneville (July 1, 1862, Mississippi; Union victory), he was promoted to brigadier general of volunteers.

Major General Philip Sheridan poses for a daguerreotype portrait by Mathew Brady. LIBRARY OF CONGRESS

Commanding the 11th Division in the Army of the Ohio, he fought with distinction at the Battle of Perryville (October 8, 1862, Kentucky; Union strategic victory) and at Stones River (December 31, 1862–January 2, 1863, Tennessee; Union victory). Promoted to major general of volunteers in 1863, he served with the Army of the Cumberland in the Tullahoma Campaign (June 24–July 3, 1863, Tennessee; Union victory), and then led the XX Corps in support of General George Henry Thomas at the Battle of Chickamauga (September 19–20, 1863, Georgia; Union defeat). He led the culminating charge at the Battle of Missionary Ridge (November 25, 1863) during the Chattanooga Campaign.

In April 1864 Sheridan was appointed commander of Cavalry Corps of the Army of the Potomac. In the Overland Campaign he fought at the Battle of the Wilderness (May 5–7, 1864, Virginia; inconclusive) and at Spotsylvania Court House (May 8–21, 1864, Virginia; inconclusive). His raid against rebel lines of supply and communications during the Spotsylvania battle resulted in the frustration if not the defeat of Confederate cavalry commander J. E. B. Stuart at Todd's Tavern (May 7, 1864, Virginia; inconclusive). The Battle of Yellow Tavern (May 11, 1864, Virginia) was a straightforward Union victory—in which Stuart, Lee's irreplaceable cavalry commander, was mortally wounded. Assigned to destroy rail lines near Charlottesville, Virginia, Sheridan engaged Confederate units at the Battle of Haw's Shop (May 28, 1864, Virginia; inconclusive) and at the Battle of Trevilian Station (June 11–12, 1864, Virginia; Union defeat).

On August 7, 1864, Sheridan assumed command of the Army of the Shenandoah, scoring victories in Virginia at the Third Battle of Winchester (September 19, 1864), the Battle of Fisher's Hill (September 21–22, 1864), the Battle of Tom's Brook (October 9, 1864), and the Battle of Cedar Creek (October 19, 1864). The swath of destruction he cut through the Shenandoah made the region virtually useless to the Confederacy.

After receiving the thanks of Congress in February 1865, Sheridan went on to raid Petersburg during February 27–March 24 in the breakthrough phase of the Siege of Petersburg (June 9, 1864–March 25, 1865, Virginia; Union victory). He was instrumental in the final battles between the Army of the Potomac and the Army of Northern Virginia, at Five Forks (April 1, 1865), Sayler's Creek (April 6, 1865), and Appomattox Court House (April 9, 1865), all Union victories. Except for a brief period in October (16–19), when Major General Horatio G. Wright held command, Sheridan led the Army of the Shenandoah until April 22, 1865.

Named commander of the Military Division of the Gulf in May 1865, Sheridan was appointed commander of the Fifth Military District in March 1867, to which was added the vast Department of the Missouri in September. He initiated a relentless military campaign against the Indian tribes of the Washita Valley in Oklahoma during 1868–69. In March 1869 Sheridan was promoted to lieutenant general with command of the Division of the Missouri. Detached from this post during the Franco-Prussian War of 1870–71, he was sent to Europe as an official war observer and liaison officer with the Prussians. On his return to the United States, he directed the 1876–77 campaign against the Southern Plains Indians. In 1878 he was named to command the Military Divisions of the West and Southwest, and in 1883 replaced his comrade and mentor William Tecumseh Sherman as commanding general of the US Army. He was promoted to general two months before his death on August 5, 1888.

Major General Alfred Thomas Archimedes Torbert assumed command of the Army of the Shenandoah in its final days, April 22–June 27, 1865. He was born in Georgetown, Delaware, in 1833 and graduated from West Point in 1855. Offered a commission in the Confederate army at the outbreak of the Civil War, he accepted instead an appointment as colonel of the 1st New Jersey Volunteers. He commanded this regiment at the Second Battle of Bull Run (August 28–30, 1862, Virginia; Union defeat) and at the Battle of South Mountain (September 14, 1862, Maryland; Union victory). He commanded a brigade in VI Corps of the Army of the Potomac at the Battle of Antietam (September 17, 1862, Maryland; Union strategic victory) and fought at Fredericksburg (December 11–15, 1862, Virginia; Union defeat), Chancellorsville (April 30–May 6, 1863, Virginia; Union defeat), and Gettysburg (July 1–3, 1863, Virginia; Union victory).

On April 10, 1864, Torbert was given command of a cavalry division under Philip H. Sheridan. He led it in the Overland Campaign (May 4–June 24, 1864, Virginia; Union strategic victory) and in Sheridan's Valley Campaigns of 1864. He was in direct command at the Battle of Tom's Brook (October 9, 1864, Virginia; Union victory). After the war Torbert served as a US consul in El Salvador (1869) and as consul general in Havana (1871) and Paris (1873). Torbert died in the sinking of the SS *Vera Cruz* off the coast of Florida on August 29, 1880.

SIZE AND ORGANIZATION

The Army of Shenandoah was at its maximum strength of approximately 40,000 men at the Third Battle of Winchester, from which the following order of battle is taken.[2]

GENERAL STAFF
Major General Philip Sheridan, commanding

VI CORPS
Major General Horatio Wright

1ST DIVISION
Brigadier General David Allen Russell,
    Brigadier General Emory Upton,
    Colonel Oliver Edwards

1st Brigade (1st New Jersey Brigade):
Lieutenant Colonel Edward L. Campbell
2nd Brigade: Brigadier General Emory Upton,
Colonel Joseph Eldridge Hamblin
3rd Brigade: Colonel Oliver Edwards,
Colonel Isaac C. Bassett

2ND DIVISION
Brigadier General George W. Getty
1st Brigade: Brigadier General Frank Wheaton
2nd Brigade (1st Vermont Brigade): Colonel
James M. Warner, Lieutenant Colonel
Amasa S. Tracy
3rd Brigade: Brigadier General
Daniel D. Bidwell

3RD DIVISION
Brigadier General James Ricketts
1st Brigade: Colonel William Emerson
2nd Brigade: Colonel J. Warren Keifer
Artillery: Colonel Charles H. Tompkins
5th Maine Light Artillery: Captain
Greenleaf T. Stevens
Battery A, 1st Massachusetts Light Artillery:
Captain William H. McCartney
Battery, 1st New York Light Artillery:
Lieutenant William H. Johnson,
Lieutenant Orsamus R. Van Etten
Battery C, 1st Rhode Island Light Artillery:
Lieutenant Jacob H. Lamb
Battery G, 1st Rhode Island Light Artillery:
Captain George W. Adams
Battery M, 5th US Artillery: Captain
James McKnight

ARMY OF WEST VIRGINIA*
Brevet Major General George Crook

1ST DIVISION
Colonel Joseph Thoburn
1st Brigade: Colonel George D. Wells
3rd Brigade: Colonel Thomas M. Harris

2ND DIVISION (KANAWHA DIVISION)
Colonel Isaac H. Duval, Colonel
Rutherford B. Hayes
1st Brigade: Colonel Rutherford B. Hayes,
Colonel Hiram F. Devol
2nd Brigade: Colonel Daniel D. Johnson,
Lieutenant Colonel Benjamin F. Coates
Artillery: Captain Henry A. du Pont
1st Ohio Light Artillery, Battery L,
Captain Frank C. Gibbs
1st Pennsylvania Light Artillery, Battery D,
Lieutenant William Munk
5th US Artillery, Battery B, Captain
Henry A. du Pont

XIX CORPS
Brigadier General William H. Emory

1ST DIVISION
Brigadier General William Dwight
1st Brigade: Colonel George L. Beal
2nd Brigade: Brigadier General
James W. McMillan
Artillery:
5th Battery, New York Light Artillery:
Lieutenant John V. Grant

2ND DIVISION
Brigadier General Cuvier Grover
1st Brigade: Brigadier General Henry W. Birge
2nd Brigade: Colonel Edward L. Molineux
3rd Brigade: Colonel Jacob Sharpe, Lieutenant
Colonel Alfred Neafie
4th Brigade: Colonel David Shunk
Artillery:
1st Battery, Maine Light Artillery: Captain
Albert W. Bradbury
Artillery Reserve: Captain Elijah D. Taft
Battery D, 1st Rhode Island Light Artillery:
Lieutenant Frederick Chase
17th Battery, Indiana Light Artillery:
Captain Milton L. Milner

*Although the Army of West Virginia was constituted as the field army of the Department of West Virginia, it functioned during Sheridan's Valley Campaigns as a corps belonging to the Army of the Shenandoah and was, in fact, often called VIII Corps. For that reason, the Army of West Virginia order of battle at the Third Battle of Winchester is included here.[3]

CAVALRY CORPS
Brevet Major General Alfred T. A. Torbert

1ST DIVISION
Brigadier General Wesley Merritt
1st Brigade: Brigadier General George
    Armstrong Custer
2nd Brigade: Brigadier General
    Thomas C. Devin
Reserve Brigade: Colonel Charles
    Russell Lowell

2ND DIVISION
Brevet Major General William W. Averell
1st Brigade: Colonel James M. Schoonmaker
2nd Brigade: Colonel William H. Powell
Artillery:
Battery L, 5th US Artillery: Lieutenant
    Gulian V. Weir

3RD DIVISION
Brigadier General James H. Wilson
1st Brigade: Brigadier General
    John B. McIntosh, Lieutenant
    Colonel George A. Purington
2nd Brigade: Brigadier General
    George H. Chapman
Horse Artillery: Captain
    La Rhett L. Livingston
Batteries K and L, 1st US: Lieutenant
    Franck E. Taylor
Batteries B and L, 2nd US: Captain
    Charles H. Pierce
Battery D, 2nd US: Lieutenant
    Edward B. Williston

MAJOR CAMPAIGNS AND BATTLES

BATTLE OF HOKE'S RUN
(JULY 2, 1861)
Major General Robert Patterson led his division across the Potomac River near Williamsport, Virginia, bound for Martinsburg. As the march neared Hoke's Run, two of Patterson's brigades engaged Confederate regiments belonging to Thomas J. Jackson's brigade. In the running battle that developed, Patterson's men drove the Confederates back, albeit slowly. Jackson, in fact, was under orders to *delay* the Union advance as the Confederates built up their forces at Manassas, so he deliberately conducted a fighting withdrawal instead of standing and fighting or counterattacking. His objective was to consume time. This notwithstanding, his withdrawal is generally counted as a Union victory.

Following the July 2 battle, Patterson occupied Martinsburg and remained there quietly until July 15, when he finally advanced to Bunker Hill. Instead of continuing on to Winchester, however, to confront Jackson, he turned east to Charles Town and then withdrew to Harpers Ferry. This allowed Confederate general Joseph E. Johnston to march to Manassas for the purpose of reinforcing Brigadier General P. G. T. Beauregard there in advance of the First Battle of Bull Run (July 21, 1861, Virginia; Union defeat), thereby contributing to the circumstances that would result in the Union's ignominious defeat in the first major battle of the Civil War.

FIRST BATTLE OF WINCHESTER
(MAY 25, 1862)
On May 24 Major General Nathaniel Banks marched with some 6,500 men of the Army of the Shenandoah and twice skirmished—at Middletown and Newton, Virginia—with elements of Stonewall Jackson's division, which consisted of some 16,000 men in all. On the next day, May 25, Jackson's division closed in on Winchester, where Banks was hurriedly preparing defenses. A Confederate division under Richard Stoddert Ewell converged on Winchester from the southeast and attacked Camp Hill. Simultaneously, the Louisiana Brigade of Jackson's division flanked and then overran Banks's other position, on Bowers Hill. The pressure on both positions created panic in the Union ranks. Many soldiers

simply ran into and through Winchester. Soon, the exodus became a rout as the disorganized Union army fled north across the Potomac River. Of the 2,419 estimated casualties of this battle, more than 2,000 were among Banks's troops.

THIRD BATTLE OF WINCHESTER (SEPTEMBER 19, 1864)

Philip Sheridan's mission in the Shenandoah Valley was clear: scorch the earth *and* defeat Jubal Early, who had free run of the valley— effectively the backyard of Washington, DC— and had even attacked the capital itself (at Fort Stevens, July 11–12, 1864). Up to this point, Sheridan and Early merely jousted in a series of minor engagements. When his reconnaissance reported that Early was spread very thin between Martinsburg and Winchester, Sheridan decided to attack him at Winchester. This town had not been kind to the Union. Twice before, on May 25, 1862, and June 13–15, 1863, Union forces had been defeated here.

Sheridan commanded approximately twice the manpower as Early, who nevertheless stubbornly held his ground during the first portion of the Union general's September 19 attack. At last, however, one of Sheridan's divisions was able to maneuver around to the rear of Early's left flank. Once in position, the division charged, splitting up the Confederate ranks. This led to a general retreat. It would prove to be the turning point in the Shenandoah campaign, as Early was now set up for additional defeats in the next three encounters between the Army of the Shenandoah and his Army of the Valley.

BATTLE OF FISHER'S HILL (SEPTEMBER 21–22, 1864)

Battered at the Third Battle of Winchester, Early's Army of the Valley dug in at Fisher's Hill, south of Strasburg, Virginia, on September 20. On September 21 Sheridan attacked Early's advance skirmishers and was able to drive them

back toward Winchester and take over their high-ground positions. On the next day, Brevet Major General George Crook's Army of West Virginia—functioning as a corps of the Army of the Shenandoah—advanced along North Mountain and, by four in the afternoon, had flanked Early. Crook attacked the Confederate cavalry, which was rapidly overwhelmed. Also taken by surprise, Early's infantry was all but defenseless, and the Confederate position folded up from west to east. Acting with maximum aggression, Sheridan continued to pile on attacking units. At length Early withdrew to Rockfish Gap near Waynesboro. This maneuver saved what remained of his army, but it opened wide the gateway to the valley, through which Sheridan now rode, burning crops and farms from Staunton to Strasburg.

BATTLE OF TOM'S BROOK (OCTOBER 9, 1864)

Sheridan did not let up on Early. After defeating him at Fisher's Hill, he pursued him to the outskirts of Staunton, and then, on October 6, began a withdrawal in which his men burned everything capable of catching fire, especially barns and mills. Having been reinforced, however, Early began harassing Sheridan as he withdrew. On October 9 Brigadier General Alfred Torbert and his Cavalry Corps suddenly turned on Early, routing two of his divisions at Tom's Brook. This brought about a fresh reversal of fortune for the Confederates, which assured Sheridan control of the Shenandoah Valley.

BATTLE OF CEDAR CREEK (OCTOBER 19, 1864)

Jubal Early had one more surprise for Sheridan. At dawn on October 19, 1864, he led his Army of the Valley in a surprise attack on the Army of the Shenandoah at Cedar Creek, quickly routing the Union's VIII and XIX Corps. Major General Sheridan, who had assumed that Early was

This L. Prang & Co. chromolithograph from about 1886 depicts "Sheridan's Ride"—from Winchester, Virginia, to rally his soldiers to victory in the Battle of Cedar Creek (October 19, 1864). LIBRARY OF CONGRESS

beaten and incapable of launching an attack, was in Winchester when he received word of what was happening at Cedar Creek. He instantly mounted his horse and galloped the ten miles toward the sound of battle. Arriving at Cedar Creek, he personally moved about his troops, rallying them to effective action. That afternoon, he mounted a spirited counterattack that drove Early from the field. It was the final blow for the Confederate Army of the Valley.

BATTLE OF APPOMATTOX COURT HOUSE (APRIL 9, 1865)

Major General Alfred Torbert, commanding the Cavalry Corps of the Army of West Virginia, participated in the final relentless pursuit of Robert E. Lee's Army of Northern Virginia, which ended at the Battle of Appomattox Court House (April 9, 1865, Virginia; Union victory) and Lee's surrender of his army to Lieutenant General Ulysses S. Grant.

AFTERWORD
THE CALCULUS OF VICTORY AND DEFEAT

Assigning numbers of stars and half stars to various aspects of the armies of the South and the North should get people arguing—perhaps even arguing in more productive directions than they otherwise might. Since what I have done in this book has produced numbers, it is difficult to resist adding them up and averaging them out on the chance that the result may actually tell us something interesting about the reasons why the Civil War ended the way it did.

I have added up the stars awarded to each rated parameter for each side, beginning with chapter 3, the first chapter that directly compares the Confederacy and the Union. Because the Confederate military was divided into fewer *major* armies than that of the Union—three armies versus eight—I have separately calculated the average number of stars for each side's armies. The Confederate average rating for its three major armies is 2.8. The Union average rating for its eight major armies is 2.6. This puts both somewhere between marginal and mission-capable, with the average of the three Confederate armies closer to mission-capable than the average of the eight Union armies.

When we add up and average *all* of the parameters rated in chapters 3 to 26, the bottom-line result is 2 (marginal) for the Confederate military versus 2.5 (between marginal and mission-capable) for the Union.

How do we interpret this result?

Let's begin by making what I readily admit is a very bold assumption—namely, that the result has real significance. If this is the case, what we discover is that the difference between victory and defeat in the Civil War was extremely narrow. That the success of the North was due mainly to its economic advantages over the South comes as no surprise. But who could have expected that these enormous economic advantages failed to make a bigger difference in the magnitude of the war's outcome? As confirmed by our bottom-line figures, in strictly military terms, the two sides were quite closely matched. Perhaps, therefore, it is best to say of the Union's victory in the Civil War what the Duke of Wellington famously said of his own victory over Napoleon at Waterloo—that it was "the nearest run thing you ever saw in your life."

Most schoolbook histories say no such thing. Instead, they paint a picture of victory for the Union that is both total and inevitable. Those of us fascinated by the Civil War have always known better than this. That the most consequential and costly military enterprise in American history was in fact such a near-run thing shocked both the South and the North during and immediately after the war. Today, this fact continues to drive the seemingly inexhaustible sensation of high drama and nearly unbearable suspense that clings to events whose outcome has been known for more than a century and a half.

ENDNOTES

PART ONE: BROTHERS IN ARMS

CHAPTER 1: REVOLUTION, 1812, AND MEXICO

1 Ulysses S. Grant, *Personal Memoirs* (1885; reprint ed., New York: Da Capo, 1982), 554–56.

CHAPTER 2: OFFICER CORPS

1 Data from Margaret E. Wagner, Gary W. Gallagher, and Paul Finkelman, eds., *The Library of Congress Civil War Desk Reference* (New York: Simon & Schuster, 2002), 376. Other commonly encountered tallies of US Army officers on the eve of the Civil War are 1,105, 1,098, and 1,008.

2 David J. Hacker, "Decennial Life Tables for the White Population of the United States, 1790-1900." In *Historical Methods* (Abingdon-on-Thames, UK: Taylor & Francis, April-May 2010), 46–47.

3 Declaration of Independence, National Archives, www .archives.gov/exhibits/charters/declaration_transcript.html.

4 "Congressman Davy Crockett's Resolution to Abolish the Military Academy at West Point," National Archives Catalog, https://research.archives.gov/id/2173241.

5 Scott Beauchamp, "Abolish West Point—and the Other Service Academies, Too," *Washington Post* (January 23, 2015), www.washingtonpost.com/opinions/why-we-dont -need-west-point/2015/01/23/fa1e1488-a1ef-11e4-9f89 -561284a573f8_story.html.

6 Jeffrey Simpson, *Officers and Gentlemen: Historic West Point in Photographs* (Tarrytown, NY: Sleepy Hollow Press, 1982), 46.

7 Wikipedia, "United States Military Academy," https:// en.wikipedia.org/wiki/United_States_Military_Academy.

8 See Herman Hathaway and Archer Jones, *How the North Won* (Urbana: University of Illinois Press, 1983), 7.

9 James M. McPherson, *Battle Cry of Freedom* (New York: Oxford University Press, 1988), 328.

10 Wikipedia, "*List of alumni of The Citadel, The Military College of South Carolina,*" *https://en.wikipedia.org/wiki/ List_of_alumni_of_The_Citadel,_The_Military_College_of _South_Carolina.*

11 Ezra J. Warner, *Generals in Blue: Lives of the Union Commanders* (Baton Rouge and London: Louisiana State University Press, 1964), xx.

12 Ibid.

CHAPTER 3: ON THE EVE OF SECESSION

1 Data from Margaret E. Wagner, Gary W. Gallagher, and Paul Finkelman, eds., *The Library of Congress Civil War Desk Reference* (New York: Simon & Schuster, 2002), 376. Other commonly encountered tallies of US Army officers on the eve of the Civil War are 1,105, 1,098, and 1,008.

2 "For the Better Regulation of the Ordnance Depart- ment," Act of February 5, 1815, quoted in Major C. E. Dutton, "The Ordnance Department," www.history.army .mil/books/r&h/R&H-OD.htm.

3 Clayton R. Newell, *The Regular Army Before the Civil War, 1845–1860* (Washington, DC: Center for Military History, United States Army, 2014), 50–51.

4 Air Force Institute of Technology, *The Logistics of Mobi- lizing and Supplying the Union Army during the Initial Stages of the Civil War* (n.p.: CreateSpace Independent Publishing Platform, 2015), 13, 14.

5 Newell, 26.

6 "Armories, Arsenals, and Foundries," in David S. Heidler and Jeanne T. Heidler, eds., *Encyclopedia of the American Civil War* (New York: W. W. Norton, 2000), 79–80.

7 Napoleon quoted in Russell F. Weigley, *The American Way of War: A History of United States Military Strategy and Policy* (Bloomington: Indiana University Press, 1977), 79.

8 Weigley, 85.

9 Scott quoted in Weigley, 76.

PART TWO: BROTHER AGAINST BROTHER

CHAPTER 4: ESPRIT AND ECONOMICS

1 William H. Seward, "Freedom in Kansas," Speech in the Senate of the United States, March 3, 1858 (Washington, DC: Buell & Blanchard, 1858), https://archive.org/stream/freedominkansass01sewa#page/n1/mode/2up.

2 James Henry Hammond, "Cotton Is King" (1858), http://cw.routledge.com/textbooks/9780415896009/data/Document6-5.pdf.

3 Ibid.

4 The historical statistics here and that follow are drawn from Mary E. Wagner, Gary W. Gallagher, and Paul Finkelman, eds., *The Library of Congress Civil War Desk Reference* (New York: Simon & Schuster, 2002), 69–90.

5 Matthew J. Gallman, *The North Fights the Civil War: The Home Front* (Chicago: Ivan R. Dee, 1994), 22–23.

6 Ibid., 26.

7 James A. Rawley, *The Politics of Union: Northern Politics during the Civil War* (Hinsdale, IL: Dryden Press, 1974), 28.

CHAPTER 5: THE SOUTH MOBILIZES

1 Michael Perman and Amy Murell Taylor, eds., *Major Problems in the Civil War and Reconstruction: Documents and Essays* (Boston: Cengage Learning, 2010), 178.

2 Quoted in William E, Freehling, *The South vs. The South: How Anti-Confederate Southerners Shaped the Course of the Civil War* (New York: Oxford University Press, 2001), 36.

3 George. C. Eggleston, *A Rebel's Recollections* (1874; reprint ed., Bloomington: Indiana University Press, 1959).

4 Earl Schenk Miers, ed., *A Rebel War Clerk's Diary, by John B. Jones, 1861–1865* (New York: Sagamore Press, 1958), 8 and 1.

5 Carlton McCarthy, *Detailed Minutiae of Soldier Life in the Army of Northern Virginia, 1861–1865* (Cambridge, MA: Riverside Press, 1882), chapter 1; Kindle ed.

6 Ibid.

7 The Confederacy could not openly purchase arms and other manufactured goods from the North during the Civil War; however, New England textile mills continued to buy surprisingly large amounts of cotton from Southern sources during the war. Some of this trade was illicit, some illegal but nevertheless allowed, and a limited portion openly sanctioned. Payment came in the form of much-needed hard currency, gold, and, in some cases, weapons. See Philip Leigh, *Trading with the Enemy: The Covert Economy during the American Civil War* (Yardley, PA: Westholme, 2014).

8 See Charles B. Dew, *Ironmaker to the Confederacy: Joseph R. Anderson and the Tredegar Iron Works* (New Haven: Yale University Press, 1966) and Nathan Vernon Madison, *Tredegar Iron Works: Richmond's Foundry on the James* (Charleston, SC: The History Press, 2015).

9 Walter Stahr, *Seward: Lincoln's Indispensable Man* (New York: Simon & Schuster, 2013), note 81, 618–19.

10 The economic statistics here and that follow are drawn from Mary E. Wagner, Gary W. Gallagher, and Paul Finkelman, eds., *The Library of Congress Civil War Desk Reference* (New York: Simon & Schuster, 2002), 668–72.

11 Kenneth Radley, *Rebel Watchdog: The Confederate States Army Provost Guard* (Baton Rouge: Louisiana State University Press, 1989), 151.

12 See Albert Burton Moore, *Conscription and Conflict in the Confederacy* (Columbia: University of South Carolina Press, 1996).

13 Frank. E. Deserino, "African-American Soldiers, C.S.A.," in David S. Heidler and Jeanne T. Heidler, eds., *Encyclopedia of the American Civil War* (New York: W. W. Norton, 2000), 16–18.

14 Ibid., 18.

CHAPTER 6: THE NORTH MOBILIZES

1 See chapter 2.

2 Quoted in Samuel W. Scott and Samuel P. Angel, *History of the Thirteenth Regiment Tennessee Volunteer Cavalry* (Philadelphia: P. W. Ziegler, 1903), 31.

3 "Uncle Sambo," in John D. Wright, *The Language of the Civil War* (Westport, CT: Oryx Press, 2001), 309.

4 Matthew J. Gallman, *The North Fights the Civil War: The Home Front* (Chicago: Ivan R. Dee, 1994), 33.

5 James W. Geary, *We Need Men: The Draft in the Civil War* (DeKalb: Northern Illinois University Press, 1991), 6.

6 "Militia Act of 1792 revised in 1795 and Lincoln," *Civil War Talk* (April 28, 2010–March 13, 2013), http://civilwartalk.com/threads/militia-act-of-1792-revised-in-1795-and-lincoln.16928.

7 United States Congress, *The Public Statutes at Large of the United States of America* (Boston: Charles C. Little and James Brown, 1850), 215.

8 Figures from James A. Huston, *The Sinews of War: Army Logistics, 1775–1953* (Washington, DC: Government Printing Office, 1966), 160–61; and from Gallman, 20.

9 Abraham Lincoln, "July 4th Message to Congress" (1861), http://millercenter.org/president/lincoln/speeches/speech-3508.

10 Ulysses S. Grant, *Personal Memoirs* (1885; reprint ed., New York: Da Capo, 1982), 114.

11 Lancaster Newspapers, "Cameron, Fritchie Are Luminaries of Era," February 7, 2012, http://lancasteronline.com/blogs/civilwar/cameron-fritchie-are-luminaries-of-era/article_f904a342-4f76-5406-8409-575f453adb17.html.

12 Huston, 163.

13 Fred A. Shannon, *The Organization and Administration of the Union Army 1861–65* (Cleveland: Arthur H. Clark, 1928), vol. 1, 23–24.

14 The account of the riot is from Joel T. Headley, *The Great Riots of New York* (New York: E. B. Treat, 1873), as excerpted at www.historyisaweapon.com/defcon1/greatriotsheadley.html.

15 Casualty estimates given in James M. McPherson, *Ordeal by Fire: The Civil War and Reconstruction* (New York: Knopf, 1982), 360.

16 Samantha Jane Gaul, "Conscription, USA," in David S. Heidler and Jeanne T. Heidler, eds., *Encyclopedia of the American Civil War* (New York: W. W. Norton, 2000), 487–88.

CHAPTER 7: THE CONFEDERATE ARMY

1 David J. Eicher, *Civil War High Commands* (Palo Alto, CA: Stanford University Press, 2001), 71.

2 E. B. Long, *The Civil War Day by Day: An Almanac, 1861–1865* (Garden City, NY: Doubleday, 1971), 705.

3 Ibid., 711.

4 Alan Axelrod, *Generals South, Generals North: The Commanders of the Civil War Reconsidered* (Guilford, CT: Lyons Press, 2011), 72.

5 The Army of Mississippi was redesignated the Army of Tennessee on November 20, 1862, and during December 1862–July 1863 was commanded by John C. Pemberton, Earl Van Dorn, and William W. Loring. By 1863 it was also known as the Army of Vicksburg, and during July 1863–June 1864 it was commanded by William J. Hardee, Leonidas Polk, and William W. Loring. In May 1864 it was officially redesignated III Corps, Army of Tennessee, but continued to call itself the Army of Mississippi.

6 Not to be confused with the Union's Army of the Potomac.

7 Not to be confused with the Union's Army of the Potomac.

8 Long, 711.

9 Wikipedia, "Native Americans in the American Civil War," https://en.wikipedia.org/wiki/Native_Americans_in_the_American_Civil_War.

10 Sons of Confederate Veterans, "Service. Honor. Pride. American Indian Confederate Veterans," http://www.scv357.org/indconf/indconf.htm.

11 Shotgun's Home of the American Civil War, "Native Americans in the Civil War," www.civilwarhome.com/nativeamericans.htm.

CHAPTER 8: THE UNION ARMY

1 Civil War Trust, "Civil War Facts," www.civilwar.org/education/history/faq/?referrer=https://www.google.com; National Park Service, "Civil War Facts," www.nps.gov/civilwar/facts.htm; Samantha Jane Gaul, "Conscription, USA," in David S. Heidler and Jeanne T. Heidler, eds., *Encyclopedia of the American Civil War* (New York: W. W. Norton, 2000), 487–88.

2 Data from Margaret E. Wagner, Gary W. Gallagher, and Paul Finkelman, eds., *The Library of Congress Civil War Desk Reference* (New York: Simon & Schuster, 2002), 376. Other commonly encountered tallies of US Army officers on the eve of the Civil War are 1,105, 1,098, and 1,008.

3 Stephen W. Sears, *George B. McClellan: The Young Napoleon* (New York: Da Capo, 1988), 95.

4 Wikipedia, "Blacks in the Army," in "Union Army," https://en.wikipedia.org/wiki/Union_Army#Blacks_in _the_army.

CHAPTER 9: JOHNNY REB AND HIS COMMANDERS

1 Abraham Lincoln, First Inaugural Address, March 4, 1861, https://en.wikisource.org/wiki/Abraham _Lincoln%27s_First_Inaugural_Address.

2 Bell I. Wiley, *The Life of Johnny Reb: The Common Soldier of the Confederacy* (Baton Rouge: Louisiana State University Press, 1943) and *The Life of Billy Yank: The Common Soldier of the Union* (Baton Rouge: Louisiana State University Press, 1952).

3 Larry M. Logue, "Who Joined the Confederate Army? Soldiers, Civilians, and Communities in Mississippi," in Michael Barton and Larry M. Logue, eds., *The Civil War Soldier: A Historical Reader* (New York: New York University Press, 2002), chapter 3; Kindle ed.; Crutcher quoted in Logue, chapter 3; Kindle ed.

4 Logue, in Barton and Logue, chapter 3; Kindle ed.

5 Ibid. See also National Park Service, "Civil War Facts," https://www.nps.gov/civilwar/facts.htm; Dorothy Denneen Volo and James M. Volo, *Daily Life in Civil War America*, 2nd ed. (Santa Barbara, CA: ABC Clio, 2009), 121.

6 Volo and Volo, 121.

7 Ibid., 122.

8 Ibid., 123.

9 Ibid., 123–24.

10 "SOUTHERN NEWS; Desperate Speech by Jeff. Davis at Macon. Two-thirds of the Rebel Army Absent Without Leave," *New York Times* (October 7, 1864), www .nytimes.com/1864/10/07/news/southern-desperate -speech-jeff-davis-macon-two-thirds-rebel-army-absent -without.html.

11 Volo and Volo, 123.

12 James H. Croushore, ed., *A Volunteer's Adventure, by Captain John W. DeForest* (New Haven: Yale University Press, 1949), 190.

13 Volo and Volo, 122.

14 Arthur J. L. Fremantle, *Three Months in the Southern States: April, June, 1863* (Edinburgh and London: William Blackwood and Sons, 1863), 293.

15 Quoted in David Donald, "The Confederate as a Fighting Man," in Barton and Logue, eds., chapter 12; Kindle ed.

16 Ibid.

17 Donald, in Barton and Logue, chapter 12; Kindle ed.

18 Herman Hattaway and Archer Jones, *How the North Won: A Military History of the Civil War* (Urbana: University of Illinois Press, 1983), 9–10.

19 Donald, in Barton and Logue, chapter 12; Kindle ed.

20 *Official Records*, series 1, XLII, part 3, 1213, quoted in Donald, in Barton and Logue, chapter 12; Kindle ed.

21 Taylor quoted in Margaret E. Wagner, Gary W. Gallagher, and Paul Finkelman, eds., *The Library of Congress Civil War Desk Reference* (New York: Simon and Schuster, 2002), 465.

22 Quoted in Wagner, Gallagher, and Finkelman, 466.

23 W. J. Hardee, *Rifle and Light Infantry Tactics* (Philadelphia: J. B. Lippincott, 1861).

24 Volo and Volo, 172–73.

25 Wagner, Gallagher, and Finkelman, 466–67.

26 Carlton McCarthy, *Detailed Minutiae of Soldier Life in the Army of Northern Virginia, 1861–1865* (Cambridge, MA: Riverside Press, 1882), chapter 4; Kindle ed.

27 Ibid.

28 John D. Wright, *The Language of the Civil War* (Westport, CT: Oryx Press, 2001), 78.

29 McCarthy, chapter 4; Kindle ed.

30 McCarthy, chapter 5; Kindle ed.

31 Ibid.

32 Letter from an unidentified father to his son, July 17, 1861, quoted in McCarthy, chapter 1; Kindle ed.

33 Wagner, Gallagher, and Finkelman, 623.

34 Telegram of William T. Sherman to Ulysses S. Grant, October 9, 1864, in William T. Sherman, *Sherman's Civil*

War: Selected Correspondence of William T. Sherman, 1860–1865 (Chapel Hill: University of North Carolina Press, 1999), 731.

35 McCarthy, chapter 6; Kindle ed.

36 Mark A. Weitz, "Desertion," in David S. Heidler and Jeanne T. Heidler, eds., *Encyclopedia of the American Civil War* (New York: W. W. Norton, 2000), 593.

37 Weitz, in Heidler and Heidler, 593.

CHAPTER 10: BILLY YANK AND HIS COMMANDERS

1 Herman Hattaway and Archer Jones, *How the North Won: A Military History of the Civil War* (Urbana: University of Illinois Press, 1983), 9–10.

2 Philip Van Doren Stern, *Soldier Life in the Union and Confederate Armies* (New York: Bonanza Books, 1961), 14.

3 The sources for the three quotations are, in order, Larry M. Logue, "Who Joined the Confederate Army? Soldiers, Civilians, and Communities in Mississippi," in Michael Barton and Larry M. Logue, eds., *The Civil War Soldier: A Historical Reader* (New York: New York University Press, 2002), chapter 3; Kindle ed. Crutcher quoted in Logue, chapter 3; Kindle ed. Dorothy Denneen Volo and James M. Volo, *Daily Life in Civil War America,* 2nd ed. (Santa Barbara, CA: ABC Clio, 2009), 124–25.

4 Stern, 18–19.

5 Massachusetts recruiting poster reproduced in Stern, 18.

6 Volo and Volo, 125.

7 Abraham Lincoln, "Address at Sanitary Fair, Baltimore, Maryland," April 18, 1864, in Roy P. Basler, ed., *Collected Works of Abraham Lincoln* (New Brunswick, NJ: Rutgers University Press, 1953), vol. 7, 301–302.

8 Volo and Volo, 121; Melissa Clyne, "Study: More New Military Recruits Are 20 or Older," *NewsMax* (April 23, 2014), www.newsmax.com/US/military-age-recruits-Army/2014/04/23/id/567274.

9 Margaret E. Wagner, Gary W. Gallagher, and Paul Finkelman, eds., *The Library of Congress Civil War Desk Reference* (New York: Simon and Schuster, 2002), 461.

10 Herbert Aptheker, "Negro Casualties in the Civil War," *The Journal of Negro History* 32, no. 1 (January 1947), 12.

11 Crispus Knight, "Almost Every Rifle Recovered at Gettysburg Was Fully Loaded and No One Knows Why," *History Buff* (January 7, 2016), http://historybuff.com/almost-90-rifles-recovered-gettysburg-fully-loaded-NlKpDL5jqJY6.

12 Dave Wilma, "Soldier Marksmanship," *Civil War Talk* (December 24, 2012), http://civilwartalk.com/threads/soldier-marksmanship.78681.

13 This and the following account is from Leander Stillwell, *A Common Soldier of Army Life in the Civil War, 1861–1865* (n.p.: Franklin Hudson Publishing Co., 1920), 30–31; Kindle ed.

14 Thomas P. Lowry, *The Story the Soldiers Wouldn't Tell: Sex in the Civil War* (Mechanicsville, PA: Peter Stackpole Books, 1994), 104.

15 Catherine Clinton, *Public Women and the Confederacy* (Milwaukee: Marquette University Press, 1999), 9.

16 Ibid., 10.

17 Alan Axelrod, *Generals South, Generals North* (Guilford, CT: Lyons Press, 2011), 229.

18 Clinton, 25–26.

19 W. J. Hardee, *Rifle and Light Infantry Tactics* (Philadelphia: J. B. Lippincott, 1861).

CHAPTER 11: CONFEDERATE UNIFORMS, EQUIPMENT, AND ARMS

1 Discussion of uniforms is based on Tom Arliskas, *Cadet Gray and Butternut Brown: Notes on Confederate Uniforms* (Gettysburg, PA: Thomas Publications, 2006); Ron Field, *The Confederate Army 1861–65,* vols. 1–5 (Oxford, UK: Osprey, 2005–2006); and Philip Katcher, *The Army of Northern Virginia* (Oxford, UK: Osprey, 1975).

2 Discussion of equipment is based on Philip Katcher, *The Army of Robert E. Lee* (London: Arms & Armour Press, 1994), 8–29.

3 US Army History Center, "US Army Field Mess Gear," www.history.army.mil/html/museums/messkits/Field_Mess_Gear(upd_Jul09).pdf.

4 Carlton McCarthy, *Detailed Minutiae of Soldier Life in the Army of Northern Virginia, 1861–1865* (Cambridge, MA: Riverside Press, 1882), chapter 1; Kindle ed.

5 Discussion of infantry weapons is based on Gordon Jones, *Confederate Odyssey: The George W. Wray Jr. Civil War Collection at the Atlanta History Center* (Athens: University of Georgia Press, 2014); Russ Pritchard, *The English Connection* (Gettysburg, PA: Thomas Publications, 2015).

6 Margaret E. Wagner, Gary W. Gallagher, and Paul Finkelman, eds., *The Library of Congress Civil War Desk Reference* (New York: Simon and Schuster, 2002), 491.

7 Information of cavalry weapons is based on William A. Albaugh III, *Confederate Edged Weapons* (New York: Harper, 1960); Joseph G. Bilby, *Small Arms at Gettysburg: Infantry and Cavalry Weapons in America's Greatest Battle* (Yardley, PA: Westholme, 2007); Philip Katcher, *Confederate Cavalryman 1861–1865* (Oxford, UK: Osprey, 2002); and Peter Schiffers, *Civil War Carbines: Myths vs. Reality* (Woonsocket, RI: Mowbray, 2007).

8 Material on Confederate artillery is drawn from Philip Katcher, *Confederate Artilleryman 1861–1865* (Oxford, UK: Osprey, 2001); Philip Katcher, *American Civil War Artillery 1861–65: Field Artillery* (Oxford, UK: Osprey, 2001); Philip Katcher, *American Civil War Artillery 1861–65: Heavy Artillery* (Oxford, UK: Osprey, 2001); Wagner, Gallagher, and Finkelman, 491.

CHAPTER 12: UNION UNIFORMS, EQUIPMENT, AND ARMS

1 Ulysses S. Grant, *Personal Memoirs* (1885; reprint ed., New York: Da Capo, 1982), 555–56.

2 The material on Union army uniforms is based on "Article LI. Uniform, Dress, and Horse Equipments," in *Revised United States Army Regulations of 1861*, 462–81, http://quod.lib.umich.edu/m/moa/AGY4285.0001.001?rgn=main;view=fulltext, and Robin Smith and Ron Field, *Uniforms of the Civil War: An Illustrated Guide for Historians, Collectors, and Reenactors* (Guilford, CT: Lyons Press, 2004).

3 Discussion of equipment is based on Jack Coggins, *Arms and Equipment of the Civil War* (Mineola, NY: Dover, 1990), and "Weapons & Equipment of the Vicksburg Campaign," *Mississippians in the Confederate Army* (blog), https://mississippiconfederates.wordpress.com/2011/07/27/weapons-equipment-of-the-vicksburg-campaign.

4 Margaret E. Wagner, Gary W. Gallagher, and Paul Finkelman, eds., *The Library of Congress Civil War Desk Reference* (New York: Simon and Schuster, 2002), 490;

Joseph G. Bilby, *Civil War Firearms: Their Historical Background and Tactical Use* (New York: Da Capo, 1997); Joseph G. Bilby, *Small Arms at Gettysburg: Infantry and Cavalry Weapons in America's Greatest Battle* (Yardley, PA: Westholme, 2007).

CHAPTER 13: THE AFRICAN-AMERICAN CIVIL WAR

1 Herbert Aptheker, "Negro Casualties in the Civil War," *Journal of Negro History* 32, no. 1 (January 1947), 12.

2 Corydon Ireland, "Black Confederates," *Harvard Gazette* (September 1, 2011), http://news.harvard.edu/gazette/story/2011/09/black-confederates.

3 See Peter Charles Hoffer, *Cry Liberty: The Great Stono River Slave Rebellion of 1739* (New York: Oxford University Press, 2010).

4 A November 7, 1775, proclamation of Virginia's royal governor Lord Dunmore declared free "all indented Servants, Negroes, or others . . . that are able and willing to bear Arms, they joining His MAJESTY'S Troops as soon as may be. . . ." (See "Lord Dunmore's Proclamation [1775]," BlackPast.org, www.blackpast.org/aah/lord-dunmore-s-proclamation-1775.) Some 800 slaves immediately joined the Tories, and many more followed in the course of the American Revolution.

5 Margaret E. Wagner, Gary W. Gallagher, and Paul Finkelman, eds., *The Library of Congress Civil War Desk Reference* (New York: Simon and Schuster, 2002), 427.

6 Ibid., 428–30.

7 "The Second Confiscation Act," Freedman & Southern Society Project, www.freedmen.umd.edu/conact2.htm.

8 Quoted in Wagner, Gallagher, and Finkelman, 429.

9 Ibid.

10 One scholar cites this figure as 12 percent of total Union forces: Gregory J. W. Unwin, "United States Colored Troops," in David S. Heidler and Jeanne T. Heidler, eds., *Encyclopedia of the American Civil War* (New York: W. W. Norton, 2000), 2002. Other authorities put the figure closer to 10 percent.

11 Wagner, Gallagher, and Finkelman, 429–30.

12 Unwin, 2002–2003. The website of the Military Order of the Loyal Legion of the United States puts the African American officer count at 120 ("at least") and provides a

list of documented officers, many of whom were chaplains. See http://suvcw.org/mollus/usctofficers.htm.

13 Unwin, 2003.

14 See Alan Axelrod, *The Real History of the Civil War* (New York: Sterling, 2012), chapter 15.

15 Quoted in Bell I. Wiley, *The Life of Billy Yank: The Common Soldier of the Union,* updated ed. (Baton Rouge: Louisiana State University, 2008), 120.

16 Unwin, 2003.

17 Quoted in "Robert Gould Shaw," Civil War Trust, www.civilwar.org/education/history/biographies/robert -gould-shaw.html?referrer=https://www.google.com.

18 The account of the Battle of Fort Wagner is based on Luis F. Emilio, *History of the Fifty-Fourth Regiment of Massachusetts Volunteer Infantry, 1863–1865* (Boston: The Boston Book Company, 1894), 105–28.

19 Unwin, 2003.

20 William A. Gladstone, *United States Colored Troops, 1863–1967* (Gettysburg, PA: Thomas Publications, 1996), 120.

21 The following is based on Frank E. Deserino, "African-American Soldiers, C.S.A.," in Heidler and Heidler, 16–18.

22 Quoted in Jonathan D. Sutherland, *African Americans at War: An Encyclopedia,* vol. 1 (Santa Barbara, CA: ABC-Clio, 2014), 113.

CHAPTER 14: MEDICS SOUTH, MEDICS NORTH

1 William A. Hammond quoted in David R. Petriello, *Bacteria and Bayonets: The Impact of Disease in American Military History* (Havertown, PA and Oxford, UK: Casemate Publishers, 2015), 169.

2 Statistics from Margaret E. Wagner, Gary W. Gallagher, and Paul Finkelman, eds., *The Library of Congress Civil War Desk Reference* (New York: Simon and Schuster, 2002), 623.

3 "Medical Department, Organization of," in Glenna R. Schroeder-Lein, *The Encyclopedia of Civil War Medicine* (Armonk, NY: M. E. Sharpe, 2008), Kindle ed.

4 "Hospitals, Wayside," in Schroeder-Lein, Kindle ed.

5 "Hospitals, Receiving and Distributing," in Schroeder-Lein, Kindle ed.

6 "Hospitals, Officers'," in Schroeder-Lein, Kindle ed.

7 "Hospitals, 'Pest' (Smallpox)," in Schroeder-Lein, Kindle ed.

8 "Hospital Ships," in Schroeder-Lein, Kindle ed.

9 Joseph K. Barnes and J. J. Woodward. *The Medical and Surgical History of the War of the Rebellion* (reprint ed., Charleston, SC: Nabu Press, 2013), vol. 2, part III, 877.

10 Adapted from Barnes, et al., *Medical and Surgical History,* vol. 1, part III, 636–40.

11 Wagner, Gallagher, and Finkelman, 637.

12 Adapted from Barnes, et al., *Medical and Surgical History,* vol. 1, part I, 710–11.

13 Wagner, Gallagher, and Finkelman, 662–63.

14 Ibid., 661–62.

CHAPTER 15: POWS SOUTH, POWS NORTH

1 Margaret E. Wagner, Gary W. Gallagher, and Paul Finkelman, eds., *The Library of Congress Civil War Desk Reference* (New York: Simon and Schuster, 2002), 583–84.

2 Based on Wagner, Gallagher, and Finkelman, 592–96, and "Civil War Military Prisons & POW Camps," http://freepages.genealogy.rootsweb.ancestry.com/~prsjr/wars/cwar/pow/0index.htm.

3 Warren Lee Goss, *A Union Captive: Andersonville, Belle Isle, and Florence Stockade* (1867; reprint ed., n.p.: Big Byte Books, 2015), "The Horror of Andersonville," Kindle ed.

4 Goss, "The Horror of Andersonville," Kindle ed.

5 Walt Whitman, "87. Releas'd Union Prisoners from the South," in *Specimen Days & Collect* (Philadelphia: Rees Welsh & Co., 1882), 69–70.

6 Based on Wagner, Gallagher, and Finkelman, 587–92, and "Civil War Military Prisons & POW Camps," http://freepages.genealogy.rootsweb.ancestry.com/~prsjr/wars/cwar/pow/0index.htm.

7 Jocelyn P. Jamison, *They Died at Fort Delaware 1861–1865* (Delaware City: Fort Delaware Society, 1997), 85–90.

PART THREE: THE PRINCIPAL ARMIES

CHAPTER 16: ARMY OF NORTHERN VIRGINIA

1 The discussion that follows is based on Philip Katcher, *The Army of Robert E. Lee* (London: Arms and Armour, 1994), 29–60 and 210–69, in addition to J. Tracy Power, "The Army of Northern Virginia," in David S. Heidler and Jeanne T. Heidler, eds., *Encyclopedia of the American Civil War* (New York: W. W. Norton, 2000), 87–90, and Margaret E. Wagner, Gary W. Gallagher, and Paul Finkelman, eds., *The Library of Congress Civil War Desk Reference* (New York: Simon and Schuster, 2002), 390–91.

CHAPTER 18: ARMY OF TENNESSEE

1 Much of the discussion that follows is based on Stanley F. Horn, *The Army of Tennessee* (Norman: University of Oklahoma Press, 1993).

2 Alan Axelrod, *Generals South, Generals North: The Commanders of the Civil War Reconsidered* (Guilford, CT: Lyons Press, 2011), 63–72.

CHAPTER 19: ARMY OF THE POTOMAC

1 David J. Eicher, *The Longest Night: A Military History of the Civil War* (New York: Simon and Schuster, 2001), 475.

2 United States War Department, *The War of the Rebellion: A Compilation of the Official Records of the Union and Confederate Armies*, series 1, vol. 27 (part I), 187, http://ebooks .library.cornell.edu/cgi/t/text/pageviewer-idx?c=moawar& cc=moawar&idno=waro0043&q1=return+of+casualties& view=image&seq=207&size=100.

3 Ulysses S. Grant, *Personal Memoirs* (1885; reprint ed., New York: Da Capo, 1982), 581.

4 United States War Department, *War of the Rebellion*, series 1, vol. 2, 309, http://ebooks.library.cornell.edu/cgi/t/ text/pageviewer-idx?c=moawar&cc=moawar&idno=waro 0002&node=waro0002%3A6&view=image&seq=325& size=100.

5 United States War Department, *War of the Rebellion*, series 1, vol. 5, 13, http://ebooks.library.cornell.edu/cgi/t/ text/pageviewer-idx?c=moawar&cc=moawar&idno=waro 0005&node=waro0005%3A6&view=image&seq=29& size=100.

6 United States War Department, *War of the Rebellion*, series 1, vol. 19 (part I), 67, http://ebooks.library.cornell .edu/cgi/t/text/pageviewer-idx?c=moawar&cc=moawar& idno=waro0027&node=waro0027%3A5&view=image& seq=83&size=100.

7 Thomas L. Livermore, *Number and Losses in the Civil War in America, 1861–65* (Boston and New York: Houghton, Mifflin and Company, 1901), 96.

8 United States War Department, *War of the Rebellion*, series 1, vol. 25 (part II), 320, http://ebooks.library.cornell .edu/cgi/t/text/pageviewer-idx?c=moawar&cc=moawar& idno=waro0040&node=waro0040%3A5&view=image& seq=322&size=100.

9 United States War Department, *War of the Rebellion*, series 1, vol. 27 (part I), 173, http://ebooks.library .cornell.edu/cgi/t/text/pageviewer-idx?c=moawar;cc =moawar;idno=waro0043;q1=return%20of%20 casualties;view=image;seq=213;size=100;page=root.

10 Eicher, *Longest Night: A Military History of the Civil War* (New York: Simon & Schuster, 2001), 660.

11 John S. Salmon, *The Official Virginia Civil War Battle-field Guide* (Mechanicsburg, PA: Stackpole, 2001), 492.

12 United States War Department, *War of the Rebellion*, series 1, vol. 27 (part I), 155–68, http://ebooks.library .cornell.edu/cgi/t/text/pageviewer-idx?c=moawar;cc =moawar;idno=waro0043;node=waro0043%3A2;view =image;seq=175;size=100;page=root.

13 United States War Department, *War of the Rebellion*, series 1, vol. 2, 327, http://ebooks.library.cornell.edu/cgi/t/ text/pageviewer-idx?c=moawar&cc=moawar&idno=waro0 002&node=waro0002%3A6&view=image&seq=343& size=100.

14 Eicher, 293.

15 United States War Department, *War of the Rebellion*, series 1, vol. 19 (part I), 189 and 810, http://ebooks.library .cornell.edu/cgi/t/text/pageviewer-idx?c=moawar&cc =moawar&idno=waro0027&node=waro0027%3A8&view =image&seq=205&size=100.

16 United States War Department, *War of the Rebellion*, series 1, vol. 25 (part I), 172.

17 United States War Department, *War of the Rebellion*, series 1, vol. 25 (part I), 806.

18 United States War Department, *War of the Rebellion*, series 1, vol. 36 (part I), 188.

CHAPTER 20: ARMY OF THE SOUTHWEST (ARMY OF SOUTHWEST MISSOURI)

1 National Park Service, "Pea Ridge National Military Park—Order of Battle," www.nps.gov/peri/learn/history culture/order-of-battle.htm.

2 William Shea and Earl Hess, *Pea Ridge: Civil War Campaign in the West* (Chapel Hill: University of North Carolina Press, 1992), 270–71.

3 Harvey Hanna, "The Battle of Cotton Plant, 7 July 1862," www.academia.edu/467854/The_Battle_of _Cotton_Plant?auto=download.

CHAPTER 21: ARMY OF THE MISSISSIPPI

1 Larry Daniel, *Shiloh: The Battle That Changed the Civil War* (NY: Simon & Schuster, 1997), 68.

2 Ulysses S. Grant, *Personal Memoirs* (1885; reprint ed., New York: Da Capo, 1982), 170.

3 Larry J. Daniel and Lynn N. Bock, *Island No. 10: Struggle for the Mississippi Valley* (Tuscaloosa: University of Alabama Press, 1996), 151–56.

4 United States War Department, *The War of the Rebellion: A Compilation of the Official Records of the Union and Confederate Armies,* series 1, vol. 17 (part I), 716–19, http:// ebooks.library.cornell.edu/cgi/t/text/pageviewer-idx?c =moawar;cc=moawar;idno=waro0024;node=waro0024 %3A2;view=image;seq=732;size=100;page=root.

CHAPTER 22: ARMY OF THE TENNESSEE

1 United States War Department, *The War of the Rebellion: A Compilation of the Official Records of the Union and Confederate Armies,* series 1, vol. 24 (part III), 249, http:// ebooks.library.cornell.edu/cgi/t/text/pageviewer-idx?c =moawar;cc=moawar;rgn=full%20text;idno=waro0038 ;didno=waro0038;view=image;seq=00251;node=waro 0038%3A1.

2 United States War Department, *War of the Rebellion,* series 1, vol. 38 (part I), 89ff, http://ebooks.library.cornell .edu/cgi/t/text/pageviewer-idx?c=moawar&cc=moawar& idno=waro0072&q1=organization+of+the&view=image& seq=111&size=100.

CHAPTER 23: ARMY OF THE CUMBERLAND

1 United States War Department, *The War of the Rebellion: A Compilation of the Official Records of the Union and Confederate Armies,* series 1, vol. 30 (part I), 40ff.

CHAPTER 24: ARMY OF THE OHIO

1 United States War Department, *The War of the Rebellion: A Compilation of the Official Records of the Union and Confederate Armies,* series 1, vol. 10 (part I), 105–108, http:// ebooks.library.cornell.edu/cgi/t/text/pageviewer-idx?c =moawar&cc=moawar&idno=waro0010&node=waro 0010%3A2&view=image&seq=111&size=100.

2 United States War Department, *War of the Rebellion,* series 1, vol. 38 (part I), 89ff, http://ebooks.library.cornell .edu/cgi/t/text/pageviewer-idx?c=moawar&cc=moawar& idno=waro0072&q1=organization+of+the&view=image& seq=111&size=100.

CHAPTER 25: ARMY OF THE JAMES

1 United States War Department, *The War of the Rebellion: A Compilation of the Official Records of the Union and Confederate Armies,* series 1, vol. 42 (part I), 133ff, http:// ebooks.library.cornell.edu/cgi/t/text/pageviewer-idx?c =moawar;cc=moawar;rgn=full%20text;idno=waro0087 ;didno=waro0087;view=image;seq=155;node=waro0087 %3A1;page=root;size=100;frm=frameset;.

CHAPTER 26: ARMY OF THE SHENANDOAH

1 Quoted in Margaret E. Wagner, Gary W. Gallagher, and Paul Finkelman, eds., *The Library of Congress Civil War Desk Reference* (New York: Simon & Schuster, 2002), 386.

2 United States War Department, *The War of the Rebellion: A Compilation of the Official Records of the Union and Confederate Armies,* series 1, vol. 43 (part I), 107–109, http:// ebooks.library.cornell.edu/cgi/t/text/pageviewer-idx?c =moawar;cc=moawar;q1=Russell;rgn=full%20text;idno =waro0090;didno=waro0090;view=image;seq=0127.

3 United States War Department, *War of the Rebellion,* series 1, vol. 43 (part I), 110–12, http://ebooks.library .cornell.edu/cgi/t/text/pageviewer-idx?c=moawar&cc =moawar&idno=waro0090&q1=Russell&view=image &seq=130&size=100.

INDEX

ABOUT THE AUTHOR

Alan Axelrod is the author of many books on leadership, history, military history, corporate history, and more. After receiving his PhD in English from the University of Iowa in 1979, Axelrod taught early American literature and culture at Lake Forest College (Lake Forest, Illinois) and at Furman University (Greenville, South Carolina). He then entered scholarly publishing in 1982 as associate editor and scholar with the Henry Francis du Pont Winterthur Museum (Winterthur, Delaware), an institution specializing in the history and material culture of America prior to 1832. Axelrod was a featured speaker at the 2004 Conference on Excellence in Government (Washington, DC), at the Leadership Institute of Columbia College (Columbia, South Carolina), and at the 2005 Annual Conference of the Goizueta Business School, Emory University (Atlanta), and the 2014 annual conference of Ecopetrol (Bogotá, Colombia).

Also by Alan Axelrod:

Patton's Drive: The Making of America's Greatest General

Miracle at Belleau Wood: The Birth of the Modern U.S. Marine Corps

Generals South, Generals North